W9-DIJ-359

CULTURE and COGNITION

Chandler Publications in Anthropology and Sociology

Leonard Broom, *General Editor*

L. L. Langness, *Editor*

CULTURE and COGNITION

Rules, Maps, and Plans

Edited by

James P. Spradley

Macalester College

CHANDLER PUBLISHING COMPANY

An Intext Publisher

SAN FRANCISCO • SCRANTON • LONDON • TORONTO

Library of Congress Cataloging in Publication Data

Spradley, James P. comp.
Culture and cognition.

(Chandler publications in anthropology and sociology)
Includes bibliographical references.
1. Cognition—Addresses, essays, lectures.
2. Personality and culture—Addresses, essays, lectures. 3. Languages—Psychology—Addresses, essays, lectures. I. Title.
GN270.S64 301.2 79-170380
ISBN 0-8102-0449-5
ISBN 0-8102-0450-9 (pbk.)

International Standard Book Number 0-8102-0449-5 (cloth)

International Standard Book Number 0-8102-0450-9 (paper)

Library of Congress Catalog Card Number 79-170380

Printed in the United States of America

To My Mother and Father

CONTENTS

Religion

PART 1 INTRODUCTION

1 FOUNDATIONS OF CULTURAL KNOWLEDGE

James P. Spradley

While attending college, I was employed at night by an egg company. There were about ten employees, and we worked together processing the eggs which were delivered from farmers and chicken ranchers. Understanding the "egg business" required considerable knowledge, which few employees besides the plant manager had. Nevertheless, we shared sufficient information to coordinate our behavior and perform the tasks set for us.

I unloaded large boxes of eggs from incoming trucks. These were classified by date and stored in a large refrigerator room. The oldest eggs were taken to another employee, who placed them in a machine which further sorted them on the basis of their size and weight. Conveyor belts delivered these eggs to individuals known as *egg candlers* who stood before machines in a long dark corridor where they could efficiently *candle* the eggs. Placing each egg momentarily before a powerful light, they could classify the eggs in terms of color, shell quality, and various internal features. On the basis of these attributes, eggs with similar characteristics were placed together in cartons or cans. Most were then returned to the refrigerator room until a truck took them to the supermarkets of the city. Some were cracked open and placed in large cans to be frozen and delivered to restaurants. Still others were thrown out with the daily trash, only to be salvaged and eaten by transients.

The performance of these tasks was facilitated by a specialized language. When someone said, "Take these jumbo cartons to the candler on number three," or "This box of checks is full," other employees could respond appropriately. On the basis of different attributes the various kinds of eggs were given names. For instance, a *check* had a defective shell, a *blood* had specks of blood on the yolk, and a *double yolker* had two yolks.

In addition to evaluating, classifying, and naming types of eggs, employees learned and used information about people, objects, places, and times at the egg company. The *manager* was evaluated differently from day

This chapter was written for this volume and has never before been published.

to day, depending on his mood. *Egg candlers* were classified in terms of their relative skills and the speed with which they worked. The first night of each week was considered *Blue Monday* and was negatively evaluated, while Friday was anticipated as the best night of the week. Smaller units of time were called such things as *break*, *lunch*, and *clean-up time*, and each came to have a meaning and value shared by employees.

When a new person began work, the operation appeared to him to be quite complex. As he listened to instructions, watched others performing similar tasks, acquired the specialized language, and learned the attributes by which to classify eggs, his actions came to resemble those of other employees. One aspect of his learning experience involved detailed explanations about eggs, their qualities, and the overall purpose of the processing plant. In fact, explanations which accounted for the quality of eggs, the moods of the boss, the breakdowns of machines, and the behavior of other employees made up a large part of all conversations. "Why are there so many checks in this batch of eggs? Because that farmer hasn't been feeding his chickens enough calcium." "I can't seem to candle eggs very fast tonight—I guess it's because it's Monday." "Fred isn't coming to work tonight. He's having family troubles again." And so life at the egg company went on—new eggs arriving each day, busy employees sorting and packaging eggs, and each of us explaining the events and actions which occurred. In a very real sense we shared a set of rules, maps, and plans for organizing our behavior individually and as a group.

It was many years later, after completing my studies in graduate school, that I began to think about life at the egg company from the viewpoint of an anthropologist. Those activities were not much different from life in every human society, where behavior is organized on the basis of a shared symbolic world. Every culture consists of categories which are used to sort and classify experience. People learn the rules for appropriate behavior. They acquire cognitive maps which enable them to interpret the behavior and events they observe. They use plans to organize their behavior in the pursuit of goals. The category systems of each culture are based on the selection of certain attributes. People are sorted and linguistically labeled. They *become* brothers, sisters, neighbors, enemies, freaks, employers, teachers, and friends by the application of the necessary cultural rules. Objects take on meaning as they are identified, classified, and named. The attributes for selecting ice for constructing an igloo, bamboo for fashioning a spear, apples for baking a pie, or eggs to pack in a carton are all based on cultural rules. Individuals learn to evaluate each experience in a way which is at least partially shared. These values become the basis for such things as avoiding snakes and poison oak, enjoying rock music and Christmas vacation, or discarding rotten eggs and tin cans. In some cultures the rules and values appear to be switched around; contact with snakes is considered desirable, vacations are unknown and therefore cannot be enjoyed, or rotten eggs are defined as a delicacy for special occasions. Whether the task is performing a wedding, driving a car, weaning a child, sentencing a drunk, smoking a joint, or processing eggs, the respective behaviors are constructed, coordinated, and interpreted by the use of cultural information systems.

The central theme of this book is the nature of this shared cognition or cultural knowledge. What is its structure? How does it function? How is it learned? By what processes does it change? How is it related to behavior? What are the empirical investigative procedures for studying it? These are some of the questions discussed in the following chapters. The authors represent many disciplines—anthropology, economics, linguistics, psychology, sociology—but underlying their diversity is a common interest in the role of cognition in human behavior. Some of the most promising developments in the social sciences are emerging from this common research interest. These are represented by the work of Jean Piaget in psychology, Noam Chomsky in linguistics, Harold Garfinkle in sociology, and Claude Lévi-Strauss in anthropology, to name but a few. During the last two decades a number of anthropologists have been working toward a more rigorous ethnographic method. Their efforts have been referred to as the new ethnography or ethnoscience (Sturtevant 1964). Because of the central concern with meaning, this work has also been called ethnographic semantics or ethnosemantics (Kay 1970). This book is intended to provide the student with an introduction to these studies in ethnoscience or culture and cognition. More than that, the following selections include several articles from other disciplines which provide a broad theoretical framework in which to place these studies. In this chapter I shall examine briefly the concept of *culture* and then outline the major aspects of human knowledge or cognition. This will involve a discussion of how sensory experience is transformed into *percepts*, the manner in which *concepts* are formed, and the way in which perceptual objects and events function as *symbols*. Finally, since these elements of knowledge and their arrangement into cognitive maps and plans are based on *rules* (Scandura 1970), I shall examine the nature of this concept, how rules are learned, and how they are used to organize behavior.

Cultural Behavior and Cultural Knowledge

One source of confusion for the student of anthropology is the much cherished but often misunderstood concept of culture. It is not misunderstood because people fail to acquire its "true" meaning but because it has so many overlapping and contradictory meanings. Social scientists have made it a regular practice to expropriate this term for their special purposes. As each new definition is added to the list, the semantic battle lines are drawn and the verbal warfare continues. Since all definitions are arbitrary, most intellectual debates over the *appropriate* usage of the concept of culture are trivial.

A brief enumeration of types of definition may clear the way for understanding the use of *culture* in this book. The *biological definition* labels a community of bacteria grown in a laboratory test tube as a culture. A *social class definition* sees culture as the refined habits and courtesies of the upper class (a definition rejected by most scholars). The *human-nature definition* is used to distinguish the behavior of man from other animals. Man, we are told, has culture; other animals do not. The referent of "human culture" is an abstract notion of socially transmitted behavior which is much more complex than the behavior of other primates. The *human-group definition* uses the concept of culture almost as a synonym for society or community. Under this definition it is possible to visit the Hawaiian culture or to be a member of Kwakiutl culture. The culture-area concept is quite closely tied up with this idea, linking the term to a geographical area. Perhaps the meaning which has had the widest usage involves an *omnibus definition:* culture is almost everything. It is emotions and works of art; it is behavior, beliefs, and institutions; it includes what people know, feel, think, make, and do. The *artifact definition* uses the concept with a qualifier—material culture, which refers to the products which man has created, including tools, paintings, houses, hypodermic needles, and hydrogen bombs.

Two other definitions are of special interest because they have come to be associated with major theoretical approaches in anthropology. These are the behavioral and cognitive definitions of culture. The *behavioral definition* focuses upon observable patterns of behavior within some social group. For this approach, "the culture concept comes down to behavior patterns associated with particular groups of peoples, that is to 'customs', or to a people's 'way of life' " (Harris 1968:16). The *cognitive definition,* on the other hand, excludes behavior and restricts the culture concept to ideas, beliefs, and knowledge. While most early definitions *included* the cognitive dimensions, they were not restricted to them. This practice emerged under the influence of linguistics and the social-systems theory of Talcott Parsons (Harris 1971). Ward Goodenough, drawing on the linguistic approach, proposed the following definition in 1957:

> A society's culture consists of whatever it is one has to know or believe in order to operate in a manner acceptable to it's members, and to do so in any role they ac-

cept for any of themselves. . . . Culture is not a material phenomenon; it does not consist of things, people, behavior, or emotions. It is rather an organization of these things. It is the forms of things that people have in mind, their models for perceiving, relating, and otherwise interpreting them (1957:167).

In sociology Talcott Parsons had begun to conceptualize culture as a symbolic system (1951). Then, in 1958, Alfred Kroeber and Parsons collaborated in writing a brief paper on "The Concept of Culture and of Social System," in which they proposed the following cognitive definition:

. . . we suggest that it is useful to define the concept of culture for most usages more narrowly than has been generally the case in the American anthropological tradition, restricting its reference to transmitted and created content and patterns of values, ideas, and other symbolic-meaningful systems as factors in the shaping of human behavior and the artifacts produced through behavior (1958:583).

In his analysis of the changing definition of culture, Marvin Harris notes this position taken by Kroeber and Parsons and observes: "The reigning academic popes of sociology and anthropology now proceeded virtually by incantation to exorcize the last devils of behavior from the culture concept" (1971:17).

Rather than continuing the debate over who has the title deed to this concept, let us concede that it is a case of joint ownership. What is important in the last two definitions is not which one is correct, but the nature of the distinctions which are being made between behavior and knowledge. Goodenough has attempted to clarify this point:

. . . in considering any society's culture, anthropologists have been talking about two different orders of reality as if they were part of the same order. Many of the disagreements among anthropological schools of thought in the past have reflected differential emphasis on one or other of these distinct orders. One is the phenomenal order of observed events and the regularities they exhibit. A human community, like any other natural universe in a state of near equilibrium, exhibits the statistical patterns characteristic of internally stable systems, as with homeostasis in the living organism. Similar, but never identical, events occur over and over again and are therefore isolable as types of event and patterned arrangement. Certain types of arrangement tend to persist and others to appear and reappear in fixed sequences. An observer can perceive this kind of statistical patterning in a community without any knowledge whatever of the ideas, beliefs, values, and principles of action of the community's members, the ideational order. The phenomenal order is a property of the community as a material system of people, their surroundings, and their behavior. The ideational order is a property not of the community but of its members. It is their organization of their experience within the phenomenal order, a product of cognitive and instrumental (habit formation) learning. The ideational order, unlike the statistical order, is nonmaterial, being composed of ideal forms as they exist in people's minds, propositions about their interrelationships, preference ratings regarding them, and recipes for their mutual ordering as means to desired ends. And as an organization of past experience, the ideational order is a means for organizing and interpreting new experience (1964:11).

In this chapter we shall follow the practice of Werner and Fenton (1970) and speak of cultural behavior and cultural knowledge. While later chapters often employ the cognitive definition of culture, the reader must be alert for changes in the semantic landscape. The concepts of image, symbolic world, cognitive map, definition of the situation, ideational order, and cultural knowledge are all used in a similar fashion. Despite the term used, there is a growing consensus that the analytical distinction between culture as behavior and culture as knowledge is a useful one. The behaviorist is then able to exclude "knowledge," or anything else which is said to go on inside the heads of those he studies. At the same time, those who find it useful to account for behavior in terms of what people know, of the information they are processing, are able to state the relationship between knowledge and behavior more clearly. We now turn to an examination of knowledge and its role in human behavior.

Knowledge: The Basic Elements

To the man in the street, reality and knowledge not only are taken for granted, but also are often equated. To be sure, he recognizes that there are differences of opinion and that others may have greater stores of knowledge. He usually knows when information comes from a dream, a novel, his imagination, or the world in which he lives. Nevertheless, it is taken for granted that reality is present in much the same form to all people. Books and stars and flowers are really there for anyone to touch and see and smell. They have qualities which are obvious: this book is large; that star is bright; those flowers are blue. Events can be seen to occur: books are burned; stars come out at night; flowers fade and die. The man in the street is a naive realist who lives in a world he can count on, a world he believes is much the same for everyone else. This view may give him a sense of security, but it must be rejected on the basis of contrary evidence. Studies in psychology have revealed that what we know of reality is constructed during the complex processes of perception and cognition. Cross-cultural studies have shown that the way people conceive of the universe differs from one society to another, and that what we take for reality is socially constructed, even though, like all peoples, we make use of sensory input (Berger and Luckmann 1967). Our knowledge results from percepts and the formation of concepts. These are then converted into a code form, which not only allows us to communicate with one another but also to create conceptual worlds of the mind which are far removed from sensory experience.

Percepts

Knowledge is stored and processed within the mind. While it has its most immediate basis in the electrochemical processes of the brain, what we know does not consist of faint copies of environmental objects. The path from a stimulus object to the brain is complex, and many transformations occur along the way. Although information moves along this path in a continuous and rapid fashion, there are several switching points where its form changes. Figure 1 shows several of the major transformations between the stimulus object or event and the mental percept (that is, representation of the object in the mind).

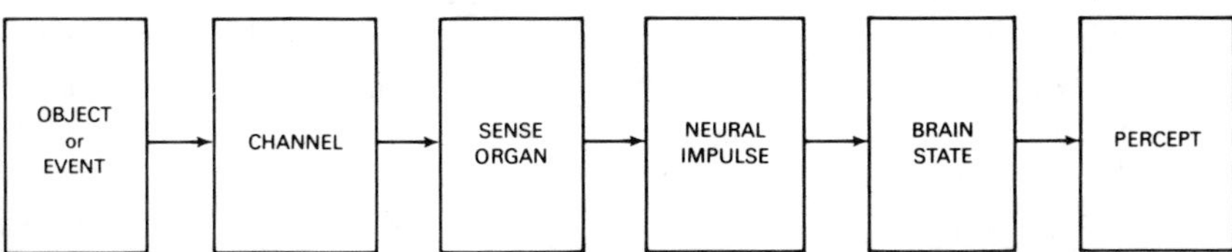

Figure 1:1. Transformations of sensory information.

Consider the following example. The blast of the factory whistle at five o'clock (*event*) serves as a signal that the workday has ended. It has various meanings to those who hear it, but before they can make use of them, they must perceive the whistle blast. The percept of this event is neither the whistle itself nor the pulsations of air it sets in motion (*channel*). When this air turbulance reaches the ear (*sense organ*) the information will again change form so that it may be transmitted to the brain (*neural impulse*). We do not know precisely the *brain state* which occurs and gives rise to a *percept* of the factory whistle, but we do know that even the most direct knowledge changes form as it moves from the external stimulus to the percept. Visual stimuli are mediated in the same way:

> Physically, this page is an array of small mounds of ink, lying in certain positions on the more highly reflective surface of the paper. . . . But the sensory input is not the page itself; it is a pattern of light rays, originating in the sun or in some artificial source, that are reflected from the page and happen to reach the eye. Suitably focused by the lens and other ocular apparatus, the rays fall on the sensitive retina, where they can initiate the neural processes that eventually lead to seeing and remembering (Neisser 1967:3).

The Formation of Concepts

But man does not live by percepts alone. The incoming stimulus information confronts us with an infinitely complex universe. Limited to percepts, we would be hopelessly enslaved to the uniqueness of each object, event, or relation. But the chaotic jumble of sensory stimuli is reduced to manageable terms by the formation of *concepts*. By this process our knowledge is transformed from a multiplicity of percepts to a limited number of informational units. We learn to pay attention to some features of an object and to ignore others. Some attributes are abstracted from the total percept and compared with those abstracted from other perceptions. Although we can discriminate among them, on the basis of these similar attributes we treat different objects *as if* they were equivalent. This is one of the ways in which concepts are formed. This process is represented in Figure 2, which shows five distinct percepts at Level I. The next step is to abstract certain features from each (Level II). Then, discriminable percepts are judged to have similar attributes and are categorized together (Level III). After this a concept is formed which includes all percepts with similar attributes (Level IV). New experiences are then perceived in terms of their attributes and are placed in the proper concept. An example should make this process clearer.

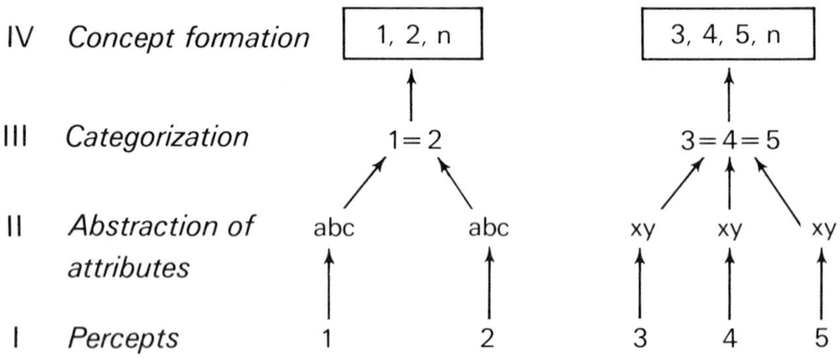

Figure 1:2. Concept formation from percepts.

In my pocket are five metal objects. My knowledge of them is based on a variety of stimulus inputs: I feel them with my fingers, sense their weight in my hand, and examine them visually. These sensations give rise to percepts of the objects, each of which is distinct from the others. Some appear smooth, others rough. Some are bright and shiny, others dull. They have different sizes and weights. The marks and designs engraved on each are slightly different from the others. In most situations I do not ponder long over these distinctions, but quickly sort the objects into one or more concepts.

The attributes of color, size, engraved designs, and monetary value are abstracted. Some of these metal objects are treated as if they were the same size, even though I know they vary slightly. Although each is a different color, two are categorized as copper color and three are seen as silver.

The information regarding a small number of their respective attributes is used to group two of the objects into one equivalence category and three into another. The result is the formation of two concepts. The fact that I have this knowledge may be inferred from my similar responses to the members of each group. I may use verbal labels, saying, "Those are pennies" and "These are dimes." On the other hand, I may simply behave in a consistent fashion with respect to each group, using objects of one class in gum machines and the other in subway meters.

A percept, as we have noted, is a mental representation of some environmental input. One way that concepts are created is by abstracting them from many percepts. Both percepts and concepts are mental events which cannot be observed directly but must be inferred from behavior or verbal report. When we note a common response to an array of objects which are discriminably different, we infer that the organism has formed a concept (Bruner et al. 1956). Kelleher (1958) has demonstrated experimentally that nonhuman primates are capable of such concept formation. Both man and other animals not only form concepts of objects and events but also of the relationships which occur among these. This cognitive process is extremely important for any adaptation to the environment. The child who moves a chair before a high shelf in order to gain access to a desired object has employed a relational concept. The *heights* of the floor, the chair, and the shelf are abstracted, as is the relationship among these different heights. The concept of this relationship is then utilized for the child's purpose. The types of relational concepts are many, including means-end, cause-effect, spatial, part-whole, and function. For example, one attribute of dimes is their function as screwdrivers, one which is not possible for many larger coins. Most coins are spatially related to objects such as banks, pockets, purses, and cash registers. They are also the means to many ends—purchasing candy, rewarding children, and paying bills. If inserted into a gum-ball machine, they become the cause which ejects the gum from the machine. Arrangements among phenomena which are perceived to occur naturally and those which result from concept formation are extremely important. They are stepping-stones to the creation of symbols, which in turn allow for an infinite number of possible relationships in symbolic thought.

The Creation of Symbols

Human knowledge, as we have said, is influenced by what we select and how it is transformed in the process of knowing. The sensory input is not everything which can be perceived, or even a random sample of it. We carefully select by one means or another the stimuli which will reach our brains. Information then changes form as it moves along the path from stimulus object to percept within the mind. The attributes used to form abstract concepts make up a limited number of the ones we could use. This means, for example, that there is a difference between our knowledge of a particular tree and the mental concept "tree." We now turn to one of the most important aspects of cognition, the creation and use of symbols. The forms of knowledge discussed thus far are closely linked to sensory experience. Although percepts and concepts are mediated, in contrast to symbols, they are still very directly tied to stimulus inputs. When something acts as a symbol, it is one step removed from this immediacy. But symbols are not the only things which represent other phenomena. The class of objects employed to refer to or represent something else is called a *sign.* Since a symbol is only one type of sign, it will be useful to examine the general nature of signs.

There has been a good deal written about the role of signs in human behavior (Pierce 1931; Morris 1938, 1946; Landar, 1965). My purpose is not to review this literature, but to clarify several points in order to contrast symbols with other kinds of signs. There are three primary factors involved in the use of signs: (1) A stimulus—that is, any object, event, quality, or relation that can be perceived—may be employed as a sign. A cloud, a wave of the hand, a factory whistle, a person snoring, a pungent odor—all may function as signs. In fact, any aspect of sensory experience may be brought into a relationship with other phenomena in such a way as to become a sign. (2) That which a sign refers to, calls attention to, or causes some organism to take account of, is called a *referent.* It may be anything conceivable in human experience. In addition to perceptual information, a referent may be abstract thoughts, ideas, and things which can never be observed. Signs thus may refer to the coins in my pocket, the curve in the road, or the green dragon with seven heads which appeared in Caesar's dream. (3) For a sign to function, some organism must grasp the relationship between it and the referent it stands for. Any such organism is an *interpreter.* Just as with percepts and concepts, the interpretation of signs is a mental process which must be inferred from behavior or verbal report. We infer that the factory worker is treating the whistle as a sign because he stops working when he hears it. When I make a hand motion to a friend, he comes toward me or waves back. Pavlov's dog responded to the bell by salivating, from which we infer that the sound functioned as a sign of food.

Now, if some object is to act as a sign, the interpreter must shift attention from the object to its referent. Every stimulus object provides us with information about itself. A sign, on the other hand, results in two types of knowledge—that which is intrinsic (knowledge about the sign) and that which is not (knowledge about the referent). During the course of a week there are several occasions when the sound of a siren reaches my ear. I am aware of a loud noise which rises and falls in both pitch and intensity. It begins slowly, continues for a few minutes, and then fades away. The percepts which I have of this event are similar to previous perceptions, and I may place them together in the concept "siren." Up to this point I have only paid attention to the intrinsic qualities of the event. But, like most city dwellers, I have learned to treat a siren as more than a mere sound. It takes little conscious effort to shift my attention away from the stimulus to the concept of "approaching fire engine, police car, or ambulance." I do not respond to the sound itself but to what it refers to. Neither do I confuse the sound with an approaching vehicle. If I am driving a car, I will probably move to the edge of the street and stop—not to avoid the sound of a siren, but to remain clear of an unseen vehicle which is the referent of the sound. This shift of attention from sign to referent, once learned, is produced unconsciously, so that we seldom stop to think, "I hear a siren; that stands for an approaching vehicle; therefore a fire engine or ambulance must be coming." Our attention is so thoroughly focused on the referent that signs are said to take on the meaning of that which they refer to.

The classification of different kinds of signs depends upon the attributes one selects. We shall focus on the relationship between a sign and its referent, to distinguish the three major kinds of signs: *icon*, *index*, and *symbol* (Nida, 1964:30–31). It was stated earlier that our percepts and concepts involve relationships among phenomena, many of which occur in nature. The leaves are under that tree; rain occurs when there are clouds; bees are associated with buzzing; if one snores, it is usually when asleep. The number of possible relationships is infinite. When one element in such a *natural association* acts as a sign by shifting attention to the other, it is an index. If I notice leaves on the ground, they are an index of a tree nearby. Clouds are a sign (index) of rain. The buzzing is a sign of bees, and if I hear snoring from a closed room, it becomes an index that someone is in there asleep. We constantly employ this type of sign in the normal course of adaptation to the environment. It enables us to extend our knowledge beyond sensory perception and anticipate the future. Tracks in the snow are an index of unseen animal life. The man who is wandering on the desert looks for green plants as a sign of water—indeed, they may even appear in his mind as a mirage. Any natural associations which occur with some degree of probability can be used as an index. When someone says, "where there's smoke, there's fire," he is expressing the essential nature of an index.

A second type of sign is an icon. It is based on some *formal association* or likeness between two elements. A statue acts as an icon of the person whose likeness it represents. The icons in Figure 3 share certain formal similarities with their referents. This resemblance enables us to interpret them with little difficulty, although this does not eliminate the need for learning. The significant feature, then, that relates an icon to its referent is physical resemblance.

Figure 1:3. Examples of icons.

The third kind of sign is a symbol. It is distinguished from the others by virtue of an *arbitrary relationship* between stimulus object and referent (Figure 4). This means, for example, that your percept of this *page* could be represented by many stimuli besides that four-letter word. If we consider only the conventional English letters and all their possible combinations as potential symbols, we can see the arbitrary nature of the word *page*. Unlike an icon, the symbol has no formal similarity to its referent. The word *page* does not resemble the piece of paper in a book which it refers to. The factory whistle does not share a likeness with the termination of a workday. There is no physical similarity between the sound of a siren and the concept of an approaching fire engine. At the same time, a symbol is not naturally associated with its referent as is the index. The wave of your hand is not related to the departure of a friend in the same way that smoke is associated with fire or clouds with rain. Buzzing is an index of a bee because that organism can make no other audible sound. Your spoken name is a symbol because an infinite number of other sounds could refer to you. The creation and use of symbols, as well as their interpretation, depend upon *rules*. A rule is an instruction to behave in a particular way. Every

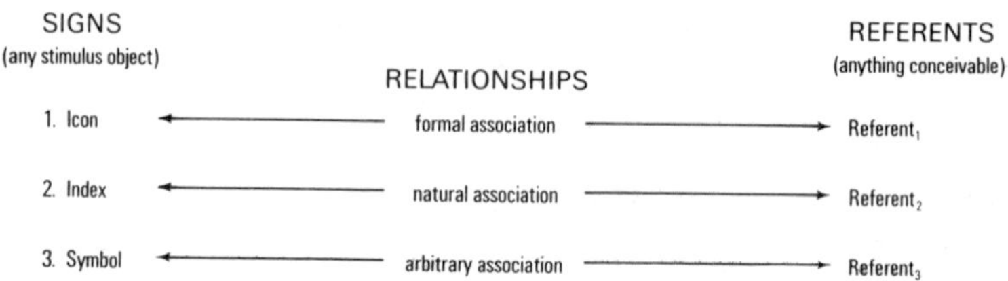

Figure 1:4. Types of relationships among signs and referents.

symbol, because it is arbitrary, implicitly involves a rule for attaching it to a particular referent. When my telephone rings, I could let it mean that someone is at my office door waiting to be admitted. Instead, I interpret it as an instruction to attach this stimulus to the concept "someone wishes to speak to me on the telephone." I then may or may not follow the related rule which instructs me to pick up the receiver and say hello.

Because of the importance of rules for both cultural knowledge and cultural behavior, we shall discuss this concept more fully, but first let us consider some of the consequences of our capacity to use symbols. The creation of symbols reduces our dependence upon immediate sensory experience. Although we can deal with present objects and events, we can also transcend them to a degree not possible for other animals. An event which occurred in the remote past, even before birth, may become part of our knowledge via symbols. Consider the person in our society who discovers that his parents, now dead, were never legally married or the man who discovers that his wife of many years is actually his sister. These past events will undoubtedly elicit their responses in the present. Similarly, we can represent the future and respond to events which may never occur. The student who attends college is anticipating the acquisition of a degree at the end of his education. The parent who saves money for an infant daughter's college tuition is likewise employing symbols to construct a tentative knowledge of the distant future. Symbols also enable us to transcend our confinement in space. We know about places we have never visited and are able to prepare for conditions we expect to encounter on trips to distant lands. When Orson Welles broadcast his fictitious report of an invasion from outer space, individuals far removed from the purported event responded to it. Man does not merely adapt to his environment, but to his symbolic environment, which may include the far reaches of the universe. As A. Irving Hallowell has said:

> This simply means that at the level of human adjustment the representations of objects and events of all kinds play as characteristic a role in man's total behavior as does the direct presentation of objects and events in perception. . . . Representative processes are at the root of man's capacity to deal with the possible or conceivable, the ideal as well as the actual, the intangible along with the tangible, the absent as well as the present object or event, with fantasy and with reality (1955:7).

A second consequence of using symbols as a code for what we know is the ability to communicate. Much of our knowledge can be converted into a set of stimuli which others can perceive. We can move our bodies in ways that can be seen: eyes can close, arms can be raised, and the head can move in a variety of directions. It is possible to make noises by vibrating the vocal cords, clapping our hands, or stamping our feet. Objects in the environment can be manipulated to create sensory information for others to perceive. Any of these humanly-produced stimuli can be employed as symbols which represent what we know. For communication to occur, it is necessary that others learn the same rules for attaching these stimuli to the appropriate concepts. As Wallace L. Chafe has pointed out, without symbols the communication of our knowledge would be impossible.

> Ideas, I assume, have some kind of electro-chemical existence in the nervous systems of individuals. Whatever their representations there may be, they cannot pass from one person to another in that form, for there is no direct neural connection between two separate organisms, no pathway over which ideas can travel in their original state. Language, like other communicative devices, provides the means of bridging this gap by converting ideas into a medium which does have the capacity to pass between one nervous system and another (1970:16).

Human interaction is essentially symbolic interaction. Nearly every movement, sound, odor, or touch of another human being acts as a symbol which we learn to interpret. And, as we move from one society to another, the code changes, and different meanings become attached to behavior. A loud belch during a meal may signal that one is pleased with the food in one society, while in another it is evidence that one is poorly socialized.

Symbolic communication is a complex phenomenon that utilizes numerous channels and many bits of information simultaneously. Let us simplify our picture of the communicative process by the use of two concepts in a common situation involving interaction. The major features in the process of transferring information from one mind to another are shown in Figure 5 and may be illustrated with an example from interaction between a child and his teacher.

In our society children communicate their desire for a teacher to recognize them and allow them to speak by using a simple symbol—a raised arm and hand. The teacher learns to interpret this symbol and to select from a variety of responses to it. For instance, she may ignore the raised hand,

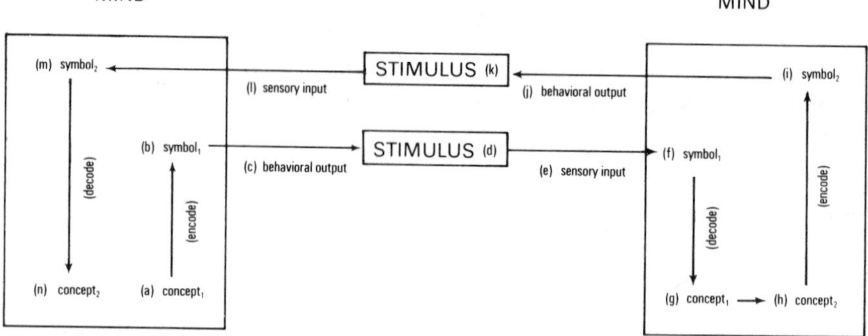

Figure 1:5. Symbolic interaction and communication.

reprimand the child for raising his hand at the wrong time, or employ his name and say, "Johnny?" If we follow the arrows in Figure 5, we may examine this simple interaction in closer detail. Johnny begins with the concept (*a*) "recognize me," which he desires to communicate. While he could stamp his feet, run out of the room, shout the teacher's name, or any number of other things, he has learned a code rule for associating this concept with a raised hand, which thus acts as a symbol (*b*). Then follows the behavioral output (*c*) when he raises his hand so that it can act as a stimulus object for the teacher (*d*). If he is especially eager, he may move his hand in short rapid movements, which not only makes it more visible, but changes his behavior into a different symbol with another meaning. The sensory input (*e*) received by the teacher is a percept which could have many meanings, but she has learned that it is a symbol (*f*) to be decoded as one representing the concept (*g*) "recognize me." The rules associated with this concept are a guide to the teacher for selecting among several alternative responses. Many responses are ruled out. She could immediately send Johnny to the principal—and indeed she would if he only varied the position of his fingers slightly! There are rules for selecting among the appropriate alternatives, and we will assume that she select the concept (*h*) "Johnny, you may speak," which in turn is encoded into a symbol (*i*) which leads to the spoken word "Johnny?" (*j*). The stimulus (*k*) is received as sensory input (*l*), treated as a symbol (*m*), and decoded into the proper concept (*n*), "Johnny, you may speak." The use of symbols has enabled two organisms to link their nervous systems and to convert concepts within their separate minds into stimulus objects which each other can interpret. This process of communication is possible because each has learned that rules for encoding information, producing symbols which carry that information, and finally decoding those same symbols.

A third consequence of symbol usage is a tremendous increase in man's capacity to generate new knowledge. The vast majority of our concepts do not result from our percepts, but rather from the recombinations of other concepts in symbolic thought. The rather simple idea of "recognize me," expressed in a raised hand, involves a combination of at least three concepts: "you," "recognize," and "me." One of the chief advantages of verbal and written symbols is the ease with which we can rearrange them to create new ideas and concepts. Symbols not only reduce our dependence upon sensory experience; they also allow us to create worlds which have no empirical reality at all. Ward H. Goodenough writes:

> Our language provides us with a set of behavioral percepts that serves as a code for our other percepts. It enables us to reduce the rest of experience to a set of coded items and propositions about them. By substituting one item of the code for another in various propositions, we can symbolically create new arrangements of

> phenomena by analogy with old ones, new arrangements that we have not experienced directly at all. Thus by substituting one coded item for another we move from the experience of purple flowers and purple hats to the vicarious experience of purple cows. Such analogies bring us to new discernments that we have not perceived in direct experience but have conceived as products of the manipulation of coded experience. These products, our concepts, may be perceivable in sensory experience or may remain, like one's more remote ancestors or like the ether of nineteenth-century physics, things whose existence can be postulated but never directly observed. Our concepts, once coded as part of language, can be manipulated along with our percepts to produce even more concepts (1963:148).

The generative capacity of symbolic thought is one of the primary factors in culture change. Most of the innovations of a culture are recombinations of old elements into new patterns, which are made possible by the use of symbols (Barnett 1953).

Rules

The versatility of symbols opens up the possibility for immense variations in human behavior. Because symbols are arbitrary, any stimulus can represent any conceivable entity in the universe. While this alone creates a staggering range of possibilities, it is increased even more by the fact that symbols can be arranged in a myriad of combinations. Imagine, if you will, that man as a species has come upon a vast ocean of sand which extends as far as the eye can see. Each unique grain of sand can be used to stand for any other, for any combination of grains, or for the entire sea of sand. Furthermore, those selected to act as symbols can be arranged in a never-ending series of combinations and patterns. It is this kind of potential variation which emerges from our capacity for symbols.

It is not surprising that man hardly begins to exploit this potential. Like a group of children who have filled their buckets from the vast expanse of sand, each society selects only a small proportion of the actions which are humanly possible. More important, these are not randomly arranged like grains of sand thrown into a container. What people do in any society follows recurring patterns. Individuals come to expect themselves and others to behave in standard ways. Each language is a selection of fewer than sixty of the indefinite number of vocal sounds which man can produce, and there are strict limitations on how these can be combined. Each society employs only a few of the possible ways to eat, sleep, give gifts, name children, arrange marriages, and organize people. Cultural behavior is customary behavior, which means that human actions are not randomly put together, that some arrangements are excluded from each society's repertoire.

In other words, there are conditions which restrict both the range and patterning of human behavior. One important class of restrictions—though by no means the only one—is the rules which are learned by members of a society. Other factors which limit behavior include human nature, the physical environment, and other kinds of learning. For example, when a person blinks one or both eyelids, it may be accounted for in terms of any of these conditions. Blinking occurs at regular intervals in most humans and is most often explained as a reflex. It could also be a result of environmental conditions such as dust in the air or a strong wind. In addition, blinking may be a conditioned reflex which results from experimental manipulation of stimuli and reinforcements. But none of these approaches can account for some aspects of blinking behavior. When a young girl meets a man for the first time and her eyelids flutter rapidly, we infer that she has learned rules for producing this behavior. If his response is appropriate, we infer that he knows the same rules and is able to interpret this blinking correctly. The movement of a single eyelid is very often governed by rules which differ from one society to another. As Robert L. Lado has remarked:

> A wink from a man to a woman in Spain might be a bold suggestion. From a woman to a man it might be even more of a suggestion. In the United States a wink does not normally have such meaning. It is difficult for the Spanish individual not to react to a wink in the United States the way he might in his own culture (1957: 144; quoted in Goodenough 1963:455).

There is considerable disagreement among social scientists over the meaning and value of the concept of rules. Some would even reject it as a useful concept for description or explanation of human behavior. Part of the problem lies in the fact that a single term has acquired a variety of meanings. For some, rules are only applicable to ideal behavior, and since they are consistently violated, it hardly seems useful to account for behavior by stating rules. For others, rules are only those prescripts which an actor can formulate with clarity; so since much of behavior is outside of awareness, they reject this notion. Another source of confusion arises from the use of many different terms to convey the same idea. For example, *norms, laws, customs, mores, expectations,* and *regulations* are all used in some instances as synonyms for rules. Accounting for behavior in terms of cultural rules has sometimes included the idea that culture uses man, in contrast to the view that man is an active agent who uses culture. Finally, rules are so much a part of our own cultural tradition that the concept has many folk meanings (Black 1962:95–139). Children are taught to obey the rules. Rules are posted around swimming pools, in locker rooms, and at the park. We have all learned there are rules for driving, parking, fighting, playing games, taking tests, mailing packages, and reporting our income taxes. We have rules for survival in the wilderness, for executing a proper turn while skiing, and for playing chess.

Much of the semantic confusion arises from a failure to recognize two things: First, all rules have certain *common features.* This is true for those formulated by the mother who tells a child, "Don't cross the street," and those employed by the anthropologist to describe marriage practices in a primitive society. Second, there are many inter- and intrasocietal *variations* among rules. Some rules are explicit; others are not. Some have a profound influence on behavior, while others are ignored by most people. The sanctions vary for the person who breaks a rule: others may simply laugh at the offender, or they may even condemn him to death for his behavior. Let us examine the nature of rules, some of their common properties, and also some of the distinctions among them. The following propositions are presented as a tentative proposal for using this concept; and let me say again, authors in later chapters sometimes use the term in other ways.

1. According to the definition previously given, *rules are instructions to behave in a particular way.* Cultural behavior is constructed by learning and following instructions. Driving a car involves numerous rules, including which side of the street is to be used and how fast one may travel. Speaking a language, performing a ceremony, baking a cake, picking up a hitchhiker—all these actions involve sets of instructions, recipes, if you will, for their performance. A recipe for baking a cake is a set of instructions for selecting ingredients, mixing them in certain proportions, placing them in a container of known size, and cooking this mixture for a specified period. Cultural rules of any sort are a similar set of instructions for putting together elements of behavior. Cultural knowledge also involves rules. We learn instructions which guide our perceptions and which specify those attributes to be used in forming concepts. Attaching symbols to their referents is regulated by rules. We also follow instructions when we interpret the behavior of others.

2. *Rules, as elements of human knowledge, have their locus in the mind.* We assume that instructions are somehow stored within the brain in the form of protein or RNA molecules. It is well known that DNA and RNA molecules can encode a very large amount of information because of their complex structures. Like the program stored in a computer, rules are made up of bits of information stored in the brain and used to process other information as well as to organize behavior. Like many other mental phenomena, rules can be represented by symbols outside the mind. While rules are known by an individual, that person may not be able to state them explicitly. Like the grammar or phonology of a language, many instructions are difficult to verbalize. Michael Polanyi considers this type of knowledge to be tacit. He writes:

> I shall reconsider human knowledge by starting from the fact that we can know more than we can tell. This fact seems obvious enough; but it is not easy to say exactly what it means. Take an example. We know a person's face, and can recognize it among a thousand, indeed among a million. Yet we usually cannot tell how we recognize a face we know. So most of this knowledge cannot be put into words (1966:4).

A major task for researchers in culture and cognition is to formulate those tacit rules which members of a society are using to organize their behavior. The fact that rules have not been encoded in symbols does not mean that individuals do not know them. While it is impossible for me to specify where each symbol on a typewriter keyboard is located, I have a tacit knowledge of where they are. Indeed, I can even type rapidly and accurately without needing visual assistance to locate these symbols. At one time I took great pains to learn the location of each and the instructions for typing, but now these rules for producing letters and words are part of my *tacit* knowledge.

3. *Rules are learned through symbolic communication and by inference from behavior.* These ways of learning are employed by the social scientist as well as the child undergoing socialization. Once a set of instructions is encoded in symbols, it is a simple matter to communicate them. The richest settings for discovering the rules of a society are those where novices of one sort or another are being instructed in appropriate behavior. Indeed, the young child in our society is the recipient of a steady stream of rules: "Wash your hands," "It is time to go to bed," "Don't cross the street," "Say 'please,'" and "Stand up straight." Schools are in the business of transmitting a host of rules to each new generation. The anthropologist in a strange society will begin to ask key informants for the rules of appropriate behavior. In every society some of the rules are made explicit and are communicated via symbols.

Rules can also be inferred from behavior. When it is observed that young couples who hold hands in our society are heterosexual or female, we infer that males learn a rule to abstain from such behavior. At a wedding, everyone stands to his feet when the bride enters, and we infer that there is a rule to this effect. Most of us have participated in at least one social event where we did not know what the rules were. Perhaps we asked someone or by careful observation inferred that certain instructions were being followed. For example, the behavior of others provided clues regarding the time to leave a party, which fork to use at a formal dinner, or whether to remain seated when someone entered the room. While the linguist infers many of the rules of grammar from samples of speech behavior, he is not the only one who uses this process to arrive at a knowledge of the rules. Children in every society acquire the instructions on how to construct and interpret sentences which are appropriate by observing the speech behavior of adults around them. One reason many of the rules we know are tacit is that they are learned from the process of observation and inference. We are seldom given verbal instructions regarding which attributes make up concepts like "tree," "street," "friend," or "blue." As we observe others using these terms, we infer the rules they are following. Then, as we use them ourselves and as others correct us, we grow more certain of the appropriate rules. The task for the anthropologist studying culture and cognition is much the same as for every child: by *inference* and *instruction* he seeks to acquire a comprehensive knowledge of both tacit and explicit cultural rules. These, taken as a guide for behavior, should enable him to act appropriately in the society he studies.

4. *Rules are learned at different levels, which determine their effect on behavior.* Intuitively we are aware that some individuals seem to follow rules more closely than others. We correct the child who says, "I was gooder cause I dranked my milk." The fact that he has not quite learned to follow some grammatical rules does not disturb us. Our reactions are stronger when someone belches loudly at a meal, when the beginning driver violates the rules of safety, or when a young professor grades examinations unfairly. One reason for the semantic quagmire which has developed around the concept of rules is the failure to recognize different degrees of learning. These levels of learning begin with a person who has just heard about a new rule. He may not understand it or have any plans to abide by it. At the other end of the scale is the individual who has internalized a rule so thoroughly that it is part of his tacit knowledge and a violation would be unthinkable. Indeed, if it is a rule for guiding complex motor activity, he may find it extremely difficult to break the rule even when instructed to! While there is undoubtedly an infinite number of gradations in the degrees to which a rule has been learned, we shall consider the five levels proposed by Spiro for learning the concepts of an ideology:

> (a) The actors have *learned about* the ideological concept, i.e., they have been exposed to it in some manner, ranging from formal instruction to informal gossip. (b) The actors have not only learned about the concept, but they also *understand* the meaning that a text or a key informant attributes to it. (c) Understanding its meaning, the actors *believe* the concept to be right or true or valid. (d) Constituting a salient element in their cognitive systems, the concept serves to inform the actors' *behavioral* environment (as Hallowell calls it) and to structure their world. (e) In addition to its cognitive salience, the concept has been *internalized* as an important element in the actor's motivational system, so that it serves not only to guide, but also to instigate, behavior (Spiro 1966:1163).

Spiro argues that if we are to assess the influence of ideology upon behavior we must discover the level at which concepts have been learned. The same is true for rules.

Consider the following example: A few years ago an anthropologist who described the cultural knowledge of a certain religious group in our society would have discovered many rules. Among them he would have noted the following: "In order to protect yourself while traveling, carry a Saint Christopher medal." This rule would have been repeated to him by priest and layman, alike. A general statement to the effect that it was part of this culture might have described their knowledge, but not necessarily their behavior. Individual variations in behavior are due, in part, to the different levels at which rules are learned. (a) Some would have only *learned about* the rule. This would have been especially true of very young children and newcomers to the group. They might have acquired this minimal knowledge by observing Saint Christopher medals in automobiles or from verbal statements of the rule. If it had only been learned to this extent, the rule would have had little influence on their behavior. (b) Second, some would have *understood the meaning* of the rule. They would have known that Saint Christopher was a saint believed to have been martyred about A.D. 250, that he should be venerated, that he was the patron saint of ferrymen and travelers, and that his day was to be celebrated on July 25 of each year. They would have known that his sainthood resulted in power to protect travelers and that this protection was granted to those who carried Saint Christopher medals. They might also have known of individuals who had escaped accidents, reportedly as a result of following this rule. But again, this kind of knowledge does not allow us to say anything about cultural behavior. Indeed, the anthropologist would probably have understood the meaning of this rule without adopting the practice of carrying medals. Likewise, many who learned the rule at this level may not have accepted it as valid for themselves.

(c) At the third level, some would have *believed* this rule to be true (that is, accepted it as right) and declared that it should be followed. Still, this in itself is no guarantee that they would always have carried a Saint Christopher medal. What if it had been stolen while the individual was on a trip and had no opportunity to acquire a new medal? Poverty or some other condition might also have prevented one from following the rule. If someone insists that his belief is sincere but consistently violates it, we may suspect that he is lying or has self-destructive wishes. At the very least, we would expect him to account for accidents while traveling in terms of his failure to abide by the rule.

Finally, there would have been some individuals who had learned this religious instruction so thoroughly that it was consistently used to organize their behavior. (d) For some, it would have been a salient part of their cognitive system. They would have carried their medals whenever they traveled. If they ever were unable to do so, our researcher would have noticed an increased sense of agitation or anxiety about accidents. Others involved in accidents while traveling would have been criticized for their failure to carry medals. When a near-accident took place for those who had learned the rule at this level, they would have offered a prayer of thanksgiving to Saint Christopher for his protection. (e) Some members of the group may have *internalized* this rule as part of their motivational system. Many rules which we learn are a *means* to some goal. Saint Christopher medals have been carried in order to reduce or eliminate accidents while traveling. Grammatical rules are followed in order to communicate with one's fellows. In some cases, the instructions are so thoroughly internalized that they become ends in themselves. If the church declared that Saint Christopher was no longer efficacious, we might still expect individuals who had internalized the rule to continue to carry their medals—and such has been the case.

There is a tendency for some researchers to write as if all rules are *cognitively salient* at the fourth level or *internalized* at the fifth level of learning. On the other hand, critics sometimes write as if all rules can only be learned at the first or second level. Harris declares:

> If permitted to develop unchecked, the tendency to write ethnographies in accord with the emic rules of behavior will result in an unintentional parody of the human condition. Applied to our own culture it would conjure up a way of life in which men tip their hats to ladies; youths defer to old people in public conveyances; unwed mothers are a rarity; citizens go to the aid of law enforcement officers; chewing gum is never stuck under tables and never dropped on the sidewalk; television repairmen fix television sets; children respect their aged parents; rich and poor get the same medical treatment; taxes are paid in full; all men are created equal; and our defense budget is used only for maintaining peace (1968:590).

In point of fact, this criticism is a parody of studies in culture and cognition. In the first place, the study of rules is not limited to instructions for ideal behavior. It has been recognized for some time that the dichotomy between ideal and real behavior is an oversimplification (Richards 1969; De Josselin de Jong 1971).

> In all societies, as many anthropologists have pointed out, there is an ideal pattern—what members of the society feel should be done when people behave "properly" or "normally"— and there is the real behavior—what people in the society actually do. In addition, however, there is the *presumed* behavior—what members of the society *think* other members do (Richards 1969:1115).

It is our contention that social interaction is largely dependent upon the presumed behavior of others. In a study of the culture of tramps in an urban setting, I focused to a large extent on the rules for presumed behavior (Spradley 1970). Informants reported their knowledge of what they believed men in this subculture actually did. It is important to point out that real behavior is what the investigator *thinks* others do. There are other important distinctions between real and presumed behavior, but the primary one is that the observer is a trained researcher in the former case and an informant in the latter. Second, the discovery of rules is not limited to verbal communication. They are formulated and tested by observation and inference, as well. An ethnography of American culture would probably include the rule "Don't stick chewing gum under tables at home," and this would emerge from inference as well as from the explicit statements of those studied. The rule, "Don't stick chewing gum under tables in public places," would be elicited for ideal conduct, but most informants would also report that many people actually do the opposite (presumed behavior), and we could formulate a rule to account for that also.

5. *The rules inferred by an observer from the behavior of an actor are not isomorphic with the rules employed by that actor.* This means that what an observer constructs to account for behavior must not be confused with the mental phenomenon which generates that behavior. There is wide agreement on the fact that cognitive models cannot be formulated with *perfect* psychological validity (Wallace and Atkins 1960; Burling 1964) in the sense that "the description is to replicate on paper what goes on neurophysiologically, or perceptually, in the heads of our subjects" (Keesing 1970:444). Nevertheless, there are differences in the way investigators talk about *mental rules*, *formulated rules*, and *behavior*, as well as relationships among these terms. Some eschew any interest in cognition or mental rules at all. Diagram 1 shows the essential features of this approach:

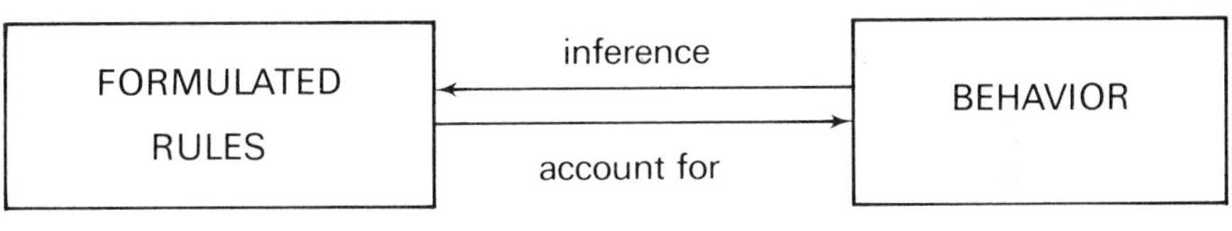

Diagram 1:1.

Robbins Burling writes:

> ...we have little idea what the processes of natural sentence production are, and it is safer to take the rules as simply a convenient and plausible mechanism in describing sentences (1970:68–69).... It certainly sounds more exciting to say we are "discovering the cognitive systems of the people" than to admit that we are just fiddling with a set of rules which allow us to use terms the way others do. Nevertheless, I think the latter is a realistic goal, while the former is not. I believe we should be content with the less exciting objective of showing how terms in language are applied to objects in the world, and stop pursuing the illusory goal of cognitive structures (1964:27).

While rejecting any claim that formulated and mental rules are isomorphic, we take the position that something does occur within the central nervous system of the actor and that we should not completely ignore it.

Several authors have suggested the helpful analogy between mental rules and computer programs. Roger M. Keesing writes:

> What we are seeking is an analog or model of some elements of what might be in the black box . . . The task is rather like communicating with a computer through an input-output device, and trying to build a theory of how it is programmed and what information is stored in it; and phrasing that theory in a metalanguage (like Fortran) that is quite different from the electronic coding in the computer (1970: 444).

Ulric Neisser, approaching the problem from the perspective of cognitive psychology, has written:

> Although a program is nothing but a flow of symbols, it has reality enough to control the operation of very tangible machinery that executes very physical operations. A man who seeks to discover the program of a computer is surely not doing anything self-contradictory! (1967:8).

We may diagram this interest in the following manner:

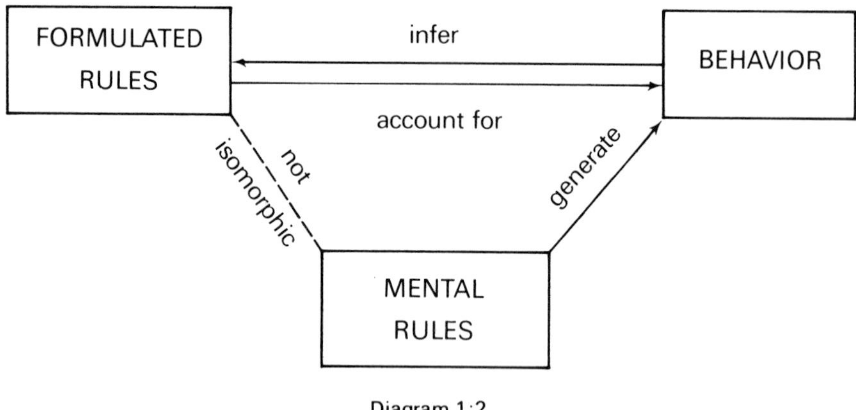

Diagram 1:2.

As we have already said, accounting for behavior by means of rules is not limited to scientific investigators. It is a *common human activity*. As Raoul Naroll has pointed out:

> All people are constantly constructing theories, testing them against reality, and forming conclusions in their minds about the probabilities concerned—the probabilities of their observations, and the probabilities of their general theories (1970:27).

As a child acquires the grammar of his language, he must infer the rules used by adults to construct and interpret messages. Social interaction requires that each of us makes sense out of the behavior of other people. We do this by formulating hypotheses that others are acting on the basis of certain rules. These hunches are tested by repeated observations, from which we arrive at the probabilities that a certain individual will act accordingly. For example, as I approach a person who is hitchhiking, I infer that he is acting in terms of cultural rules. If I offer him a ride, I anticipate that he will act as a friendly passenger. It may turn out that he intends to threaten me with a gun and steal my car, but, since I have estimated this to be a very low probability, I often pick up hitchhikers. In most of our encounters we can reliably anticipate how others will behave. When our theories are not confirmed, we generally revise them and change our behavior in the future. George Kelly, in an unpublished paper, has proposed that this behavior is not different in kind from the work of scientists. He suggests that many textbooks actually contain two theories of human behavior, one to explain what scientists do and one to explain the behavior of others. He then asks:

> But what would happen if one were to envision all human endeavor in those same terms the psychologists have found so illuminating in explaining themselves to their students? And, indeed, might it not be that in doing so one would see the course of individual life, as well as human progress over the centuries, in clearer perspective? Scientists are men, and, while it does not follow that men are scientists, it is quite appropriate to ask if it is not their human character that makes scientists what they are. This leads us to the question of how that human character can better be construed so as to account for scientists, and whether our construction can still explain as well the accomplishments that fall far short of what we, at this transient moment in our history, think good science is (Kelly 1966, quoted in Bannister & Mair 1968:3).

In order to understand the game of chess or any other social activity, the scientist as well as the novice must begin by learning the rules for appropriate behavior. As they watch others play and listen to their instructions, each learns the rules of the game. Both will discover things outside the awareness of those who are playing, that is, the tacit rules. The scientist may be more skilled at this and perhaps seek to develop a comprehensive theory of games in general—something few chess players will do. In addition, he is trained to make exceptionally careful observations and to formulate the rules in an uncommonly elegant and precise manner. But the essential activity is the same—both will formulate theories about the rules for chess, predict the behavior of chess players, and test their theories by observations.

Now, if all people are inferring the rules used by others, and if these rules are not isomorphic with the ones employed by actors, it raises an important question for any theory of culture: To what extent can it be said that culture is *shared* by members of a society? Cultural behavior is shared in the sense that we can indicate the extent to which individuals in the same role engage in similar behavior. For example, we can report that 99 percent of all men arraigned for public drunkeness in a particular court plead guilty to the charge. But do these men share a body of cultural knowledge? Because the judge and those arraigned interact in a predictable manner, it is often inferred that they also share the same *cultural knowledge*, the same definition of the situation. But it is not necessarily so that cognitive sharing occurs in either case. Men plead guilty for a host of reasons. The judge sentences men on the basis of rules he has learned, which are often at odds with those used by drunks.

Let us consider this interaction in more detail. In a study of sentencing drunks, the following rule was inferred from observations and interviews with the judge: "Drunks who admit they have a drinking problem and desire professional help should be sentenced to a treatment center rather than jail" (Spradley 1970). While this study was in progress, more than two hundred men were sentenced to the treatment center, largely on the basis of this rule. A study of the cultural knowledge of these men revealed that many operated with rules which were quite different from those the judge used. The treatment center was a pleasant place to spend several months, especially during the winter. It was doing "easy time" instead of the "hard time" done in jail. Yet men who did not feel they had a drinking problem and who furthermore did not want help were also sentenced to the treatment center. How did this happen? They used the rule, "In order to do easy time, convince the judge you have a drinking problem and want professional help." Although the judge sometimes suspected this to be the operating principle used by drunks, it was difficult to be sure and even harder to believe that such men would not earnestly desire professional treatment for their illness. The drunk who used this rule only did so after anticipating the length of time the judge would sentence him to jail. This was done by inferring the rules for length of sentence used by the judge, an inference which was extremely accurate. On each successive arraignment, sentences were increased in magnitude; but if a man could stay out of court for six months, the judge would begin anew and only give him a two-day suspended sentence. One man volunteered for treatment on the basis of the following calculation: "If I'd done my time in jail I might have been back in there doing time now. I think I'm ahead coming out here because I had sixty days hanging [his anticipated sentence] and might have gotten another sixty days [after release from jail]." After four months at the treatment center, he planned to go to another city for two more months, so that when he returned to Seattle an arrest would result in a minimum sentence! In the courtroom drama both judge and drunk play their parts with the satisfaction of knowing they have followed the rules, even though they are often unaware that these are quite different from each other's. A.F.C. Wallace has proposed the notion of equivalence structures to account for this kind of symbolic interaction (1970). Cognitive nonsharing is even seen as functional because it "liberates the participants in a system from the heavy burden of learning and knowing each other's motivations and cognitions" (1970:35). An adequate description of culture, whether one focuses on behavior or on knowledge, must take seriously the fact that similar behavior or predictable interaction *may* be based on cognitive systems which are not shared.

5. *Cultural rules are instructions for constructing, combining, interpreting, and otherwise dealing with symbols.* When you construct a symbol —be it a word, a wave of the hand, a red light, or a ritual—it must be done in a certain way. Rules tell us how. There is a range of variation: a word may be whispered or shouted, a hand may be waved slowly or rapidly, a light can be many different shades of red, and a ritual allows for some flexibility. Rules are instructions for staying within those limits. In addition, they tell us what arrangements are permissible for symbolic behavior. Food has meaning in every society, and individuals learn instructions for arranging it at mealtime. Our culture, for example, prohibits mixing all items of food and drink in a single container. Likewise, cultural rules determine the way we combine all symbols, whether letters, words, clothes, furniture, books, sounds, gestures, or ceremonies. Every symbol stands for *some*thing, not merely *any*thing, so there are rules for interpreting each one. Social life is a continuous stream of symbolic behavior in which we are unendingly constructing, combining, interpreting, storing, and processing symbols in a myriad of different ways. This stream of behavior is organized by cultural rules.

Rules are instructions which act as constraints on behavior—say "cat" by using *those* muscles; identify *that* object as a tree; show agreement by nodding your head in *that* way; express your loyalty by displaying *that* flag in *that* position. They tell us, for each symbol, to include some things and exclude others. John Atkins and Luke Curtis have emphasized this function of rules:

> Let us begin by postulating that rules of every sort share at least one common property: they all may be said to *rule in* something or other, while *ruling out* something else. This assertion does not report any startling empirical discovery, of course; it merely constitutes a proposal that attention be shifted from the abstract noun "rule" to the pair of verbs "to rule in (out)." We are claiming, in effect, that ruling in and out is what rules "do" and are at minimum "for," whatever else may be said of them (1969:217).

Even when some action is not generated by rules, it is usually assigned a meaning—some interpretations are ruled in and others out. The woman with an armload of packages who stumbles on a busy street has not learned rules for this action, but she and those nearby will interpret her accident.

Stuttering, while not the result of instructions, will take on cultural meaning which varies from one society to another.

As we learn the concepts which constitute our cultural knowledge, we inevitably learn rules.

> A category or a concept is a rule for identifying the parts of one's world, physical, and ideational, and it always refers to a class of events, objects, ideas, or whatever. A given rule or category invokes those attributes necessary for the identification of each member of the class to which the category refers (Zajonc 1968:332).

Implicit in the category "dog" is the attribute of having four legs. Two legs, six legs, or any combination except four is ruled out of this concept. The concept "aunt" involves a rule which invokes the attribute of female and rules out males. "Cousin," on the other hand, rules in persons of either sex and uses other attributes to rule out certain kinds of relatives. The use of concepts always involves information-processing rules (Geoghegan 1971). This means that the study of cultural knowledge is similar to the work of cryptographers. Each seeks to discover the rules used to convey information and thus to crack the code someone else is using.

6. *Cultural rules are employed by the individual in conjunction with other information.* Much of the literature of anthropology has perpetuated the myth that *culture uses man*. Homo sapiens is seen as an oversocialized creature of habit. He is a slave who unerringly conforms to the rules of his culture. But this is not the case. Rules are much more like the tools of a craftsman than the whip of a slavemaster. In other words, *man uses culture*. He does so in order to organize his behavior, and primarily in the course of intentional behavior. Moreover, the use of rules is always dependent on a multitude of environmental conditions and internal states. "Plead guilty to drunkenness *if* you want treatment"; "Drive faster than the speed limit *if* it is an emergency"; "Don't stick gum under the table in a restaurant *if* someone is watching"; "Don't marry her *if* you do not love her." As Goodenough has remarked, "Every recipe requires certain states of affairs in the phenomenal world for people to be able to act in accordance with it" (1963:267). Information about the sanctions for rule violation, the goals we pursue, the behavior of others, rules we have previously applied, the time of day, and many other things are used in decisions about which rule to apply. When we say that every culture has rules for breaking rules, we simply mean that the application of any rule is contingent upon a great deal of other information. Although man cannot be equated with a computer, even computer programs operate in terms of input information, as Neisser has pointed out:

> A program is not a device for measuring information, but a recipe for selecting, storing, recovering, combining, outputting, and generally manipulating it . . . We

must be careful not to confuse the program with the computer that it controls. Any single general-purpose computer can be "loaded" with an essentially infinite number of different programs. On the other hand, most programs can be run, with minor modifications, on many physically different kinds of computers. A program is not a machine; it is a series of instructions for dealing with symbols: "If the input has certain characteristics . . . then carry out certain procedures . . . otherwise other procedures . . . combine their results in various ways . . . store or retrieve various items . . . . depending on prior results . . . use them in further specified ways . . . etc." (1967:8).

Take an example using a simple flow chart similar to those used in computer programing. I have learned a rule for ideal conduct—"Don't pick up hitchhikers." The importance of this rule is continually reinforced by stories of the tragedy which comes to those who violate it. Only recently a teacher in the city where I live was killed by three youths he picked up. Nevertheless, I do not always use this rule. My behavior is influenced by input information, other rules, and, undoubtedly, things outside my awareness.

As I drive to and from my office each day, I observe individuals who have moved off the sidewalk and into the street. The particular interpretations and actions which are a consequence of this and other sensory information are themselves dependent upon the application of numerous rules. Whatever I do, we are engaged in some form of symbolic interaction. I may wave my hand, stop, turn the vehicle, honk the horn, or any number of other things. If I decode the person's behavior as a request for a ride, I either offer one or ignore him and drive on.

Some of the conditions and rules for selecting one of these two responses from among all those open to me are shown in the flow chart in Figure 6. Each diamond shows some of the information I am processing. The arrows represent instructions for attending to new information and selecting appropriate responses. If the person is not hitchhiking (and there are ways to identify this), I ignore him and drive by. I may select some other response such as stopping suddenly to avoid collision. Once he is identified as a hitchhiker, I then determine if he is an acquaintance by using the tacit rules I have learned for this kind of recognition. If he is, I immediately apply instructions to stop the car and offer him a ride. For persons I do not know, I usually determine the time of day. If daylight has passed, I continue traveling; if not, I estimate the distance I must travel on that particular street. If it is only a few blocks, I decide not to stop; otherwise I estimate the relative age of the person who seeks the ride. If he is a "kid," roughly from 10 to 15 years of age, I offer him a ride. If he is older, I check to see whether he is carrying books or not. If so, I infer that he is a student and probably a good risk as a passenger. Once I decide to offer a ride to a stranger, I must still observe whether traffic is heavy or light. If it appears

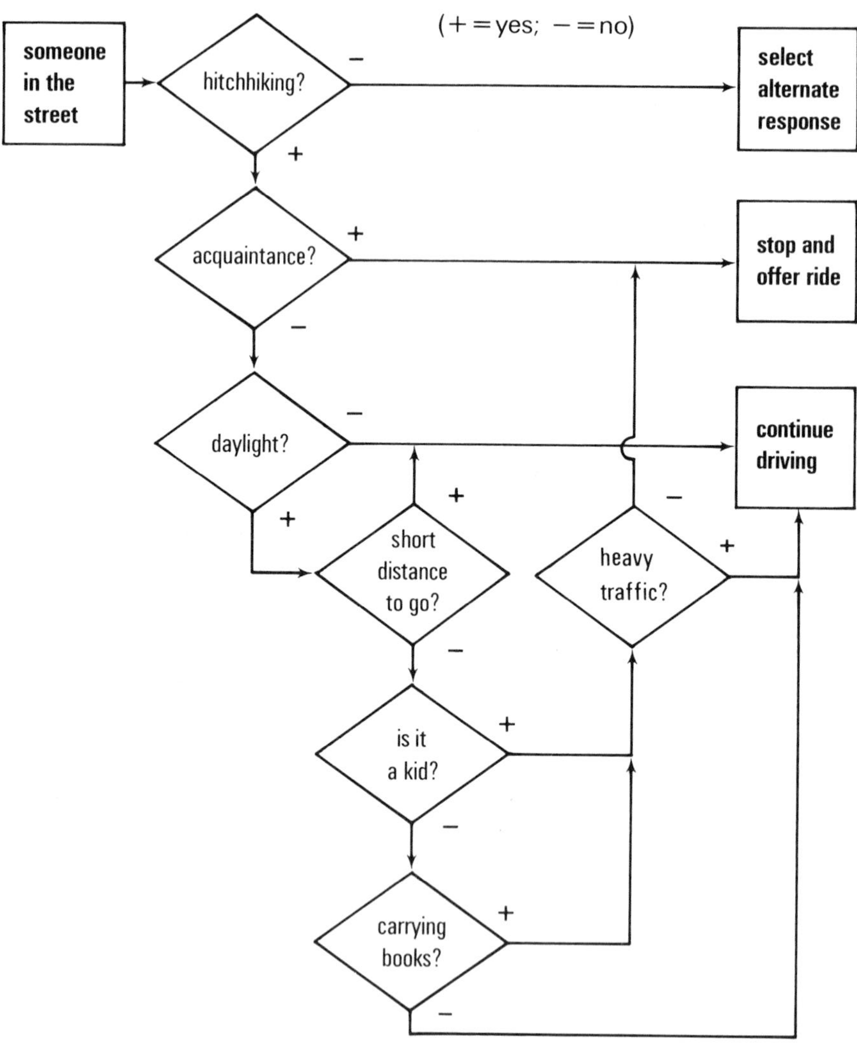

Figure 1:6.

to be dangerous or difficult to stop, I will reverse my decision and continue driving. This is only a partial description of how cultural rules are used to direct perceptual faculties, guide interpretation of environmental events, and organize motor responses.

7. *Finally, rules are recursive, a feature which accounts for the individual's ability to generate and interpret a potentially infinite set of cultural acts.* Any behavior which falls within the limits of variability

recognized by members of a society is a cultural act. People can tell when someone is speaking properly, treating his children in the right manner, espousing the correct ideas, and interacting appropriately. This does not mean that performances are identical, since for any act there is a recognized *range of variation*. The limits may be fuzzy or precise, but behavior which is outside this variance is inappropriate, or noncultural. There are many responses which indicate that people recognize noncultural behavior. They may raise their eyebrows, whisper, laugh, cry, label the deviant as crazy, or sentence him to death in the gas chamber.

The set of behavior which includes all cultural acts for any society is potentially infinite in size. No individual can possibly observe all members of this set. You have not heard all the sentences which could be constructed from the English language. Neither have you observed all the possible combinations for serving even those foods which you regularly eat. Even a simple act like shaking hands is unique each time it is performed, and no one has experienced all the variations of this behavior which are acceptable in our society. The investigator of cultural behavior is faced with two problems: First, how shall we account for the ability to generate and interpret *novel* acts, ones which have never been encountered before and yet which are culturally appropriate? Second, how is it possible to describe a set of behavior which is indefinitely large? A list of all cultural acts could only be started in the lifetime of the investigator. Consider the task of stating all the acceptable utterances which are possible for any language. Both of these problems are resolved by the fact that rules have the property of recursiveness:

> . . . the property of reapplicability indefinitely many times over, each successive application enumerating another member of the set. It is exactly in this sense that a simple rule for addition is said to generate, or enumerate, the infinite set of whole positive integers in mathematics (Stockwell 1969:261).

The rules of our culture enable us to tell whether others are properly dressed, even when they wear different clothes each day. New objects we have never seen before are easily sorted into their respective categories by means of recursive rules. Take reading, for example, not only must one learn the rules for recognizing each letter of the alphabet—and there is wide variation in the way each may be constructed—but he learns to apply one rule over and over again: read words from left to right. Sentences may appear on the television screen, in books and magazines, on packages and boxes of all sorts, in the sky, and any number of other places. They may be written in different ways with a variety of materials. Yet, once a person learns the rule for moving his eyes from left to right, he can generate acceptable reading behavior in all these situations and in any new ones which are encountered. A simple recursive rule thus can be used to generate, interpret, or describe a large set of cultural acts.

It is this property of rules which enables us to anticipate the behavior of other people. We infer the rules they are following and mentally generate the actions which the application of those rules would produce. Frake has cogently summarized this feature of cultural knowledge, and we agree with him that anticipation of behavior should be the basis for evaluating the adequacy of formulated rules:

> When an ethnographer first enters a strange society, each encountered event is new, unanticipated, improbable, and hence, highly informative in the communication-theory sense. As he learns the culture of the society, more and more of what happens becomes familiar and anticipatable. The ethnographer can plan his own activities on the basis of these anticipations. The more he learns of a culture, the more his anticipations match those of his informants. Similarly for a person born in a society, as he learns his culture, the events of his life become more probable, becoming parts of familiar *scenes* which he and his fellows plan for, stage, and play their roles in. To describe a culture, then, is not to recount the events of a society but to specify what one must know to make those events maximally probable. The problem is not to state what someone did but to specify the conditions under which it is culturally appropriate to anticipate that he, or persons occupying his role, will render an equivalent performance. This conception of a cultural description implies that an ethnography should be a theory of cultural behavior in a particular society, the adequacy of which is to be evaluated by the ability of a stranger to the culture (who may be the ethnographer) to use the ethnography's statements as instructions for appropriately anticipating the scenes of the society. I say "appropriately anticipate" rather than "predict" because a failure of an ethnographic statement to predict correctly does not necessarily imply descriptive inadequacy as long as the members of the described society are as surprised by the failure as is the ethnographer. The test of descriptive adequacy must always refer to informants' interpretations of events, not simply to the occurrence of events (Frake 1964:112).

Conclusion

The customary behavior which occurs in each society results, in part, from the cultural knowledge learned by its members. This chapter has presented the basic elements of such knowledge and examined some of the relationships between cognition and behavior. While much of what we know comes through sensory experience, it is never identical with environmental objects. Information is transformed before it arises as percepts in the mind. Furthermore, as we select, abstract, and arrange the properties of objects to form concepts, our knowledge is even further removed from the empirical world. But the most significant transformation comes when we employ objects and events to act as signs which refer to other phenomena, including those which have no physical reality. Symbols—those signs which are arbitrarily attached to referents—open up a myriad of possibilities for man. They free us from our dependence upon the immediate sensory world. They allow us to link our minds with those of other human beings and thus communicate what we know. Then, too, we can manipulate and arrange them in an infinite variety of patterns to create symbolic worlds which are independent of or superimposed on the world of sensory experience. But none of this would be possible without consistent behavior with respect to percepts, concepts, and symbols. This is accomplished by means of rules—instructions to behave in some ways, while excluding others. Rules are like a program stored within the brain for constructing, combining, interpreting, and otherwise dealing with symbols. In themselves they do not determine behavior, since human action results from processing a great deal of other information in addition to using rules. While it is impossible to formulate rules which are identical to those someone is using, a primary goal of cultural and cognition research is to decipher the codes and discover the tacit rules which each society uses to maintain its distinct symbolic world.

Bibliography

Atkins, John, and Curtis, Luke
1969 "Game Rules and the Rules of Culture." In *Game Theory in the Behavioral Sciences*, I. R. Buchler and H. G. Nutini, eds., pp. 213–234. Pittsburgh: University of Pittsburgh Press.

Bannister, D., and Mair, J. M. M.
1968 *The Evaluation of Personal Constructs*. New York: Academic Press, Inc.

Barnett, Homer G.
1953 *Innovation: the Basis of Cultural Change*. New York: McGraw-Hill Book Company.

Berger, Peter L. and Luckmann, Thomas
1967 *The Social Construction of Reality*. Garden City, N.Y.: Doubleday & Company, Inc.

Black, Max
1962 *Models and Metaphors: Studies in Language and Philosophy*. Ithaca, New York: Cornell University Press.

Bruner, Jerome S.; Goodnow, Jacqueline J.; and Austin, George A.
1956 *A Study of Thinking*. New York: John Wiley and Sons, Inc.

Burling, Robbins
1964 "Cognition and Componential Analysis: God's Truth or Hocus-pocus?" *American Anthropologist* 66:113–132.
1970 *Man's Many Voices: Language in Its Cultural Context*. New York: Holt, Rinehart & Winston, Inc.

CHAFE, WALLACE L.
1970 *Meaning and the Structure of Language.* Chicago: University of Chicago Press.
DE JOSSELIN DE JONG, P. E.
1971 "Presumed Behavior: Comments on Cara E. Richards' Brief Communication." *American Anthropologist* 73:270–273.
FRAKE, CHARLES O.
1964 "A Structural Description of Subanun 'Religious Behavior.'" In *Explorations in Cultural Anthropology*, Ward Goodenough, ed., pp. 111–129. New York: McGraw-Hill Book Company.
GEOGHEGAN, WILLIAM H.
1971 "Information Processing Systems in Culture." In *Explorations in Mathematical Anthropology*, Paul Kay, ed., pp. 3–35. Cambridge, Mass.: The M.I.T. Press.
GOODENOUGH, WARD H.
1957 "Cultural Anthropology and Linguistics." In *Report of the Seventh Annual Round Table Meeting on Linguistics and Language Study*, P. L. Garvin, ed. Washington: Georgetown University Monograph Series on Languages and Linguistics No. 9.
1963 *Cooperation in Change.* New York: Russell Sage.
1964 "Introduction." In *Explorations in Cultural Anthropology*, Ward Goodenough, ed., pp. 1–24. New York: McGraw-Hill Book Company.
HALLOWELL, A. IRVING
1955 *Culture and Experience.* Philadelphia: University of Pennsylvania Press.
HARRIS, MARVIN
1968 *The Rise of Anthropological Theory.* New York: Thomas Y. Crowell Company.
1971 "The History and Ideological Significance of the Separation of Social and Cultural Anthropology." Unpublished manuscript.
KAY, PAUL
1970 "Some Theoretical Implications of Ethnographic Semantics." In *Current Directions in Anthropology.* Bulletin of the American Anthropological Association, Vol. 3, No. 3, Part 2, pp. 19–35.
KEESING, ROGER M.
1970 "Toward a Model of Role Analysis." In *A Handbook of Method in Cultural Anthropology*, Raoul Naroll and Ronald Cohen, eds., pp. 423–453. Garden City, N.Y.: Natural History Press.
KELLEHER, ROGER T.
1958 "Concept Formation in Chimpanzees." *Science* 128:777–778.
KELLY, G. A.
1966 "A Brief Introduction to Personal Construct Theory." Unpublished manuscript. Brandeis University.
KROEBER, ALFRED, and PARSONS, TALCOTT
1958 "The Concept of Culture and of Social System." *American Sociological Review* 23:582–583.
LADO, ROBERT L.
1957 "Problems in Learning the Culture." In *Report of the Seventh Annual Round Table Meeting of Linguistics and Language Study.* Monograph

Series on Language and Linguistics, No. 9. Washington: Georgetown University Press.

LANDAR, HERBERT
1965 *Language and Culture*. New York: Oxford University Press, Inc.

MORRIS, CHARLES W.
1938 "Foundations of the Theory of Signs." *International Encyclopedia of Unified Science* 1:63–75. Chicago: University of Chicago Press.
1946 *Signs, Language and Behavior*. New York: Prentice-Hall, Inc.

NAROLL, RAOUL
1970 "Epistemology." In *A Handbook of Method in Cultural Anthropology*, Raoul Naroll and Ronald Cohen, eds., pp. 25–30. Garden City, N.Y: Natural History Press.

NEISSER, ULRIC
1967 *Cognitive Psychology*. New York: Appleton-Century-Crofts.

NIDA, EUGENE A.
1964 *Toward a Science of Translating*. Leiden: E. J. Brill.

PIERCE, CHARLES SANDERS
1931 *Collected Papers*. Cambridge, Mass.: Harvard University Press.

PARSONS, TALCOTT
1951 *The Social System*. New York: The Free Press.

POLANYI, MICHAEL
1966 *The Tacit Dimension*. Garden City, N.Y.: Doubleday & Company, Inc.

RICHARDS, CARA E.
1969 "Presumed Behavior: Modification of the Ideal-Real Dichotomy." *American Anthropologist* 71:1115–1117.

SCANDURA, JOSEPH M.
1970 "Role of Rules in Behavior: Toward an Operational Definition of What (Rule) Is Learned." *Psychological Review* 77:516–533.

SPIRO, MELFORD E.
1966 "Buddhism and Economic Action in Burma." *American Anthropologist* 68:1163–1173.

SPRADLEY, JAMES P.
1970 *You Owe Yourself A Drunk: An Ethnography of Urban Nomads*. Boston: Little, Brown and Company.

STOCKWELL, ROBERT P.
1969 "Generative Grammar." In *Linguistics Today*, Archibal A. Hill, ed., pp. 259–269. New York: Basic Books, Inc.

STURTEVANT, WILLIAM C.
1964 "Studies in Ethnoscience." In *Transcultural Studies in Cognition*, A. K. Romney and R. G. D'Andrade, eds. *American Anthropologist* 66(3) pt. 2:99–131.

WALLACE, ANTHONY F. C.
1970 *Culture and Personality*. Second Edition. New York: Random House, Inc.

______ and JOHN ATKINS
1960 "The Meaning of Kinship Terms." *American Anthropologist* 62:58–80.

WERNER, OSWALD and JOANN FENTON
1970 "Method and Theory in Ethnoscience or Ethnoepistemology." In

A Handbook of Method in Cultural Anthropology, Raoul Naroll and Ronald Cohen, eds., 537–578. Garden City, N.Y.: Natural History Press.

ZAJONC, ROBERT B.

1968 "Cognitive Theories in Social Psychology." In *The Handbook of Social Psychology*, Gardner Lindzey and Elliot Aronson, eds., 1:320–411. Second Edition. Reading, Mass.: Addison-Wesley Publishing Co., Inc.

PART 2 INTERDISCIPLINARY PERSPECTIVES

2 THE IMAGE

Kenneth E. Boulding

This chapter is an introduction to "an organic theory of knowledge." That which is known by the individual constitutes his image of the world. It locates one in the complex worlds of space, time, personal relations, nature, and emotions. The image is both more and less than cultural knowledge. From the individual's point of view, his image contains information which is entirely private and also cultural knowledge which is public. From the investigator's perspective, the cultural knowledge of a society is more than the public image of any single individual. Chapter 1 emphasized the fundamental elements of knowledge and how these are organized into larger structures. In this chapter Kenneth E. Boulding stresses the processes by which the image develops and changes over time. The behavior of an individual at any moment depends on his image; as this changes with time, so does his behavior. Each society, including science, develops a collective image. As Boulding points out, "Science is a subculture among subcultures. It can claim to be useful. It may claim rather more dubiously to be good. It cannot claim to give validity." One aim of the research in culture and cognition is to develop an image of the many different images which have grown up in human societies.—EDITOR'S NOTE

As I sit at my desk, I know where I am. I see before me a window; beyond that some trees; beyond that the red roofs of the campus of Stanford University; beyond them the trees and the roof tops which mark the town of Palo Alto; beyond them the bare golden hills of the Hamilton Range. I know, however, more than I see. Behind me, although I am not looking in that direction, I know there is a window, and beyond that the little campus of the Center for the Advanced Study in the Behavioral Sciences; beyond that the Coast Range; beyond that the Pacific Ocean. Looking ahead of me again, I know that beyond the mountains that close my present hori-

Reprinted from *The Image: Knowledge in Life and Society*, pp. 3–18, by permission of the author and the publisher.

zon, there is a broad valley; beyond that a still higher range of mountains; beyond that other mountains, range upon range, until we come to the Rockies; beyond that the Great Plains and the Mississippi; beyond that the Alleghenies; beyond that the eastern seaboard; beyond that the Atlantic Ocean; beyond that is Europe; beyond that is Asia. I know, furthermore, that if I go far enough I will come back to where I am now. In other words, I have a picture of the earth as round. I visualize it as a globe. I am a little hazy on some of the details. I am not quite sure, for instance, whether Tanganyika is north or south of Nyasaland. I probably could not draw a very good map of Indonesia, but I have a fair idea where everything is located on the face of this globe. Looking further, I visualize the globe as a small speck circling around a bright star which is the sun, in the company of many other similar specks, the planets. Looking still further, I see our star the sun as a member of millions upon millions of others in the Galaxy. Looking still further, I visualize the Galaxy as one of millions upon millions of others in the universe.

I am not only located in space, I am located in time. I know that I came to California about a year ago, and I am leaving it in about three weeks. I know that I have lived in a number of different places at different times. I know that about ten years ago a great war came to an end, that about forty years ago another great war came to an end. Certain dates are meaningful: 1776, 1620, 1066. I have a picture in my mind of the formation of the earth, of the long history of geological time, of the brief history of man. The great civilizations pass before my mental screen. Many of the images are vague, but Greece follows Crete, Rome follows Assyria.

I am not only located in space and time, I am located in a field of personal relations. I not only know where and when I am, I know to some extent who I am. I am a professor at a great state university. This means that in September I shall go into a classroom and expect to find some students in it and begin to talk to them, and nobody will be surprised. I expect, what is perhaps even more agreeable, that regular salary checks will arrive from the university. I expect that when I open my mouth on certain occasions people will listen. I know, furthermore, that I am a husband and a father, that there are people who will respond to me affectionately and to whom I will respond in like manner. I know, also, that I have friends, that there are houses here, there, and everywhere into which I may go and I will be welcomed and recognized and received as a guest. I belong to many societies. There are places into which I go, and it will be recognized that I am expected to behave in a certain manner. I may sit down to worship, I may make a speech, I may listen to a concert, I may do all sorts of things.

I am not only located in space and in time and in personal relationships, I am also located in the world of nature, in a world of how things operate.

I know that when I get into my car there are some things I must do to start it; some things I must do to back out of the parking lot; some things I must do to drive home. I know that if I jump off a high place I will probably hurt myself. I know that there are some things that would probably not be good for me to eat or to drink. I know certain precautions that are advisable to take to maintain good health. I know that if I lean too far backward in my chair as I sit here at my desk, I will probably fall over. I live, in other words, in a world of reasonably stable relationships, a world of "ifs" and "thens," of "if I do this, then that will happen."

Finally, I am located in the midst of a world of subtle intimations and emotions. I am sometimes elated, sometimes a little depressed, sometimes happy, sometimes sad, sometimes inspired, sometimes pedantic. I am open to subtle intimations of a presence beyond the world of space and time and sense.

What I have been talking about is knowledge. Knowledge, perhaps, is not a good word for this. Perhaps one would rather say my *Image* of the world. Knowledge has an implication of validity, of truth. What I am talking about is what I believe to be true; my subjective knowledge. It is this Image that largely governs my behavior. In about an hour I shall rise, leave my office, go to a car, drive down to my home, play with the children, have supper, perhaps read a book, go to bed. I can predict this behavior with a fair degree of accuracy because of the knowledge which I have: the knowledge that I have a home not far away, to which I am accustomed to go. The prediction, of course, may not be fulfilled. There may be an earthquake, I may have an accident with the car on the way home, I may get home to find that my family has been suddenly called away. A hundred and one things may happen. As each event occurs, however, it alters my knowledge structure or my image. And as it alters my image, I behave accordingly. *The first proposition of this work, therefore, is that behavior depends on the image.*

What, however, determines the image? This is the central question of this work. It is not a question which can be answered by it. Nevertheless, such answers as I shall give will be quite fundamental to the understanding of how both life and society really operate. One thing is clear. The image is built up as a result of all past experience of the possessor of the image. Part of the image is the history of the image itself. At one stage the image, I suppose, consists of little else than an undifferentiated blur and movement. From the moment of birth if not before, there is a constant stream of messages entering the organism from the senses. At first, these may merely be undifferentiated lights and noises. As the child grows, however, they gradually become distinguished into people and objects. He begins to perceive himself as an object in the midst of a world of objects. The conscious image has begun. In infancy the world is a house and, perhaps, a few streets or a park. As the child grows his image of the world expands. He sees himself in a town, a country, on a planet. He finds himself in an increasingly complex web of personal relationships. Every time a message reaches him his image is likely to be changed in some degree by it, and as his image is changed his behavior patterns will be changed likewise.

We must distinguish carefully between the image and the messages that reach it. The messages consist of *information* in the sense that they are structured experiences. *The meaning of a message is the change which it produces in the image.*

When a message hits an image one of three things can happen. In the first place, the image may remain unaffected. If we think of the image as a rather loose structure, something like a molecule, we may imagine that the message is going straight through without hitting it. The great majority of messages is of this kind. I am receiving messages all the time, for instance, from my eyes and my ears as I sit at my desk, but these messages are ignored by me. There is, for instance, a noise of carpenters working. I know, however, that a building is being built nearby and the fact that I now hear this noise does not add to this image. Indeed, I do not hear the noise at all if I am not listening for it, as I have become so accustomed to it. If the noise stops, however, I notice it. This information changes my image of the universe. I realize that it is now five o'clock, and it is time for me to go home. The message has called my attention, as it were, to my position in time, and I have re-evaluated this position. This is the second possible effect or impact of a message on an image. It may change the image in some rather regular and well-defined way that might be described as simple addition. Suppose, for instance, to revert to an earlier illustration, I look at an atlas and find out exactly the relation of Nyasaland to Tanganyika. I will have added to my knowledge, or my image; I will not, however, have very fundamentally revised it. I still picture the world much as I had pictured it before. Something that was a little vague before is now clearer.

There is, however, a third type of change of the image which might be described as a revolutionary change. Sometimes a message hits some sort of nucleus or supporting structure in the image, and the whole thing changes in a quite radical way. A spectacular instance of such a change is conversion. A man, for instance, may think himself a pretty good fellow and then may hear a preacher who convinces him that, in fact, his life is worthless and shallow, as he is at present living it. The words of the preacher cause a radical reformulation of the man's image of himself in the world, and his behavior changes accordingly. The psychologist may say, of course, that these changes are smaller than they appear, that there is a great mass of the unconscious which does not change, and that the relatively small change in behavior which so often follows intellectual conversion is a testimony to this fact. Nevertheless, the phenomenon of reorganization of the image is an important one, and it occurs to all of us and in ways that are much less spectacular than conversion.

The sudden and dramatic nature of these reorganizations is perhaps a result of the fact that our image is in itself resistant to change. When it receives messages which conflict with it, its first impulse is to reject them as in some sense untrue. Suppose, for instance, that somebody tells us something which is inconsistent with our picture of a certain person. Our first impulse is to reject the proffered information as false. As we continue to receive messages which contradict our image, however, we begin to have doubts, and then one day we receive a message which overthrows our previous image and we revise it completely. The person, for instance, whom we saw as a trusted friend is now seen to be a hypocrite and a deceiver.

Occasionally, things that we see, or read, or hear, revise our conceptions of space and time, or of relationships. I have recently read, for instance, Vasiliev's *History of the Byzantine Empire*. As a result of reading this book I have considerably revised my image of at least a thousand years of history. I had not given the matter a great deal of thought before, but I suppose if I had been questioned on my view of the period, I would have said that Rome fell in the fifth century and that it was succeeded by a little-known empire centering in Constantinople and a confused medley of tribes, invasions, and successor states. I now see that Rome did not fall, that in a sense it merely faded away, that the history of the Roman Empire and of Byzantium is continuous, and that from the time of its greatest extent the Roman Empire lost one piece after another until only Constantinople was left; and then in 1453 that went. There are books, some of them rather bad books, after which the world is never quite the same again. Veblen, for instance, was not, I think, a great social scientist, and yet he invented an undying phrase: "conspicuous consumption." After reading Veblen, one can never quite see a university campus or an elaborate house in just the same light as before. In a similar vein, David Riesman's division of humanity into inner-directed and other-directed people is no doubt open to serious criticism by the methodologists. Nevertheless, after reading Riesman one has a rather new view of the universe and one looks in one's friends and acquaintances for signs of inner-direction or other-direction.

One should perhaps add a fourth possible impact of the messages on the image. The image has a certain dimension, or quality, of certainty or uncertainty, probability or improbability, clarity or vagueness. Our image of the world is not uniformly certain, uniformly probable, or uniformly clear. Messages, therefore, may have the effect not only of adding to or of reorganizing the image. They may also have the effect of clarifying it, that is, of making something which previously was regarded as less certain more certain, or something which was previously seen in a vague way, clearer.

Messages may also have the contrary effect. They may introduce doubt or uncertainty into the image. For instance, the noise of carpenters has just stopped, but my watch tells me it is about four-thirty. This has thrown a certain amount of confusion into my mental image. I was under the impression that the carpenters stopped work at five o'clock. Here is a message which contradicts that impression. What am I to believe? Unfortunately, there are two possible ways of integrating the message into my image. I can believe that I was mistaken in thinking that the carpenters left work at five o'clock and that in fact their day ends at four-thirty. Or, I can believe that my watch is wrong. Either of these two modifications of my image gives meaning to the message. I shall not know for certain which is the right one, however, until I have an opportunity of comparing my watch with a timepiece or with some other source of time which I regard as being more reliable.

The impact of messages on the certainty of the image is of great importance in the interpretation of human behavior. Images of the future must be held with a degree of uncertainty, and as time passes and as the images become closer to the present, the messages that we receive inevitably modify them, both as to content and as to certainty.

The subjective knowledge structure or image of any individual or organization consists not only of images of "fact" but also images of "value." We shall subject the concept of a "fact" to severe scrutiny in the course of the discussion. In the meantime, however, it is clear that there is a certain difference between the image which I have of physical objects in space and time and the valuations which I put on these objects or on the events which concern them. It is clear that there is a certain difference between, shall we say, my image of Stanford University existing at a certain point in space and time, and my image of the value of Stanford University. If I say "Stanford University is in California," this is rather different from the statement "Stanford University is a good university, or is a better university than X, or a worse university than Y." The latter statements concern my image of values, and although I shall argue that the process by which we obtain an image of values is not very different from the process whereby we obtain an image of fact, there is clearly a certain difference between them.

The image of value is concerned with the *rating* of the various parts of our image of the world, according to some scale of betterness or worseness. We, all of us, possess one or more of these scales. It is what the economists call a welfare function. It does not extend over the whole universe. We do not now, for instance, generally regard Jupiter as a better planet than Saturn. Over that part of the universe which is closest to ourselves, however, we all erect these scales of valuation. Moreover, we change these scales of valuation in response to messages received much as we change our image of the world around us. It is almost certain that most people possess not merely one scale of valuation but many scales for different purposes. For instance, we may say A is better than B for me but worse for the country, or it is better for the country but worse for the world at large. The notion of a hierarchy of scales is very important in determining the effect of messages on the scales themselves.

One of the most important propositions of this theory is that the value scales of any individual or organization are perhaps the most important single element determining the effect of the messages it receives on its image of the world. If a message is perceived that is neither good nor bad it may have little or no effect on the image. If it is perceived as bad or hostile to the image which is held, there will be resistance to accepting it. This resistance is not usually infinite. An often repeated message or a message which comes with unusual force or authority is able to penetrate the resistance and will be able to alter the image. A devout Moslem, for instance, whose whole life has been built around the observance of the precepts of the Koran will resist vigorously any message which tends to throw doubt on the authority of his sacred work. The resistance may take the form of simply ignoring the message, or it may take the form of emotive response: anger, hostility, indignation. In the same way, a "devout" psychologist will resist strongly any evidence presented in favor of extrasensory perception, because to accept it would overthrow his whole image of the universe. If the resistances are very strong, it may take very strong, or often repeated messages to penetrate them, and when they are penetrated, the effect is a realignment or reorganization of the whole knowledge structure.

On the other hand, messages which are favorable to the existing image of the world are received easily and even though they may make minor modifications of the knowledge structure, there will not be any fundamental reorganization. Such messages either will make no impact on the knowledge structure or their impact will be one of rather simple addition or accretion. Such messages may also have the effect of increasing the stability, that is to say, the resistance to unfavorable messages, which the knowledge structure or image possesses.

The stability or resistance to change of a knowledge structure also depends on its internal consistency and arrrangement. There seems to be some kind of principle of minimization of internal strain at work which makes some images stable and others unstable for purely internal reasons. In the same way, some crystals or molecules are more stable than others because of the minimization of internal strain. It must be emphasized that it is not merely logical consistency which gives rise to internal cohesiveness of a knowledge structure, although this is an important element. There are important qualities of a nonlogical nature which also give rise to stability. The structure may, for instance, have certain aesthetic relationships among the parts. It may represent or justify a way of life or have certain consequences which are highly regarded in the value system, and so on. Even in mathematics, which is of all knowledge structures the one whose internal consistency is most due to logic, is not devoid of these nonlogical elements. In the acceptance of mathematical arguments by mathematicians there are important criteria of elegance, beauty, and simplicity which contribute toward the stability of these structures.

Even at the level of simple or supposedly simple sense perception we are increasingly discovering that the message which comes through the senses is itself mediated through a value system. We do not perceive our sense data raw; they are mediated through a highly learned process of interpretation and acceptance. When an object apparently increases in size on the retina of the eye, we interpret this not as an increase in size but as movement. Indeed, we only get along in the world because we consistently and persistently disbelieve the plain evidence of our senses. The stick in water is not bent; the movie is not a succession of still pictures; and so on.

What this means is that for any individual organism or organization, there are no such things as "facts." There are only messages filtered through a changeable value system. This statement may sound rather startling. It is inherent, however, in the view which I have been propounding. This does not mean, however, that the image of the world possessed by an individual is a purely private matter or that all knowledge is simply subjective knowledge, in the sense in which I have used the word. Part of our image of the world is the belief that this image is shared by other people like ourselves who also are part of our image of the world. In common daily intercourse we all behave as if we possess roughly the same image of the world. If a group of people are in a room together, their behavior clearly shows that they all think they are in the same room. It is this shared image which is "public" knowledge as opposed to "private" knowledge. It follows, however, from the argument above that if a group of people are to share the same image of the world, or to put it more exactly, if the various images of the world which they have are to be roughly identical, and if this group of people are exposed to much the same set of messages in building up images of the world, the value systems of all individuals must be approximately the same.

The problem is made still more complicated by the fact that a group of individuals does not merely share messages which come to them from "nature." They also initiate and receive messages themselves. This is the characteristic which distinguishes man from the lower organisms—the art of conversation or discourse. The human organism is capable not only of having an image of the world, but of talking about it. This is the extraordinary gift of language. A group of dogs in a pack pursuing a stray cat clearly share an image of the world in the sense that each is aware to some degree of the situation which they are all in, and is likewise aware of his neighbors. When the chase is over, however, they do not, as far as we know, sit around and talk about it and say, "Wasn't that a fine chase?" or, "Isn't it too bad the cat got away?" or even, "Next time you ought to go that way and I'll go this way and we can corner it." It is discourse or conversation which makes the human image public in a way that the image of no lower animal can possibly be. The term "universe of discourse" has been used to describe the growth and development of common images in conversation and linguistic intercourse. There are, of course, many such universes of discourse, and although it is a little awkward to speak of many universes, the term is well enough accepted so that we may let it stay.

Where there is no universe of discourse, where the image possessed by the organism is purely private and cannot be communicated to anyone else, we say that the person is mad (to use a somewhat old-fashioned term). It must not be forgotten, however, that the discourse must be received as well as given, and that whether it is received or not depends upon the value system of the recipient. This means that insanity is defined differently from one culture to another because of these differences in value systems and that the schizophrenic of one culture may well be the shaman or the prophet of another.

Up to now I have sidestepped and I will continue to sidestep the great philosophical arguments of epistemology. I have talked about the image. I have maintained that images can be public as well as private, but I have not discussed the question as to whether images are *true* and how we know whether they are true. Most epistemological systems seek some philosopher's stone by which statements may be tested in order to determine their "truth," that is, their correspondence to outside reality. I do not claim to have any such philosopher's stone, not even the touchstone of science. I have, of course, a great respect for science and scientific method—for careful observation, for planned experience, for the testing of hypotheses and for as much objectivity as semirational beings like ourselves can hope to achieve. In my theoretical system, however, the scientific method merely stands as one among many of the methods whereby images change and develop. The development of images is part of the culture or the subculture in which they are developed, and it depends upon all the elements of that culture or subculture. Science is a subculture among subcultures. It can claim to be useful. It may claim rather more dubiously to be good. It cannot claim to give validity.

In summation, then, my theory might well be called an organic theory of knowledge. Its most fundamental proposition is that knowledge is what somebody or something knows, and that without a knower, knowledge is an absurdity. Moreover, I argue that the growth of knowledge is the growth of an "organic" structure. I am not suggesting here that knowledge is simply an arrangement of neuronal circuits or brain cells, or something of that kind. On the question of the relation between the physical and chemical structure of an organism and its knowledge structure, I am quite prepared to be agnostic. It is, of course, an article of faith among physical scientists that there must be somewhere a one-to-one correspondence between the structures of the physical body and the structures of knowledge. Up to now, there is nothing like empirical proof or even very good evidence for this hypothesis. Indeed, what we know about the brain suggests that it is an extraordinarily unspecialized and, in a sense, unstructured object; and that if there is a physical and chemical structure corresponding to the knowledge structure, it must be of a kind which at present we do not understand. It may be, indeed, that the correspondence between physical structure and mental structure is something that we will never be able to determine because of a sort of "Heisenberg principle" in the investigation of these matters. If the act of observation destroys the thing observed, it is clear that there is a fundamental obstacle to the growth of knowledge in that direction.

All these considerations, however, are not fundamental to my position. We do not have to conceive of the knowledge structure as a physico-chemical structure in order to use it in our theoretical construct. It can be inferred from the behavior of the organism just as we constantly infer the images of the world which are possessed by those around us from the messages which they transmit to us. When I say that knowledge is an organic structure, I mean that it follows principles of growth and development similar to those with which we are familiar in complex organizations and organisms. In every organism or organization there are both internal and external factors affecting growth. Growth takes place through a kind of metabolism. Even in the case of knowledge structures, we have a certain intake and output of messages. In the knowledge structure, however, there are important violations of the laws of conservation. The accumulation of knowledge is not merely the difference between messages taken in and messages given out. It is not like a reservoir; it is rather an organization which grows through an active internal organizing principle much as the gene is a principle or entity organizing the growth of bodily structures.

The gene, even in the physico-chemical sense may be thought of as an inward teacher imposing its own form and "will" on the less formed matter around it. In the growth of images, also, we may suppose similar models. Knowledge grows also because of inward teachers as well as outward messages. As every good teacher knows, the business of teaching is not that of penetrating the student's defenses with the violence or loudness of the teacher's messages. It is, rather, that of co-operating with the student's own inward teacher whereby the student's image may grow in conformity with that of his outward teacher. The existence of public knowledge depends, therefore, on certain basic similarities among men. It is literally because we are of one "blood," that is, genetic constitution, that we are able to communicate with each other. We cannot talk to the ants or bees; we cannot hold conversations with them, although in a very real sense they communicate to us. It is the purpose of this work, therefore, to discuss the growth of images, both private and public, in individuals, in organizations, in society at large, and even with some trepidation, among the lower forms of life. Only thus can we develop a really adequate theory of behavior.

3 PLANS

George A. Miller, Eugene Galanter, and Karl H. Pribram

The sciences of human behavior are divided over two conflicting approaches. There are the strict empiricists, who only accept as data those events and behavior which are observable. On the other hand, there are those who would also include in their data the meanings which subjects assign to those phenomena. Each discipline has these divergent schools: psychology has behaviorists and cognitivists; sociology has a variety of behavioral theorists in contrast to its symbolic interactionists; anthropology has cultural materialists and cultural idealists. Undoubtedly, the debates, differences of perspective, and attempts to build more inclusive theories will continue for many years to come. In this chapter the authors discuss some of the issues involved from the viewpoint of psychology and give their reasons for rejecting the behaviorist formulation. They recognize that an enduring problem for the cognitive approach is the difficulty in making the relationship between knowledge and behavior explicit. To say that what we know "influences" what we do or that actions "depend" upon the image leaves something to be desired. These authors make an important contribution to the eventual resolution of the problem with their concept of plans. As a set of instructions, the notion of plans is very simliar to the concept of rules which was developed in Chapter 1. Perhaps the major difference is that plans refer to cognitive structures of greater complexity—they are a hierarchy of instructions. After reviewing some of the conflicts between the behavioral and cognitive approaches, they outline the nature of plans and consider how this concept is related to the idea of the image, discussed in Chapter 2.—EDITOR'S NOTE

Consider how an ordinary day is put together. You awaken, and as you lie in bed, or perhaps as you move slowly about in a protective shell of morning habits, you think about what the day will be like—it will be hot, it

Reprinted from *Plans and the Structure of Behavior* by George A. Miller, Eugene Galanter, and Karl H. Pribram, pp. 5–19, by permission of the senior author and the publisher.

will be cold; there is too much to do, there is nothing to fill the time; you promised to see him, she may be there again today. If you are compulsive, you may worry about fitting it all in, you may make a list of all the things you have to do. Or you may launch yourself into the day with no clear notion of what you are going to do or how long it will take. But, whether it is crowded or empty, novel or routine, uniform or varied, your day has a structure of its own—it fits into the texture of your life. And as you think what your day will hold, you construct a plan to meet it. What you expect to happen foreshadows what you expect to do.

The authors of this chapter believe that the plans you make are interesting and that they probably have some relation to how you actually spend your time during the day. We call them "plans" without malice—we recognize that you do not draw out long and elaborate blueprints for every moment of the day. You do not need to. Rough, sketchy, flexible anticipations are usually sufficient. As you brush your teeth you decide that you will answer that pile of letters you have been neglecting. That is enough. You do not need to list the names of the people or to draft an outline of the contents of the letters. You think simply that today there will be time for it after lunch. After lunch, if you remember, you turn to the letters. You take one and read it. You plan your answer. You may need to check on some information, you dictate or type or scribble a reply, you address an envelope, seal the folded letter, find a stamp, drop it in a mailbox. Each of these subactivities runs off as the situation arises—you did not need to enumerate them while you were planning the day. All you need is the name of the activity that you plan for that segment of the day, and from that name you then proceed to elaborate the detailed actions involved in carrying out the plan.

You *imagine* what your day is going to be and you make *plans* to cope with it. Images and plans. What does modern psychology have to say about images and plans?

Presumably, the task of modern psychology is to make sense out of what people and animals do, to find some system for understanding their behavior. If we, as psychologists, come to this task with proper scientific caution, we must begin with what we can see and we must postulate as little as possible beyond that. What we can see are movements and environmental events. The ancient subject matter of psychology—the mind and its various manifestations—is distressingly invisible, and a science with invisible content is likely to become an invisible science. We are therefore led to underline the fundamental importance of behavior and, in particular, to try to discover recurrent patterns of stimulation and response.

What an organism does depends on what happens around it. As to the way in which this dependency should be described, however, there are, as in most matters of modern psychology, two schools of thought. On the one hand are the optimists, who claim to find the dependency simple and straightforward. They model the stimulus-response relation after the classical, physiological pattern of the reflex arc and use Pavlov's discoveries to explain how new reflexes can be formed through experience. This approach is too simple for all but the most extreme optimists. Most psychologists quickly realize that behavior in general, and human behavior in particular, is not a chain of conditioned reflexes. So the model is complicated slightly by incorporating some of the stimuli that occur after the response in addition to the stimuli that occur before the response. Once these "reinforcing" stimuli are included in the description, it becomes possible to understand a much greater variety of behaviors and to acknowledge the apparently purposive nature of behavior. That is one school of thought.

Arrayed against the reflex theorists are the pessimists, who think that living organisms are complicated, devious, poorly designed for research purposes, and so on. They maintain that the effect an event will have upon behavior depends on how the event is represented in the organism's picture of itself and its universe. They are quite sure that any correlations between stimulation and response must be mediated by an organized representation of the environment, a system of concepts and relations within which the organism is located. A human being—and probably other animals as well—builds up an internal representation, a model of the universe, a schema, a simulacrum, a cognitive map, an Image. Sir Frederic C. Bartlett, who uses the term "schema" for this internal representation, describes it in this way:

> "Schema" refers to an active organisation of past reactions, or of past experiences, which must always be supposed to be operating in any well-adapted organic response. That is, whenever there is any order or regularity of behavior, a particular response is possible only because it is related to other similar responses which have been serially organised, yet which operate, not simply as individual members coming one after another, but as a unitary mass. Determination by schemata is the most fundamental of all the ways in which we can be influenced by reactions and experiences which occurred some time in the past. All incoming impulses of a certain kind, or mode, go together to build up an active, organised setting: visual, auditory, various types of cutaneous impulses and the like, at a relatively low level; all the experiences connected by a common interest: in sport, in literature, history, art, science, philosophy, and so on, on a higher level.[1]

The crux of the argument, as every psychologist knows, is whether anything so mysterious and inaccessible as "the organism's picture of itself and its universe," or "an active organisation of past reactions," etc., is really necessary. Necessary, that is to say, as an explanation for the behavior that can be observed to occur.

The view that some mediating organization of experience is necessary has a surprisingly large number of critics among hardheaded, experimentally trained psychologists. The mediating organization is, of course, a theoretical concept and, out of respect for Occam's Razor, one should not burden the science with unnecessary theoretical luggage. An unconditional proof that a completely consistent account of behavior cannot be formulated more economically does not exist, and until we are certain that simpler ideas have failed we should not rush to embrace more complicated ones. Indeed, there are many psychologists who think the simple stimulus-response-reinforcement models provide an adequate description of everything a psychologist should concern himself with.

For reasons that are not entirely clear, the battle between these two schools of thought has generally been waged at the level of animal behavior. Edward Tolman, for example, has based his defense of cognitive organization almost entirely on his studies of the behavior of rats—surely one of the least promising areas in which to investigate intellectual accomplishments. Perhaps he felt that if he could win the argument with the simpler animal, he would win it by default for the more complicated ones. If the description of a rodent's cognitive structure is necessary in order to understand its behavior, then it is just that much more important for understanding the behavior of a dog, or an ape, or a man. Tolman's position was put most simply and directly in the following paragraph:

> [The brain] is far more like a map control room than it is like an old-fashioned telephone exchange. The stimuli, which are allowed in, are not connected by just simple one-to-one switches to the outgoing responses. Rather, the incoming impulses are usually worked over and elaborated in the central control room into a tentative, cognitivelike map of the environment. And it is this tentative map, indicating routes and paths and environmental relationships, which finally determines what responses, if any, the animal will finally release.[2]

We ourselves are quite sympathetic to this kind of theorizing, since it seems obvious to us that a great deal more goes on between the stimulus and the response than can be accounted for by a simple statement about associative strengths. The pros and cons cannot be reviewed here—the argument is long and other texts[3] exist in which an interested reader can pursue it—so we shall simply announce that our theoretical preferences are all on the side of the cognitive theorists. Life is complicated.

Nevertheless, there is a criticism of the cognitive position that seems quite important and that has never, so far as we know, received an adequate answer. The criticism is that the cognitive processes Tolman and others have postulated are not, in fact, sufficient to do the job they were supposed to do. Even if you admit these ghostly inner somethings, say the critics, you will not have explained anything about the animal's behavior.

Guthrie has made the point about as sharply as anyone:

> Signs, in Tolman's theory, occasion in the rat *realization* or *cognition*, or *judgment*, or *hypotheses*, or *abstraction*, but *they do not occasion action.* In his concern with what goes on in the rat's mind, Tolman has neglected to predict what the rat will do. So far as the theory is concerned the rat is left buried in thought; if he gets to the food-box at the end that is his concern, not the concern of the theory.[4]

Perhaps the cognitive theorists have not understood the force of this criticism. It is so transparently clear to them that if a hungry rat knows where to find food—if he has a cognitive map with the food-box located on it—he will go there and eat. What more is there to explain? The answer, of course, is that a great deal is left to be explained. The gap from knowledge to action looks smaller than the gap from stimulus to action—yet the gap is still there, still indefinitely large. Tolman, the omniscient theorist, leaps over that gap when he infers the rat's cognitive organization from its behavior. But that leaves still outstanding the question of the rat's ability to leap it. Apparently, cognitive theorists have assumed that their best course was to show that the reflex theories are inadequate; they seem to have been quite unprepared when the same argument—that things are even more complicated than they dared to imagine—was used against them. Yet, if Guthrie is right, more cognitive theory is needed than the cognitive theorists normally supply. That is to say, far from respecting Occam's Razor, the cognitive theorist must ask for even *more* theoretical luggage to carry around. Something is needed to bridge the gap from knowledge to action.

It is unfair to single out Tolman and criticize him for leaving the cognitive representation paralytic. Other cognitive theorists could equally well be cited. Wolfgang Köhler, for example, has been subjected to the same kind of heckling. In reporting his extremely perceptive study of the chimpanzees on Tenerife Island during the first World War, Köhler wrote:

> We can . . . distinguish sharply between the kind of behavior which from the very beginning arises out of a consideration of the structure of a situation, and one that does not. Only in the former case do we speak of insight, and only that behavior of animals definitely appears to us intelligent which takes account from the beginning of the lay of the land, and proceeds to deal with it in a single, continuous, and definite course. Hence follows this criterion of insight: *the appearance of a complete solution with reference to the whole lay-out of the field.*[5]

Other psychologists have been less confident that they could tell the difference between behavior based on an understanding of the whole layout and behavior based on less cognitive processes, so there has been a long and rather fruitless controversy over the relative merits of trial-and-error and of insight as methods of learning. The point we wish to raise here, however, is that Köhler makes the standard cognitive assumption: once the animal has grasped the whole layout he will behave appropriately. Again, the fact that grasping the whole layout may be necessary, but is certainly not sufficient as an explanation of intelligent behavior, seems to have been ignored by Köhler. Many years later, for example, we heard Karl Lashley say this to him:

> I attended the dedication, three weeks ago, of a bridge at Dyea, Alaska. The road to the bridge for nine miles was blasted along a series of cliffs. It led to a magnificent steel bridge, permanent and apparently indestructible. After the dedication ceremonies I walked across the bridge and was confronted with an impenetrable forest of shrubs and underbrush, through which only a couple of trails of bears led to indeterminate places. In a way, I feel that Professor Köhler's position is somewhat that of the bridge.... The neurological problem is in large part, if not entirely, the translation of the afferent pattern of impulses into the efferent pattern. The field theory in its present form includes no hint of the way in which the field forces induce and control the pattern of efferent activity. It applies to perceptual experience but seems to end there.[6]

Many other voices could be added to this dialogue. Much detailed analysis of different psychological theories could be displayed to show why the cognitive theorists feel they have answered the criticism and why their critics still maintain that they have not. But we will not pursue it. Our point is that many psychologists, including the present authors, have been disturbed by a theoretical vacuum between cognition and action. The present book is largely the record of prolonged—and frequently violent—conversations about how that vacuum might be filled.

No doubt it is perfectly obvious to the reader that we have here a modern version of an ancient puzzle. At an earlier date we might have introduced the topic directly by announcing that we intended to discuss the will. But today the will seems to have disappeared from psychological theory, assimilated anonymously into the broader topic of motivation. The last serious attempt to make sense out of the will was the early work of Kurt Lewin and his students. Lewin's contributions are so important that . . . we cannot dismiss them summarily by a paragraph in this introduction. In order to show what a psychology of will might be like, therefore, it is necessary to return to an earlier and more philosophical generation of psychologists. William James provides the sort of discussion that was once an indispensable part of every psychology text, so let us consider briefly how he handled the topic.

The second volume of *The Principles* contains a long chapter (106 pages) entitled "Will." The first third of it is James's struggle against theories based on "sensations of innervation"—the notion that the innervation required to perform the appropriate action is itself a part of the cognitive representation. James maintains instead that it is the anticipation of the kinesthetic effects of the movement that is represented in consciousness. He then turns to the topic of "ideo-motor action," which provides the foundation for his explanation of all phenomena of will. If a person forms a clear image of a particular action, that action tends to occur. The occurrence may be inhibited, limited to covert tensions in the muscles, but in many cases having an idea of an action is sufficient for action. If there is anything between the cognitive representation and the overt action, it is not represented in consciousness. Introspectively, therefore, there seems to be no vacuum to be filled, and James, had he heard them, would have felt that criticisms of the sort made by Guthrie and Lashley were not justified.

But what of the more complicated cases of willing? What occurs when we force ourselves through some unpleasant task by "the slow dead heave of the will?" According to James, the feeling of effort arises from our attempt to keep our attention focused on the unpleasant idea. "The essential achievement of the will," he tells us, "is to *attend* to a difficult object and hold it fast before the mind."[7] If an idea can be maintained in attention, then the action that is envisioned in the idea occurs automatically—a direct example of ideo-motor action. All of which helps us not in the least. The bridge James gives us between the *ideo* and the *motor* is nothing but a hyphen. There seems to be no alternative but to strike out into the vacuum on our own.

The problem is to describe how actions are controlled by an organism's internal representation of its universe. If we consider what these actions are in the normal, freely ranging animal, we must be struck by the extent to which they are organized into patterns. Most psychologists maintain that these action patterns are punctuated by goals and subgoals, but that does not concern us for the moment. We wish to call attention to the fact that the organization does exist—configuration is just as important a property of behavior as it is of perception. The configurations of behavior, however, tend to be predominantly temporal—it is the *sequence* of motions that flows onward so smoothly as the creature runs, swims, flies, talks, or whatever. What we must provide, therefore, is some way to map the cognitive representation into the appropriate *pattern* of activity. But how are we to analyze this flowing pattern of action into manageable parts?

The difficulty in analyzing the actions of an animal does not arise from any lack of ways to do it but from an embarrassment of riches. We can describe an action as a sequence of muscle twitches, or as a sequence of movements of limbs and other parts, or as a sequence of goal-directed actions, or in even larger units. Following Tolman, most psychologists distinguish the little units from the big units by calling the little ones "molecular," the big ones, "molar." Anyone who asks which unit is the correct size to use in describing behavior is told that behavioral laws seem more obvious when molar units are used, but that just how molar he should be in any particular analysis is something he will have to learn from experience and observation in research.

The implication is relatively clear, however, that the molar units must be composed of molecular units, which we take to mean that a proper description of behavior must be made on *all levels simultaneously*. That is to say, we are trying to describe a process that is organized on several different levels, and the pattern of units at one level can be indicated only by giving the units at the next higher, or more molar, level of description. For example, the molar pattern of behavior X consists of two parts, A and B, in that order. Thus, $X = AB$. But A, in turn, consists of two parts, a and b; and B consists of three, c, d, and e. Thus, $X = AB = abcde$, and we can describe the same segment of behavior at any one of the three levels. The point, however, is that we do not want to pick one level and argue that it is somehow better than the others; the complete description must include all levels. Otherwise, the configurational properties of the behavior will be lost—if we state only *abcde*, for example, then (*ab*) (*cde*) may become confused with (*abc*)(*de*), which may be a very different thing.

This kind of organization of behavior is most obvious, no doubt, in human verbal behavior. The individual phonemes are organized into morphemes, morphemes are strung together to form phrases, phrases in the proper sequence form a sentence, and a string of sentences makes up the utterance. The complete description of the utterance involves all these levels. The kind of ambiguity that results when all levels are not known is suggested by the sentence, "They are flying planes." The sequence of phonemes may remain unchanged, but the two analyses (*They*)(*are flying*) (*planes*) and (*They*)(*are*)(*flying planes*) are very different utterances.[8]

Psychologists have seldom demonstrated any reluctance to infer the existence of such molar units as "words" or even "meanings" when they have dealt with verbal behavior, even though the actual responses available to perception are merely the strings of phones, the acoustic representations of the intended phonemes. Exactly the same recognition of more molar units in nonverbal behavior deserves the same kind of multilevel description. Unfortunately, however, the psychologist usually describes behavior—or some aspect of behavior—at a single level and leaves his colleagues to use their own common sense to infer what happened at other levels. The meticulous recording of every muscle twitch, even if anyone were brave enough to try it, would still not suffice, for it would not contain the structural features that characterize the molar units—and those structural features must be *inferred* on the basis of a *theory* about behavior. Our theories of behavior, in this sense of the term, have always remained implicit and intuitive. (It is rather surprising to realize that after half a century of behaviorism this aspect of the problem of describing behavior has almost never been recognized, much less solved.)

In those fortunate instances that do give us adequate descriptions of behavior—instances provided almost entirely by linguists and ethologists—it is quite obvious that the behavior is organized simultaneously at several levels of complexity. We shall speak of this fact as the "hierarchical organization of behavior."[9] The hierarchy can be represented in various ways. The diagram of a hierarchy usually takes the form of a tree, the arborizations indicating progressively more molecular representations. Or it can be cast as an outline:

X.
- *A.*
  - *a.*
  - *b.*
- *B.*
  - *c.*
  - *d.*
  - *e.*

This outline shows the structure of the hypothetical example introduced on page 59. Or it can be considered as a collection of lists: *X* is a list containing the two items, *A* and *B*; *A* is a list containing two items, *a* and *b*; *B* is a list containing three items, *c*, *d*, and *e.*[10] Or it can be considered as a set of rules governing permissible substitutions: Where *X* occurs, we can substitute for it *AB*; where *A* occurs we can substitute *ab*; etc.[11] Each of these methods of presentation of a hierarchy has its special advantages in special situations.

Now, if the hierarchical nature of the organization of behavior can be taken as axiomatic, the time has come to set aside a few terms for the special purposes of the present discussions. Because definitions make heavy reading, we shall keep the list as short as possible.

Plan. Any complete description of behavior should be adequate to serve as a set of instructions, that is, it should have the characteristics of a plan that could guide the action described. When we speak of a Plan in these pages, however, the term will refer to a *hierarchy* of instructions, and the capitalization will indicate that this special interpretation is intended. *A Plan is any hierarchical process in the organism that can control the order in which a sequence of operations is to be performed.*

A Plan is, for an organism, essentially the same as a program for a computer, especially if the program has the sort of hierarchical character described above. Newell, Shaw, and Simon have explicitly and systematically used the hierarchical structure of lists in their development of "information-processing languages" that are used to program high-speed digital computers to simulate human thought processes. Their success in this direction—which the present authors find most impressive and encouraging—argues strongly for the hypothesis that a hierarchical structure is the basic form of organization in human problem-solving. Thus, we are reasonably confident that "program" could be substituted everywhere for "Plan" in the following pages. However, the reduction of Plans to nothing but programs is still a scientific hypothesis and is still in need of further validation. For the present, therefore, it should be less confusing if we regard a computer program that simulates certain features of an organism's behavior as a theory about the organismic Plan that generated the behavior.[12]

Moreover, we shall also use the term "Plan" to designate a rough sketch of some course of action, just the major topic headings in the outline, as well as the completely detailed specification of every detailed operation.[13]

Strategy and Tactics. The concept of the hierarchical organization of behavior was introduced earlier with the distinction between molar and molecular units of analysis. Now, however, we wish to augment our terminology. The molar units in the organization of behavior will be said to comprise the behavioral *strategy*, and the molecular units, the *tactics*.

Execution. We shall say that a creature is executing a particular Plan when in fact that Plan is controlling the sequence of operations he is carrying out. When an organism executes a Plan he proceeds through it step by step, completing one part and then moving to the next. The execution of a Plan need not result in overt action—especially in man, it seems to be true that there are Plans for collecting or transforming information, as well as Plans for guiding actions. Although it is not actually necessary, we assume on intuitive grounds that only one Plan is executed at a time, although relatively rapid alternation between Plans may be possible. An organism may—probably does—store many Plans other than the ones it happens to be executing at the moment.

Image. The Image is all the accumulated, organized knowledge that the organism has about itself and its world. The Image consists of a great deal more than imagery, of course. What we have in mind when we use this term is essentially the same kind of private representation that other cognitive theorists have demanded. It includes everything the organism has learned—his values as well as his facts—organized by whatever concepts, images, or relations he has been able to master.

In the course of prolonged debates the present authors heard themselves using many other terms to modify "Plan" in rather special ways, but they will not be listed here. New terms will be defined and developed as they are needed in the course of the argument that follows. For the moment, however, we have defined enough to be able to say that the central problem . . . is *to explore the relation between the Image and the Plan.*

Stated so, it may seem to imply some sharp dichotomy between the two, so that it would be meaningful to ask, "Is such-and-such a process exclusively in the Plan or exclusively in the Image?" That the two points of view cannot be used in that way to classify processes into mutually exclusive categories should become apparent from such considerations as these:

—A Plan can be learned and so would be a part of the Image.

—The names that Plans have must comprise a part of the Image for human beings, since it must be part of a person's Image of himself that he is able to execute such-and-such Plans.

—Knowledge must be incorporated into the Plan, since otherwise it could not provide a basis for guiding behavior. Thus, Images can form part of a Plan.

—Changes in the Images can be effected only by executing Plans for gathering, storing, or transforming information.

—Changes in the Plans can be effected only by information drawn from the Images.

—The transformation of descriptions into instructions is, for human beings, a simple verbal trick.

Psychologists who are accustomed to think of their problem as the investigation of relations between Stimulus and Response are apt to view the present undertaking in a parallel way—as an investigation of relations between a subjective stimulus and a subjective response. If that were all we had to say, however, we would scarcely have written a book to say it. Stimulus and response are physiological concepts borrowed from the discussion of reflexes. But we have rejected the classical concept of the reflex arc as the fundamental pattern for the organization of all behavior, and consequently we do not feel a need to extend the classic disjunction between stimulus and response variables into the realm of Images and Plans. To assume that a Plan is a covert response to some inner Image of a stimulus does nothing but parallel objective concepts with subjective equivalents and leaves the reflex arc still master—albeit a rather ghostly master—of the machinery of the mind. We are not likely to overthrow an old master without the help of a new one, so it is to the task of finding a successor that we must turn next.

Notes

1. Frederic C. Bartlett, *Remembering, A Study in Experimental and Social Psychology* (Cambridge: Cambridge University Press, 1932), p. 201.

2. Edward C. Tolman, Cognitive maps in rats and men, *Psychological Review*, 1948, 55, 189–208.

3. See, for example, either E. R. Hilgard, *Theories of Learning* (New York: Appleton-Century-Crofts, ed. 2, 1956), or W. K. Estes *et al.*, *Modern Learning Theory* (New York: Appleton-Century-Crofts, 1954), or D. O. Hebb, *The Organization of Behavior* (New York: Wiley, 1949).

4. E. R. Guthrie, *The Psychology of Learning* (New York: Harper, 1935), p. 172.

5. Wolfgang Köhler, *The Mentality of Apes* (translated from the second edition by Ella Winter; London: Routledge and Kegan Paul, 1927), pp. 169–170.

6. Lloyd A. Jeffress, ed., *Cerebral Mechanisms in Behavior* (New York: Wiley, 1951), p. 230.

7. William James, *The Principles of Psychology*, Vol. II (New York: Holt, 1890), p. 561.

8. The traditional method of parsing a sentence is the prototype of the kind of behavioral description we demand. Noam Chomsky, in Chapter 4 of his monograph, *Syntactic Structures* (The Hague: Mouton, 1957), provides a formal representation of this kind of description, which linguists refer to as "constituent analysis." We shall discuss Chomsky's method of representing verbal behavior in more detail in Chapter 11. The suggestion that linguistic analysis provides a model for the description of all kinds of behavior, is of course, no novelty; it has been made frequently by both linguists and psychologists. For example, in *The Study of Language* (Cambridge: Harvard University Press, 1953), John B. Carroll, a psychologist, observed that, "From linguistic theory we get the notion of a hierarchy of units—from elemental units like the distinctive feature of a phoneme to large units like a sentence-type. It may be suggested that stretches of any kind of behavior may be organized in somewhat the same fashion" (p. 106).

9. Many psychologists are familiar with the notion that behavior is hierarchically organized because they remember Clark Hull's use of the phrase "habit-family hierarchy." We must hasten to say, therefore, that Hull's use of the term "hierarchy" and our present use of that term have almost nothing in common. We are talking about a hierarchy of levels of representation. Hull was talking about an ordering of alternative (interchangeable, substitutable) responses according to their strengths. See, for example, C. L. Hull, The concept of the habit-family hierarchy and maze learning, *Psychological Review*, 1934, 41, 33–54; 134–152. Closer to the spirit of the present discussion is the system of behavioral episodes used by Roger G. Barker and Herbert F. Wright, in *Midwest and Its Children* (Evanston: Row, Peterson, 1954), to describe the molar behavior of children in their natural habitats. The work of Barker and Wright is a noteworthy exception to our assertion that psychologists have not tried to describe the structural features of behavior.

10. The tree and outline forms of representation are quite ancient and familiar, but the use of list structures for representing such organizations is, we believe, relatively new. We first became acquainted with it through the work of Newell, Shaw, and Simon on the simulation of cognitive processes by computer programs. See, for example, Allen Newell and Herbert A. Simon, The logic theory machine: A complex information processing system, *IRE Transactions on Information Theory*, 1956, Vol. IT-2, No. 3, 61–79. Also, Allen Newell and J. C. Shaw, Programming the logic theory machine, *Proceedings of the Western Joint Computer Conference*, Los Angeles, February 1957, pp. 230–240.

11. Chomsky, *Syntactic Structures*, p. 26.

12. It should be clearly recognized that, as Newell, Shaw, and Simon point out, comparing the sequence of operations executed by an organism and by a properly programmed computer is quite different from comparing computers with brains, or electrical relays with synapses, etc. See Allen Newell, J. C. Shaw, and Herbert A. Simon, Elements of a theory of human problem solving. *Psychological Review*, 1958, 65, 151–166. Also, Herbert A. Simon and Allen Newell, Models, their uses and limitations, in L. D. White, ed., *The State of the Social Sciences* (Chicago: University of Chicago Press, 1956), pp. 66–83.

13. Newell, Shaw, and Simon have also used "plan" to describe a general strategy before the details have been worked out, but they distinguish between such a plan and the program that enables a computer to use planning as one of its problem-solving techniques. See Allen Newell, J. C. Shaw, and Herbert A. Simon, A report on a general problem solving program. *Proceedings of the International Conference on Information Processing*, Paris, 1959 (in press).

Other workers have used the term "machine" rather loosely to include both the Plan and the instrument that executes it. For example, see M. L. Minsky, *Heuristic Aspects of the Artificial Intelligence Problem*, Group Report 34-55, Lincoln Laboratory, Massachusetts Institute of Technology, 17 December 1956, especially Section III. 3.

4 SYMBOLIC INTERACTION

Herbert Blumer

The debate over the adequacy of behaviorist approaches versus that of cognitive ones is continued here—this time from a sociological perspective. Blumer contends that behavior cannot be explained merely in terms of factors such as age, race, social status, and income, which are imputed to actors. It is necessary to consider their meanings and each actor's definition of his situation. He maintains a relativist position—that is, that objects and events do not imply their own meanings. Then the author makes an extremely important shift in emphasis. In contrast to the previous focus upon the individual who uses knowledge to organize his behavior, he places social interaction at the center of the stage. As individuals interact with each other, their definitions of the situation emerge. Cultural knowledge is not limited to information which is socially transmitted from one generation to the next. Rather, it is socially created by the members of each new generation as they engage in continuous symbolic interaction. Furthermore, human acts are *constructed* during this process. Rules are not rigid molds into which behavior is poured. It is the "group life that creates and upholds the rules, not the rules that create and uphold group life." Symbolic interaction takes place among actors who receive messages, interpret them, define the situation, anticipate how others will act, formulate plans, make decisions to act, receive new information, and revise their plans. We noted earlier that science is a subculture with its own image of the world. Symbolic interactionism, as a scientific theory, has several basic images which are very general in nature. Blumer discusses the more important "root images" of this position.

At this point an observation about symbolic interactionism and ethnoscience is in order. In later chapters the methods of ethnoscience receive considerable attention. Several studies in Part 4 are explicit applications of these methods. It has appeared to me that the data gathered by ethnoscience techniques is sometimes divorced from the reality of social interaction. Symbolic-interaction studies, on the other hand, often present cogent statements about the way human behavior is organized with reference to meaning, but then resort to sterile research methods. For instance, questionnaires which are far removed from the language and meaning of those studied are often used. In short, ethnoscience appears to be a method in search of a theory, and symbolic interactionism, a theory in search of a method. While this is an overstatement, those who are concerned with either of these fields would be well advised to acquaint themselves with the writings of the other.—EDITOR'S NOTE

The term "symbolic interactionism" has come into use as a label for a relatively distinctive approach to the study of human group life and human conduct.[1] The scholars who have used the approach or contributed to its intellectual foundation are many, and include such notable American figures as George Herbert Mead, John Dewey, W. I. Thomas, Robert E. Park, William James, Charles Horton Cooley, Florian Znaniecki, James Mark Baldwin, Robert Redfield, and Louis Wirth. Despite significant differences in the thought of such scholars, there is a great similarity in the general way in which they viewed and studied human group life. The concept of symbolic interactionism is built around this strand of general similarity. There has been no clear formulation of the position of symbolic interactionism, and above all, a reasoned statement of the methodological position of this approach is lacking. This essay is an effort to develop such a statement. I rely chiefly on the thought of George Herbert Mead who, above all others, laid the foundations of the symbolic interactionist approach, but I have been compelled to develop my own version, dealing explicitly with many crucial matters that were only implicit in the thought of Mead and others, and covering critical topics with which they were not concerned. Thus, to a major extent I must bear full responsibility for the views and analyses presented here. This is especially true of my treatment of methodology; the discussion of this topic is solely my own. My scheme of treatment is first to outline the nature of symbolic interactionism, next to identify the guiding principles of methodology in the case of empirical science, and finally to deal specifically with the methodological position of symbolic interactionism.

The Nature of Symbolic Interactionism

Symbolic interactionism rests in the last analysis on three simple premises. The first premise is that human beings act toward things on the basis of the meanings that the things have for them. Such things include everything that the human being may note in his world—physical objects, such as trees or chairs; other human beings, such as a mother or a store clerk; categories of human beings, such as friends or enemies; institutions, as a school or a government; guiding ideals, such as individual independence or honesty; activities of others, such as their commands or requests; and such situations as an individual encounters in his daily life. The second premise is that the meaning of such things is derived from, or arises out of, the social interaction that one has with one's fellows. The third premise is that these meanings are handled in, and modified through, an interpretative process used by the person in dealing with the things he encounters. I wish to discuss briefly each of these three fundamental premises.

It would seem that few scholars would see anything wrong with the first premise—that human beings act toward things on the basis of the meanings which these things have for them. Yet, oddly enough, this simple view is ignored or played down in practically all of the thought and work in contemporary social science and psychological science. Meaning is either taken for granted and thus pushed aside as unimportant or it is regarded as a mere neutral link between the factors responsible for human behavior and this behavior as the product of such factors. We can see this clearly in the predominant posture of psychological and social science today. Common to both of these fields is the tendency to treat human behavior as the product of various factors that play upon human beings; concern is with the behavior and with the factors regarded as producing them. Thus, psychologists turn to such factors as stimuli, attitudes, conscious or unconscious motives, various kinds of psychological inputs, perception and cognition, and various features of personal organization to account for given forms or instances of human conduct. In a similar fashion sociologists rely on such factors as social position, status demands, social roles, cultural prescriptions, norms and values, social pressures, and group affiliation to provide such explanations. In both such typical psychological and sociological explanations the meanings of things for the human beings who are acting are either bypassed or swallowed up in the factors used to account for their behavior. If one declares that the given kinds of behavior are the result of the particular factors regarded as producing them, there is no need to concern oneself with the meaning of the things toward which human beings act; one merely identifies the initiating factors and the resulting behavior. Or one may, if pressed, seek to accommodate the element of meaning by lodging it in the initiating factors or by regarding it as a neutral link intervening between the initiating factors and the behavior they are alleged to produce. In the first of these latter cases the meaning disappears by being merged into the initiating or causative factors; in the second case meaning becomes a mere transmission link that can be ignored in favor of the initiating factors.

The position of symbolic interactionism, in contrast, is that the meanings that things have for human beings are central in their own right. To ignore the meaning of the things toward which people act is seen as falsifying the behavior under study. To bypass the meaning in favor of factors alleged to produce the behavior is seen as a grievous neglect of the role of meaning in the formation of behavior.

The simple premise that human beings act toward things on the basis of the meaning of such things is much too simple in itself to differentiate symbolic interactionism—there are several other approaches that share this premise. A major line of difference between them and symbolic interactionism is set by the second premise, which refers to the source of meaning. There are two well-known traditional ways of accounting for the origin of meaning. One of them is to regard meaning as being intrinsic to the thing that has it, as being a natural part of the objective makeup of the thing. Thus, a chair is clearly a chair in itself, a cow a cow, a cloud a cloud, a rebellion a rebellion, and so forth. Being inherent in the thing that has it, meaning needs merely to be disengaged by observing the objective thing that has the meaning. The meaning emanates, so to speak, from the thing and as such there is no process involved in its formation; all that is necessary is to recognize the meaning that is there in the thing. It should be immediately apparent that this view reflects the traditional position of "realism" in philosophy—a position that is widely held and deeply entrenched in the social and psychological sciences. The other major traditional view regards "meaning" as a psychical accretion brought to the thing by the person for whom the thing has meaning. This psychical accretion is treated as being an expression of constituent elements of the person's psyche, mind, or psychological organization. The constituent elements are such things as sensations, feelings, ideas, memories, motives, and attitudes. The meaning of a thing is but the expression of the given psychological elements that are brought into play in connection with the perception of the thing; thus one seeks to explain the meaning of a thing by isolating the particular psychological elements that produce the meaning. One sees this in the somewhat ancient and classical psychological practice of analyzing the meaning of an object by identifying the sensations that enter into perception of that object; or in the contemporary practice of tracing the meaning of a thing, such as let us say prostitution, to the attitude of the person who views it. This lodging of the meaning of things in psychological elements limits the processes of the formation of meaning to whatever processes are involved in arousing and bringing together the given psychological elements that produce the meaning. Such processes are psychological in nature, and include perception, cognition, repression, transfer of feelings, and association of ideas.

Symbolic interactionism views meaning as having a different source than those held by the two dominant views just considered. It does not regard meaning as emanating from the intrinsic makeup of the thing that has meaning, nor does it see meaning as arising through a coalescence of psychological elements in the person. Instead, it sees meaning as arising in the process of interaction between people. The meaning of a thing for a person grows out of the ways in which other persons act toward the person with regard to the thing. Their actions operate to define the thing for the person. Thus, symbolic interactionism sees meanings as social products, as creations that are formed in and through the defining activities of people as they interact. This point of view gives symbolic interactionism a very distinctive position, with profound implications that will be discussed later.

The third premise mentioned above further differentiates symbolic interactionism. While the meaning of things is formed in the context of social interaction and is derived by the person from that interaction, it is a mistake to think that the use of meaning by a person is but an application of the meaning so derived. This mistake seriously mars the work of many scholars who otherwise follow the symbolic interactionist approach. They fail to see that the use of meanings by a person in his action involves an interpretative process. In this respect they are similar to the adherents of the two dominant views spoken of above—to those who lodge meaning in the objective makeup of the thing that has it and those who regard it as an expression of psychological elements. All three are alike in viewing the use of meaning by the human being in his action as being no more than an arousing and application of already established meanings. As such, all three fail to see that the use of meanings by the actor occurs through *a process of interpretation*. This process has two distinct steps. First, the actor indicates to himself the things toward which he is acting; he has to point out to himself the things that have meaning. The making of such indications is an internalized social process in that the actor is interacting with himself. This interaction with himself is something other than an interplay of psychological elements; it is an instance of the person engaging in a process of communication with himself. Second, by virtue of this process of communicating with himself, interpretation becomes a matter of handling meanings. The actor selects, checks, suspends, regroups, and transforms the meanings in the light of the situation in which he is placed and the direction of his action. Accordingly, interpretation should not be regarded as a mere automatic application of established meanings but as a formative process in which meanings are used and revised as instruments for the guidance and formation of action. It is necessary to see that meanings play their part in action through a process of self-interaction.

It is not my purpose to discuss at this point the merits of the three views that lodge meaning respectively in the thing, in the psyche, and in social action, nor to elaborate on the contention that meanings are handled flexibly by the actor in the course of forming his action. Instead, I wish merely to note that by being based on these three premises, symbolic interaction is necessarily led to develop an analytical scheme of human society and human conduct that is quite distinctive. It is this scheme that I now propose to outline.

Symbolic interactionism is grounded on a number of basic ideas, or "root images," as I prefer to call them. These root images refer to and depict the nature of the following matters: human groups or societies, social interaction, objects, the human being as an actor, human action, and the interconnection of the lines of action. Taken together, these root images represent the way in which symbolic interactionism views human society and conduct. They constitute the framework of study and analysis. Let me describe briefly each of these root images.

Nature of Human Society or Human Group Life

Human groups are seen as consisting of human beings who are engaging in action. The action consists of the multitudinous activities that the individuals perform in their life as they encounter one another and as they deal with the succession of situations confronting them. The individuals may act singly, they may act collectively, and they may act on behalf of, or as representatives of, some organization or group of others. The activities belong to the acting individuals and are carried on by them always with regard to the situations in which they have to act. The import of this simple and essentially redundant characterization is that fundamentally human groups or society *exists in action* and must be seen in terms of action. This picture of human society as action must be the starting point (and the point of return) for any scheme that purports to treat and analyze human society empirically. Conceptual schemes that depict society in some other fashion can only be derivations from the complex of ongoing activity that constitutes group life. This is true of the two dominant conceptions of society in contemporary sociology—that of culture and that of social structure. Culture as a conception, whether defined as custom, tradition, norm, value, rules, or such like, is clearly derived from what people do. Similarly, social structure in any of its aspects, as represented by such terms as social position, status, role, authority, and prestige, refers to relationships derived from how people act toward each other. The life of any human society consists necessarily of an ongoing process of fitting together the activities of its members. It is this complex of ongoing activity that establishes and portrays structure or organization. A cardinal principle of symbolic interactionism is that any empirically oriented scheme of human society, however derived, must respect the fact that in the first and last instances human society consists of people engaging in action. To be empirically valid the scheme must be consistent with the nature of the social action of human beings.

Nature of Social Interaction

Group life necessarily presupposes interaction between the group members; or, put otherwise, a society consists of individuals interacting with one another. The activities of the members occur predominantly in response to one another or in relation to one another. Even though this is recognized almost universally in definitions of human society, social interaction is usually taken for granted and treated as having little, if any, significance in its own right. This is evident in typical sociological and psychological schemes—they treat social interaction as merely a medium through which the determinants of behavior pass to produce the behavior. Thus, the typical sociological scheme ascribes behavior to such factors as status position, cultural prescriptions, norms, values, sanctions, role demands, and social system requirements; explanation in terms of such factors suffices without paying attention to the social interaction that their play necessarily presupposes. Similarly, in the typical psychological scheme such factors as motives, attitudes, hidden complexes, elements of psychological organization, and psychological processes are used to account for behavior without any need of considering social interaction. One jumps from such causative factors to the behavior they are supposed to produce. Social interaction becomes a mere forum through which sociological or psychological determinants move to bring about given forms of human behavior. I may add that this ignoring of social interaction is not corrected by speaking of an interaction of societal elements (as when a sociologist speaks of an interaction of social roles or an interaction between the components of a social system) or an interaction of psychological elements (as when a psychologist speaks of an interaction between the attitudes held by different people). Social interaction is an interaction between actors and not between factors imputed to them.

Symbolic interactionism does not merely give a ceremonious nod to social interaction. It recognizes social interaction to be of vital importance in its own right. This importance lies in the fact that social interaction is a process that *forms* human conduct instead of being merely a means or a setting for the expression or release of human conduct. Put simply, human beings in interacting with one another have to take account of what each other is doing or is about to do; they are forced to direct their own conduct or handle their situations in terms of what they take into account. Thus, the activities of others enter as positive factors in the formation of their own conduct; in the face of the actions of others one may abandon an intention or purpose, revise it, check or suspend it, intensify it, or replace it. The actions of others enter to set what one plans to do, may oppose or prevent such plans, may require a revision of such plans, and may demand a very different set of such plans. One has to *fit* one's own line of activity in some manner to the actions of others. The actions of others have to be taken into account and cannot be regarded as merely an arena for the expression of what one is disposed to do or sets out to do.

We are indebted to George Herbert Mead for the most penetrating analysis of social interaction—an analysis that squares with the realistic account just given. Mead identifies two forms or levels of social interaction in human society. He refers to them respectively as "the conversation of gestures" and "the use of significant symbols"; I shall term them respectively "non-symbolic interaction" and "symbolic interaction." Non-symbolic interaction takes place when one responds directly to the action of another without interpreting that action; symbolic interaction involves interpretation of the action. Non-symbolic interaction is most readily apparent in reflex responses, as in the case of a boxer who automatically raises his arm to parry a blow. However, if the boxer were reflectively to identify the forthcoming blow from his opponent as a feint designed to trap him, he would be engaging in symbolic interaction. In this case, he would endeavor to ascertain the meaning of the blow—that is, what the blow signifies as to his opponent's plan. In their association human beings engage plentifully in non-symbolic interaction as they respond immediately and unreflectively to each other's bodily movements, expressions, and tones of voice, but their characteristic mode of interaction is on the symbolic level, as they seek to understand the meaning of each other's action.

Mead's analysis of symbolic interaction is highly important. He sees it as a presentation of gestures and a response to the meaning of those gestures. A gesture is any part or aspect of an ongoing action that signifies the larger act of which it is a part—for example, the shaking of a fist as an indication of a possible attack, or the declaration of war by a nation as an indication of a posture and line of action of that nation. Such things as requests, orders, commands, cues, and declarations are gestures that convey to the person who recognizes them an idea of the intention and plan of forthcoming action of the individual who presents them. The person who responds organizes his response on the basis of what the gestures mean to him; the person who presents the gestures advances them as indications or signs of what he is planning to do as well as of what he wants the respondent to do or understand. Thus, the gesture has meaning for both the person who makes it and for the person to whom it is directed. When the gesture has the same meaning for both, the two parties understand each other. From this brief account it can be seen that the meaning of the gesture flows out along three lines (Mead's triadic nature of meaning): It signifies what the person to whom it is directed is to do; it signifies what the person who is making the gesture plans to do; and it signifies the joint action that is to arise by the articulation of the acts of both. Thus, for illustration, a robber's command to his victim to put up his hands is (a) an indication of what the victim is to do; (b) an indication of what the robber plans to do, that is, relieve the victim of his money; and (c) an indication of the joint act being formed, in this case a holdup. If there is confusion or misunderstanding along any one of these three lines of meaning, communication is ineffective, interaction is impeded, and the formation of joint action is blocked.

One additional feature should be added to round out Mead's analysis of symbolic interaction, namely, that the parties to such interaction must necessarily take each other's roles. To indicate to another what he is to do, one has to make the indication from the standpoint of that other; to order the victim to put up his hands the robber has to see this response in terms of the victim making it. Correspondingly, the victim has to see the command from the stand-point of the robber who gives the command; he has to grasp the intention and forthcoming action of the robber. Such mutual role-taking is the *sine qua non* of communication and effective symbolic interaction.

The central place and importance of symbolic interaction in human group life and conduct should be apparent. A human society or group consists of people in association. Such association exists necessarily in the form of people acting toward one another and thus engaging in social interaction. Such interaction in human society is characteristically and predominantly on the symbolic level; as individuals acting individually, collectively, or as agents of some organization encounter one another they are necessarily required to take account of the actions of one another as they form their own action. They do this by a dual process of indicating to others how to act and of interpreting the indications made by others. Human group life is a vast process of such defining to others what to do and of interpreting their definitions; through this process people come to fit their activities to one another and to form their own individual conduct. Both such joint activity and individual conduct are formed *in* and *through* this ongoing process; they are not mere expressions or products of what people bring to their interaction or of conditions that are antecedent to their interaction. The failure to accommodate to this vital point constitutes the fundamental deficiency of schemes that seek to account for human society in terms of social organization or psychological factors, or of any combination of the two. By virtue of symbolic interaction, human group life is necessarily a formative process and not a mere arena for the expression of pre-existing factors.

Nature of Objects

The position of symbolic interactionism is that the "worlds" that exist for human beings and for their groups are composed of "objects" and that these objects are the product of symbolic interaction. An object is anything that can be indicated, anything that is pointed to or referred to—a cloud, a book, a legislature, a banker, a religious doctrine, a ghost, and so forth. For purposes of convenience one can classify objects in three categories: (a) physical objects, such as chairs, trees, or bicycles; (b) social objects, such as students, priests, a president, a mother, or a friend; and (c) abstract objects, such as moral principles, philosophical doctrines, or ideas such as justice, exploitation, or compassion. I repeat that an object is anything that can be indicated or referred to. The nature of an object—of any and every object—consists of the meaning that it has for the person for whom it is an object. This meaning sets the way in which he sees the object, the way in which he is prepared to act toward it, and the way in which he is ready to talk about it. An object may have a different meaning for different individuals: a tree will be a different object to a botanist, a lumberman, a poet, and a home gardener; the President of the United States can be a very different object to a devoted member of his political party than to a member of the opposition; the members of an ethnic group may be seen as a different kind of object by members of other groups. The meaning of objects for a person arises fundamentally out of the way they are defined to him by others with whom he interacts. Thus, we come to learn through the indications of others that a chair is a chair, that doctors are a certain kind of professional, that the United States Constitution is a given kind of legal document, and so forth. Out of a process of mutual indications common objects emerge—objects that have the same meaning for a given set of people and are seen in the same manner by them.

Several noteworthy consequences follow from the foregoing discussion of objects. First, it gives us a different picture of the environment or milieu of human beings. From their standpoint the environment consists *only* of the objects that the given human beings recognize and know. The nature of this environment is set by the meaning that the objects composing it have for those human beings. Individuals, also groups, occupying or living in the same spatial location may have, accordingly, very different environments; as we say, people may be living side by side yet be living in different worlds. Indeed, the term "world" is more suitable than the word "environment" to designate the setting, the surroundings, and the texture of things that confront them. It is the world of their objects with which people have to deal and toward which they develop their actions. It follows that in order to understand the action of people it is necessary to identify their world of objects—an important point that will be elaborated later.

Second, objects (in the sense of their meaning) must be seen as social creations—as being formed in and arising out of the process of definition and interpretation as this process takes place in the interaction of people. The meaning of anything and everything has to be formed, learned, and transmitted through a process of indication—a process that is necessarily a social process. Human group life on the level of symbolic interaction is a vast process in which people are forming, sustaining, and transforming the objects of their world as they come to give meaning to objects. Objects have no fixed status except as their meaning is sustained through indications and definitions that people make of the objects. Nothing is more apparent than that objects in all categories can undergo change in their meaning. A star in the sky is a very different object to a modern astrophysicist than it was to a sheepherder of biblical times; marriage was a different object to later Romans than to earlier Romans; the president of a nation who fails to act successfully through critical times may become a very different object to the citizens of his land. In short, from the standpoint of symbolic interactionism human group life is a process in which objects are being created, affirmed, transformed, and cast aside. The life and action of people necessarily change in line with the changes taking place in their world of objects.

The Human Being as an Acting Organism

Symbolic interactionism recognizes that human beings must have a makeup that fits the nature of social interaction. The human being is seen as an organism that not only responds to others on the non-symbolic level but as one that makes indications to others and interprets their indications. He can do this, as Mead has shown so emphatically, only by virtue of possessing a "self." Nothing esoteric is meant by this expression. It means merely that a human being can be an object of his own action. Thus, he can recognize himself, for instance, as being a man, young in age, a student, in debt, trying to become a doctor, coming from an undistinguished family and so forth. In all such instances he is an object to himself; and he acts toward himself and guides himself in his actions toward others on the basis of the kind of object he is to himself. This notion of oneself as an object fits into the earlier discussion of objects. Like other objects, the self-object emerges from the process of social interaction in which other people are defining a person to himself. Mead has traced the way in which this occurs in his discussion of role-taking. He points out that in order to become an object to himself a person has to see himself from the outside. One can do this only by placing himself in the position of others and viewing himself or acting toward himself from that position. The roles the person takes range from that of discrete individuals (the "play stage"), through that of discrete organized groups (the "game stage") to that of the abstract community (the "generalized other"). In taking such roles the person is in a position to address or approach himself—as in the case of a young girl who in "playing mother" talks to herself as her mother would do, or in the case of a young priest who sees himself through the eyes of the priesthood. We form our objects of ourselves through such a process of role-taking. It follows that we see ourselves through the way in which others see or define us—or, more precisely, we see ourselves by taking one of the three types of roles of others that have been mentioned. That one forms an object of himself through the ways in which others define one to himself is recognized fairly well in the literature today, so despite its great significance I shall not comment on it further.

There is an even more important matter that stems from the fact that the human being has a self, namely that this enables him to interact with himself. This interaction is not in the form of interaction between two or more parts of a psychological system, as between needs, or between emotions, or between ideas, or between the id and the ego in the Freudian scheme. Instead, the interaction is social—a form of communication, with the person addressing himself as a person and responding thereto. We can clearly recognize such interaction in ourselves as each of us notes that he is angry with himself, or that he has to spur himself on in his tasks, or that he reminds himself to do this or that, or that he is talking to himself in working out some plan of action. As such instances suggest, self-interaction exists fundamentally as a process of making indications to oneself. This process is in play continuously during one's waking life, as one notes and considers one or another matter, or observes this or that happening. Indeed, for the human being to be conscious or aware of anything is equivalent to his indicating the thing to himself—he is identifying it as a given kind of object and considering its relevance or importance to his line of action. One's waking life consists of a series of such indications that the person is making to himself, indications that he uses to direct his action.

We have, then, a picture of the human being as an organism that interacts with itself through a social process of making indications to itself. This is a radically different view of the human being from that which dominates contemporary social and psychological science. The dominant prevailing view sees the human being as a complex organism whose behavior is a response to factors playing on the organization of the organism. Schools of thought in the social and psychological sciences differ enormously in which of such factors they regard as significant, as is shown in such a diverse array as stimuli, organic drives, need-dispositions, conscious motives, unconscious motives, emotions, attitudes, ideas, cultural prescriptions, norms, values, status demands, social roles, reference group affiliations, and institutional pressures. Schools of thought differ also in how they view the organization of the human being, whether as a kind of biological organization, a kind of psychological organization, or a kind of imported societal organization incorporated from the social structure of one's group. Nevertheless, these schools of thought are alike in seeing the human being as a responding organism, with its behavior being a product of the factors playing on its organization or an expression of the interplay of parts of its organization. Under this widely shared view the human being is "social" only in the sense of either being a member of social species, or of responding to others (social stimuli), or of having incorporated within it the organization of his group.

The view of the human being held in symbolic interactionism is fundamentally different. The human being is seen as "social" in a much more profound sense—in the sense of an organism that engages in social interaction with itself by making indications to itself and responding to such indications. By virtue of engaging in self-interaction the human being stands in a markedly different relation to his environment than is presupposed by the widespread conventional view described above. Instead of being merely an organism that responds to the play of factors on or through it, the human being is seen as an organism that has to deal with what it notes. It meets what it so notes by engaging in a process of self-indication in which it makes an object of what it notes, gives it a meaning, and uses the meaning as the basis for directing its action. Its behavior with regard to what it notes is not a response called forth by the presentation of what it notes but instead is an action that arises out of the interpretation made through the process of self-indication. In this sense, the human being who is engaging in self-interaction is not a mere responding organism but an acting organism—an organism that has to mold a line of action on the basis of what it takes into account instead of merely releasing a response to the play of some factor on its organization.

Nature of Human Action

The capacity of the human being to make indications to himself gives a distinctive character to human action. It means that the human individual confronts a world that he must interpret in order to act instead of an environment to which he responds because of his organization. He has to cope with the situations in which he is called on to act, ascertaining the meaning of the actions of others and mapping out his own line of action in the light of such interpretation. He has to construct and guide his action instead of merely releasing it in response to factors playing on him or operating through him. He may do a miserable job in constructing his action, but he has to construct it.

This view of the human being directing his action by making indications to himself stands sharply in contrast to the view of human action that dominates current psychological and social science. This dominant view, as already implied, ascribes human action to an initiating factor or a combination of such factors. Action is traced back to such matters as motives, attitudes, need-dispositions, unconscious complexes, stimuli configurations, status demands, role requirements, and situational demands. To link the action to one or more of such initiating agents is regarded as fulfilling the scientific task. Yet, such an approach ignores and makes no place for the process of self-interaction through which the individual handles his world and constructs his action. The door is closed to the vital process of interpretation in which the individual notes and assesses what is presented to him and through which he maps out lines of overt behavior prior to their execution.

Fundamentally, action on the part of a human being consists of taking account of various things that he notes and forging a line of conduct on the basis of how he interprets them. The things taken into account cover such matters as his wishes and wants, his objectives, the available means for their achievement, the actions and anticipated actions of others, his image of himself, and the likely result of a given line of action. His conduct is formed and guided through such a process of indication and interpretation. In this process, given lines of action may be started or stopped, they may be abandoned or postponed, they may be confined to mere planning or to an inner life of reverie, or if initiated, they may be transformed. My purpose is not to analyze this process but to call attention to its presence and operation in the formation of human action. We must recognize that the activity of human beings consists of meeting a flow of situations in which they have to act and that their action is built on the basis of what they note, how they assess and interpret what they note, and what kind of projected lines of action they map out. This process is not caught by ascribing action to some kind of factor (for example, motives, need-dispositions, role requirements, social expectations, or social rules) that is thought to initiate the action and propel it to its conclusion; such a factor, or some expression of it, is a matter the human actor takes into account in mapping his line of action. The initiating factor does not embrace or explain how it and other matters are taken into account in the situation that calls for action. One has to get inside of the defining process of the actor in order to understand his action.

This view of human action applies equally well to joint or collective action in which numbers of individuals are implicated. Joint or collective action constitutes the domain of sociological concern, as exemplified in the behavior of groups, institutions, organizations, and social classes. Such instances of societal behavior, whatever they may be, consist of individuals fitting their lines of action to one another. It is both proper and possible to view and study such behavior in its joint or collective character instead of in its individual components. Such joint behavior does not lose its character of being constructed through an interpretative process in meeting the situations in which the collectivity is called on to act. Whether the collectivity be an army engaged in a campaign, a corporation seeking to expand its operations, or a nation trying to correct an unfavorable balance of trade, it needs to construct its action through an interpretation of what is happening in its area of operation. The interpretative process takes place by participants making indications to one another, not merely each to himself. Joint or collective action is an outcome of such a process of interpretative interaction.

Interlinkage of Action

As stated earlier, human group life consists of, and exists in, the fitting of lines of action to each other by the members of the group. Such articulation of lines of action gives rise to and constitutes "joint action"—a societal organization of conduct of different acts of diverse participants. A joint action, while made up of diverse component acts that enter into its formation, is different from any one of them and from their mere aggregation. The joint action has a distinctive character in its own right, a character that lies in the articulation or linkage as apart from what may be articulated or linked. Thus, the joint action may be identified as such and may be spoken of and handled without having to break it down into the separate acts that comprise it. This is what we do when we speak of such things as marriage, a trading transaction, war, a parliamentary discussion, or a church service. Similarly, we can speak of the collectivity that engages in joint action without having to identify the individual members of that collectivity, as we do in speaking of a family, a business corporation, a church, a university, or a nation. It is evident that the domain of the social scientist is constituted precisely by the study of joint action and of the collectivities that engage in joint action.

In dealing with collectivities and with joint action one can easily be trapped in an erroneous position by failing to recognize that the joint action of the collectivity is an interlinkage of the separate acts of the participants. This failure leads one to overlook the fact that a joint action always has to undergo a process of formation; even though it may be a well-established and repetitive form of social action, each instance of it has to be formed anew. Further, this career of formation through which it comes into being necessarily takes place through the dual process of designation and interpretation that was discussed above. The participants still have to guide their respective acts by forming and using meanings.

With these remarks as a background I wish to make three observations on the implications of the interlinkage that constitutes joint action. I wish to consider first those instances of joint action that are repetitive and stable. The preponderant portion of social action in a human society, particularly in a settled society, exists in the form of recurrent patterns of joint action. In most situations in which people act toward one another they have in advance a firm understanding of how to act and of how other people will act. They share common and pre-established meanings of what is expected in the action of the participants, and accordingly each participant is able to guide his own behavior by such meanings. Instances of repetitive and pre-established forms of joint action are so frequent and common that it is easy to understand why scholars have viewed them as the essence or natural form of human group life. Such a view is especially apparent in the concepts of "culture" and "social order" that are so dominant in social science literature. Most sociological schemes rest on the belief that a human society exists in the form of an established order of living, with that order resolvable into adherence to sets of rules, norms, values, and sanctions that specify to people how they are to act in their different situations.

Several comments are in order with regard to this neat scheme. First, it is just not true that the full expanse of life in a human society, in any human society, is but an expression of pre-established forms of joint action. New situations are constantly arising within the scope of group life that are problematic and for which existing rules are inadequate. I have never heard of any society that was free of problems nor any society in which members did not have to engage in discussion to work out ways of action. Such areas of unprescribed conduct are just as natural, indigenous, and recurrent in human group life as are those areas covered by pre-established and faithfully followed prescriptions of joint action. Second, we have to recognize that even in the case of pre-established and repetitive joint action each instance of such joint action has to be formed anew. The participants still have to build up their lines of action and fit them to one another through the dual process of designation and interpretation. They do this in the case of repetitive joint action, of course, by using the same recurrent and constant meanings. If we recognize this, we are forced to realize that the play and fate of meanings are what is important, not the joint action in its established form. Repetitive and stable joint action is just as much a result of an interpretative process as is a new form of joint action that is being developed for the first time. This is not an idle or pedantic point; the meanings that underlie established and recurrent joint action are themselves subject to pressure as well as to reinforcement, to incipient dissatisfaction as well as to indifference; they may be challenged as well as affirmed, allowed to slip along without concern as well as subjected to infusions of new vigor. Behind the facade of the objectively perceived joint action the set of meanings that sustains that joint action has a life that the social scientists can ill afford to ignore. A gratuitous acceptance of the concepts of norms, values, social rules, and the like should not blind the social scientist to the fact that any one of them is subtended by a process of social interaction—a process that is necessary not only for their change but equally well for their retention in a fixed form. It is the social process in group life that creates and upholds the rules, not the rules that create and uphold group life.

The second observation on the interlinkage that constitutes joint action refers to the extended connection of actions that make up so much of human group life. We are familiar with these large complex networks of action involving an interlinkage and interdependency of diverse actions of diverse people—as in the division of labor extending from the growing of grain by the farmer to an eventual sale of bread in a store, or in the elaborate chain extending from the arrest of a suspect to his eventual release from a penitentiary. These networks with their regularized participation of diverse people by diverse action at diverse points yields a picture of institutions that have been appropriately a major concern of sociologists. They also give substance to the idea that human group life has the character of a system. In seeing such a large complex of diversified activities, all hanging together in a regularized operation, and in seeing the complementary organization of participants in well-knit interdependent relationships, it is easy to understand why so many scholars view such networks or institutions as self-operating entities, following their own dynamics and not requiring that attention be given to the participants within the network. Most of the sociological analyses of institutions and social organization adhere to this view. Such adherence, in my judgment, is a serious mistake. One should recognize what is true, namely, that the diverse array of participants occupying different points in the network engage in their actions at those points on the basis of using given sets of meanings. A network or an institution does not function automatically because of some inner dynamics or system requirements; it functions because people at different points do something, and what they do is a result of how they define the situation in which they are called on to act. A limited appreciation of this point is reflected today in some of the work on decision-making, but on the whole the point is grossly ignored. It is necessary to recognize that the sets of meanings that lead participants to act as they do at their stationed points in the network have their own setting in a localized process of social interaction–and that these meanings are formed, sustained, weakened, strengthened, or transformed, as the case may be, through a socially defining process. Both the functioning and the fate of institutions are set by this process of interpretation as it takes place among the diverse sets of participants.

A third important observation needs to be made, namely, that any instance of joint action, whether newly formed or long established, has necessarily arisen out of a background of previous actions of the participants. A new kind of joint action never comes into existence apart from such a background. The participants involved in the formation of the new joint action always being to that formation the world of objects, the sets of meanings, and the schemes of interpretation that they already possess. Thus, the new form of joint action always emerges out of and is connected with a context of previous joint action. It cannot be understood apart from that context; one has to bring into one's consideration this linkage with preceding forms of joint action. One is on treacherous and empirically invalid grounds if he thinks that any given form of joint action can be sliced off from its historical linkage, as if its makeup and character arose out of the air through spontaneous generation instead of growing out of what went before. In the face of radically different and stressful situations people may be led to develop new forms of joint action that are markedly different from those in which they have previously engaged, yet even in such cases there is always some connection and continuity with what went on before. One cannot understand the new form without incorporating knowledge of this continuity into one's analysis of the new form. Joint action not only represents a horizontal linkage, so to speak, of the activities of the participants, but also a vertical linkage with previous joint action.

Summary Remarks

The general perspective of symbolic interactionism should be clear from our brief sketch of its root images. This approach sees a human society as people engaged in living. Such living is a process of ongoing activity in which participants are developing lines of action in the multitudinous situations they encounter. They are caught up in a vast process of interaction in which they have to fit their developing actions to one another. This process of interaction consists in making indications to others of what to do and in interpreting the indications as made by others. They live in worlds of objects and are guided in their orientation and action by the meaning of these objects. Their objects, including objects of themselves, are formed, sustained, weakened, and transformed in their interaction with one another. This general process should be seen, of course, in the differentiated character which it necessarily has by virtue of the fact that people cluster in different groups, belong to different associations, and occupy different positions. They accordingly approach each other differently, live in different worlds, and guide themselves by different sets of meanings. Nevertheless, whether one is dealing with a family, a boy's gang, an industrial corporation, or a political party, one must see the activities of the collectivity as being formed through a process of designation and interpretation.

Notes

[1]The term "symbolic interactionism" is a somewhat barbaric neologism that I coined in an offhand way in an article written in *Man and Society* (Emerson P. Schmidt, ed. New York: Prentice-Hall, 1937). The term somehow caught on and is now in general use.

5 RULES IN LINGUISTICS AND ETHNOGRAPHY

Robbins Burling

The science of linguistics has provided numerous models for those who seek to describe other aspects of cultural behavior and knowledge. In his monumental work *Language in Relation to a Unified Theory of the Structure of Human Behavior* (1967), Kenneth L. Pike made one of the first attempts to use the advances in linguistics to further the study of behavior generally. He distinguished between "emic" and "etic" analyses on the basis of the analogy of phonological studies. Phon*emics* deals with the sounds recognized and used by a particular language group, while phon*etics* describes the sounds used by all the world's languages. Emic descriptions of behavior thus depend upon discovering the native's categories and perceptions. Etic analyses, on the other hand, are based upon categories created by the investigator for comparing behavior cross-culturally. Other concepts such as componential analysis (Chapter 16) have also been borrowed from linguistics.

In this chapter Robbins Burling suggests that ethnographic descriptions in general are analogous to grammatical descriptions. He presents the goals of grammar and shows how these also apply to other kinds of cultural behavior. Of particular importance is the concept of rules in both linguistic and ethnographic descriptions. In addition to discussing the similarities, Burling points out some of the differences. For example, while the linguist depends upon examples of speech behavior, from which he infers rules, the ethnographer is more likely to use statements about behavior. In a comment on this article, Alice B. Kehoe argues that there is a higher frequency of observable utterances available to investigators than other behavior samples. Thus, "the linguist obtains a statistically more reliable sample for analysis than does the ethnographer" (1970:1461), and therefore the ethnographer must rely more on descriptions of cases and rules made by informants. In response Burling writes: "Ethnographers do rely more heavily (though not exclusively) on verbal explanations. Linguists do rely more heavily (though not exclusively)

Reprinted from "Linguistics and Ethnographic Description," *American Anthropologist*, vol. 71, no. 4 (1969), pp. 817–827, by permission of the author and the American Anthropological Association.

on observation of examples. But rules that account for some sort of human activity (whether language, or residence, or anything else) are not justified by the way we get them, but by whether they work. To this extent I feel that linguistic and ethnographic descriptions have the same logical status. The number of examples observed while working up the rules is entirely irrelevant either to a child or to an ethnographer, as long as the rules work once he gets them" (1970:1462).—EDITOR'S NOTE

Introduction

Anthropologists have long turned to linguistics for techniques by which they have hoped to solve their own problems—techniques for learning an exotic field language, for recording myths in an adequate transcription, for classifying languages so as to make inferences about migrations, for providing glottochronological dates—but I believe that the deepest influence of linguistics upon anthropology has not been to provide these specialized techniques but to suggest far more general view-points from which other aspects of culture than language alone might be considered. In whatever way we define culture, it is difficult to exclude language from the scope of our definition, and anthropologists and linguists share many assumptions about their respective subjects. Language, like culture, is seen as being perpetuated within a social group, as having continuity through time but also as undergoing continual change. Both language and culture are regarded as having "structure" but both are subject to diffusion (or borrowing). Anthropologists and linguists even share the term "informant" to describe the man from whom they learn, and for me this symbolizes the similarity of their approach. An "informant" is regarded as a collaborator, as a man who has an intelligence entirely comparable to the investigator's. The "subject" of some other social sciences always runs the risk of being mistaken for a rat. An informant does not share the subject's peril.

If language must be accepted as one aspect of culture, it is still, in some ways, a very special aspect. It can be argued that of all the many aspects of culture, language is the easiest to study and its description the easiest to formalize. To the extent that language is easier to study than the rest of culture, it may be strategic first to try out new viewpoints and theoretical approaches on language and then see whether these same approaches might also be applied elsewhere. The extension of linguistic approaches to other aspects of culture has in fact been a regular anthropological habit, and there is hardly a generalized theoretical viewpoint in anthropology without its rather direct analogue in linguistics. Just as some anthropologists have been interested in the synchronic structure of a society at a particular point in time, some linguists have been concerned to describe a language synchronically. Other anthropologists have been interested in the changes that culture undergoes through time, and other linguists have shared this interest with respect to language. In language as in the rest of culture, one can make a distinction between the cumulative evolution associated with long-term trends, and the fine scale evolution of shorter periods—those that can involve systematic changes without implying any accumulated complexity. Both in linguistics and in anthropology the relationship of the individual to his culture (or to his language) raises some rather complex issues, but practitioners of both fields frequently study their subject matter as if it were divorced from particular individuals, even if both must finally recognize that it is individual speakers and actors who carry their language and their culture and who exemplify them in their behavior.

The Goals of Grammar

In the last decade linguists have suddenly become far more articulate than formerly in considering the goals and purposes of linguistic description. This development has been stimulated by Chomsky and his disciples, but it has by no means been confined to them. Anthropologists might benefit by trying to understand the attitude that linguists are taking toward the role of linguistic description, to see whether this attitude might have implications for anthropological endeavors in the way other linguistic attitudes so often have had.

In this paper I explore one way in which I believe linguistic viewpoints can clarify anthropological ideas. Specifically, I ask whether the writing of ethnographic descriptions, which I take to be one characteristic activity of anthropologists, might be illuminated by a clear understanding of the comparable task of the linguist: the writing of a grammatical description. So that my comparison between grammar and ethnography will be as unambiguous as possible, I must first discuss with some care just what a grammatical description amounts to. The following points seem to me to be the most important ones:

(1) A grammar is a theory of how a language works. We can refine this by saying that a grammar is a theory that in some manner specifies what can be said in a particular language. Still more explicitly we might say that a grammar constitutes a device that distinguishes between those sequences of vocal noises that are allowable ("grammatical") in some particular language and other sequences that are not allowable ("ungrammatical").

(2) It is important to note that a grammar does *not* specify what *is* said on any particular occasion, but only what *can* potentially be said. At any particular moment a great many things might be said, and linguists have

had little or nothing to say about how the choice among the enormously large number of grammatical sequences is to be made. If linguistics is a predictive science, it can only be predictive in a much looser sense than that of predicting what somebody is actually going to say. Instead, linguists have usually been quite content if they could predict whether native speakers would accept or reject various sequences of noises. Since an enormous number of sequences will be accepted as grammatical, any explicit grammatical formulation must provide for these alternatives, but it cannot predict which of these many alternatives will actually be chosen at a particular time.

(3) All linguists use some criteria of simplicity, though these are rarely clearly stated. Other things being equal, the grammatical description that covers the situation in a simple way is better than one that does the same job in a more complicated fashion. We must admit the enormous complexities of defining simplicity, but at the very least a grammar should be simpler than the full set of data for which it accounts. One might try to argue that the total list of possible sentences in a language would constitute a grammar of that language. To find out whether any particular sequence was grammatical we would simply have to check it against the list. If a sentence was found in the list it would be grammatical and so the list would do a job of specifying grammaticality, and this is what we ask a grammar to do. But no linguist would be satisfied with such a list, for he wants his description to be briefer or more parsimonious than the total list of possible sentences, and in general the simpler or briefer the description, the better it is judged to be. Any decent grammar, in other words, should provide for (generate) a larger amount of data than it contains itself.

(4) A grammar accomplishes its task by a system of rules. These rules account for or "predict" back to the known data, but beyond this they also predict or "generate" new data that are not contained in the original body of information with which a linguist begins. Any body of data is limited in quantity, but the rules a linguist formulates to account for these limited data are expected to have such generality that they will predict new grammatical sequences as well. This allows an investigator to check his formulation against empirical evidence, i.e., against the judgment of a native speaker as to whether or not the new sequences generated by his grammatical rules are in fact acceptable.

(5) The rules of a grammar are justified by their predictive utility, not by the procedure used in working them out. Rules, to be sure, are constructed by a linguist on the basis of his knowledge, but in the final analysis it is not how he goes about finding the rules but whether or not they work that decides their status. Most linguists today have accepted the idea that the discovery procedures they use are ultimately irrelevant and they even

tend to believe that the discovery of grammatical rules is, *in principle*, not capable of systematization. There is no algorithm for writing grammars. Of course, linguists develop skills, and they try to communicate these skills when teaching their students, but if a rule finally works and if it does account for data, it matters not one jot if it first came to the linguist in a trance. It is the ability of rules, acting together in the grammatical system, to generate grammatical sequences that is their justification, not the way in which they were discovered.

(6) A difficult question remains open: just what is the locus of these grammatical rules? One can argue that the rules are simply devices, schemes, tricks, constructed by the linguist to do the job of accounting for acceptable sentences. It is easy, however, to begin speaking as if one were actually working out rules that are in the heads of speakers of the language and that have just been waiting to be discovered. In practice it seems to make very little difference what attitude a linguist takes. He can perform the same sort of operations and construct the same sort of rules whether he regards them simply as devices that work to generate sentences or whether he takes them more seriously as a real part of the language he is investigating. Linguistics has developed and will no doubt continue to de-develop without all linguists agreeing on this question.

I will return to these points later and I will argue that ethnographic descriptions have the same general characteristics, but first I wish to present some concrete ethnographic data so as to give some flesh to the abstract bones of my arguments.

Garo Household Composition

I shall take as my data certain facts about household composition among the Garo of Assam, India.[2] I shall offer some rules that will account for the varied composition of these households, and I shall then ask whether the rules are in any way analogous to grammatical rules. I start with rather concrete data (analogous to linguistic texts), set out in the form of kinship diagrams that show the kinship ties binding the members of real households to one another (Figure 1). These are households that are, or were in 1956, "on the ground." The symbols used in the diagrams are conventional except that in a few diagrams I have used a curving dotted line to indicate a kinship relationship between coresident women through other relatives (always women) who do not actually live in the household in question.

In spite of the considerable diversity among households shown in the diagrams, inspection leads rather easily to a few generalizations. Most,

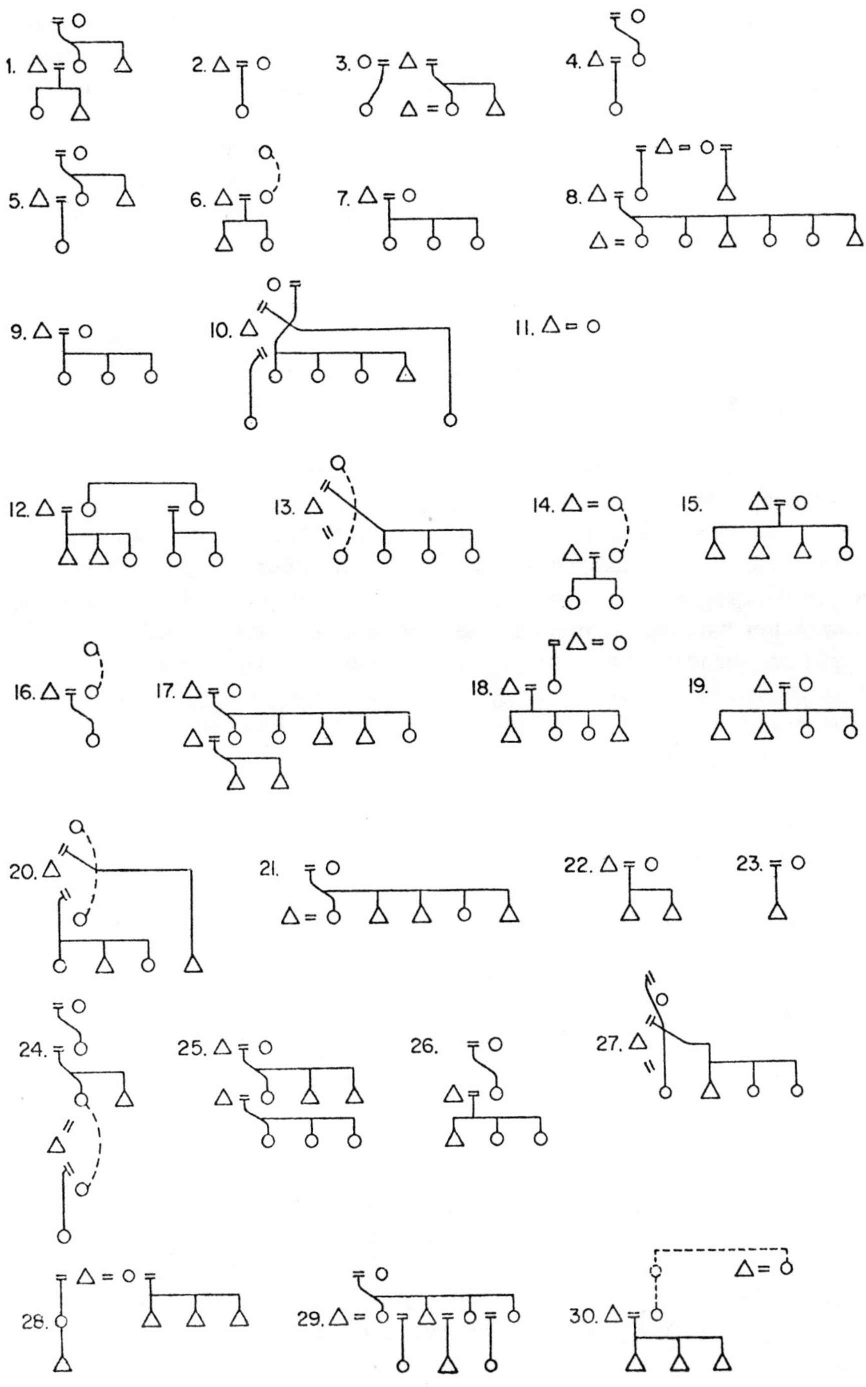
1.
2.
3.
4.
5.
6.
7.
8.
9.
10.
11.
12.
13.
14.
15.
16.
17.
18.
19.
20.
21.
22.
23.
24.
25.
26.
27.
28.
29.
30.

Figure 5:1.

though not quite all, households have at least one married couple, and a good many have two; but more than two couples is unusual. In a household with two married couples, the two wives are most often mother and daughter, or at least they are related to each other through women; and in only one example do two married sisters live together. More striking perhaps, no married son lives with either of his parents. A few men have two living wives, and the wives always seem to be related, occasionally as mother and daughter. The reader can easily add other statements of this sort, and if data on more households were available, they might be refined and extended, but they are not the kind of generalizations most anthropologists really like. They are statements of statistical probability, and they seem to leave out any real explanation for the presence of some kinds of households but the absence of others. I suspect that most anthropologists would be happier with a set of rules such as the following:

(1) Marriage constitutes a particular relationship between a man and a woman, which among other things requires common residence.

(2) Unmarried children reside with their mother and, when she is married, with her husband who is usually their father.

(3) After marriage, one daughter must continue to live permanently with her parents. (It follows as a corollary from rules 1 and 3 that this girl's husband must move in with his wife and his parents-in-law.)

(4) All other daughters may live temporarily with their parents after marriage (e.g., household 29) but within a year or so they establish a separate household.

(5) Couples with no daughters will "adopt" a girl to act as a daughter. Adoptions are always made from among the close matrilineal kinsmen of the daughterless woman, and the ideal choice is her sister's daughter (households 6, 14, 16). (As is implied by this rule and by rule 3, the adopted daughter lives permanently with her adopted parents.)

(6) A young mother who, whether through divorce, widowhood, or illegitimacy, has no husband may live with her parents or if her parents are dead with her sister (12, 29).

(7) A widower may remarry and bring his new wife to live in the house he had shared with his first wife and their children. If the new wife has unmarried children she will bring them along (3, 8, 28).

(8) Widows may remain unmarried for a time and live only with their children (23); unless they marry a widower, their new husband must always be simultaneously married to or at least promised to a younger woman. (Garos rationalize this by saying that every man, at some time in his life, should have a "new" wife.) If a remarrying widow has a daughter, she is felt to be a suitable cowife for her mother's new husband (10, 27), otherwise a younger matrilineally related woman must be adopted as the widow's

daughter to serve as her cowife (13, 20, 24). (The cowives are virtually always approximately a generation apart in age even if not real mother and daughter, for Garos feel that the women will quarrel less if they are not too close in age.)

(9) A widow who has already acquired a resident son-in-law before she is widowed will not remarry, although she will henceforth be described slightly metaphorically as the "wife" of her son-in-law (1, 4, 5, 6, 16, 21, 24, 26).

(10) Widowers who already have a resident son-in-law may remarry (3, 8, 18) but they do not always do so. Widowers without resident sons-in-law, virtually always remarry rapidly (28).

With one exception (30) the households shown in the diagram conform to the possibilities provided by these ten rules. I will return to this exceptional household later but first I will try to suggest how these rules can be regarded as similar to grammatical rules.

Household Composition Rules

I must be very clear on one point: I do not regard the treatment of household composition given in the last section as deviating in any substantial way from general ethnographic practice. Except for setting my rules off with numbers and making an extra effort toward precision and parsimony, I mean to provide an entirely conventional description of some ethnographic phenomena. My purpose is *not* to suggest that we can give better ethnographic descriptions by following some sort of "linguistic technique" but merely to suggest that we may be able to get a clearer view of what we have been doing all along if we look at our conventional ethnographic practice from the same vantage point as linguists use for viewing their endeavors. To this extent only, I believe the nature of the rules for household composition can be clarified if they are seen in the light of the points already made about grammar rules:

(1) The rules of household composition can be said to constitute a theory. They are a device that specifies the possible composition of a household, or more explicitly, they provide a means for distinguishing between proper and improper assemblages of people who might live together.

(2) The rules do *not* specify the composition of any particular household. Like grammatical rules, which specify the range of possible grammatical sentences without predicting any particular sentence, these composition rules specify the range of proper households, but do not predict any particular household. As in any sequence of grammatical rules, these rules of household composition contain alternatives that allow for a broad range of final results.

(3) In some sense (a sense that need not be defined very closely) the rules of household composition are simpler than the data for which they provide. The rules are of limited length, but they will provide a very wide range of households. One can list these rules in less space and with greater parsimony than would be needed to list all the possible household types separately.

(4) Households have been accounted for by a system of rules that predict back ("generate") the original data, but they also predict additional data in the form of other household types that were not included in the original sample. Just as one can use grammatical rules to generate new sentences that can then be tested against the judgment of a native speaker, so one can use these composition rules to generate new household types. These newly generated types could be tested against empirical data, either by checking on additional real households, or by testing their acceptance among informants to find out if they would be regarded as proper and reasonable hypothetical households even if they do not happen to be known to have occurred.

(5) The composition rules cannot be justified by reference to any particular methodology used in working them out. They stand or fall entirely by their utility in accounting for the data. To be sure, it would be exceedingly difficult to work out these rules if one were limited to bare descriptions of particular households such as are available from the diagrams. As a practical matter it is easier to ask informants for their explanation and to try these out against the data. But the methods by which we work out the rules are, in the end, irrelevant; and if the rules an ethnographer comes up with can be used to "explain" the households that do exist and to suggest additional plausible household types, that is entirely sufficient to justify the rules.

(6) Just as with grammatical rules, we are left with some difficult questions about the locus of the composition rules. Anthropologists, like linguists, seem to have been divided in their attitudes. Do we, as anthropologists, rest content with a system that simply accounts for our data? Or do we want to discover rules that the people themselves use, rules that in some way already exist in the culture independent of the analysis. I will return briefly to this problem later but must first consider some more specific implications of the composition rules and point out a few ways in which they have particularly close parallels with grammatical rules.

Ethnographic Parallels to Linguistic Description

If one examines the composition rules closely, he will discover that in two cases households having the same composition can arise in two different ways. First, a simple nuclear family consisting of a single married couple and their children can come about either through the marriage of a girl who leaves her parents and establishes a new and separate household with her husband or through the survival of an in-living daughter and her husband and children after the time of her parents' death and after the departure of all her brothers and sisters at the time of their respective marriages. Second, a household consisting of a woman, her real or adopted daughter, and a man who is said to be the husband of both of them, can also arise in two ways. If a woman is widowed after her daughter has been married, Garos speak as if the son-in-law "inherits" his mother-in-law. They describe the son-in-law as being married to both women at once. A household with identical composition occurs when a woman is widowed before she acquires a resident son-in-law; for after she is remarried, she must take her real or adopted daughter as a second wife for her new husband.

The composition of the households is the same in these two cases, but their status in Garo society is different. Garos describe the surviving nuclear family as having quite different ties to related households than the newly established nuclear family, and these differences are symbolized in a number of ways that I need not give here in detail. Similarly, the two kinds of families in which a man is said to be married to both a mother and her daughter by a previous marriage are actually quite different. Among other things, if the husband is first married to the daughter and only later "inherits" the mother-in-law, he is not expected to engage in sexual relations with the older woman, although Garos use the usual terms for "husband" and "wife" to describe their relationship. If a man marries the older woman first, however, and then or subsequently acquires her daughter as his second wife, Garos do expect that he will engage in sexual relations with both women. Garos show nothing but approval if such a man should father children by both women.

These superfically identical but fundamentally distinct households can be compared, with some reason, to "structurally homonymous" sentences. The famous sentence "The shooting of the hunters was terrible" can mean either "It was bad that the hunters got shot," or "the aim of the hunters was poor." The superficial sentence can reflect two different derivational histories, and it is best to say that there are really two different sentences, produced by different sequences of rules which in the end culminate in homonymous forms. Similarly, by applying different sequences of composition rules, we can generate superfically identical households that for some purposes are not regarded as identical at all. Somewhat metaphorically, we might even describe these households as having "homonymous composition."

I have already pointed out that one of the households included in the diagram does not fit the rules as I have given them. This is household 30, in which a woman and her husband have moved in with the family of her sister's daughter, the intervening sister having died. Since the rules do not account for this very real household, the rules must seem imperfect and one's first impulse might be to modify or expand the rules until they can account for household 30 along with all the others. To do this, however, would require either a rule with extremely peculiar limitations (e.g., a married woman and her husband are allowed to move into her deceased sister's daughter's family) or a rule of a more general character that would run the danger of simultaneously providing for a large number of other household types that never seem to occur (e.g., matrilineally related women may live together after marriage).

Neither of these alternatives by which the rules might be modified is at all attractive, but unless the rules are modified somehow, household 30 is left as an exception to them. But perhaps this is a realistic way to look at this household. Perhaps it simply does not conform to plausible rules, and in this way is comparable to an ungrammatical sentence. We know that people do utter ungrammatical sentences. When asked about them they may edit them out and confess that they spoke in a broken fashion that was not really correct. Similarly when I inquired about this rather deviant household, my informants admitted that it did not fit their conception of a proper household. People freely predicted that it would soon split up and that it certainly would not remain in its present form for long. Just as I was led to recognize "homonymous households," perhaps this deviant assemblage of people could be labeled "ungrammatical."

To characterize this household as ungrammatical is to assert something utterly different than simply to characterize it as statistically unusual or extreme. If one simply wanted to give a statistical summary of household composition, the data from this particular household would have to be fed into the statistical maw along with the data from all the other households. This one might prove to be very unusual in terms of certain statistical measures, but it could never, by such means alone, be characterized as "wrong." From the view point of the composition rules, however, it can indeed be labeled "wrong." Here we have a difference between a set of rules, on the one hand, and a statistical summary, which adds up cases, finds averages, and charts frequencies, on the other. It is probably fair to say that most anthropologists, like most linguists, have been partial to descriptions by rules, which like my composition rules introduce few or no measures of probability for the occurrence of various alternatives. By contrast, both anthropologists and linguists have tended to dislike measures that involve counting proportions and reporting frequencies.

However, the rules I have given, like most ethnographic descriptions, are surely deficient in some respects. The composition rules cannot tell us what percentage of households have two married couples or specify the average number of unmarried children per household or answer any number of other similar and reasonable questions that could nevertheless be readily determined from the same sort of data on households to which the rules apply. Analogously, conventional grammatical rules give us no means for summarizing or predicting the proportion of nouns to verbs in running discourse or of describing the relative frequency of bilabial stops.

A statistical summary and the usual description by rules tell us different things about our subject matter, but they are by no means irreconcilable. In particular it would seem promising to try to combine them by introducing some sort of probabilistic parameters into the sequences of rules for either grammar or household composition. One could specify the frequency with which each choice should be made at each point where the rules leave alternatives. For household composition we would have to specify such things as life expectancy, fertility, and divorce rate and then weave these into the composition rules. For grammar we would have to specify such things as the proportion of selections of transitive and intransitive verbs and frequency of application of negative and question transformations. If statements of probability were woven into a set of rules in a clear enough way, it might conceivably be possible to develop rules that would generate either sentences or households in which the proportions of word classes or of marriages would approximate the proportions found in the empirical data. Therefore, I see no incompatability between a rule-based description and measures of probability. I simply feel it to be a fair generalization that, whether explicitly or not, most anthropologists like most linguists have expressed their descriptions in a manner that can be seen as consisting of sets of rules, and they have rarely been strong on specifying the probability of their application.

Culturally Explicit Rules and Rules of an Observer

I have pointed out several close analogies between the grammatical description of sentences and the cultural description of household composition, but the differences between them should not be glossed over. Perhaps the greatest difference lies in the way in which an investigator works out the rules. I have no intention of compromising with my claim that the discovery procedures by which rules are worked out are ultimately irrelevant, but it cannot be denied that linguists and anthropologists have different habits of investigation, and these varying habits make it easy to *imagine* that they are following different principles. The contrast in our work habits lies in the differing ways linguists and anthropologists use informants, and

I believe this depends in turn upon the different techniques by which everyone first learns his own culture.

I have pointed out that both anthropologists and linguists use the term "informant" to describe the person from whom they learn, but it must be admitted that they typically use their informants in rather different ways. The linguist characteristically uses an informant to elicit *examples* of behavior, while the anthropologist is more apt to elicit statements that *describe* behavior. The difference is not absolute. Sometimes linguists ask their informants for explanations of why they say the things they do, and anthropologists sometimes look at their informant's behavior and try to interpret it without relying upon the informant's own description, but by and large the difference is there. I believe that these differing methodologies rest upon and correspond to the differing ways in which all human beings learn their own culture. If presented with enough examples, a normal child will always learn to speak, and he need never be given any explicit instruction at all. As a result, when people do formulate explicit generalizations about their own language these generalizations are often rather wildly different from anything that a linguist would be willing to recognize as a valid description. Explicit grammatical generalizations have no real pedagogical use to the people of the culture, since language can be perpetuated without them or even in spite of them. If children can learn the grammar of their language without explicit instruction, the linguist should be able to do the same. What he needs for his work are examples of linguistic behavior from which he can make his own generalizations, and this is what a linguist looks for from his informants.

Children learn many other aspects of their culture with the help of explicit verbal instructions, or at least in a context in which activities are constantly discussed and described. Garos may never formulate rules of household composition quite as explicitly or concisely as I have done in this paper, but they do talk about household composition. When asked to describe appropriate behavior, or to consider alternative possibilities, they can articulate their own rules quite successfully. It may be unlikely that rules of behavior of this sort could be successfully passed from one generation to the next without at least some verbal formulation, whether this comes in the form of explicitly stated rules or less explicitly in descriptions and discussions of actual behavior. To the extent that a child requires a verbal context and verbal instruction to learn his own culture, an anthropologist would seem to be forced to rely upon similar sorts of verbal description. For this reason it is probably absolutely necessary for the cultural anthropologist, unlike the linguist, to elicit *statements about* behavior, from his informants. He cannot expect to rely entirely upon *examples of* behavior as a linguist can generally do. As a result of these contrasting uses of informants, the rules that an ethnologist formulates tend superficially to look much more like the rules that are explicitly known and used in the culture than do the rules worked out by a linguist. The natives do not need to be able to articulate anything about the grammatical rules of their language, but they can certainly articulate many statements that bear upon the rules of most other sorts of behavior.

I think it would be a mistake, however, to overstate this difference, and it is here, above all, that I find the linguistic analogy helpful in clarifying our ethnographic assumptions. If, in the end, it does not matter how we arrive at our rules, then whether we use an informant's explicit verbal statements to give us hints or extract the rules instead entirely from examples of observed behavior is a matter of no importance at all. What matters is whether or not our rules do somehow correspond to the data we seek to describe, and my rules for household composition, in the working out of which I was surely helped by informant's statements, have exactly the same formal status as a linguist's grammatical rules. In both cases we may have differences of opinion about whether the rules are simply convenient devices by which an observer can account for the data or are in some more important way a part of the language or the culture of the people that was waiting there to be discovered and that enters into the cognitive processes of the people. But the degree of correspondence between the rules of the observer and the explicit criteria that the natives themselves use has no more bearing upon the status of the rules than the procedures by which rules are worked out. This is simply to say that disconformity between the explicit rules of the native and the rules worked out by ethnographers will not lead us to reject our rules so long as the rules work (natives can be wrong about their own behavior) and by the same token agreement between the native's and the ethnographer's rules amounts to no confirmation of the latter.[3]

Of course it should still be an interesting empirical question to ask how closely the explicit rules of the people correspond to the rules of an ethnologist or linguist. I suspect that they will tend to be much closer to each other in some areas of culture (such as household composition) than in others (such as language). But this empirical question can never even be raised in a clear fashion unless the explicit rules that are formulated and articulated by the people themselves are first clearly differentiated from those other rules the enthologist and linguist construct when they try to account for their respective fields of human behavior.

Notes

1. I am indebted to my colleague Roy A. Rappaport not only for the original suggestion that I organize my ideas on this subject for presentation to one of our classes, but also for numerous cogent ideas that emerged in our many subsequent discussions. Joseph Jorgensen

has tried to help me untangle a few notions I had about the relationship between statistics and rules.

2. The data on Garo residence patterns was obtained in the field while I held a fellowship from the Ford Foundation between 1954 and 1956 and have been more fully presented in Burling 1963.

3. In this connection, I believe that Marvin Harris's recent work (1968: Chapter 20, "Emics, Etics, and the New Ethnography"), which contrasts what he calls the "emic" and "etic" points of view, seems to me to unnecessarily polarize our alternatives. Claiming to go back to Pike's original definitions of "emic" and "etic" Harris bypasses whole schools of linguistics in which these terms came to be understood. In Harris's words:

> Emic statements refer to logico-empirical systems whose phenomenal distinctions or 'things' are built up out of contrasts and discriminations significant, meaningful, real, accurate, or in some other fashion regarded as appropriate by the actors themselves [1968:571].

> Etic statements depend upon phenomenal distinctions judged appropriate by the community of scientific observer [1968:575].

By these definitions, the Bloomfieldian phoneme is not an "emic" unit, since the Bloomfieldians were firmly, even obstinately, opposed to any sort of mentalistic interpretation of language. Furthermore not all of the anthropologists concerned with semantics whose work Harris dismisses as "emic" have been concerned with cognition. Lounsbury, for instance, has never made cognitive claims for his rules, and indeed he has not cared in the least whether or not his rules have any sort of cognitive status. By Harris's definition, therefore, Lounsbury's rules should not be called "emic." It is true, of course, that some of the generative grammarians have been making extensive claims for the innate or cognitive or psychological importance of their rules, but the accomplishments of linguistics hardly stand or fall upon these particular and by no means undisputed claims. By indifferently dismissing ethnosemantics, Lounsbury rules, and indeed much or all of linguistics, as "emic" and therefore as idealistic, Harris makes it difficult to salvage a non-idealistic but rule-based description, of any sort. Whatever Pike's original definition of "emic," most linguists and most anthropologists other than Harris would surely grant "emic" status to both the Bloomfieldian phoneme and to Lounsbury's rules. By the same token I think it not unreasonable, and in accordance with general usage, to call all ordinary grammatical rules and my rules of household composition "emic," because they represent theoretical statements, separated in certain respects from (and not algorithmically derivable from) the more directly observable "etic" data, such as households on the ground or sequences of noise, but at the same time the rules provide a means of interpreting and understanding the observable (and "etic") data of real households or real sentences. Of course it is silly to argue about the meaning of a word, but even if we decide that "emic" is not appropriate for such descriptions, it is still important to keep them distinct from the more directly observable "etic" phenomena, and Harris's simplistic bifurcation into idealist "emics" and materialist "etics" is in danger of squeezing out the middle ground between them. The rules of household composition, the Bloomfieldian phoneme, grammatical rules, and Lounsbury's rules stand or fall on their ability to account for observable phenomena, though none may be directly observable themselves. Whether or not they are in any sense cognitively or psychologically real is in an entirely separate question.

References Cited in Editor's Note

BURLING, ROBBINS.
1970. "Burling's Reply to Kehoe." *American Anthropologist* 72:1462.

KEHOE, ALICE B.
1970. "A Significant Difference Between Linguistics and Ethnographic Description." *American Anthropologist* 72:1461-1462.
PIKE, KENNETH L.
1967. *Language in Relation to a Unified Theory of the Structure of Human Behavior*. 2nd. rev. ed. The Hague: Mouton. (1st ed. 1954, Glendale: Summer Institute of Linguistics.)

References Cited

BURLING, ROBBINS
1963 *Rengsanggri: family and kinship in a Garo village*. Philadelphia: University of Pennsylvania Press.
HARRIS, MARVIN
1968 *The rise of anthropological theory*. New York: Thomas Y. Crowell Co.

6 COGNITION IN CULTURE-AND-PERSONALITY

Melford E. Spiro

The limited goals of culture and cognition studies often seem at odds with the holistic emphasis of traditional anthropology. As we noted earlier, such studies sometimes appear methodologically rigorous but theoretically truncated. In this chapter Melford E. Spiro places cognition in proper perspective as one member of a set of variables which are necessary for a more comprehensive explanatory task. Culture-and-personality is a subfield of anthropology concerned with the psychological conditions which promote stability and change in human sociocultural systems. Cultural knowledge is certainly one of those conditions, but not the only one; learning, perception, and motivation are equally important. While cognition regulates behavior, it is not identical with it. The author makes a distinction between cognitive learning and behavioral learning. This is important, since it is possible to learn the rules for behavior without the skills necessary for its performance. This overview of the variables needed to account for sociocultural systems should be kept in mind as one proceeds to the more specific studies in the following chapters.—EDITOR'S NOTE

Culturally constituted social groups are as necessary for human existence as are any of man's vital organs. Nevertheless, as even cursory observation of children reveals, the acquisition of culture is often accompanied by conflict and struggle; and conformity with cultural rules and norms is frequently associated with frustration and tension. These two facets of culture—its capacity for both gratifying and frustrating human needs—constitute the basis for the two major axes of social science inquiry, stability and change; together, they constitute the generic problems of culture-and-personality research: What are the psychological conditions that promote persistence and innovation in human social and cultural systems?

"Culture and Personality" by Melford E. Spiro. Reprinted with permission of the author and the publisher from the *International Encyclopedia of the Social Sciences*, David L. Sills, editor. Volume 3, pages 558–563.

Historical Background

Despite the evident importance of its problems, culture-and-personality, as a formal discipline, is the youngest and smallest branch of anthropology. With some few exceptions, it hardly exists outside of the United States. Culture-and-personality, like biochemistry, falls between two academic stools, in this case anthropology on the one hand and the psychological sciences on the other. Thirty-five years ago there was no way of bridging the gap between them. Anthropology, to the extent that it was theoretically oriented, was concerned with such macroproblems as historical developments and evolutionary trends, for which the concepts of academic psychology were, or were deemed to be, irrelevant. The psychological sciences, on the other hand, were tied to the *a*historical, *a*cultural laboratory; their molecular concepts were obviously unrelated to the sociocultural concepts of anthropology. Only psychoanalytic psychology—not part of the academic establishment—seemed to see a bridge between the data obtained in the clinic and the social sciences. Earlier, Freud had made periodic forays into anthropology, but attempts to link the disciplines met with strong opposition on the part of social scientists.

The raw data of anthropological field work exposed living human beings in all their complexity, acting within a specified historical—cultural matrix. It is no accident that it was the field anthropologists, confronted with the necessity of relating traditional descriptive cultural constructs to the ongoing social life about them, who first attempted to build this bridge in their search for the psychologically "genotypic" bases of their "phenotypic" cultural constructs. It is no accident, either, that psychoanalytic theory, however modified, was seized upon first as a possible theoretical tool. For psychoanalysis, unlike academic psychology, is concerned with molar rather than molecular psychological variables. Despite its *a*historicism, psychoanalysis anchors its patients in their own ontogenetic histories, thereby providing a link with the anthropological notion of culture as a configuration of learned customs. Hence, Edward Sapir, the generally acknowledged founder of the field, was influenced by his personal contacts with the psychiatrist H. S. Sullivan; Margaret Mead, by her contacts with E. H. Erikson; Ralph Linton and Cora DuBois, by collaboration with Abram Kardiner.

Personality studies 35 years ago were unsystematic; and cultural studies, with their heavy descriptive and empirical emphases, were self-consciously nontheoretical. Hence, a large share of culture-and-personality theory was, and continues to be, devoted to the exploration of empirical and analytic relationships. At that time, anthropologists had few techniques for the study of personality. The time-honored techniques of gross observation and informant interviews were inadequate for personality investigation. Again anthropology looked to the psychological sciences for assistance: depth interviews, Rorschach tests, doll-play, dreams, life histories, systematic observation of family interaction, and other techniques were borrowed in whole or in part from clinical psychology and psychiatry. Where disciplinary boundaries are rigidly drawn, this influx of exotic tools—combined with the exotic concepts of psychoanalytic theory and learning theory—could hardly have been expected to attract discipline-bound researchers.

Some anthropologists avoided culture-and-personality because of the imprecise and inconclusive nature of its findings. This is not to say, as is sometimes charged, that its studies are "soft," or lacking in rigor—the best of its studies are certainly as rigorous, conceptually and methodologically, as their counterparts in other branches of social and cultural anthropology. It is, rather, that the very nature of its problems, given the research tools available, results in findings that sometimes lack the unqualified conviction characteristic of research in more structured fields.

As the field has matured, its initial period of heavy borrowing has come to an end. Methods and theories borrowed from other fields have become transformed by the new discipline for its own problems and its specific theoretical aims—and, although it continues to be catholic in its sources of stimulation, it has been developing its own. Increasingly, data cited in favor of a theory, and theories used for hypothesis derivation, originate in culture-and-personality research, rather than in the psychiatric clinic or the experimental laboratory. Moreover, as data accumulate, it is becoming increasingly possible to test hypotheses statistically by means of large-scale, cross-cultural samples. Although these studies, pioneered by Whiting and Child (1953), have been subjected to serious criticism, their findings have been sufficiently suggestive to hazard the prediction that such studies will increase both in number and in importance.

Despite its small number of practitioners, culture-and-personality has been extraordinarily diversified in its research interests. Although culture-and-personality has explored many topics that have been neglected by other anthropologists, it has also explored many of the topics that are of greatest interest to them. In both cases, psychological variables have played a prominent role in its research. The rationale for this emphasis must be sought within the explanatory framework of anthropological thought.

Explanation in Anthropology

Anthropological theory has, in general, been cast in four explanatory modes—historical, structural, causal, and functional—that, when analyzed, can be reduced to the causal or the functional mode. Thus, historical explanations, to the extent that they are scientific explanations rather than uncontrolled speculations, are really causal explanations. The mere listing of a series of events that are chronologically prior to the appearance of the custom to be explained does not constitute explanation, unless it can be shown that one or more of these events was a condition—either necessary and/or sufficient—for the appearance of the custom. If this can be demonstrated, the explanation of the custom's origin is causal, the fact that it originated in the past being incidental to the theoretical aim, which is to provide an explanation for a certain type of social or cultural innovation.

Structural explanations can also be shown to be either causal or functional. Those which show the configuration (or interrelationships) in a set of customs are essentially descriptive. The data are ordered according to a coherent plan. If a theory is offered to explain the configuration (structure), then this theory is necessarily either causal or functional. Structural explanations that purport to explain a custom or set of customs in terms of some "principle" that it embodies are either verbal labels, serving to classify a set of data according to a heuristic scheme (such as the "principle" of the unity of the sibling group), or phenomenological principles of the actors (cognitive maps), in which case they are members of a cognitive subset in a set of causal variables. Similarly, explanations that stipulate either the structural requirements of a system or its structural "implications" are either causal or functional. Causal explanations are concerned with the antecedents of a system; functional explanations, with its consequences.

If anthropological explanations can be classified as either causal or functional, what role has culture-and-personality played in either or both types of explanation?

The Human Social Order as a Normative Order

Social systems are characterized by a configuration of reciprocal roles that are shared by the members of a social group and are acquired from a previous generation. These roles serve to satisfy the three functional requirements of any society—adaptation, adjustment, and integration. Within zoological perspective, the unique feature of human social systems does not reside in the fact that their constituent roles are acquired through learning—for this is probably characteristic, although not to the same degree, of all mammalian social systems—but that many of the customs comprising these roles are based on rules and norms.

A custom, as this term is used by anthropologists, refers to any socially acquired behavior pattern that is widely, if not uniformly, performed by the members of a society or by one of its constituent social groups. In general, it is possible to distinguish two types of customs. First, there are those customs whose occurrence is based on prescriptive or proscriptive norms. Their performance may thus be characterized as being *isomorphic* with a norm or set of norms. These may be termed Type-1 customs. Second, there are customs whose occurrence, although not based on norms, nevertheless reflects them. If a norm, or set of norms, is proscriptive with respect to one subclass of behavior patterns but permissive with respect to all other members of the class, the latter, if they occur, reflect the norms but are not isomorphic with them. For example, marriage with any female not included in incest proscriptions reflects, but is not isomorphic with, the proscriptive norms. These customs may be termed Type-2 customs.

Although the occurrence of Type-1 customs is mandatory and the occurrence of Type-2 customs is voluntary, the performance of the latter is also normative in the sense that behavior falls within a normative, i.e., permissible, range of variability. Type-2 customs are also governed by socially shared rules that define proper performance. In the absence of such rules, behavior patterns are habits that describe individual action; they are not customs, which describe social interaction. Knowledge of habits and customs enables us to predict behavior.

The Human Social Order as a Cognitive Order

Culture, as a normative system, is a functional requirement of a human social order. Because of the enormous degrees of biological plasticity and cognitive ingenuity that, together, produce the broad variability characteristic of human behavior, the absence of this normative dimension would render human social systems impossible. The range of behavior patterns potential in any individual is much broader than the limited range required for the performance of any custom or set of customs. Beyond a certain critical point, whose limits are still unknown, variability in behavior precludes the very possibility of custom. In other words, human societies have had to set limits (by means of prescriptive and proscriptive norms, and of rules) to the range of permitted variability in customary behavior. The cultural dimension of human social systems is made possible by the very capacity for symbolization. It is to human societies what limited plasticity and biological determination are to insect and mammalian societies. By selecting the optimal range required by the operation of a particular social system, from the potential range of variability characteristic of the species, it ensures an important degree of uniformity and predictability, thereby rendering social order possible. In short, the invention of culture allowed man to combine the short-run adaptive value of social order with the long-run advantage of flexibility.

A human social order, then, is a cognitive order. The set of customs that comprise the constituent roles of a human social system consist, in the first instance, of a set of norms and rules—cognitive variables—that either prescribe or regulate behavior. These norms and rules must be cognized by the members of the society if the social system is to be maintained. The acquisition of cognitions, then, as well as of complete cognitive maps, is a necessary psychological condition (cause) for the performance of single customs and for the maintenance of an entire social system. Cognitions can regulate behavior, but they are not identical with it. The conventional statement "Social behavior is learned" implies two kinds of learning, cognitive and behavioral. That is, the performance of a custom requires that the actors learn about the custom (acquisition of cognitions) and that they learn to perform what they have learned (acquisition of behavior). In general, culture-and-personality has devoted less attention to the former type of learning than to the latter. Nevertheless, the recent interest in cognition and in ethnoscience, and the development of such techniques as componential analysis, will probably redress the balance.

Since customary behavior is governed by rules, proper performance of customs requires that the actors be capable of evaluating and regulating their own behavior in terms of these rules. Evaluation, then, is yet another cognitive basis for the maintenance of social systems, although it has received little attention from culture-and-personality.

Despite their importance, cognition, learning, and evaluation do not constitute necessary and sufficient psychological prerequisites for the performance of customs. For, although anthropological informants are entitled to explain their own behavior by the ubiquitous "It is our custom," anthropologists cannot abdicate their scientific responsibility by this obviously redundant explanation. Customs cannot compel the occurrence of behavior; they can only channel behavior once it occurs. Unless the actors are more highly motivated to perform a custom than to perform competing, alternative behavior patterns that compose their behaviorial repertoire, the learning of a custom, however normative, will not ensure its performance. In short, the performance of customs, like other forms of behavior, must be instigated by the intention or expectation of satisfying a need or set of needs. A great deal of culture-and-personality research has been devoted to the study of motivation and its ontogenesis in the socialization process.

In sum, cognition, learning, motivativation, and evaluation—all psychological variables—constitute necessary and sufficient conditions (causes) for the proper performance of customs and, hence, for the maintenance of social systems. This analysis becomes much more complicated when it is observed that the relationship between the performance of customs and the satisfaction of needs is not always a simple one. For Type-2 customs—in which "performance" means the practice of personally preferred behavior patterns—this analysis, with proper qualifications, will serve as a simplified model. For Type-1 customs, in which "performance" means compliance with prescriptive or proscriptive norms, further elaboration is required.

The Human Social Order as a Moral Order

A normative order, it has been indicated, consists of two related, but discrete, variables: norms and rules. "Norms" prescribe the occurrence of behavior; proscriptive norms prescribe avoidance behavior. "Rules" regulate or govern behavior (whether it is prescribed or permissive) once it occurs. Norms and rules ensure the uniformity, and hence the predictability, of behavior. Rules are ethically neutral; norms implicitly incorporate a set of moral values and, therefore, also function to preclude the overt expression of motives that are, or are deemed to be, socially harmful or disruptive. Norms also ensure the performance of activities that are, or are deemed to be, socially desirable, if not necessary. In terms of the moral order, deviation from norms is viewed as an offense to the social order. The limits that norms impose on behavioral variability are intended to ensure the occurrence of *culturally* normative behavior, as well as to regulate the performance of *socially* normative behavior.

Because of man's plasticity and cognitive ingenuity, what any actor *must* do, as defined by cultural norms, in order to participate in his social system is not the same as what he *can* do; thus, what he must do may conflict with what he would *like* to do. Hence, tension between personal needs and cultural norms, as well as the internal pressures to eliminate this tension, are omnipresent in any society. In general, tension is resolved in favor of the norms, resolution being mediated by anxiety. This will be moral anxiety, if the norms have been internalized (superego); or social anxiety, if punishment is known to be the consequence of deviation. Although anxiety can serve to motivate compliance with Type-2 customs, the source of deviation (the original need) is inhibited but not extinguished. For the existence of these norms implies that the motivational systems of the actors are either indifferent to, or opposed to, the prescriptive or proscriptive behavior. If the latter is the case, the frustration of the proscribed motive has important consequences for cultural stability and change.

Frustration, Sociocultural Persistence, Change

If the expectation of gratifying drives, including anxiety, constitutes a necessary (although not a sufficient) condition for the persistence of social systems, the frustration of drives constitutes a necessary (although not a sufficient) condition for the disruption of and change in these systems. Cultural norms, which proscribe the satisfaction of certain drives, constitute one important source of frustration. The social structure is another important source. For example, if a structural arrangement such as stratification prevents certain groups in society from satisfying culturally approved needs by denying them access to those roles whose performance can satisfy these needs, the attendant frustration may be as great as frustration induced by proscriptive norms. Both types of frustration constitute potential sources of social and cultural deviation, innovation, and change.

Paradoxically, they also constitute sources of cultural and social persistence. If motives cannot be satisfied directly, because of cultural or social impediments, need-frustration may be averted by distortions in any of the motive's four dimensions—drive, goal, act, and agent. These changes may sufficiently alter the original meaning of the motive so that, in its disguised form, the need may seek gratification in indirect, but culturally approved, ways. Frequently, the means for such distortion of motives, and consequent gratification of needs, are found in elements of the social and cultural systems. Although customs—and even roles—making up the social system are often used in this fashion, it is the cultural system that, *par excellence*, serves the function of gratifying these forbidden motives. For example, forbidden dependency or hostility motives are often disguised and, consequently, gratified in subservient or dominant political roles, respectively. Religion, art, folklore, ritual, and the like may function as culturally constituted defense mechanisms by which frustrated motives may be disguised and, hence, gratified in a culturally approved manner. This, of course, is not their only function. They have other latent, not to mention manifest, functions of a nondefensive character. When elements of the social and cultural systems serve to gratify otherwise frustrated and potentially disruptive needs, the needs, in turn, constitute powerful motivational causes for the persistence of these systems. Culture-and-personality research has only begun a systematic exploration of this important field of research.

Sometimes, however, socially and culturally induced need-frustrations are not resolved in this manner; and this frustration results in deviation, either cultural or psychological. In defending the self against internal conflict, some defense mechanisms are adopted in which the cognitive distortion of motives is of sufficient magnitude to cause behavior that, psychologically bizarre and/or socially disruptive, may be diagnosed as mental illness. In other cases, defense mechanisms may be avoided in favor of direct expression of forbidden motives, resulting in crime and delinquency. This type of deviation has received less attention from culture-and-personality research than has psychological deviation, probably because its incidence is much less frequent in the primitive societies whose study has engaged traditional anthropological attention.

Need-frustration is a necessary (but not a sufficient) condition for social and cultural change, as well as for psychological and cultural deviation. Indeed, the border line between change and deviation is often a tenuous one. If certain cultural norms or structural arrangements systematically frustrate important needs, indigenous or borrowed innovations in norms or in social structure, which might otherwise have been ignored or labeled as deviation, become the basis for sociocultural cumulation and change. In general, culture-and-personality research has paid more attention to dramatic change than it has to gradual change. (This is found, for example, in studies of nativistic and revivalistic movements.)

If motivation is a necessary stimulus to change, cognition is a necessary basis for change. Any change entails cognitive restructuring; the more dramatic the change, the greater the restructuring required. Although cognitive maps, or perceptual sets, seem to be highly resistant to change, it is frequently observed that the acceptance of innovations is impeded by cognitive blocks. If innovations are accepted, they are sufficiently assimilated to traditional cognitive orientations, often rendering dramatic changes that are more apparent than real. Culture-and-personality has devoted relatively little attention to cognitive variables in studies of sociocultural change.

Psychological variables, such as learning, cognition, perception, and motivation, are as important in causal explanations of change in sociocultural systems as they are in explanations of structural persistence.

Functionalism in Culture-and-personality

Culture-and-personality theory, by the very nature of its explanatory concepts, is both causal and functional in character. If customs are performed because of the expectations of satisfying needs, at least one of their functions (manifest and/or latent) is the satisfaction of the biological and psychological requirements of the actors. However, customs are units within a sociocultural system; functionalism, as a theory that purports to explain the maintenance of social and cultural systems, is concerned with the functional requirements of social groups taken collectively. Since the functional requirements of group existence are satisfied not by the *existence* of customs but by their *performance*, and since performance is caused by the expectation of satisfying needs (personal functions), social functions are served in the process of serving personal functions. Obviously, an explanation of the latter is contingent upon an explanation of the former. Thus, when personal functional requirements are not satisfied by the performance of customs, these customs may not occur. When this happens, their functions are not served, and changes and/or disruptive influences may take place in both the social and the cultural systems.

Personality variables, although always causal, may not always be important for understanding social functions. If all of the functions of a custom are recognized (manifest functions), motivation may be taken for granted; an understanding of a custom's social functions does not entail explicit knowledge of the needs that instigate its performance. This is not true of unrecognized (latent) functions, especially of those which are served by the performance of customs whose motivation is at least partially unconscious. Since unconscious motives are frequently expressed in the performance of customs whose manifest functions are unrelated to these motives, and since the motives are disguised because of the disruptive sociocultural impact of their undisguised expression, the latent social functions served by the performance of these customs are of the utmost importance for an understanding of sociocultural persistence.

Bibliography

BENEDICT, RUTH 1934 *Patterns of Culture*. Boston and New York: Houghton Mifflin. A paperback edition was published in 1961.

DUBOIS, CORA A. (1944) 1960 *The People of Alor: A Social-psychological Study of an East Indian Island*. Cambridge, Mass.: Harvard Univ. Press.

HALLOWELL, A. IRVING 1955 *Culture and Experience*. Philadelphia: Univ. of Pennsylvania Press.

HARING, DOUGLAS (editor) (1948) 1956 *Personal Character and Cultural Milieu: A Collection of Readings*. 3d rev. ed. Syracuse Univ. Press.

HSU, FRANCIS L. K. (editor) 1961 *Psychological Anthropology: Approaches to Culture and Personality*. Homewood, Ill.: Dorsey Press.

KAPLAN, BERT (editor) 1961 *Studying Personality Cross-culturally*. Evanston, Ill.: Row, Peterson.

KARDINER, ABRAM 1939 *The Individual and His Society: The Psychodynamics of Primitive Social Organization*. New York: Columbia Univ. Press.

KLUCKHOHN, CLYDE et al. (editors) (1948) 1953 *Personality in Nature, Society, and Culture*. 2d ed., rev. & enl. New York: Knopf.

LABARRE, WESTON 1954 *The Human Animal*. Univ. of Chicago Press.

MEAD, MARGARET 1939 *From the South Seas; Studies in Adolescence and Sex in Primitive Societies*. New York: Morrow.

OPLER, MARVIN K. (editor) 1959 *Culture and Mental Health: Cross-cultural Studies*. New York: Macmillan.

SAPIR, EDWARD (1910–1944) 1949 *Selected Writings in Language, Culture, and Personality*. Edited by David G. Mandelbaum. Berkeley: Univ. of California Press.

SIEGEL, BERNARD J. (editor) 1959–1962 *Biennial Review of Anthropology*. 2 vols. Stanford Univ. Press.

WALLACE, ANTHONY F. C. 1961 *Culture and Personality*. New York: Random House.

WHITING, JOHN W. M.; and CHILD, IRVIN L. 1953 *Child Training and Personality: A Cross-cultural Study*. New Haven: Yale Univ. Press. A paperback edition was published in 1962 by Yale University Press.

7 CULTURE AND COGNITION

Anthony F. C. Wallace

Cultural anthropology has always maintained a cross-cultural perspective. Although each investigator may only study a few societies himself, he is constantly comparing them with others around the world. Cross-cultural surveys on hundreds of groups have been used to test hypotheses about human behavior. While this work will undoubtedly continue, it is becoming clear that it suffers from inadequate ethnographic descriptions. The data which have been gathered are not easily comparable, and what anthropologists have labeled marriage in one society is not the same as the behavior which receives that name in another. As Anthony F. C. Wallace points out, thorough and precise ethnographic description is a prerequisite to the anthropologist's comparative and theoretical work. In this chapter he surveys some of the advances which have been made toward adequate descriptions. The attempt to represent cultural rules as a structured set of cognitive calculi is seen as an important step. One method to this end is componential analysis, which seeks to discover the rules for classifying phenomena into sets. The author illustrates this method with an analysis of kinship terms and shows clearly the steps in the procedure. The formal structures of taxonomies, values, and plans may eventually provide a more adequate basis for cross-cultural comparison.—EDITOR'S NOTE

Cultural anthropology has as its central interest the description and analysis of a certain kind of regularities in human social behavior. The regularities in question are the customs—or, to use the technical term, the culture—of the group. The work of describing such regularities within the boundaries of a particular society during a brief cross-section of time is called ethnography. All of the comparative and theoretical work of cultural anthropology depends upon thorough and precise ethnographic description.

Reprinted from "Culture and Cognition," *Science*, vol. 135, no. 3501 (February 2, 1962), pp. 351–357, by permission of the author and the publisher.

Systematic ethnography began about a century ago. The early ethnographic works were exercises in natural history and were of theoretical interest chiefly insofar as they provided materials for crude calendars of cultural evolution. The naturalistic phase was succeeded in the early twentieth century by a Linnaean period during which interest in cultural evolution flagged and intense effort was directed toward the exact and detailed description, or at least classification, of thousands of languages, of various aspects of culture, and of hundreds of whole cultures on the basis of more or less objective morphological criteria. The heyday of "pure" ethnography was succeeded by the development of more sophisticated theories of cultural change, of cultural structure and function, and of the relation of cultural processes to processes in other analytical domains, such as personality structure and development, psychopathology, hominid physical evolution, and so forth. But ethnography remains the minimum essential task of cultural anthropology and continues to be the subject of intensive methodological study and experimentation.

One of the products of modern studies in ethnographic method has been an increasing awareness that the research operations of the ethnographer produce primarily not naturalistic or statistical descriptions of regularities in overt behavior but descriptions of the rules which the actors are presumably employing, or attempting to employ, in the execution and mutual organization of this behavior. A second product of these methodological studies is the recognition that a set of such related rules forms a calculus which describes cognitive process.

The work of the ethnographer, in describing the cognitive processes which have been culturally standardized in society, may perhaps best be made clear by an analogy. Let us suppose that a nonmathematician is given the task of describing a new mathematical calculus which is in active use by a group of people who have not bothered to formulate their system of calculation in a text or monograph. It has, in other words, been developing informally over the years, is currently being used in developed form, and is being taught to new users by example and by oral instruction. The investigator is allowed to interview and observe—that is, he may ask questions during coffee breaks, watch people computing, save scraps of paper from wastebaskets, take photographs of the machines employed, talk a few times with a project director, listen to people teaching one another the right way of doing things, and make other such minimally interfering kinds of observation and inquiry. He may even be permitted—and he will certainly be well advised—to join the group as a novice and learn to use the calculus himself.

Now, as he analyzes the data collected in these various ways, he does not merely tabulate the frequencies and intercorrelations of various classes of observed behavior in order to arrive at the calculus; if he did this, he would be giving equal weight to misunderstood jokes, learners' mistakes, slips of the pen, plain sloppy work, gibberish produced by broken computers, legpulling, and competent professional operations. What he does, instead, is to infer the system of rules which these people are attempting to apply. The assurance that he is on the way to an adequate understanding of these rules will be given him by the logical completeness of the system he infers and by his ability, when using it, to produce behavior which an expert will reward by saying, in effect, "That's right; that's good; now you've got it." Sometimes, of course, a sociologist or a psychologist will say to him, "But it is the behavior that is real, not this abstract system which no one actually applies perfectly and completely and which is merely the asymptote of the real curve of behaviors." To this the investigator simply replies that culture—conceived in this sense as a collection of formal calculi—is just as real as algebra, Euclidean geometry, and set theory, which are also "merely" the asymptotes of the "real" behavior of fallible students, professional mathematicians, and machines. Indeed, he will point out, these other calculi *are* aspects of a culture, and their apparently greater tangibility is attributable to the incidental circumstance that they have been the object of more intensive study, in order to make their elements and operations explicit, than the undescribed calculus which he has just been investigating.

Let us now look at the ways in which anthropologists are actually attempting to formulate the calculi of culture. We shall consider first the method of componential analysis as applied to kinship systems.

Componential Analysis of Kinship Terminologies

The study of kinship is an anthropological specialty on which considerable labor and ingenuity have been lavished for many years. In particular, the terms by which the individual refers to his kinfolk have attracted attention, both because of the variety of observed arrangements from culture to culture and because of the rigor and elegance with which these relatively restricted taxonomies can be described. The problem of description is not simply to translate an exotic nomenclature into English or some other, scientific language. In fact, exact translations can rarely be made. The problem is to define the taxonomic system itself—that is, to explicate the rules by which the users of the terms group various social and genealogical characteristics into concepts. It is a problem in cultural semantics, then, not in practical or structural linguistics, and as a semantic problem it is of cognitive and logical interest.

The meaning of kinship terms has been traditionally rendered, among English-speaking ethnologists, by a straightforward procedure: each term is matched with a primitive English term (for example *mother*), with a relative product of two or more primitives (for example, *mother's brother*), or (in most cases) with a group of single terms or of relative-product terms, or of both. Each primitive term and each relative product denotes a "kintype." There are eight basic primitive kintypes, and they are conventionally represented by the first two letters of the corresponding English term (*Fa, Mo, Br, Si, So, Da, Hu, Wi*); there are an indefinitely large number of relative products in which each antecedent primitive is read as possessing the subsequent primitive (for example, *MoBr* is read as "mother's brother") (*1*). The English term *uncle* thus may be defined in kintype notation by the expression:

Uncle = *FaBr, MoBr, FaFaBr, MoFaBr, FaMoBr, MoMoBr, etc.*

The definition of English *uncle* is, however, not semantically satisfactory because it does not identify the principles by which the kintypes (and the corresponding kinfolk) have been grouped into the set of denotata, and because the set of kintypes which it denotes has no finite boundary. Since kintype definitions in all languages are in general semantically ambiguous and often unbounded, anthropologists have been dissatisfied with them.

Componential analysis, as developed in the original papers of Goodenough (*2*) and Lounsbury (*3*), is a method of determining the semantic components of the concept for which a given term is a rubric. The componential analysis of a kinship lexicon commonly consists of five steps: (i) the recording of a complete set of the terms of reference; (ii) the definition of these terms in the traditional kintype notation (*Fa, FaBr*, and so on); (iii) the identification, in the principles of grouping of kintypes by terms, of two or more conceptual dimensions each of whose values ("components") is signified by one or more of the terms; (iv) the definition of each term, in a symbolic notation, as a specific combination, or set of combinations, of the components; and (v) a statement of the semantic relationships among the terms and of the structural principles of the taxonomy. To give a simple example of the method, let us take, in their formal and referential sense, a familiar group of American-English terms denoting degrees of consanguinity and perform a componential analysis of their meaning.

Stage 1: We select *grandfather, grandmother, father, mother, brother, sister, son, daughter, grandson, granddaughter, uncle, aunt, nephew, niece,* and *cousin* as a group of terms in American English used to refer to consanguineal relatives.

Stage 2. We define these terms, employing the primitive kintypes *Fa, Mo, Br, Si, So,* and *Da:*

Grandfather = *FaFa, MoFa*
Grandmother = *FaMo, MoMo*
Father = *Fa*
Mother = *Mo*
Brother = *Br*
Sister = *Si*
Son = *So*
Daughter = *Da*
Grandson = *SoSo, DaSo*
Granddaughter = *SoDa, DaDa*
Uncle = *FaBr, MoBr, FaFaBr, MoFaBr*, etc.
Aunt – *FaSi, MoSi, FaFaSi, MoFaSi*, etc.
Nephew – *BrSo, SiSo, BrSoSo, SiSoSo*, etc.
Niece = *BrDa, SiDa, BrDaDa, SiDaDa*, etc.
Cousin = *FaBrSo, FaBrDa, MoBrSo, MoBrDa, FaSiSo, FaSiDa, MoSiSo, MoSiDa, FaFaBrSo, FaMoBrSo, MoFaSiDa*, etc.

Stage 3. We observe that all but one of these terms (*cousin*) specifies sex of relative; all but one makes some discrimination with respect to generation; all specify whether the relative is lineally or nonlineally related to ego; and nonlineal terms specify whether or not all the ancestors of the relative are ancestors of ego, or whether all the ancestors of ego are ancestors of the relative, or whether neither is the case. From these observations we hypothesize that three dimensions (A, B, and C) will be sufficient to define all the terms. Sex of relative (A): male (a_1), female (a_2). Generation (B): two generations above ego (b_1), one generation above ego (b_2), ego's own generation (b_3), one generation below ego (b_4), two generations below ego (b_5). Lineality (C): lineal (c_1), colineal (c_2), ablineal (c_3). We use Goodenough's definition of the values on this dimension of lineality: lineals are persons who are ancestors or descendants of ego; colineals are nonlineals all of whose ancestors include, or are included in, all the ancestors of ego; ablineals are consanguineal relatives who are neither lineals nor colineals (*4*).

Stage 4. We define the terms now by components, adopting the convention that where a term does not discriminate on a dimension, the letter for that dimension is given without subscript.

Grandfather, $a_1b_1c_1$
Grandmother, $a_2b_1c_1$
Father, $a_1b_2c_1$
Mother, $a_2b_2c_1$
Brother, $a_1b_3c_2$
Sister, $a_2b_3c_2$
Son, $a_1b_4c_1$
Daughter, $a_2b_4c_1$
Grandson, $a_1b_5c_1$
Granddaughter, $a_2b_5c_1$
Uncle, $a_1b_1c_2$ and $a_1b_2c_2$
Aunt, $a_2b_1c_2$ and $a_2b_2c_2$
Nephew, $a_1b_4c_2$ and $a_1b_5c_2$
Niece, $a_2b_4c_2$ and $a_2b_5c_2$
Cousin, abc_3

The definitions are represented paradigmatically in Fig. 7:1.

As is evident, each term has been so defined, with respect to the compo-

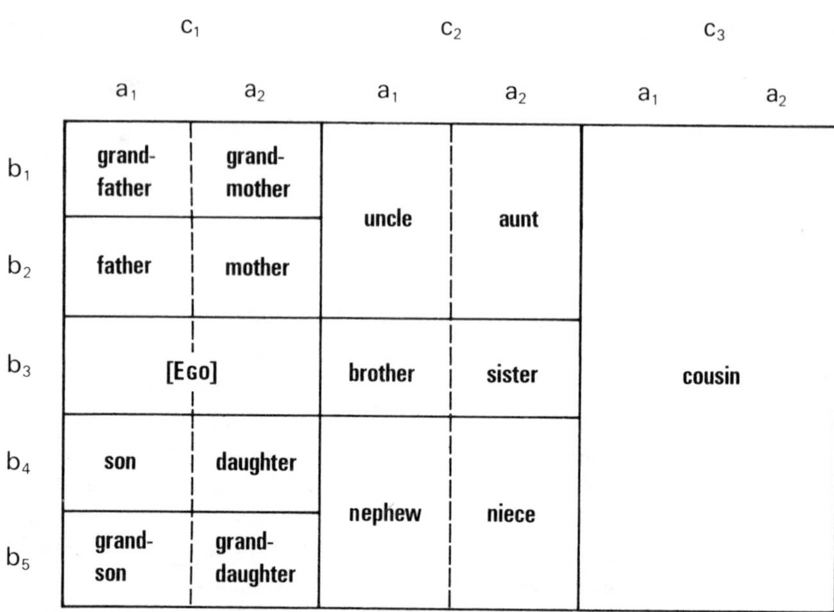

Figure 7:1. A componential paradigm of American-English terms denoting degrees of consanguinity. [After Wallace and Atkins (6).]

nents selected, that no term overlaps or includes another; every component is discriminated by at least one term; and all terms can be displayed on the same paradigm. We do not argue that this is the only or even the best representation—only that it is adequate to define the set of terms chosen (*5, 6*).

Study of Folk Taxonomies

The principles of componential analysis, and the label "componential analysis" itself, have been used in linguistics in the construction of grammatic and phonemic paradigms (*7*). Componential analysis has also been used for the exposition of the meaning of color terms, of concepts of disease, and of the nomenclature of folk botanical taxonomies (*8*). It is evident that the general method of componential analysis is applicable not merely to kinship taxonomies but to taxonomies of any kind, whether the taxonomy is associated with a nomenclature or with other kinds of differential behavior, and indeed, whether the taxonomies are folk taxonomies or more explicit and self-conscious scientific taxonomies such as the schemata of biological taxonomy and the periodic table of the elements.

Now from the standpoint of interest in cognitive process, the value of componential analysis as a method lies not merely in its utility in clarifying what a certain group of speakers "mean" when they use a set of terms but in its ability to reveal the structure of the logical calculus which is employed in the given taxonomy associated with the terms. Implicit in the procedures of componential analysis is the statement of the semantic structure in a symbolic code. At first, no doubt, the semantic structure was stated in code for the sake of convenience, in order to avoid the cumbersome task of scribbling elaborate verbal definitions after each term in the nomenclature. But then it was realized that liberating the analysis from its concern with the original nomenclature and with its particular semantic freight makes it much easier to consider the cognitive structure (just as it is easier to consider the structure of language if one ignores the particular semantic content of the utterances).

The semantic paradigm which is the product of a componential analysis is merely a mapping of a particular set of behaviors (such as a set of words) on a logical space. The logical spaces actually employed in folk (and scientific) taxonomies seem to differ considerably in detail (though not in principle) from the kinds of logical spaces that are conventionally recommended for mathematical and other systematic practical thinking by Western logicians (although the principles by which they are constructed are no doubt well enough recognized). A logical space may be generally characterized as a group of values (logical predicates) related by certain rules. Each of these values refers to a subset of a set of empirical phenomena (such as the set of all living and remembered members of a community).

Many logical spaces are class-product spaces. In class-product spaces, any values which refer to mutually exclusive subsets of the universe, and are therefore mutual contraries of one another, are said to belong to a single dimension. In fact, the group of values represented in a space will usually divide into two or more dimensions. At least one of these dimensions will be logically independent of at least one other (that is, no value or group of values on that dimension implies, or rules out, a value or group of values on the other). Logical spaces may, however, in principle also be constructed of values whose product relations are relative products rather than class products, and furthermore, dimensions can be constructed of values which do not follow the two-valued rule of mutual exclusiveness of referential subsets. Even when class-product spaces are considered alone (and this is the usual preference in componential analysis), considerable variation is possible: dimensions may be nonordered or ordered (and of course they can be ordered in various ways, such as continuous-variable, discrete-variable, or partial ordering); dimensions can be finite or infinite; and the "shape" of the space may be of at least three types. The simplest shape (and probably the rarest in folk taxonomies) is the orthogonal space, which is constructed from independent dimensions, and which may be defined as the set of class products formed by all unique combinations of values from the several dimensions, each product including one value from each dimension and each product being non-self-contradictory. Non-orthogonal spaces are constructed from a group of dimensions of which at least one pair is nonindependent. There are at least two types of non-orthogonal spaces: in the first type, all the dimensions span the same set of referents, but at least two values from different dimensions are mutual contraries; in the second type, at least one value on one dimension and each of the values on another dimension are mutual contraries. The three types of class-product spaces may be represented, for purposes of discussion here, by three simple diagrams, constructed in each case from two dimensions (Fig. 7:2).

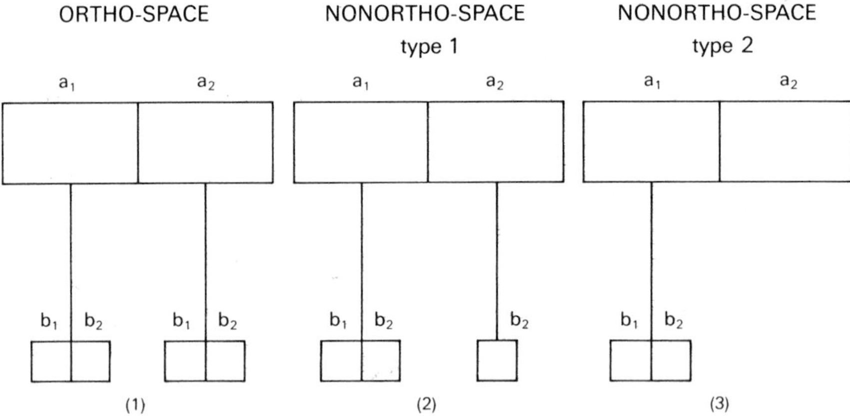

Figure 7:2. Types of class-product spaces formed of two binary dimensions. [After Wallace and Atkins (6).]

An orthogonal space may be neatly mapped as a "solid" rectangular matrix; a rectangular matrix displaying a nonorthogonal space will have "holes" representing the impossible class-products.

Evidently, then, the range of logical models available for choice by a particular culture in the construction of a folk taxonomy is considerable. Ethnologists should not, and in fact do not any longer, expect the shape and other characteristics of the logical space on which a folk taxonomy is mapped to be necessarily the simple and convenient orthogonal class-product space so familiar in textbook expositions of social science methodology. And that human folk taxonomies in general cannot be said to be confined to that logical structure known as the orthogonal class-product space is in itself something of a discovery.

Class-product spaces have the additional convenience, for the scientist, of being readily measurable. It is possible to count the number of dimensions, of values on each dimension, and of cells in the space, and to compute a measure of semantic information. The unit of semantic information, by analogy with the unit of statistical information, is the binary choice, and it can be easily shown that the value for the logarithm of L to the base 2, where L is the number of terms in a taxonomic lexicon, is the minimum number of binary dimensions necessary to define each term on an orthogonal space.

Even rough measurements of the quantity of semantic information contained in such folk taxonomies as kinship lexicons and the phonemes of language suggest strongly that human folk taxonomies rarely require more than the equivalent of six binary dimensions on any given level of abstraction. This number is not far from the "magical number seven" which apparently limits the complexity of binary conceptual discriminations possible for experimental subjects in the psychological laboratory (*9*). The possible existence of a 2^n rule, limiting the complexity of taxonomic systems practicable for cultural standardization, has interesting implications for human physical and cultural evolution and for mental health (*10*).

Other Kinds of Logical Calculi in Cultural Systems

Taxonomy is just one of the cognitive structures necessary to organized "meaningful" behavior (including cultural behavior, where taxonomies are shared or at least complementary among the members of large groups). Three other kinds of calculi may be mentioned as having already received some, and as deserving more, attention from the cognitive standpoint from anthropologists: the hierarchical ordering of states in terms of differential desirability; calculi of transformations of state; and systems of deductive and inductive logic employed in folk science and technology.

The anthropological study of "values" (that is, of customary formulations, on a highly abstract level, of what are the desirable and undesirable human experiences) has included some partial and incomplete formal taxonomic efforts which are in the technical tradition of componential analysis (*11*). The development of a scientific taxonomy of values for cross-cultural use, and the mapping of the major values of a particular society on the cross-cultural taxonomic matrix, is not of much use in culture and cognition research, however. The relevant problem has been more clearly defined in psychoanalytic theory and in role theory. To introduce this problem, let us argue that each society should (optimally) be so designed that the fewest possible number of value dilemmas exist for its members.

Thus, if a set of values is given ($a, b, c, \ldots, n$), they should be mapped onto an absolute order of levels of desirability in such a way that the fewest number of pairs will occupy the same levels. Perhaps the simplest of the solutions is the partial ordering exemplified (in truncated form) in such formulas as:

This above all; to thine own self be true,
Thou canst not then be false to any man

which has the form:

$$[a \rightarrow \sim(\sim b)] \rightarrow [a \rightarrow b]$$

But while religious and political systems of ethics strive to establish partial orderings of values in the form:

$$a \rightarrow b \rightarrow c \rightarrow \cdots \rightarrow n$$

in which one can start with a supreme value and derive all other values from it lineally, various circumstances of personal history and social and situational complexity generally work to unravel such utopian formulations. The logical net of values actually observed thus usually branches, often asymmetrically. Branching, on the one hand, leads to the possibility of value conflicts (in the effort to resolve which there may even be created independent value domains, as when one system of ethics applies to the ingroup, another to the outgroup) and, on the other hand, merges values, sometimes with unhappy consequences (as in the case of the involuntary establishment of equivalences in the transference neurosis). The value dilemmas imposed by discontinuities in cultural conditioning, and by innovation and acculturation, and the consequent effort by social reformers to create internally consistent calculi of values, have been of particular interest to anthropologists concerned with national character and with culture change.

The cultural calculi which describe transformations of state are embodied in processual descriptions of how things happen and in rules, techniques, recipes, or programs for getting things done. Given a set of entities defined on appropriate taxonomic spaces, and given a goal specified in a value hierarchy, and process equation integrates a sequence of events in what some psychological theorists call a Plan (*12*). Much of culture, then, can be regarded as an archive of Plans. The formal nature of these Plans has been approached by anthropologists in four principal ways: (i) by attempting to contrast the logical structure of primitive and civilized, or magical and rational, thinking; (ii) by summarizing the cognitive representation of a behavioral system as a stochastic, and particularly a Markov, statistical process, which can in principle be evaluated in terms of the quantity of organization of the system; (iii) by treating Plans as problem solutions in decision theory and applying to them such mathematical models as the theory of games; and (iv) by treating sets of related transformations as Galois groups.

The assumption that primitive peoples think according to radically different roles of logic, and that these "primitive" logical calculi are needful to account for such irrational beliefs about process in the natural world as mana and taboo, magic, witchcraft, and so forth, is an old one. It has been unfortunately coupled with a psychiatric theory that the psychotic regresses not merely in the direction of his own infancy but in the direction of the infancy of the species, and that—to complete the circle—thought processes of psychotics in modern mental hospitals can be studied as a means of understanding primitive thought. There is, however, no real evidence that any primitive people characteristically and conventionally employs what Western logicians would define as a logical fallacy. And to suppose that the primitive is *unable* to think rationally, for instance, would lead to the expectation that the primitive hunter would perform the following feat of cerebration, with suicidal consequences:

A rabbit has four legs.
That animal has four legs.
Therefore that animal is a rabbit.

This fallacious piece of reasoning follows the so-called law of Von Domarus (subjects are identical if they have a common predicate). Such reasoning has been attributed to primitives and schizophrenics alike (*13*), and, had it been in fact widely applied during the Paleolithic period, it would long ago have been the death of our ancestors. A more profitable approach is to explain the scientifically demonstrable nonvalidity of certain pieces of native theory (as, for instance, notions of taboo and of magic) as arising from a lack of empirical knowledge rather than from a peculiarity of the logical forms. The theories of natural process implicit in beliefs about taboo, magic, and witchcraft are not illogical; they are simply wrong.

The analysis of the cognitive representation of complex processes and relationships as stochastic process has been suggested, but there would be major difficulties in securing appropriate bodies of data. The periodic Markov process in particular (in distinction to the aperiodic process emphasized by Shannon in his work on information theory) seems, in principle, appropriate for the representation of cognitive models of sociocultural systems, which are largely composed of alternative events probabilistically related in repeated fixed-order sequences. The standard formula for such a system would be that given in Fig. 7:3, with each conditional probability (designated by an arrow) somewhat less than 1. One advantage of this model is that it collapses, as the set of probabilities ap-

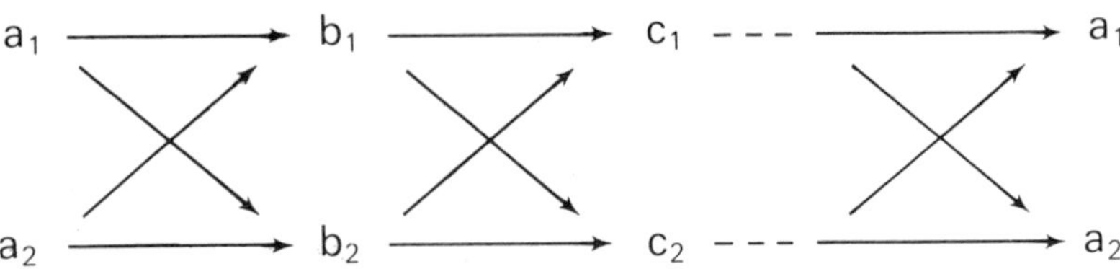

Figure 7:3. The standard formula for a sociocultural system.

proaches unity, into simple logical structures, and that at all levels of probability the total system can be measured with respect to the quantity of statistical information, or (complementarily) the quantity of statistical organization, it "contains." The measure of organization is potentially of great interest in considering the processes of cultural and personality change, since one may inquire whether certain types of pattern changes in systems are associated with increases or decreases in their quantity of organization (*14*).

The use of mathematical decision theory models—such as game theory—has also been proposed for analysis of certain ethnographic materials. Moore, for instance, has suggested that scapulimancy—divining from the pattern of cracks in the scapula of a roasted animal—may be interpreted as a method for maximizing the probability of success in hunting, when empirical knowledge of game movements is lacking, by randomizing decisions as to hunting grounds, time of hunt, and so on (*15*).

The abstract mathematical model of related transformations provided by Galois group theory is potentially of considerable significance. For instance, native theories of historical cycles (as in the Near Eastern cycles of reincarnation and of world degeneration and renewal), and Hindu concepts of ritual pollution and cleansing, may be usefully analyzed by means of group theory. Group theory has in other branches of science proved to be convenient for clarifying the logical structure of transformations, and it will probably turn out to be equally useful in the domain of culture and cognition.

The study of ethnoscience has an interesting role in the study of culture and cognition. Nowhere in our own culture are the logical structures of cognitive processes more explicitly formulated than in science. Hence, comparison of "primitive" science and technology, from the standpoint of logic and cognitive process, with contemporary science is apt to be profitable. Already some interesting bodies of material are becoming available: Hallowell's observations on measurement of space and time among the Ojibwa (*16*); the work of Goodenough on native astronomy in Micronesia (*17*); Barnett's work on the logical structure of technological innovation (*18*); my own investigation of the Iroquois theory of dreams (which anticipated essential features of Freud's dream theory by at least 300 years) (*19*); the study of calendrics and arithmetic of the Maya [who independently invented a positional notation and the zero (*20*)]; and so on.

Despite the anthropologist's tendency to question the universal applicability of psychological principles, the most useful methodological assumption with which to approach the study of the logical calculi in folk sciences is that these calculi are already contained in logical structures familiar to, or at least implicit in, Western symbolic logic. Cultural relativism, with respect to logic, applies more forcefully to the content of propositions than to this form of their relationships. Perhaps this can be made clear by citing the example of Handsome Lake, a Seneca Indian prophet of the late eighteenth century, who (successfully) preached temperance to his people. Handsome Lake did not speak or read English and received no training in Western logic or scientific method. Yet he said (*21*):

> . . . Good food is turned into evil drink. Now some have said that there is no harm in partaking of fermented liquids.
>
> Then let this plan be followed: let men gather in two parties, one having a feast of food, apples and corn, and the other cider and whiskey. Let the parties be equally divided and matched and let them commence their feasting at the same time. When the feast is finished you will see those who drank the fermented juices murder one of their own party but not so with those who ate food only.

His was hardly a prelogical mentality. Handsome Lake's experimental design follows precisely Mill's Second Canon of Inductive Logic (the Method of Differences), which states, "If an instance in which the phenomenon under investigation occurs, and an instance in which it does not occur, have every circumstance in common save one, that one occurring only in the former; the circumstance in which alone the two instances differ, is the effect, or the cause, or an indispensable part of the cause, of the phenomenon" (*22*).

Methodological Problems and Theoretical Implications

The use which is made of symbolic logic, algebraic notation, set theory, and other formalisms in studies of culture and cognition should not permit a confusion of these enterprises with other logicomathematical analyses of social and cultural phenomena which aim simply at precise and accurate description of overtly observable phenomena.

The commitment to describe the psychological reality of culture requires that not just any model which predicts some overt class of action be accepted, but only that model which is used as a system of reckoning by the actor. Not infrequently it can be demonstrated that two systems of reckoning will yield the same result in overt behavior. For example, there are several different ways to compute the square root of a number; the task in culture and cognition would be, not simply to find *a* way, but to find *the* way being actively employed by a person or a group. The technical problem of determining which of two equally predictive models corresponds best to the model actually being used by the subject requires the introduction of problems of choice which were not a part of the originally predicted behavior and which precede it in the chain of reckoning.

Now, just as the ethnographer may invent a taxonomic model which will predict satisfactorily how a speaker will refer to his kinsmen but which does not describe how the speaker reckons kinfolk, so it is possible that two members of the same society may produce similar or complementary behaviors without sharing the same cognitive model. Indeed, if one makes the conservative assumption that no set of people all share the same cognitive model requisite to a type of behavior, one may ask the larger question: How are diverse cognitive models (of values, plans, taxonomies, and so on) articulated in a functioning cultural system? This question leads to a consideration of the properties of a metacalculus whose components are the diverse calculi of particular individuals or subgroups cooperating to maintain stable systems of relationships (or, for that matter, failing to do so). It has been demonstrated that a family of such metacalculi exists (we shall call it the family of equivalence structures), each of whose members is the sum of the plans of two or more individuals. Each component plan minimally consists of an instrumental action by the planner, followed by a facilitating action by his partner and a consummatory action by the planner. The intriguing feature is that neither partner's plan need include an awareness of the other's in order for the two plans to sum to a stable and mutually rewarding interaction system (see Fig. 7:4 for an analysis of the simplest equivalence structure). In fact, except where plans are shared, the metacalculus is always a more complex system than is included in the

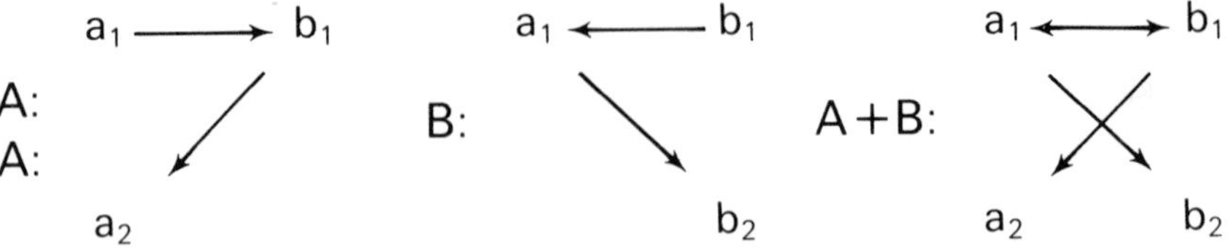

Figure 7:4. The summation of nonshared plans (*A*, *B*) in an equivalence structure (*A* + *B*). [After Wallace (23).]

plan of either partner. This suggests several interesting functional properties of sociocultural systems, among them the dual properties (i) that an effective and viable sociocultural system can evolve which is categorically beyond the capacity of any of its members to incorporate in a single plan, and (ii) that the maximum size of a sociocultural system is associated with a minimal level of cognitive sharing.

Conclusion

Anthropologists are turning their attention to the cognitive structures which are basic to customary behavior in society (*24*). In general, these studies work to expose the abstract calculus underlying the specific content of behavior by the use of a symbolic notation and the application of available logical-mathematical models as hypotheses. Particular attention has been paid to the semantic analysis of folk taxonomies, such as kinship terminologies, but formal analysis of other aspects of culture, such as values, the program of behavior released in particular situations, and folk science, is also a promising area of work. The principles of the metacalculi to which the diverse cognitive structures of individuals sum in stable social systems are, then, to be regarded as principles of sociocultural organization itself.

References and Notes

1. G. P. Murdock, *Social Structure* (Macmillan, New York, 1949).
2. W. H. Goodenough, *Language* **32,** 195 (1956).
3. F. G. Lounsbury, *ibid.* **32,** 158 (1956).
4. W. H. Goodenough, private communication (1959).
5. The analysis of English consaguineal terms given here is taken from A. F. C. Wallace and J. Atkins (*6*).
6. A. F. C. Wallace and J. Atkins, *Am. Anthropologist* **62, 58** (1960).
7. C. F. Hockett, *Intern. J. Am. Linguistics* **13, 258** (1947); Z. S. Harris, *Language* **24,** 87 (1948).
8. H. Conklin, *Southwestern J. Anthropol.* **11,** 339 (1955); C. O. Frake, *Am. Anthropologist* **63,** 113 (1961); H. Conklin, work paper for the Conference on Lexicography, Indiana University, 1960.
9. G. A. Miller, *Psychol. Rev.* **63,** 81 (1956).
10. A. F. C. Wallace, *Proc Natl. Acad. Sci. U.S.* **47,** 458 (1961); *Intern. Record Med.* **173,** 700 (1960).
11. C. M. Kluckhohn, in *The State of the Social Sciences,* L. D. White, Ed. (Univ. of Chicago Press, Chicago, 1956).
12. G. A. Miller, E. Galanter, K. H. Pribram, *Plans and the Structure of Behavior* (Holt, New York, 1960).
13. S. Arieti, *Am. Anthropologist* **58,** 26 (1956).

14. A. F. C. Wallace, in *Studying Personality Cross-Culturally*, B. Kaplan, Ed. (Row, Peterson, Evanston, Ill., 1961), p. 129.

15. O. K. Moore, *Am. Anthropologist* **59,** 69 (1957).

16. A. I. Hallowell, *ibid.* **44,** 62 (1942); *Culture and Experience* (Univ. of Pennsylvania Press, Philadelphia, 1955).

17. W. H. Goodenough, *Native Astronomy in the Central Carolines* (University Museum, Phiadelphia, 1953); *Sci. Monthly* **73,** 105 (1951).

18. H. G. Barnett, *Innovation: The Basis of Cultural Change* (McGraw-Hill, New York, 1953).

19. A. F. C. Wallace, *Am. Anthropologist* **60,** 234 (1958).

20. S. G. Morley, *The Ancient Maya* (Stanford Univ. Press, Stanford, Calif., 1946); L. Satterthwaite, *Concepts and Structures of Maya Calendrical Arithmetics* (University Museum and Philadelphia Anthropological Society, Philadelphia, 1947).

21. A. C. Parker, *N.Y. State Museum Bull. No. 163* (1913).

22. J. S. Mill, *A System of Logic* (1881), p. 280.

23. A. F. C. Wallace, *Culture and Personality* (Random House, New York, 1961).

24. See also D. French, in *Psychology: A Study of a Science*, vol. 6, S. Koch, Ed. (Mc-Graw-Hill, New York, 1963), for a review of the role of anthropology in studies of perception and cognition.

PART 3 ETHNOSCIENCE

8 STUDIES IN ETHNOSCIENCE

William C. Sturtevant

During the past two decades a number of anthropologists have developed methods for more rigorous ethnographic research. In this chapter William C. Sturtevant surveys the major principles of their work and many of the studies which have resulted. The ideas presented here are further developed in Chapters 9 and 10. In order to avoid losing sight of the forest because of the trees, the student should gain a clear idea of certain major concepts.

An example which provides a brief overview may be of value at this point: Ethnoscience is primarily an *emic* approach. A study of your college or university would seek to discover the student's own definition of experience. It would not examine variables defined by the investigator for a study of all the world's campuses. Students sort their experience into large chunks or *domains*, the boundaries of which could not be defined ahead of time. Domains might include kinds of students like "freaks" and "jocks" or kinds of courses like "snap," "mickey-mouse," and "tough." These labels for experience are called *lexemes*, and they would provide a ready entrance into the meaning-system of students. Sets of terms which are used in similar ways make up *contrast sets*, which are arranged into *terminological systems*. The investigator seeks to discover the nature of these systems. Some names for things are included in others; that is, a *jock* is a kind of *student* and can be referred to by either term. Terms related in this way form a *taxonomy*. But how do students distinguish among a set of related terms? They use certain *criteria* or attributes which can be discovered by the method of *componential analysis*. Buildings, for example, might be distinguished by size, color, function, and who uses them. When the attributes have been discovered for a set of terms, they can be mapped onto the terms, and this information represented in a *paradigm*. Whether those studied are college students or cannibals, the principles discussed in this chapter for discovering and representing their respective systems of cultural knowledge would be much the same.—EDITOR'S NOTE

Reproduced from *American Anthropologist*, vol. 66(2), no. 1 (1964), pp. 99–131, by permission of the author and the American Anthropological Association.

This paper[1] is a survey and explication of a new approach in ethnography—of what one might well call "the New Ethnography" were it not for that label's pejorative implications for practitioners of other kinds of ethnography. The method has no generally accepted name, although one is clearly required. "Ethnoscience" perhaps has the widest acceptance, in conversation if not in print, and has the advantage of freshness. However, some of this word's undesirable implications should be disavowed: "The term 'ethnoscience' is unfortunate for two reasons—first, because it suggests that other kinds of ethnography are *not* science, and second because it suggests that folk classifications and folk taxonomies *are* science" (Spaulding 1963). Although the name may have been chosen partly because of the first of these implications, it would be impolitic if not impolite to insist on it; in any case, the method should stand or fall on its own merits. To dispose adequately of the second implication would require a discourse on the definition and philosophy of science. It is perhaps sufficient to remark that the most appropriate meaning to assign to the element "science" here (but not necessarily elsewhere) is, essentially, "classification." This restricted implication has been well expressed by G. G. Simpson in a somewhat similar context:

> The necessity for aggregating things (or what is operationally equivalent, the sensations received from them) into classes is a completely general characteristic of living things. . . . Such generalization, such classification in that sense, is an absolute, minimal requirement of adaptation, which in turn is an absolute and minimal requirement of being or staying alive. . . . We certainly order our perceptions of the external world more fully, more constantly, and more consciously than do any other organisms. . . . Such ordering is most conspicuous in the two most exclusively human and in some sense highest of all our activities: the arts and sciences. . . . The whole aim of theoretical science is to carry to the highest possible and conscious degree the perceptual reduction of chaos. . . . the most basic postulate of science is that nature itself is orderly. . . . All theoretical science is ordering (Simpson 1961:3–5).

"Ethnoscience" is appropriate as a label because it may be taken to imply one interpretation of such terms as "ethnobotany," "ethnogeography," etc.—although it is important to emphasize that the approach is a general ethnographic one, by no means limited to such branches of ethnography as are often called by the names of recognized academic "arts and sciences" coupled with the prefix "ethno-" This prefix is to be understood here in a special sense: it refers to the system of knowledge and cognition typical of a given culture. Ethnoscience differs from Simpson's "theoretical science" in that it refers to the "reduction of chaos" achieved by a particular culture, rather than to the "highest possible and conscious degree" to which such chaos may be reduced. To put it another way, a culture itself amounts to the sum of a given society's folk classifications, all of that society's ethnoscience, its particular ways of classifying its material and social universe. Thus, to take an extreme example, the "ethnopornography" of the Queensland aborigines is what *they* consider pornography—if indeed they have such a category—rather than what was considered pornography by the Victorian ethnologist who titled the last chapter of his monograph on Queensland aboriginal culture "ethno-pornography," warned that "the following chapter is not suitable for perusal by the general reader," and described under this heading such topics as marriage, pregnancy and childbirth, menstruation, "foul language," and especially genital mutilations and their social and ceremonial significance (Roth 1897:169–84). Similarly, "ethnohistory" is here the conception of the past shared by the bearers of a particular culture, rather than (the more usual sense) the history (in our terms) of "ethnic groups"; "ethnobotany" is a specific cultural conception of the plant world, rather than (again the more usual sense) a description of plant uses arranged under the binomials of our own taxonomic botany.

It is not a new proposal that an important aspect of culture is made up of the principles by which a people classify their universe. A rather clear statement to this effect was made by Boas (1911:24–26); the notion was hinted at by Durkheim and Mauss (1903:5–6); Malinowski clearly stated that "the final goal, of which an Ethnographer should never lose sight. . . . is, briefly, to grasp the native's point of view, his relation to life, to realise *his* vision of *his* world" (1922:25). Even E. B. Tylor can be understood in the same sense, when he warned that the ethnologist "must avoid that error which the proverb calls measuring other people's corn by one's own bushel" (1881:410). However, the explicit definition of culture as a whole in these terms, and the proposition that ethnography should be conceived of as the discovery of the "conceptual models" with which a society operates, was first stated quite recently in an elegant, brief paper by Goodenough:

> A society's culture consists of whatever it is one has to know or believe in order to operate in a manner acceptable to its members, and to do so in any role that they accept for any one of themselves. . . . It is the forms of things that people have in mind, their models for perceiving, relating, and otherwise interpreting them. . . . Ethnographic description, then, requires methods of processing observed phenomena such that we can inductively construct a theory of how our informants have organized the same phenomena. It is the theory, not the phenomena alone, which ethnographic description aims to present (Goodenough 1957:167–68).

It has long been evident that a major weakness in anthropology is the underdeveloped condition of ethnographic method. Typologies and generalizations abound, but their descriptive foundations are insecure. Anthropology is in the natural history stage of development rather than the "stage of deductively formulated theory" (Northrop 1947), it is history rather than science (Kroeber 1952:52–78), it has not discovered a fundamental unit comparable to the physicists' atom (a common complaint, variously worded; e.g., Kluckhohn 1953:517, Spuhler 1963). One may try to make the best of this situation by insisting that one prefers to remain a historian or a humanist, or one may look for improvement in ethnography. Taking the latter choice, the best strategy is not, I think, to seek to modify existing generalizations on the basis of intensive field work of the traditional sort in one or two societies (Leach 1961a, 1961b), nor to elaborate *a priori* typologies and apply them to more and more old descriptions by means of fancy retrieval procedures, hoping that the errors and incommensurabilities in the descriptive sources will balance out in the statistical manipulations used to yield generalizations. It is on this latter score that Needham (1962) attacks Murdock's methods (e.g., 1953, 1957), justifiably although intemperately. An interesting methodological contrast of this sort is provided by the exchange between Goodenough (1956b) and Fischer (1958) on Trukese residence rules: Goodenough pointed out the discrepancies resulting from his and Fischer's attempts to apply the usual *a priori* typology of residence in their independent censuses of Truk as a basis for urging that ethnographers should drop this method and substitute the search for the rules significant to the bearers of a particular culture in their own choices of residence. Fischer responded by tinkering with the *a priori* typology to take account of the Trukese peculiarities Goodenough had noted—yet there is no guarantee that the next culture examined will fit his new typology any better than Truk fitted the old one.

What is needed is the improvement of ethnographic method, to make cultural descriptions replicable and accurate, so that we know what we are comparing. Ethnoscience shows promise as the New Ethnography required to advance the whole of cultural anthropology.[2]

The ethnoscientific approach is now about ten years old[3] and has a rapidly growing body of practitioners in general agreement on methods and aims, in close communication with each other, and sharing an enthusiasm for the rehabilitation and revivification of ethnography. There are several excellent programmatic general statements about ethnoscience (Conklin 1962a; Frake 1962; Wallace 1962), which include (usually simplified) examples. However, most previous discussions and exemplifications have been couched in such terms that many anthropologists assume that what is being described is not ethnography but some kind of linguistics or "kinship algebra" or both, so that there may now be room for a more informal, less technical characterization.

The sections which follow attempt to present briefly and in rather general terms the main features of ethnoscience as a method, and to indicate some of the areas in which further work is needed. Usually, examples are either not given, or not described in sufficient detail for adequate comprehension of their relevance. The sources cited should be examined for more complete exemplification.

Principles

1. *Etics and Emics*

If a folk classification is ever to be fully understood, an ethnoscientific analysis must ultimately reduce to a description in terms approximating culture-free characteristics. Colors may be among the significant features in a folk taxonomy of plants; but color itself is classified by principles which differ from culture to culture, hence is a domain which must be analyzed ethnoscientifically before the botanical folk taxonomy is translatable into our terms (Conklin 1955). Enough is known about color, and the classificatory features involved are ordinarily sufficiently concrete, so that the color classification of a given culture may be relatable to culture-free physical and physiological features. Obviously there are very few aspects of culture where reductionism of this type is even remotely foreseeable. In domains where such reduction is not yet possible, the local perceptual structure may nevertheless be largely discoverable, even though incompletely translatable (see now Frake 1964:134). In fact, in some domains the very difficulties in observation which prevent the outside observer from analyzing the significant features in culture-free terms also force the bearers of the culture to utilize explicit verbalized defining attributes in learning and communicating about their own folk classification—hence make easier the discovery of attributes on this level—in contrast to classifications where the objects and their attributes are so concrete and frequent that the classifications may be well learned by exemplification rather than description (Frake 1961:124–25). Nevertheless, full understanding of a culture or an aspect of a culture and particularly its full description in a foreign language require the ultimate reduction of the significant attributes of the local classifications into culture-free terms. Lamb's discussion of the relationship between his semantic and sememic strata, and the parallel relationship between the phonetic and phonemic strata (Lamb 1964:75–77), is highly relevant here.

Culture-free features of the real world may be called "etics" (Pike 1954). The label may also be applied to features which are not truly culture-free, but which at least have been derived from the examination of more than one culture, or to the sum of all the significant attributes in the folk classifications of all cultures. Most of ethnography has operated with characteristics of this sort; ethnology has devoted much attention to the accumulation and systematization of features which *might* be significant in any folk classification, but it has given little attention to comparison of folk classifications or their principles as such. These results are by no means wasted from the point of view of ethnoscience: the ethnographer's knowledge of etics assists him in discovering the locally-significant features by guilding his initial observations and formulation of hypotheses.

Pike contrasts an etic approach with one which he calls emic, which amounts to an ethnoscientific one: an attempt "to discover and describe the behavioral system [of a given culture] in its own terms, identifying not only the structural units but also the structural classes to which they belong" (French 1963:398). An emic description should ultimately indicate which etic characters are locally significant. The more we know of the etics of culture, the easier is the task of ethnoscientific analysis. Thus the great attention to kinship in the past, as well as the great amount of knowledge concerning cultural variability in kinship terminologies (the basic paper on the etics of kinship being a half century old [Kroeber 1909]) is one reason why emic analyses of kinship are easier than those of art, or law, or religion. Better knowledge, at least among anthropologists, of the physiology and physics of color than of taste or smell more readily permits an ethnoscientific analysis of color, even though it is clear (Conklin 1955) that a folk domain including color need not be congruent with what the physicists understand by color. It seems probable that the vast accumulation of anthropological (both ethnological and archeological) knowledge of the etics of material culture will allow the ethnoscientific approach to be quite readily applied in this presently-neglected field. Furthermore, in material culture the objects classified are concrete and easily examined and usually readily observable in many examples during the time available for normal field work—in contrast to diseases, deities, etc. In classifications of concrete but natural, noncultural phenomena such as plants and animals, the range of variation which is classified is both extreme and beyond the direct control of the classifiers, who must select only certain features to which classificatory significance is given (Lévi-Strauss 1962b: 73–74). But with cultural artifacts the corpus is smaller and the significant features are largely produced by the classifiers and hence should be more distinctive and more readily recognizable; also the ethnographer can here subject at least some of the features to controlled variation in order to test informants' reactions to their significance (cf. Berlin and Romney 1964 for an illustration of some of these advantages).

The nature of learning and of communication implies that a culture consists of shared classifications of phenomena, that not every etic difference is emic. But it should be emphasized that an emic analysis refers to one society, to a set of interacting individuals. Cross-cultural comparison, if we take culture in Goodenough's sense, is another level of analysis which involves the comparison of different emic systems. There is no reason why one should expect to find emic regularities shared by cultures differing in space or time. Thus Dundes' "emic units in the structural study of folktales" (1962) are not emic units in the sense here intended, insofar as the "system" of which they are analytical units is comparative (an etically defined "motif," "tale," or "tale type," whose actual manifestations in different cultures are treated as "variants"). On the other hand, Lévi-Strauss' brief characterization of some of the defining attributes of the "gustèmes" of the English, French, and Chinese cuisines (1958: 99–100) is a comparison of the emics of different cultures, although the emic analysis of each of the three cuisines is not presented in sufficient detail to be convincing. Even so, "slippage back and forth between individual systems, and any and all systems, as context for structural relevance, recurs in his [Lévi-Strauss'] work" also; "the first step in a resolution of the problem . . . is to refer structural contrast exclusively to within the domains of individual systems, where its cognitive basis can be empirically warranted" (Hymes 1964:45, 16).

2. Domains

One of the most important principles of ethnoscience, and one of those most often overlooked, is the necessity for determining in a nonarbitrary manner the boundaries of the major category or classification system being analyzed, i.e., for discovering how a domain is bounded in the culture being described rather than applying some external, cross-cultural definition of the field. If this is not done, the description of the internal structuring of the domain is likely to be incomplete if not entirely erroneous, and the utility of the analysis for predicting the classificatory placement of new instances will suffer. (See now Hymes 1964:16–18.)

Any two cultures differ in the way they classify experience. Everyone with any familiarity with more than one realizes that this is true for the lower, more specific classificatory categories, and trivial examples are easily found. But we cannot assume that the higher, more general levels of the folk classifications of different cultures will coincide either; there is no reason to suppose that the total range of a set of categories will match that of the "corresponding" set in another culture even though the ranges of the lower categories in the two sets are different.

Thus every anthropologist recognizes that "uncle" is not a universal category, but most seem to suppose that "relative" or "kinship" is—i.e., that a set of categories defined by consanguinity and affinity is everywhere a "natural" set, that features such as ritual relationships must somehow be always outside the core system; the term "fictive kinship" is significant of the analytical bias. In contrast, Conklin (1964) specifically does not assume that "kinship" is a domain everywhere bounded in the same manner.

It is also customary to assume that everywhere there are just two systems of kinship terms: those used in "reference" and those used in "address." Thus an *a priori* decision is made as to the significant defining features and the number of coexistent systems. Such an analysis of the American kinship system blurs many distinctions: "mother's brother" and "father's brother" are required instead of "uncle" in some referential contexts; different forms of address are often used to differentiate co-resident "grandmothers" or "mothers" (Mo vs WiMo/HuMo); such terms as "father, dad, daddy, pop, old man" are not synonymous.

> The classic distinction between terms of address and terms of reference is not of much help in dealing with the American system. It tends to obscure certain important processes, partly, at least, because it presumes that there is a single term used in all referential contexts. . . . In the contemporary American system the wide variety of alternate forms allows them to differentiate a variety of different contexts (Schneider and Homans 1955:1195–96).

It seems probable that these "alternate forms" would turn out to be quite systematically structured, that several domains could be specified, were the contexts to be analyzed ethnoscientifically. One would expect a higher degree of agreement between informants in the usage of these terms if the contexts were discovered by the observation of natural situations or the asking of natural questions than is the case when informants are asked (e.g. Lewis 1963) to sort the "alternates" into contexts which are supplied ahead of time by the investigator, even though he himself is an American.

Frake (1960:58–59) has made the same point with regard to the Eastern Subanun. Conklin (1951) described several Tagalog "co-existing sets of relationship terms," with their defining contexts. Swartz (1960) shows the relevance of situational environments to the choice between two Trukese terms. According to Chao's analysis (1956), there are three major sets of Mandarin Chinese kinship terms, which are not entirely synonymous even in their kin-term referents; furthermore, the contexts in which Chinese "terms of address" (pronouns, kinship terms, proper names, and titles) are used can be analyzed in terms of the intersection of seven main categories of hearers and ten main categories of person spoken of or addressed (Chao 1956). Presumably this kind of situation is quite general. Yet Norbeck can still conclude a discussion of the "errors" in Morgan's schedule of Japanese kinship terms by urging "the importance of making clear distinctions between terms of address and terms of reference" (1963:214) when it is clear from his preceding discussion (and from Befu and Norbeck 1958) that there are many more than two systems here, and that some of Morgan's "errors" in fact represent accurate reporting of one of these systems.

The arbitrary delimitation of major domain boundaries persists in kinship studies even though the analytical procedures here are the most developed ones in ethnography. It is an even more obvious fault in other areas. Many of the difficulties, for example, in discussions of "primitive art" are seen in a new light when one ceases to assume that "art" is a universal category. The assumption that "cultures . . . have in common . . . a uniform system of classification. . . . a single basic plan" (Murdock 1945:125) is stifling to ethnoscientific analysis.

There may be domains—perhaps kinship is one of them—which are more nearly universal than others, where cross-cultural comparison would show greater sharing of significant features for higher level taxa than for lower level ones. But this is a significant hypothesis to be tested by the comparison of domains from different cultures, each analyzed without prejudice, rather than being a postulate determining the delimitation of domains to be analyzed. Prior assumption of the universality of domains, as in much work on kinship and other domains (e.g. color), prejudges the case and masks some of the variability the explication of which is a classical task of anthropology.

But procedures for the definition of domains are not yet well worked out—this remains one of the more difficult problem areas of ethnoscience (Conklin 1962a:124, 1964; Öhman 1953; Voegelin and Voegelin 1957). However, the problems do not differ in kind from those involving the identification of categories on lower levels, or the discovery of significant contexts or environments.

3. *Terminological Systems*

Research in ethnoscience so far has concentrated on classifications as reflected by native terminology, on "discerning how people construe their world of experience from the way they talk about it" (Frake 1962:74).

> The analysis of a culture's terminological systems will not, of course, exhaustively reveal the cognitive world of its members, but it will certainly tap a central portion of it. Culturally significant cognitive features must be communicable between persons in one of the standard symbolic systems of the culture. A major share of these features will undoubtedly be codable in a society's most flexible and productive communication device, its language (Frake 1962:75, cf. Conklin 1962a, Goodenough 1957, Lounsbury 1963).

The main evidence for the existence of a category is the fact that it is named. As a result, the analyst faces the problem of locating *segregates* (segregate: "any terminologically-distinguished . . . grouping of objects," Conklin 1962a:120–21; Frake 1962:76). Much work on the "Sapir-Whorf hypothesis" has assumed that any morpheme, word, or grammatical construction labels a category of meaning, that the semantic structure of a language is built up only of these units. But it is clear that contrasting categories within a terminological system, and within a single level of a system, are frequently named with units whose positions in the strictly linguistic system vary markedly—morpheme, word, phrase, etc. (Conklin 1962a; Frake 1961, 1962; Lounsbury 1956:190–92). These labels of classificatory categories, whatever their grammatical status, have been called "lexemes." Alternatively, a lexeme is a "meaningful form whose signification cannot be inferred from a knowledge of anything else in the language" (Conklin 1962a:121; see also Weinreich 1963:145–46; Lamb's use of the term [1964] is nearly equivalent). Thus for example "stool" is a lexeme in English, and kwêi chêi ('stool') is a lexeme in Burmese labelling an approximately equivalent segregate, even though kwei ('dog') and chei ('leg(s)') are also nouns occurring independently as labels for other segregates. The analyst must differentiate between lexemes and other linguistic forms of similar grammatical status which do not serve as segregate lables. The solution of this problem depends partly on knowledge of the language, both comprehension of it and technical knowledge of its structure. Comprehension is required because translation prior to semantic analysis causes insuperable difficulties because of the incommensurability of the semantics of any two languages (Conklin 1962a:125–27 gives a nice example). Furthermore, in practice much of the best data comes from observing linguistic behavior outside the formal eliciting situation with an informant. One task of ethnoscience, in fact, can be viewed as the solution of the old problem of translation.

Knowledge of the linguistic structure is necessary because the category names belong to two systems, one linguistic and one nolinguistic; or, in Lamb's terms (1964), because lexemes are related by representation to both the morphemic and sememic strata. "While identity between the two planes is incomplete, it is a useful starting-point from which to describe the lack of isomorphism actually found" (Weinreich 1963:117). Lamb (1964: 62–66) catalogs the different possible discrepancies between units on different strata.

The many discussions within linguistics of the relevance of meaning to the analysis of phonology and grammar apply here also; even if form and meaning are in principle independent, or at least not isomorphic, and if (as some have maintained) an appeal to meaning is methodologically unsound in linguistic analysis, nevertheless the practice of linguistic field work has established that in order to get the job done within a reasonable time, on the basis of a corpus of practical size, it is essential to appeal to meaning in some manner—by the same or different test, the pair test, or some less explicit test where the linguist is analyzing his own native language (see Voorhoeve 1961:41–42 on the semantic element in such tests). The converse applies to ethnoscientific analysis: although the two systems are not entirely congruent, the overlap is sufficient so that an "appeal to linguistic form" is a very useful field technique in working out a terminological system. In fact, the development of ethnoscience will certainly eventually assist strict linguistics in handling the "problem of meaning."

Efforts to discover nonterminological systems in such areas as behavior units (Barker 1963; Barker and Barker 1961; Barker and Wright 1955), folktales (Lévi-Strauss 1955; Leach 1961c), and values (Kluckhohn 1956, 1958) have not employed rigorous, replicable procedures for identifying units without the application of criteria foreign to the cultures analyzed; in this regard they differ little from many previous ethnographies. These studies attempt to discover classifications without first establishing the communication systems by which they are transmitted.

Nonlinguistic communication systems are also structured. Birdwhistell's work with kinesics (1952) and Hall's with proxemics (the structuring of space in interpersonal relations) (1963a, 1963b) are concerned with establishing the units of the codes, and to some extent with discovering categories of meanings, but both jump to rather anecdotal cross-cultural comparisons before working out the structure of any one system. The nonisomorphism of sememic and lower strata can be expected to hold here also. Other communication systems are also relevant, including paralanguage (voice qualities and nonlinguistic vocalizations; see Trager 1958). Material culture resembles language in some important respects: some artifacts—for example, clothing—serve as arbitrary symbols for meanings (i.e., noniconic signs [Goodenough 1957]) and occur in a limited number of discrete units whose combinability is restricted. Possibly complex phenomena of esthetics would yield to a similar approach. Studies in these areas are potentially of much importance for ethnography, and it seems wise not to restrict the meaning of ethnoscience to the study of *terminological* systems.

4. Paradigms and Componential Analysis

A key concept in ethnoscience is that of the contrast set. This is a class of mutually exclusive segregates which occur in the same culturally relevant environment (setting, context, substitution frame, surroundings, situation, etc.). These segregates "share exclusively at least one defining feature"—

i.e., that which characterizes the environment in which they occur (Conklin 1962a:124; cf. Frake 1962:78–79). The domain of the set is the total range of meanings of its segregates.

The notion of contrast is relative to the environment within which it occurs. Thus the mutual exclusion in English between 'ant' and 'ship' (Conklin 1962a:127) or between 'hamburger' and 'rainbow' (Frake 1962: 79) is not contrast in this sense, because the environment which they share is not culturally relevant. As Frake (1962:79) puts it, "In writing rules for classifying hamburgers I must say something about hot dogs, whereas I can ignore rainbows. Two categories contrast only when the difference between them is significant for defining their use. The segregates 'hamburger' and 'rainbow,' even though they have no members in common, do not function as distinctive alternates in any uncontrived classifying context." Although 'ant,' 'ship,' 'hamburger,' and 'rainbow' are all 'things,' the sub-sets of 'things' to which they belong are so far removed from each other that these four segregates themselves are never distinctive alternates. Any culturally significant partitioning of 'things' would involve contrasts between segregates on a much higher level. Lower level environments are of primary importance—in this case, for example, the environment in which such segregates as 'hamburger,' 'hot dog,' and 'cheeseburger' contrast, and the environments in which such adjacent segregates as 'sandwich,' 'pie,' and 'something to eat' occur (Frake 1962:78–82).

One may conceive of a contrast set containing only one segregate; if, as seems likely, there are no complete synonyms, then every segregate does occur in an environment which no other segregate shares. But "contrast" implies that the set contain at least two segregates, and the term is normally understood in this way. Since these minimal two contrast in the same environment, each must have some unique feature of meaning.

A paradigm is a set of segregates which can be partitioned by features of meaning, i.e., a set some members of which share features not shared by other segregates in the same set (Chafe 1962; Conklin 1962a:132; Goodenough 1956a:197, 202; Lounsbury 1960:127–28, 1964a). A set of only two segregates can be considered a paradigm, but normally the term is applied to sets of three or more segregates, so that at least some of the sub-sets consist of two or more segregates sharing some feature of meaning.

It is important to note that while all contrast sets are paradigmatic, not all paradigmatic sets are *complete* contrast sets. A paradigmatic set may not be equivalent to its containing contrast set: it is possible to analyze paradigmatically a collection of items which do not *exclusively* share any feature, which do not exhaust the membership of a class occurring in a single environment (Conklin 1964). Thus Burling (1963a) has made a paradigmatic analysis of a set of "core kinship terms" which however do not form a complete contrast set—there is no culturally relevant environment which differentiates these terms from the other Garo kinship terms. A parallel example from phonology (where a paradigm involves phonetic rather than semantic features) is Chafe's (1962:338–39) paradigm of English consonant phonemes, which excludes some phonemes (*l*, *r*, perhaps also *y*, *w*, *h*) which are included in the relevant contrast set.

This difference between a paradigm and a contrast set is not always recognized in ethnoscientific work. Yet if the analysis is required to reflect the cognitive system of the bearers of the culture, before attempting a paradigmatic analysis one should show that one is dealing with a complete contrast set, that there is a culturally relevant environment in which all and only the segregates in the set occur. This is the problem of definition of domains seen from a somewhat different angle.

A componential analysis is an analysis of a paradigm in terms of the defining features, the "dimensions of contrast" or "criterial attributes" of the segregates in the set. The aim is to discover the "rules for distinguishing newly encountered specimens of [a] category from contrasting alternatives" (Frake 1962:83). The procedure is to search for the minimum features of meaning which differentiate segregates in the set. Each feature has two or more contrasting values, termed "components." Each segregate is then defined in terms of the presence or irrelevance of each component; i.e., a bundle of components defines the segregate. It is normally assumed that the number of componential dimensions will be smaller than the number of segregates they define. The paradigm may then be viewed as a multidimensional structure, in which the categories are placed according to the componential dimensions. (Useful references on componential analysis include Conklin 1962a, 1964; Frake, 1962; Wallace 1962; Lounsbury 1956, 1964a; Goodenough 1956a; Sebeok 1946; Chafe 1962. Lamb's [1964] sememes are similar to, if not identical with, the semantic components of these authors.)

There are two points of view regarding such componential analyses (Burling 1964). According to one of them, the componential analysis should reflect the classificatory principles utilized by the bearers of the culture, the components should be "cognitively salient"; such an approach has been labeled an aim for "psychological reality" (Wallace and Atkins 1960:64). However, this is a difficult requirement: such features are often not consciously formulated,[4] and furthermore different bearers of the same culture may utilize different features and yet share the same categories and communicate perfectly (Wallace 1962). The other position is what Wallace and Atkins (1960:64) refer to as an aim for "structural reality," and what Lounsbury (1964b) calls a "formal account." This position drops at this point the requirement that an ethnoscientific analysis should reflect the cognitive world of the bearers of the culture being analyzed. Having discovered the culturally significant sets and their included units, say these workers, we now try to determine the most economical componential analysis which will define (or "generate") their paradigmatic relationship—we are concerned only with predictability, economy, and inclusiveness, not any longer with cognitive saliency. Others take an intermediate position, and allow the use of hints from the culture in deciding between variant componential solutions which are equally or nearly equally economical—for there will often (if not always) be such variants, and furthermore the criterion of economy (simplicity, parsimony) is not an easy one to define and apply (see Wells 1963:42 on this last point). Romney and D'Andrade (1964) discuss this problem, and illustrate some testing procedures for determining the cognitive saliency of alternate componential analyses of the same set of terms. Cancian (1963) has illustrated another method, which may be used to evaluate a componential analysis of a multi-position classification. If it is possible to determine the position in this classification of some items whose exact position is not known to all informants familiar with the classification, the correctness of the components used in setting up the classification can be tested by means of the magnitude of informants' errors in placing items unknown to them. If errors are extreme, the classification is shown to be erroneously understood by the ethnographer. "When an informant makes an error that results from lack of precise information, he is most likely to approximate the truth in terms that are meaningful to him" (Cancian 1963:1073).

Weinreich (1963:148–49) points out that componential analysis is more appropriate in some domains than in others. In a given culture, some domains will be more highly patterned; in these, "distinguishing components recur in numerous sets of signs, [whereas] the bulk of the vocabulary is of course more loosely structured and is full of components unique to single pairs, or small numbers of pairs," of segregates. While componential analysis is still possible in these latter "non-terminologized fields," Weinreich suggests that the cognitive saliency of components will be greater in the more structured domains and the validity of the componential analysis can be more readily checked by informants' reactions in these domains.

It is important to note that not every componential analysis is ethnoscientific. Semantic and ethnoscientific studies have adapted the method from its use in another area, phonology (e.g. Harris 1944). When semantic componential analysis is applied to paradigms which are not complete contrast sets, the results are not strictly ethnoscientific. Furthermore, the method essentially amounts to focussing on the differentiating features of a classification rather than on its categories or pigeonholes. Hence any classification is amenable to analysis resembling a componential one, and the technique is very useful for extending and elaborating purely etic typologies having nothing to do with ethnoscience. Thus, for example, Pike (1943) was able to improve greatly on existing compendia of articulatory phonetics by attending to the distinctive features of previous phonetic typologies, and extending and recombining them to produce new phonetic types and a more logical classification. Similarly, Balfet (1952) produced the best available typology of basketry techniques by abstracting the components of previous classifications and re-arranging them to produce logical grids with many new classificatory slots, some of them as yet unknown in actual specimens even though fully possible. Malkiel (1962) describes a typology of dictionaries which explicitly borrows from the method of componential analysis.

5. *Taxonomies*

Different segregates within a folk classification may be related to each other in various ways: as part to whole, as sequential or developmental stage to stage, as different grades of intensity, etc. (Conklin 1962a:129, 1962b; Frake 1964). The kind of relationship between segregates which has so far received the most attention is that of inclusion; segregates related in this way form a taxonomy—a folk taxonomy in the case of folk classifications. In a taxonomy, there is a series of heirarchical levels, with each segregate at one level included in (only) one segregate at the next higher level. It is sometimes possible to analyze componentially a contrast set which forms one level of a folk taxonomy, but it is impossible to analyze in this way the whole taxonomy, even though the boundaries of the whole must define a domain: a single contrast set is limited to one taxonomic level (Conklin 1962a:128, 1964; Frake 1962).

A single folk classification may contain sets of segregates interrelated in different ways. From one point of view, any folk classification is a taxonomy since the domain or environment of the whole classification may be taken to define the most inclusive taxonomic level. But if the segregates within such a classification are not further related by inclusion, the taxonomy has only two levels and is relatively uninteresting as such; what is then more interesting is the kind of non-taxonomic relationship between the lower level segregates. A folk taxonomy of more than two levels, interesting as such, may also contain within it segregates which are interrelated in some nontaxonomic way (e.g., as developmental stages) which together form a domain which itself is placed within a taxonomic series.

Some attention has been devoted to folk taxonomies, particularly in ethnobotany, and the prospects are good for comparisons of folk taxonomic principles intra- and interculturally, but much of the methodology still requires attention. Further discussion will be found in Conklin's recent (1962a) excellent general treatment of folk taxonomies.

6. Discovery Procedures

Since the ethnoscientific method aims at discovering culturally relevant discriminations and categorizations, it is essential that the discovery procedures themselves be relevant to the culture under investigation. While arbitrary stimuli—i.e., stimuli foreign to the culture—may yield nonrandom responses, the patterning involved derives from the cognitive system of the bearers of the culture, and the principles of this system are not likely to be made clear by answers to the wrong questions. Regularities will appear if one measures continental European manufactured goods with an American or British yardstick, but measuring with a meter stick will much more readily reveal the principles of the system relevant in European culture.

If an ethnography is to reflect the cognitive system of the bearers of a culture, the validity of the description depends on the discovery procedures. Hypotheses must be checked in the field situation, and revised if they turn out not to fit the field data. Thus it is impossible to make a strictly ethnoscientific analysis of data previously collected, by oneself or by someone else, according to different procedures. Any componential or similar analysis made of such old data must be treated as an inadequately checked hypothesis. Structural restatements of even the best old field data may prove impossible. Lévi-Strauss illustrates some difficulties which

> result from our ignorance of the observations (real or imaginary), facts, or principles which inspire the [folk] classifications. The Tlingit Indians say that the wood worm is "clever and neat," and that the land-otter "hates the smell of human excretion." The Hopi believe that owls exert a favorable influence on peach trees. If these attributes were taken into account in placing these animals in a [folk] classification of beings and objects, one could search indefinitely for the key, were not these minute but precious indications furnished by chance (Lévi-Strauss 1962b:81, my translation).

Criterial attributes must be investigated in the field.

The general principle here is widely recognized, but only very recently has attention been devoted to making explicit the discovery procedures involved. Discussion and exemplification so far have concentrated on the use of questions in the native language and *chosen from the customary repertory* of the culture being studied. Frake's explication of interlinked topics and responses of queries in Subanun is an excellent example. His general suggestions on distinguishing questions which are appropriate to particular topics from those which are inappropriate (1964:143–144) should be particularly noted. Sarles (1963) describes a related procedure, in this case applied to Tzotzil, for identifying questions and their responses in conversational texts, determining acceptable permutations of the questions, and manipulating these to discover classes of appropriate responses. Metzger and Williams, in a series of papers as yet only partly published, have emphasized the discovery, selection, and use of question "frames" appropriate for eliciting specific folk classifications, particularly among the Tzeltal and Ladinos of Chiapas (Metzger 1963; Metzger and Williams 1962a, 1962b, 1962c, 1963a, 1963b). These papers are important particularly in that the frames utilized are explicitly stated, as a means of ensuring replicability and demonstrating the reliability of the analyses. Conklin (1964) has suggested some improvements in the genealogical method applicable to field studies of kinship systems, including the use of question frames, the recording of conversations in native settings,[5] and the use of "ethnomodels" or native metaphors and diagrams of classifications (including diagrams volunteered by informants to aid in explaining to the ethnographer and influenced by observation of the ethnographer's charting attempts).

The emphasis on the classes of responses elicited by appropriate questions is beginning to show the expectable extreme complexity of the cognitive map of any culture, with multitudinous interlocking and overlapping contrast sets. Even so, these papers concentrate on the discovery of categories and their significant environments; as yet insufficient attention has been devoted to the development of reliable techniques for elucidating the further underlying complexities in cognitively salient semantic components.

I have already mentioned the relevance of ethnoscientific methods to material culture, where the possibility of pointing to and manipulating concrete objects may partially replace the use of question frames and the reliance on terminological systems in eliciting significant categories and contrasts. Another area where similar comparison of concrete cultural manifestations may be possible is music. Recent published discussions by ethnomusicologists of their problems in developing appropriate notation systems imply, at least to a nonspecialist, that the etics in this field have developed to the point where the application of ethnoscientific methods would resolve many difficulties and lead to a true *ethno*-musicology (see Bright 1963:28–31).

Examples

Despite considerable discussion of ethnoscience in recent years, there have been relatively few applications of the methods in the only context in which they matter: intensive field work. This section provides an annotated bibliography of most but not all of the published or nearly-published ethnographic reports which qualify as ethnoscience, insofar as I am aware of them. I comment also on some publications which will not so qualify, but which are of interest in this connection because of similarities or contrasts in method or theory.

1. Pronominal and Case Paradigms

Analysis in terms of semantic components was first applied to paradigms of affixes, particularly to sets where the components are at least sometimes overt, i.e., components "with separate phonemic identities" (Lounsbury 1956:161–62; in Lamb's [1964] terms, where there is simple representation between the sememic, lexemic, and morphemic strata). In these instances, the contrast set is defined morphologically, in terms of its linguistic environment. The first development of the methods is due to Roman Jakobson, who applied them in an analysis of the semantic components of the Russian case system (Jakobson 1936). This was followed by Trubetzkoy's (1937) componential analysis of the Slovak case system (with some comparison of Slavic case systems on the same basis), and by Sebeok's (1946) analysis of the Finnish and Hungarian case systems and comparison of the structural principles of the two.

Lotz (1949) followed with an analysis of the Hungarian pronominal suffixes, which included a diagram exhibiting the suffixes in a structure whose dimensions consist of semantic oppositions. Wonderly, pointing out (in effect) that Sebeok's components are much less overt than Lotz's, analyzed the pronominal suffixes of two dialects of Quechua in terms of semantic components which are covert in that each morpheme is associated with two components, but where the distributional classes of the morphemes are associated with the components on a one-to-one basis (Wonderly 1952). In the use of distribution to validate the semantic components, Wonderly's treatment resembles Harris' (1948) analysis of the Hebrew pronominal paradigm—but Harris identified the components solely in terms of the shared linguistic environments of the morphemes, and did not attempt to identify shared features of meaning (Lounsbury 1956:162). D. Thomas (1955) gives a componential analysis of Ilocano pronouns which utilizes both semantic and distributional criteria. A similar analysis for another Philippine language, Maranao, is briefly outlined by McKaughan

(1959); but according to his analysis the forms are not affixes, yet he gives no evidence that the paradigm is a complete contrast set. A very similar componential structure is indicated for the pronominals of a third Philippine language, Hanunóo, where the morphemes are also not affixes; but Conklin (1962:134–36) is careful to demonstrate that the paradigm is a complete contrast set. He includes a dimensional diagram of the type introduced by Lotz (1949), as does Berlin (1963) in his componential analysis of Tzeltal pronominals (a more complex system than the Philippine ones), and Austerlitz (1959) in his componential analysis of Gilyak pronouns. In a footnote, Austerlitz (1959:104) notes the possibility of reducing the three pairs of oppositions of his analysis to two, by introducing a rule of order of application of the oppositions. The semantic components involved make clear the implications of an alternative application of forms glossed 'thou' and 'ye' in addressing a single person, and an alternative between 'he, she' and 'thou' in addressing one's spouse.

In a fascinating paper, Brown and Gilman (1960) have analyzed in detail a somewhat similar alternative in European languages (English, French, Italian, Spanish, and German; Slobin [1963] finds the analysis to be applicable to Yiddish also). They describe the rules for selecting, now and in the past, between the two singular pronouns normally glossed 'familiar' and 'polite.' There turn out to be a whole series of correlates of choice between the two, which Brown and Gilman reduce to two basic semantic binary oppositions, power or status (superior-inferior) and solidarity or intimacy (solidary-nonsolidary), discussing their association with features of social structure, political ideology, and affective style. The relationship between these dimensions is complex enough so that it would be difficult to diagram, and further complexities are introduced by ongoing changes which the authors demonstrate both by historical data and by data on individual variation in present usage. In another paper, Brown and Ford (1961) show the relevance of the same dimensions to choices between a variety of forms of address in modern American English which are not grammatically obligatory, unlike the pronouns previously analyzed (the dimensions governing the selection of pronouns are here said to hold for 20 languages of Europe and India, and for Japanese). Brown's emphasis on social correlates and his detailed examination of the semantic dimensions in various behavioral contexts might well be combined with a more explicitly componential analysis and more careful delimitation of domain boundaries. Probably some of Brown's methods are adaptable to the problem of determining the cognitive saliency of semantic components in this and similar domains. Brown alludes to some interconnections between usages of kinship terms and other terms of address. An approach similar to his might elucidate some of the semantic dimensions of choice between alternative or "variant" kinship terms, and it would be particularly interesting to apply similar techniques to the study of the complex and often interrelated kinship, status, and personal address terminological systems of Southeast and Eastern Asia (see Koentjaraningrat 1960:107–14, for an example).

2. Kinship Terminologies

Componential analysis was first applied to kinship terminologies in simultaneous and independent inventions by Ward H. Goodenough and Floyd G. Lounsbury in 1947–1949. In each case the breakthrough was the result of training by Murdock in the etics of kinship, plus thorough knowledge of descriptive linguistics (where componential analysis was then used in phonology), plus an acquaintance with the philosopher Charles W. Morris' work on the theory of signs. Both shared also some exposure to mathematics and learning theory (Lounsbury, in conversation, November, 1960). Goodenough published first, giving a methodological statement together with a componential analysis of the Trukese kinship terminology he had collected in the field (1951:103–10). In a pair of important papers appropriately published in a 1956 issue of *Language* dedicated to A. L. Kroeber, both authors set out careful theoretical and methodological treatments, Goodenough's illustrated by a revision of his Trukese analysis and Lounsbury's by a structural analysis of the Pawnee terminology collected by an Indian Agent in 1863 for Lewis Henry Morgan (Goodenough 1956a, Lounsbury 1956). Wallace and Atkins (1960) have analyzed and compared the methods of these two papers in some detail. An important difference not noted by Wallace and Atkins—although it is related to the problem of metaphors which they do discuss—is that Goodenough makes plain (more so in his earlier monograph [1951:103–107] than in his methodological paper [1956a]) that the paradigm he is analyzing is also a complete contrast set. He is able to do this because he was concerned while in the field with identifying the boundaries of the domain glossed 'kinship.' Lounsbury (1956), however, is not able to do this, since he is analyzing a set of terms collected long ago with unknown sampling procedures. He goes further, and explicitly excludes some of the terms listed by Morgan, making his selection on the basis of *a priori* criteria (1956:163).

Since these ground-breaking papers, a number of other kinship terminologies have been analyzed componentially, with variations in techniques of analysis, in methods of presentation, and in the extent of discussion of methodological problems. Conklin's unpublished Ph.D. thesis (1954:80) included a brief componential analysis of Hanunóo consanguineal terms of reference, influenced by Goodenough's monograph (1951) and by knowledge of Lounsbury's Pawnee analysis prior to its publication. Romney and Epling (1958) gave a componential analysis of Kariera kinship terminology, pointing out some of the behavioral correlates of the semantic features. Pospisil (1960) gave componential definitions for the Kapauku terminology, and followed this with a classification of the terms in an outline which has some of the characteristics of a key (cf. Conklin 1962b, 1964). Frake's treatment of Subanun kinship (1960:58–63) emphasizes the nonarbitrary delimitation of domains, the determination of complete contrast sets, the environmental features determining selection between alternative sets of terms, and the investigation of behavioral correlates of the kinship categories, as well as presenting a well-diagrammed componential analysis. Wallace and Atkins (1960) illustrate their theoretical discussion with a componential analysis of some American-English consanguineal terms of reference, admitting that for purposes of simplified illustration they use an arbitrarily delimited paradigmatic set.

Conant (1961) presented an interesting "componential comparison" of "Jarawa kin systems of reference and address," emphasizing eliciting procedures for maintaining the Jarawa distinctions between the two systems, pointing out that the system of address here involves "non-kin terms" ("which have meanings and usages not restricted to kinship") in the same contrast set with kin terms, and discussing problems of establishing the psychological reality of the componential analysis (including evaluation of disagreements between informants). One of his conclusions from the comparison is that the Jarawa address system has more behavioral correlates than the reference system. In contrast, Grimes and Grimes (1962) restrict their componential analysis of Huichol terminology to those terms of reference "that are amenable to simple structural statement" (1962:104). Yet within this arbitrary boundary, they are concerned with criteria of cultural relevance—for example, in setting up an unusual dimension of "distance from ego" because it accords well with some other characteristics of the social structure.

Epling (1961) published a detailed analysis of Njamal terminology, in which he assumed that his componential description is the psychologically real one. Burling (1962) challenged this assumption by presenting an alternative componential analysis of the same set of terms. He greatly simplified the componential formulae required, mainly by defining components specifically relevant to this system rather than following Epling (1961:155) in using only dimensions as defined by Kroeber (1909) plus one from Lounsbury (1956). Burling also discussed some of the problems in applying the criterion of economy in choosing between different componential analyses, and emphasized that this criterion, difficult as it is, is not the same as the criterion which demands cognitive saliency for a componential analysis. In a later paper using his own Garo data and influenced by recent developments in linguistics, Burling (1963) modified the usual procedures of componential analysis by selecting a set of "core terms" which are readily analyzable componentially, then using these terms "as building blocks to provide definitions for the remaining kinship terms used by the Garo," these latter being labelled "derived terms" (1963:80). He disavowed any implication of psychological reality for this scheme. A third paper combines the two points, in an analysis of Burmese kinship terminology (Burling 1965). Here he presents two full analyses of a set of referential terms, one of them componential in the usual sense, and the other using a method similar to the one he had previously applied to the Garo system. While Burling gives some evidence that certain features of the second analysis better reflect the Burmese cognitive system, he again disavows an interest in using this kind of criteria to choose between alternative analyses.

Lounsbury's recent work (1964a, 1964b) has concentrated on increasing the parsimony of componential analyses. The two papers cited deal with the Seneca consanguineal terminology (1964a) and with some general techniques for simplifying analyses by the application of "generative rules" resembling those used by Burling but more elegantly stated and of more general application. As before, Lounsbury is concerned with improving the logic of the analytical method. He does point out possible sociological correlates, but he views "formal accounts" such as his, which operate with criteria of parsimony and sufficiency, as logically prior to "functional accounts" (Lounsbury 1964b). The criterion of sufficiency requires that the analysis correctly account for all the empirical data in hand; but since the data he uses derive from fieldwork not oriented towards his problems (e.g., his Seneca data are largely from Lewis Henry Morgan) he cannot be certain that his paradigms represent complete contrast sets—thus the "root meaning" or common semantic feature defining the domain of a paradigm is that feature shared by all the forms of the set, but the additional phrase "and no others" which would define a complete contrast set is missing (Lounsbury 1964a)—and the adequacy of his analytical models is tested by their ability to account for data which is at least secondary as compared to the primary field data against which ethnographic theories should be tested if they are to be adequate cultural descriptions. There can be little doubt, however, that Lounsbury's improvements in analytical method will be very valuable to ethnographers interested in gauging the cognitive saliency of structural analyses: procedures for developing additional alternative models should help in discovering the one (or more than one) which is the most "real" for a given culture, and it is not difficult to conceive of cognitive saliency for generative rules such as Lounsbury's.

Furthermore, his models are already enabling him to devise ethnological typologies much more powerful than previous ones for cross-cultural comparisons of kinship terminologies and their correlates.

Romney and D'Andrade (1964) have again demonstrated the possibility of alternative componential analyses of the same paradigm—in this case, the restricted set of American-English terms previously analyzed by Wallace and Atkins (1960). The results of their testing of informants to determine the cognitive saliency of the variant analyses imply that it might be useful to use some such tests as an aid in the construction of models, rather than using tests to compare formal models previously devised.

Conklin (1964) emphasizes the desirability of combining "in actual field situations, recording activities, analytic operations, and evaluative procedures." The evaluative procedures on which he concentrates involve "the discovery of locally recognized contrasts, within recurrent ethnogenealogical settings." This paper is important for its many suggestions for methodological improvement, particularly in the development of more rigorous field techniques. It is illustrated by a detailed presentation of the Hanunóo kinship system as analyzed by these methods.

An advance in a new direction has been made by Friedrich (1963), who uses componential analyses to reconstruct the evolution of the Russian kinship system from the Proto-Indo-European period to the present, giving particularly detailed analyses of the Old Russian and Modern Russian terminologies. He demonstrates the advantages of such an approach over previous methods for reconstructing the history of kinship terminologies.

3. Color Terminologies

Useful contrasts with the problems of ethnoscientific analysis of kinship are provided by recent work on color terminologies. Some such domain is probably universal, but it is very clear here that domain boundaries vary from culture to culture. Conklin's analysis of Hanunóo color terminology (1955) provides a good starting point. Several features of this overly-brief account are too often overlooked: (1) The culturally relevant domain, for which Hanunóo lacks a covering lexeme, is *not* equivalent to that labelled "color" in English, since it involves semantic dimensions additional to those of hue, saturation, and brightness which delimit the domain in English; (2) This being the case, the basic structure of the terminological system would not have been discovered had the ethnographer restricted his investigation to the use of artificial stimuli such as color chips; (3) Discovery of the taxonomic nature of the system required observation of Hanunóo behavior in contrastive situations normal to them, (4) The "two levels" of contrast described for this system are relevant to it, not proposed as a cultural universal, and even the Hanunóo second, more specific, level (not here analyzed) is said to include several sublevels. The first two points particularly have not been attended to in other studies—including those which cite this paper as a model. Eliciting procedures such as those recommended by Ray (1952, 1953) and those used by Lenneberg and Roberts (1956), Landar, Ervin, and Horowitz (1960), and Goodman (1963) will not reveal such criterial attributes as moisture, surface texture, etc., as may exist (cf. Newman's remarks quoted by Lenneberg and Roberts 1956:23), nor will they make evident the nature of different coexisting systems which may occur (e.g., special color terminologies for horses in Navaho [Landar, Ervin, and Horowitz 1960:371 n. 12] and Papago [O'Neale and Dolores 1943], or for cattle in Nuer [Evans-Pritchard 1940:41–45]). Nevertheless, work to date provides nice illustrations of the cultural relativity of semantic distinctions. Taking only the spectral dimension of hue, the most central feature for cross-cultural equating of 'color' domains, one could now add Hanunóo (Conklin 1955), Navaho (Landar, Ervin, and Horowitz 1960), Malayalam (Goodman 1963), and perhaps Zuni (Lenneberg and Roberts 1956) to the chart Gleason (1955:4 and 1961:4) gives comparing the very different placement and number of basic categorizations made by English, Shona, and Bassa.

Probably color terminologies are everywhere taxonomies of at least three levels. The relation of inclusion which defines a taxonomy is well illustrated by the specific studies of Hanunóo, Navaho, and Malayalam. All have a domain 'color' (sometimes lacking a lexeme) at the most inclusive level, with a small number of basic or primary terms at "Level I," and with a great number of more specific terms, all included under one or another of the basic terms, at "Level II" (probably usually with further levels below this). However, the Zuni research did not investigate this point but evidently assumed that the artificial testing situation itself would elicit terms on the same taxonomic level; deductions as to probable primary terms in Zuni can be made from the data provided as to which terms were most frequently used, but neglect of levels of contrast certainly accounts for some of the variability between subjects in the Zuni experiments.

Conklin (1955) gives a componential analysis of the four Level I Hanunóo terms; the other authors are prevented from making such analyses by their concentration on contrasts along the dimension of hue. The Navaho study gives more detail than the others on more specific Level II color terminology and mentions several dimensions on this level, but does not analyze them componentially. One step which should now be taken is to investigate levels below the primary level in a folk taxonomy of color; it is evident that this will be a considerably more difficult task than the analysis of Level I terms.

The research of Lenneberg and others (Lenneberg 1961; Landar, Ervin, and Horowitz 1960; and references in both) on "color codability" has shown interesting variation between speakers of the same and of different languages in the extent of agreement on the application of terms to specific colors, on the width of overlap of terms measured against scaled stimuli, and on the relationship between the folk terminology and abilities to recognize and discriminate between colors. The domain would seem to be particularly useful for such tests of the effects of folk classification—culture—on behavior, because different areas of the same taxonomy vary in the extent to which individuals agree on categorization, and vary in the discreteness and degree of criteriality of semantic features, and because at least some of the distinguishing features are relatively easy to codify and display in testing materials.

4. Other Domains

It is instructive to compare what has been accomplished and what can be envisaged in the analysis of color terminologies with the possibilities in the domain of smell and taste. In these areas English has a relatively small and weakly terminologized vocabulary, and, particularly in comparison to color, the etics involved are very poorly known. Thus Aschmann (1946) lists a number of Totonac stems in a domain which may reasonably be glossed 'smell,' in the form of a taxonomy with eight primary categories each labelled with a basic root, with a quite vague characterization of the meaning of each of these eight roots. Each class is in turn subdivided by terms for more specific 'smells,' but the lack of relevant etics forces Aschmann to define each more specific term merely by listing objects characterized by that 'smell.' Each term on this lower level consists of the root labelling the higher class, plus an affix; these affixes recur with the different roots in the set, but the lack of etics prohibits the recognition of any features of meaning which may be associated with the affixes. It would be possible to determine, with informants, whether Aschmann's analysis represents a true folk taxonomy and whether this has more than three levels, but the lack of appropriate etics would make it exceedingly difficult if not impossible to identify criterial attributes.

A domain in which smells and tastes in turn might be expected to serve frequently as criterial attributes is that of cuisine. Lévi-Strauss' brief suggestion for the analysis of "gustèmes" (1958:99–100) influenced L.-V. Thomas (1960) in a description of the Diola cuisine. But this first attempt of any length must be said to have failed. Thomas listed and described the principal Diola recipes, but grouped them according to an arbitrary imposed scheme. He then took up the binary oppositions suggested by Lévi-Strauss, plus a few of his own, and applied them as *a priori* descriptive devices to the whole cuisine—without any effort to account exhaustively for the corpus he had just presented, and without any attempt to discover any Diola classifications of foods or recipes other than that implicitly recognized by his (incomplete) mention of Diola names for the recipes described. The oppositions were not even related to the distinctions between individual recipes. As Thomas remarks, it is surprising that more attention has not been devoted to cuisines by ethnographers. The domain should yield readily to an ethnoscientific approach.

Ethnobiology is frequently cited in illustration of ethnoscientific methods, particularly the study of folk taxonomies. A great deal of work in this field is partially relevant, in that it has frequently been realized (although also too often ignored) that the species and genus categorizations of other cultures normally do not coincide with those of Western science. A good example is Bulmer's (1957) discussion of bird naming practices among the Kyaka of the New Guinea highlands. He recognizes differences between the Kyaka and scientific classifications, but tends to assume, for example, that apparent synonymy represents ignorance or confusion without testing for levels of contrast or the effects of setting (he does note that names for hawks are more accurately—i.e., more consistently—applied to specimens seen in flight than to the rare specimens seen dead). Malkin's papers on the ethnozoology of the Seri, Sumu, and Cora (1956a, 1956b, 1958) are unusual in the attention devoted to the higher level taxa in the folk taxonomies, and to native knowledge of such subjects as the sex differentiation, development, and food habits of local animals. But Malkin's approach is to evaluate ethnozoological knowledge in terms of scientific zoology—to see whether the distinctions and characteristics known to scientific zoologists are locally recognized—rather than to investigate the nature and principles of the local systems of zoological knowledge. An early work which exhibits some of the same merits and faults, and is still worth attention for its detailed description of a system of ethnozoological knowledge, is that by Henderson and Harrington (1914).

Studies of any sort in ethnozoology are rare. There are, however, hundreds of publications relating to ethnobotany, which are emic or ethnoscientific in varying degrees (again, an unusually sophisticated early example must be credited to Harrington: Robbins, Harrington, and Freire-Marreco 1916). Despite the importance of the domain, the previous interest in the topic, the usual explicit taxonomic structure of the terminology, and the relative ease with which names may be tied to specimens and 'translated' into scientific terminology, there is only one full-scale ethnoscientific investigation of ethnobotany: that in Conklin's dissertation on the Hanunóo (1954). Some of this material as well as ethnoscientific analyses of many related domains appears in his monograph on Hanunóo agriculture (1957). But the analysis of the Hanunóo classification of plants together with the corpus of terms on which it is based, and a great deal of material on the significance of plants in other areas of Hanunóo culture, remain unpublished. Some illustrations taken from this research are presented in a methodological context in Conklin's recent paper on folk taxonomies (1962a).

Frake's ethnoscientific treatment of Subanun disease diagnosis (1961) is important as a demonstration of the utility of the new methods in a quite different domain, but even more so for its emphasis on ethnographic analytic techniques. The system is a multilevel taxonomy. Among the points taken up by Frake are problems involved in the extensive occurrence of the same term at different levels of contrast, the relation between hierarchic levels and sets consisting of stage names, and methods for the discovery of the significant attributes of categories via verbal descriptions (possible because other methods for learning distinctive features here are difficult for both Subanun and ethnographer). To explain why some areas of the Subanun folk taxonomy of diseases are more elaborated than others, Frake advances the general hypothesis that "the greater the number of distinct social contexts in which information about a particular phenomenon must be communicated, the greater the number of different levels of contrast into which that phenomenon is categorized" (1961:121).

In another ethnoscientific study of medicine, Metzger and Williams (1963a) have investigated several aspects of the roles of Tzeltal curers. Again, emphasis is placed on discovery procedures—in this case particularly question frames. One interesting feature of the Tzeltal situation is that while there are clear criteria for placing curers into two classes, one more highly valued than the other, these are not in general groups with fixed and widely recognized membership; yet the choice of a curer is clearly very important to the patient, and Metzger and Williams succeed in indicating how such choices are made.

The research of Barker and his coworkers in the "psychological ecology" of the "behavior systems" of American and English children (Barker and Wright 1955; Barker and Barker 1961; Barker 1963) converges in several respects with ethnoscience (awareness of the convergence is apparently one-sided: Barker *et al.* do not cite ethnographers or linguists, nor relevant work in systematic biology). These authors emphasize their concern with the inherent segments of the normally-occurring "stream of behavior," as opposed to the artificial "tesserae" into which behavior is segmented in more usual psychological investigations. They are interested in the discovery and analysis of natural "behavior units" and in the classification and interrelationships of such units, the identification and segmentation of their significant behavioral and nonbehavioral environments or "settings," and the relations between these environments and the behavior units. Their requirements for a "natural unit" are less stringent than those of ethnoscience: it is sufficient for them that the investigator does not himself influence the behavior he is observing, and that his segmentation is not entirely arbitrary. It is not required that the units be cognitively salient to the subjects. Thus, speaking of behavior settings, Barker and Barker (1961:467) write:

> Because the list of settings which we have identified reads, for the most part, like a common-sense directory of a town's businesses, organization meetings, school classes, and so forth, it is sometimes overlooked that their identification involves highly technical operations and precise ratings of interdependence. . . . . the precise quantitative criterion which we have used to establish the limits of behavior settings. . . . was selected so that the settings would fall within the usual range of laymen's discrimination. Nevertheless, the criteria for their identification are not lay criteria.

Reliability is measured by agreement between observers trained in the special analytical method, and while subjects are observed in detail, their own terminology for units of behavior or environment is not thoroughly investigated and their own perception of units is otherwise deemphasized. It is assumed that there is a "normal behavior perspective," i.e., a normal size for perceived units, which varies between subjects, rather than that the size of perceived units is determined by the environment (with variations in judgments on artificial questionnaires being more the result of varying interpretations of the directions given than of differences between individuals' behavior perspectives). The behavior units are not viewed as a separate system, a folk classification, which is actualized in the stream of behavior. Quite plainly, familiarity with the notions of contrast sets, and of levels of contrast, would be advantageous.

The "behavioral segments" investigated by Richard N. Adams in rural Guatemala (1962) superficially resemble Barker's "behavior units." But Adams' approach is explicitly ethnoscientific, he concentrates on local terminology as an indicator of "reported acts," and says his segments must be distinguished from the preceding and following phases of the continuum by formal attribute differences recognized by the actors. He is concerned also that the classification of these acts reflects the participants' cognition. Adams' early results indicate considerable success in identifying natural segments and their sequential arrangements; he recognizes the existence of unsolved problems in componential analysis (including that of the cognitive saliency of components).

O. E. Klapp (1962) has published an intriguing study of American "social types"—more than 800 "informal" roles which have explicit colloquial names. The domain makes good sense intuitively to an American.

Klapp fully recognizes that his social types represent a terminological folk classification specific to American culture, and he approaches a non-rigorous analysis of the semantic components involved. But he provides no explicit description of the boundaries of the domain, his higher level taxa are artificial rather than folk taxa, and he is little concerned with the structural relations between social types. While this folk classification is certainly more "weakly terminologized" than such domains as kinship or "institutionalized offices" (both excluded by Klapp), it seems probable that a more ethnoscientific approach, with attention to complementary distribution and levels of contrast, would show it to be more highly structured and more hierarchical than does Klapp's description.

I stop at this point, in the hope that sufficient examples have been given to illustrate the new approach; however, I do not mean to imply that there are not a number of other studies which are clearly ethnoscientific, and many more which are partially so.

Conclusions

It is claimed that ethnoscience is a general ethnographic method. It may be useful to indicate a few of the classical interests of ethnology to which the relevance of the new methods is already quite obvious. The measurement and significance of individual variation among bearers of a culture is touched on in ethnoscientific contexts by Frake (1964), Romney and D'Andrade (1964), and Metzger (1963), among others. Lévi-Strauss (1962a, 1962b) has devoted much attention recently to symbolism seen as the equating and movement between folk classifications in different domains. It seems likely that there are great differences between cultures in the pervasiveness of symbolic or metaphoric equation between folk classifications; the Dogon (Hopkins 1963; Griaule and Dieterlen 1954; Palau Marti 1957:53ff.) and the Ancient Chinese (Bodde 1939) seem to exhibit such symbolism to a higher degree than is indicated by the usual ethnographic literature for most other cultures. Perhaps this is best viewed as one aspect of the interlinking of domains noted by Frake (1964:140–141); the manner in which these networks may be revealed by Frake's interlinking queries promises to clarify some of the meanings of the concept of function in cultural analysis. Barnett's view of the process of innovation makes particularly obvious the relevance of ethnoscience to the study of culture change. He sees innovation as essentially a process of cognitive reorganization, where innovators substitute an element from one folk classification into another, and this often by a sort of idiosyncratic metaphorical equating of different domains (Barnett 1961; see Wallace 1961:ch. 4 for a critical expansion of this idea). Adams (1962), in a somewhat similar approach to culture change, is examining changes in the formal definitions and the frequency of occurrence of behavioral segments.

Ethnoscience raises the standards of reliability, validity, and exhaustiveness in ethnography. One result is that the ideal goal of a complete ethnography is farther removed from practical attainment. The full ethnoscientific description of a single culture would require many thousands of pages published after many years of intensive field work based on ethnographic methods more complete and more advanced than are now available. The emphases in ethnography will therefore continue to be guided by ethnological, comparative, interests. Some domains will receive more attention than others.

In the present state of interest in cross-cultural comparisons, continued ethnoscientific emphasis on domains such as kinship is assured. Existing generalizations require testing, and new theories require development, by the comparison of ethnographic statements which reveal the relevant structural principles. It is the classificatory principles discovered in ethnography which should be compared, not the occurrence of categories defined by arbitrary criteria whose relevance in the cultures described is unknown (cf. Goodenough 1956b:36–37).

But fuller development of ethnographic method and theory, and also intracultural comparisons to determine the "nature of culture" or the nature of cognition, the generality and interrelations of classificatory and other cognitive principles and processes within any one culture, both require that the New Ethnography be applied to a variety of domains, not just to areas of much current interest in ethnological theory.

Cross-cultural comparison of the logic of classification requires a great deal more knowledge of the varying logics of different domains in the same culture, as well as better ethnographies of different cultures.

> It is probable that the number, kind, and "quality" of these logical axes [of relations between classificatory categories] are not the same in different cultures, and that the latter could be classed as richer or poorer according to the formal properties of the reference systems they appeal to in erecting their classificatory structures. However even cultures less endowed in this respect operate with logics of several dimensions, of which the inventorying, analysis, and interpretation require a richness of ethnographic and general data which is too often lacking. (Levi-Strauss 1962b:85–86; my translation.)

Ethnoscientific work so far has concentrated on the sorts of cognitive structure involved in selection classes: the interrelations of categories considered as sets of possible alternatives under varying environmental conditions. Little attention has yet been paid to the methods required for the investigation of the sort of structures involved in rules of combination, the temporal or spatial ordering of co-occurring categories from different selection classes. To understand "how natives think"[6] we need to know about both kinds of structure.

Notes

1. In revising the original version of this paper I have profited greatly from the papers, discussion, and criticism presented by the other participants in the Conference on Trans-Cultural Studies of Cognitive Systems. I acknowledge also my debt to many discussions over several years with Harold C. Conklin, Charles O. Frake, Dell H. Hymes, and Floyd G. Lounsbury. Helpful written criticisms of the earlier version of this paper were provided by the editors, and by Conklin (at first from the field), Hymes, Richard N. Adams, Robbins Burling, Wallace L. Chafe, Paul Friedrich, Ward H. Goodenough, and Duane Metzger. I thank them all, and do not intend to commit any of them to agreement with everything said here.

2. I use the term cultural anthropology to include ethnology (of which social anthropology is one variety) and archeology. Obviously ethnology/social anthropology generalizes and typologizes on the basis of ethnographies, and it is a commonplace that archeology depends ultimately on ethnography for its cultural interpretations.

3. It is significant that Olmsted in a general survey of the relations between linguistics and ethnology made in 1950 envisaged nothing like the present adaptation of linguistic methods to ethnography.

4. I well remember once asking my father, a specialist on the taxonomy of the Diptera, how he could so readily identify Drosophila to the species in a glance at his collecting bottle. He replied, "How do you tell a horse from a cow?" The answer may at first seem surprising, coming from one intimately familiar with precisely those characters taxonomically significant for differentiating the species, but the situation is surely quite an ordinary one for biological systematists no less than for others.

5. Definitions of categories in response to an explicit question about classification may differ from the definitions implicit in the actual conversational use of the same categories. Thus I recently heard my sister's husband refer to my wife in speaking to a friend of his who does not know her; he said, "My sister-in-law is a good cook." I then asked him, "Do you call your wife's brother's wife your sister-in-law?" "No," he immediately replied, and remarked that he had done so "because it was easier than explaining."

6. The phrase is the translator's title of one of Lévy-Bruhl's books. But of course, as Lévi-Strauss stresses (1962b), "la pensée sauvage" is typical of us all.

References Cited

Adams, Richard N.
1962 The formal analysis of behavioral segments: A progress report. MS. read at the 61st Annual Meetings of the American Anthropological Association, Chicago, November 16, 1962.

Aschmann, Herman
1946 Totonac categories of smell. Tlalocan 2(2):187–189. Azcapotzalco, D. F., México.

AUSTERLITZ, ROBERT
1959 Semantic components of pronoun systems: Gilyak. Word 15(1): 102–109.
BALFET, HÉLÈNE
1952 La Vannerie: Essai de classification. L'Anthropologie 56(3–4):259–280.
BARKER, ROGER G., ed.
1963 The stream of behavior: Explorations of its structure & content. New York, Appleton-Century-Crofts.
BARKER, ROGER G. and LOUISE SHEDD BARKER
1961 Behavior units for the comparative study of cultures. *In* Studying Personality Cross-culturally, B. Kaplan, ed. New York, Row, Peterson, pp. 457–476.
BARKER, ROGER G. and HERBERT F. WRIGHT
[n.d.; 1955] Midwest and its children: The psychological ecology of an American town. Evanston, Row, Peterson.
BARNETT, H. G.
1961 The innovative process. Kroeber Anthropological Society Papers 25:25–42. Berkeley.
BEFU, HARUMI and EDWARD NORBECK
1958 Japanese usages of terms of relationship. Southwestern Journal of Anthropology 14(1):66–86.
BERLIN, BRENT
1963 A possible paradigmatic structure for Tzeltal pronominals. Anthropological Linguistics 5(2):1–5.
BERLIN, BRENT and A. KIMBALL ROMNEY
1964 Descriptive semantics of Tzeltal numeral classifiers. American Anthropologist 66(3) pt. 2:79–98.
BIRDWHISTELL, RAY L.
[n.d.; preface dated 1952] Introduction to kinesics: An annotation system for analysis of body motion and gesture. Louisville, University of Louisville.
BOAS, FRANZ
1911 Introduction. *In* Handbook of North American Indian Languages, part 1, Boas, ed. Bureau of American Ethnology Bulletin 40.
BODDE, DIRK
1939 Types of Chinese categorical thinking. Journal of the American Oriental Society 59(2):200–219.
BRIGHT, WILLIAM
1963 Language and music: Areas for cooperation. Ethnomusicology 7(1):26–32.
BROWN, ROGER and MARGUERITE FORD
1961 Address in American English. Journal of Abnormal and Social Psychology 62(2):375–385.
BROWN, ROGER and ALBERT GILMAN
1960 The pronouns of power and solidarity. *In* Style in Language, T. A. Sebeok, ed. Cambridge, Massachusetts, Technology Press of M. I. T.; New York, John Wiley, pp. 253–276.
BULMER, RALPH
1957 A primitive ornithology. Australian Museum Magazine 12(7): 224–229.

BURLING, ROBBINS

1962 A structural restatement of Njamal kinship terminology. Man 62:122–124 (art. 201).

1963 Garo kinship terms and the analysis of meaning. Ethnology 2(1): 70–85.

1964 Cognition and componential analysis: God's truth or hocus pocus. American Anthropologist 66(1):20–28.

1965 Burmese kinship terminology. American Anthropologist 67(5) pt. 2:106–117.

CANCIAN, FRANK

1963 Informant error and native prestige ranking in Zinacantan. American Anthropologist 65(5):1068–1075.

CHAFE, WALLACE L.

1962 Phonetics, semantics, and language. Language 38(4):335–344.

CHAO, YUEN REN

1956 Chinese terms of address. Language 32(1):217–241.

CONANT, FRANCIS P.

1961 Jarawa kin systems of reference and address; a componential comparison. Anthropological Linguistics 3(2):19–33.

CONKLIN, HAROLD C.

1951 Co-existing sets of relationship terms among the Tanay Tagalog. Unpublished MS., read at the 50th Annual Meetings of the American Anthropological Association, Chicago.

1954 The relation of Hanunóo culture to the plant world. Unpublished Ph.D. dissertation in anthropology, Yale University.

1955 Hanunóo color categories. Southwestern Journal of Anthropology 11(4):339–344.

1957 Hanunóo agriculture: A report on an integral system of shifting cultivation in the Philippines. FAO Forestry Development Paper No. 12. Rome, Food and Agriculture Organization of the United Nations.

1962a Lexicographical treatment of folk taxonomies. *In* Problems in Lexicography, F. W. Householder and S. Saporta, eds., Indiana University Research Center in Anthropology, Folklore, and Linguistics Publication 21 [and] International Journal of American Linguistics 28 (2) part 4, pp. 119–141.

1962b Comment [on Frake 1962]. *In* Anthropology and Human Behavior, T. Gladwin and W. C. Sturtevant, eds., Washington, Anthropological Society of Washington, pp. 86–91.

1964 Ethnogenealogical method. *In* Explorations in Cultural Anthropology: Essays in honor of George Peter Murdock. W. H. Goodenough, ed. New York, McGraw-Hill, pp. 25–55.

DUNDES, ALAN

1962 From etic to emic units in the structural study of folk-tales. Journal of American Folklore 75(296):95–105.

DURKHEIM, EMILE and M. MAUSS

1903 De quelques formes primitives de classification; contribution à l'étude des représentations collectives. L'Année Sociologique 6:1–72.

EPLING, P. J.

1961 A note on Njamal kin-term usage. Man 61:152–159 (art. 184).

EVANS-PRITCHARD, E. E.

1940 The Nuer: A description of the modes of livelihood and political institutions of a Nilotic people. Oxford, Clarendon Press.

FISCHER, J. L.

1958 The classification of residence in censuses. American Anthropologist 60(3):508–517.

FRAKE, CHARLES O.

1960 The Eastern Subanun of Mindanao. *In* Social Structure in Southeast Asia, G. P. Murdock, ed. Viking Fund Publications in Anthropology 29, pp. 51–64.

1961 The diagnosis of disease among the Subanun of Mindanao. American Anthropologist 63(1):113–132.

1962 The ethnographic study of cognitive systems. *In* Anthropology and Human Behavior, T. Gladwin and W. C. Sturtevant, eds. Washington, Anthropological Society of Washington, pp. 72–85, 91–93.

1964 Notes on queries in ethnography. American Anthropologist 66 (3) pt. 2:132–145.

FRENCH, DAVID

1963 The relationship of anthropology to studies in perception and cognition. *In* Psychology: A Study of a Science, vol. 6, S. Koch, ed. New York, McGraw-Hill, pp. 388–428.

FRIEDRICH, PAUL

1963 An evolutionary sketch of Russian kinship. Proceedings of the 1962 Annual Spring Meeting of the American Ethnological Society, pp. 1–26.

GLEASON, H. A., JR.

1955, 1961 An introduction to descriptive linguistics. 1st ed., New York, Henry Holt & Co., 1955; Rev. ed., New York, Holt, Rinehart & Winston, 1961.

GOODENOUGH, WARD H.

1951 Property, kin, and community on Truk. Yale University Publications in Anthropology 46.

1956a Componential analysis and the study of meaning. Language 32(2): 195–216.

1956b Residence rules. Southwestern Journal of Anthropology 12(1): 22–37.

1957 Cultural anthropology and linguistics. *In* Report of the 7th Annual Round Table Meeting on Linguistics and Language Study, Paul L. Garvin, ed. Monograph Series on Languages and Linguistics No. 9, Institute of Languages and Linguistics, Georgetown University, Washington, pp. 167–173. [Also published in Bulletin of the Philadelphia Anthropological Society 9(3):3–7, 1956, Philadelphia.]

GOODMAN, JOHN STUART

1963 Malayalam color categories. Anthropological Linguistics 5(5):1–12.

GRIAULE, MARCEL and GERMAINE DIETERLEN

1954 The Dogon. *In* African Worlds: Studies in the Cosmological Ideas and Social Values of African Peoples, Daryll Forde, ed. London, Oxford University Press for the International African Institute, pp. 83–110.

GRIMES, JOSEPH E. and BARBARA F.

1962 Semantic distinctions in Huichol (Uto-Aztecan) kinship. American Anthropologist 64:104–114.

HALL, EDWARD T.
1963a Field methodology in proxemics. Unpublished lecture before the Anthropological Society of Washington, March 19, 1963.
1963b Proxemics: The study of man's spatial relations. *In* Man's Image in Medicine and Anthropology, Iago Galdston, ed. Monograph IV, Institute of Social and Historical Medicine, The New York Academy of Medicine, New York, International Universities Press, Inc, pp. 422–445.

HARRIS, ZELLIG S.
1944 Simultaneous components in phonology. Language 20(4):181–205.
1948 Componential analysis of a Hebrew paradigm. Language 24(1): 87–91. (Reprinted on pp. 272–274 of Readings in Linguistics, 2nd ed., M. Joos, ed. New York, American Council of Learned Societies, 1958.)

HENDERSON, JUNIUS and JOHN PEABODY HARRINGTON
1914 Ethnozoology of the Tewa Indians. Bureau of American Ethnology Bulletin 56.

HOPKINS, NICHOLAS S.
1963 Dogon classificatory systems. Anthropology Tomorrow 9(1):48–54. Chicago.

HYMES, DELL H.
1964 Directions in (ethno-) linguistic theory. American Anthropologist 66(3) pt. 2:6–56.

JAKOBSON, ROMAN
1936 Beitrag zur allgemeinen Kasuslehre; Gesamtbedeutungen der russischen Kasus. Travaux du Cercle Linguistique de Prague 6 (Études dédiées au Quatrième Congrès de Linguistes):240–288. Prague.

KLAPP, ORRIN E.
1962 Heroes, villains, and fools: The changing American character. Englewood Cliffs, New Jersey, Prentice-Hall, Inc.

KLUCKHOHN, CLYDE K. M.
1953 Universal categories of culture. *In* Anthropology Today: An Encyclopedic Inventory, A. L. Kroeber, ed. Chicago, University of Chicago Press, pp. 507–523.
1956 Toward a comparison of value-emphases in different cultures. *In* The State of the Social Sciences, L. D. White, ed. Chicago, University of Chicago Press, pp. 116–132.
1958 The scientific study of values. *In* University of Toronto Installation Lectures: Three Lectures (by N. Frye, C. K. M. Kluckhohn, and V. B. Wigglesworth), Toronto, University of Toronto Press, pp. 26–54.

KOENTJARANINGRAT, R. M.
1960 The Javanese of south central Java. *In* Social Structure in Southeast Asia, G. P. Murdock, ed. Viking Fund Publications in Anthropology 29, pp. 88–115.

KROEBER, A. L.
1909 Classificatory systems of relationship. Journal of the Royal Anthropological Institute 39:77–84. [Reprinted on pp. 175–181 of Kroeber 1952.]
1952 The nature of culture. Chicago, University of Chicago Press.

LAMB, SYDNEY M.
1964 The sememic approach to structural semantics. American Anthropologist 66(3) pt. 2:57–78.

LANDAR, HERBERT J., SUSAN M. ERVIN, and ARNOLD E. HOROWITZ

1960 Navaho color categories. Language 36(3):368–382.

LEACH, E. R.

1961a Pul Eliya, a village in Ceylon. Cambridge, University Press.

1961b Rethinking anthropology. London School of Economics Monographs on Social Anthropology 22.

1961c Lévi-Strauss in the Garden of Eden: An examination of some recent developments in the analysis of myth. Transactions of the New York Academy of Sciences, ser. 2, 23(4):386–396.

LENNEBERG, ERIC H.

1961 Color naming, color recognition, color discrimination: A re-appraisal. Perceptual and Motor Skills 12(3):375–382. Missoula, Montana.

LENNEBERG, ERIC H. and JOHN M. ROBERTS

1956 The language of experience; a study in methodology. Indiana University Publications in Anthropology and Linguistics 13 [and] International Journal of American Linguistics Memoir 13.

LÉVI-STRAUSS, CLAUDE

1955 The structural study of myth. Journal of American Folklore 68(270):428–444.

1958 Anthropologie structurale. Paris, Plon.

1962a Le Totémisme aujourd'hui. Paris, Presses Universitaires de France.

1962b La Pensée sauvage. Paris, Plon.

LEWIS, LIONEL S.

1963 Kinship terminology for the American parent. American Anthropologist 65(3):649–652.

LOTZ, JOHN

1949 The semantic analysis of the nominal bases in Hungarian. Travaux du Cercle Linguistique de Copenhague 5:185–197. Copenhagen.

LOUNSBURY, FLOYD G.

1956 A semantic analysis of the Pawnee kinship usage. Language 32(1):158–194.

1960 Similarity and contiguity relations in language and in culture. *In* Report on the 10th Annual Round Table Meeting on Linguistics and Language Studies, Richard S. Harrell, ed. Georgetown University Monograph Series on Languages and Linguistics, No. 12. Washington, pp. 123–128.

1963 Linguistics and psychology. *In* Psychology: A Study of a Science, vol. 6, S. Koch, ed. New York, McGraw-Hill, pp. 552–582.

1964a The structural analysis of kinship semantics. *In* Proceedings of the Ninth International Congress of Linguists, Horace B. Lunt, ed., The Hague, Mouton & Co., pp. 1073–1090.

1964b A formal account of the Crow- and Omaha-type kinship terminologies. *In* Explorations in Cultural Anthropology: Essays in honor of George Peter Murdock, W. H. Goodenough, ed. New York, McGraw-Hill, pp. 351–393.

MALINOWSKI, BRONISLAW

1922 Argonauts of the Western Pacific. London, George Routledge & Sons, Ltd.

MALKIEL, YAKOV

1962 A typological classification of dictionaries on the basis of distinctive features. *In* Problems in Lexicography, Fred W. Householder and Sol Saporta, eds., Indiana University Research Center in Anthropology, Folklore, and Linguistics Publication 21 [and] International Journal of American Linguistics 28(2), part 4, pp. 3–24.

MALKIN, BORYS

1956a Seri ethnozoology: A preliminary report. Davidson Journal of Anthropology 2(1): 73–83. Seattle.

1956b Sumu ethnozoology: Herpetological knowledge. *Ibid.* 2(2): 165–180.

1958 Cora ethnozoology, herpetological knowledge; a bioecological and cross cultural approach. Anthropological Quarterly 31(3):73–90. Washington.

MCKAUGHAN, HOWARD P.

1959 Semantic components of pronoun system: Maranao. Word 15(1): 101–102.

METZGER, DUANE

1963 Some ethnographic procedures. MS. read at annual meeting of Southwestern Anthropological Association, Riverside, California, April 11–13.

METZGER, DUANE and GERALD WILLIAMS

1962a The patterns of primary personal reference in a Tzeltal community. Unpublished paper, Anthropology Research Projects, Preliminary Report, Stanford.

1962b Procedures and results in the study of native cognitive systems: Tzeltal firewood. Unpublished paper, Anthropology Research Projects, Preliminary Report, Stanford.

1962c Tenejapa medicine II: Sources of illness. Unpublished paper, Anthropology Research Projects, Preliminary Report, Stanford.

1963a Tenejapa medicine I: The curer. Southwestern Journal of Anthropology 19(2):216–34.

1963b A formal ethnographic analysis of Tenejapa Ladino weddings. American Anthropologist 65(5), pp. 1076–1101.

MURDOCK, GEORGE PETER

1945 The common denominator of cultures. *In* The Science of Man in the World Crisis, Ralph Linton, ed. New York, Columbia University Press, pp. 123–142.

1953 The processing of anthropological materials. *In* Anthropology Today, A. L. Kroeber, ed. Chicago, University of Chicago Press, pp. 476–487.

1957 World ethnographic sample. American Anthropologist 59:664–87.

NEEDHAM, RODNEY

1962 Notes on comparative method and prescriptive alliance. Bijdragen tot de Taal-, Land- en Volkenkunde 118(1) (Anthropologica 3):160–82. 's-Gravenhage.

NORBECK, EDWARD

1963 Lewis Henry Morgan and Japanese terms of relationship: Profit through error. Southwestern Journal of Anthropology 19(2):208–15.

NORTHROP, F. S. C.

1947 The logic of the sciences and the humanities. New York, Macmillan.

ÖHMAN, SUZANNE

1953 Theories of the "linguistic field." Word 9(2):123–34.

OLMSTED, DAVID L.

1950 Ethnolinguistics so far. Studies in Linguistics, Occasional Papers 2. Norman, Oklahoma.

O'Neale, Lila M. and Juan Dolores
1943 Notes on Papago color designations. American Anthropologist 45(3):387–97.

Palau Marti, Montserrat
1957 Les Dogon. [Ethnographic Survey of Africa, Western Africa, French Series, No. 4.] Paris, Presses Universitaires de France [for the] Institut International Africain.

Pike, Kenneth L.
1943 Phonetics: A critical analysis of phonetic theory and a technic for the practical description of sounds. University of Michigan Publications, Language and Literature vol. 21.
1954 Emic and etic standpoints for the description of behavior. *In* his Language in Relation to a Unified Theory of the Structure of Human Behavior, Part I, Preliminary Edition. Glendale, Summer Institute of Linguistics, pp. 8–28.

Pospisil, Leopold
1960 The Kapauku Papuans and their kinship organization. Oceania 30(3):188–205.

Ray, Verne F.
1952 Techniques and problems in the study of human color perception. Southwestern Journal of Anthropology 8(3):251–259.
1953 Human color perception and behavioral response. Transactions of the New York Academy of Sciences, ser. 2, 16(2):98–104.

Robbins, Wilfred William, John Peabody Harrington, and Barbara Freire-Marreco
1916 Ethnobotany of the Tewa Indians. Bureau of American Ethnology Bulletin 55.

Romney, A. Kimball and Roy Goodwin D'Andrade
1964 Cognitive aspects of English kin terms. American Anthropologist 66(3) pt. 2:146–170.

Romney, A. Kimball and Philip J. Epling
1958 A simplified model of Kariera kinship. American Anthropologist 60(1):59–74.

Roth, Walter E.
1897 Ethnological studies among the north-west-central Queensland aborigines. Brisbane, Edmund Gregory; and London, Queensland Agent-General's Office.

Sarles, Harvey B.
1963 The question-response system in language. Manuscript.

Schneider, David M. and George C. Homans
1955 Kinship terminology and the American kinship system. American Anthropologist 57(6):1194–1208.

Sebeok, Thomas A.
1946 Finnish and Hungarian case systems: Their form and function. Acta Instituti Hungarici Universitatis Holmiensis, Series B, Linguistica 3. Stockholm.

Simpson, George Gaylord
1961 Principles of animal taxonomy. New York, Columbia University Press.

Slobin, Dan I.
1963 Some aspects of the use of pronouns of address in Yiddish. Word 19(2):193–202.

SPAULDING, ALBERT C.
1963 The course of anthropological research as viewed from the National Science Foundation. Unpublished paper, read before the annual meeting of the Central States Anthropological Society, Detroit, Michigan, May 17.
SPUHLER, J. N.
1963 *Review of* Mankind Evolving by Th. Dobzhansky. American Anthropologist 65(3):683–84.
SWARTZ, MARC J.
1960 Situational determinants of kinship terminology. Southwestern Journal of Anthropology 16(4):393–97.
THOMAS, D.
1955 Three analyses of the Ilocano pronoun system. Word 11(2):204–208.
THOMAS, L.-V.
1960 Essai d'analyse structurale appliquée à la cuisine diola. Bulletin de l'Institut Français d'Afrique Noire, sér. B, 22(1–2):328–345.
TRAGER, GEORGE L.
1958 Paralanguage: A first approximation. Studies in Linguistics 13(1–2):1–12. Buffalo.
TRUBETZKOY, N. S.
1937 Gedanken über die slovakische Deklination. Sborník Matice Slovenskej 15:39–47. [Not seen.]
TYLOR, EDWARD B.
1881 Anthropology, an introduction to the study of man and civilization. New York, D. Appleton & Co.
VOEGELIN, CHARLES F. and FLORENCE M. VOEGELIN
1957 Hopi domains; a lexical approach to the problem of selection. Indiana University Publications in Anthropology and Linguistics 14 [and] International Journal of American Linguistics Memoir 14.
VOORHOEVE, JAN
1961 Linguistic experiments in syntactic analysis. *In* Creole Language Studies No. II, Proceedings of the Conference on Creole Language Studies . . . , R. B. Le Page, ed. London, Macmillan & Co., Ltd., pp. 37–60.
WALLACE, ANTHONY F. C.
1961 Culture and personality. Studies in Anthropology [1], New York, Random House.
1962 Culture and cognition. Science 135(3501):351–57.
WALLACE, ANTHONY F. C. and JOHN ATKINS
1960 The meaning of kinship terms. American Anthropologist 62(1):58–80.
WEINREICH, URIEL
1963 On the semantic structure of language. *In* Universals of Language, Joseph H. Greenberg, ed. Cambridge, Massachusetts, The M. I. T. Press, pp. 114–171.
WELLS, RULON
1963 Some neglected opportunities in descriptive linguistics. Anthropological Linguistics 5(1):38–49.
WONDERLY, WILLIAM L.
1952 Semantic components in Kechua person morphemes. Language 28(3):366–376.

9 CATEGORIES AND COGNITION

Jerome S. Bruner, Jacqueline J. Goodnow, and George A. Austin

Chapter 8 surveyed studies in ethnoscience. This chapter focuses in detail upon the nature and function of categories. Chapter 10 discusses an explicit methodology for the study of a culture's terminological systems. If there is one core idea in ethnoscience that emerges again and again in each of these chapters, it is the *category*. Lexemes are the names given to categories; taxonomies are one way they are arranged; their properties are called attributes; domains are very large ones; rules are instructions for what to include in them; and using categories is a universal process of human cognition. There are other names for the category; it is a group, a set, a concept, and a collection. It is a plurality which is treated as if it were singular.

In the following discussion the authors examine the various facets of this amazing cognitive element. They categorize it, show how new ones are invented in each society, and examine the way categories guide the behavior of scientist and layman, alike. An understanding of categories and the cognitive processes related to their use is essential for the study of cultural knowledge.—EDITOR'S NOTE

We begin with what seems a paradox. The world of experience of any normal man is composed of a tremendous array of discriminably different objects, events, people, impressions. There are estimated to be more than seven million discriminable colors alone, and in the course of a week or two we come in contact with a fair proportion of them. No two people we see have an identical appearance and even objects that we judge to be the same object over a period of time change appearance from moment to moment with alterations in light or in the position of the viewer. All of these differences we are capable of seeing, for human beings have an exquisite capacity for making distinctions.

Reprinted from *A Study of Thinking* by Jerome S. Bruner, Jacqueline J. Goodnow, and George A. Austin, pp. 1–22, by permission of the senior author and the publisher.

But were we to utilize fully our capacity for registering the differences in things and to respond to each event encountered as unique, we would soon be overwhelmed by the complexity of our environment. Consider only the linguistic task of acquiring a vocabulary fully adequate to cope with the world of color differences! The resolution of this seeming paradox—the existence of discrimination capacities which, if fully used, would make us slaves to the particular—is achieved by man's capacity to categorize. To categorize is to render discriminably different things equivalent, to group the objects and events and people around us into classes, and to respond to them in terms of their class membership rather than their uniqueness. Our refined discriminative activity is reserved only for those segments of the environment with which we are specially concerned. For the rest, we respond by rather crude forms of categorial placement. In place of a color lexicon of seven million items, people in our society get along with a dozen or so commonly used color names. It suffices to note that the book on the desk has a "blue" cover. If the task calls for finer discrimination, we may narrow the category and note that it is in the class of things called "medium blue." It is rare indeed that we are ever called upon to place the book in a category of colors comprising *only* the unique hue-brightness-saturation combination it presents.

The process of categorizing involves, if you will, an act of invention. This hodgepodge of objects is comprised in the category "chairs," that assortment of diverse numbers is all grouped together as "powers of 2," these structures are "houses" but those others are "garages." What is unique about categories of this kind is that once they are mastered they can be used without further learning. We need not learn *de novo* that the stimulus configuration before us is another house. If we have learned the class "house" as a concept, new exemplars can readily be recognized. The category becomes a tool for further use. The learning and utilization of categories represents one of the most elementary and general forms of cognition by which man adjusts to his environment. It was in this belief that the research reported in this volume was undertaken. For it is with the categorizing process and its many ramifications that this book is principally concerned.

Identity and Equivalence Categories

The full moon, the moon in quarter, and the crescent moon all evoke the same nominative response, "moon." From a common response made by a person to an array of objects we infer that he "has" an equivalence or identity category. The similar responses from which we draw such an inference need not be verbal. An air-raid siren, a dislodged piton while climbing, and a severe dressing-down by a superior may all produce a common autonomic response in a man and by this fact we infer that they are all grouped as "danger situations." Indeed, the person involved may not be able to verbalize the category. While this is in itself interesting, it is not crucial to our point, which is simply that an equivalence range is inferred from the presence of a common response to an array of discriminably different events. This leaves many technical questions unsettled (cf. Klüver, 1933), but it serves to get the inquiry under way.

Two broad types of categorizing responses are obviously of interest. One of them is the identity response, the other the equivalence response, and each points to a different kind of category.

Without belaboring the obvious, identity categorization may be defined as classing a variety of stimuli as *forms of the same thing.* What lies behind the identity response is not clear, save that it is obviously a response that is affected by learning. It does not do to say simply that an object is seen as the identical object on a later encounter if it has not "changed its characteristics too much." The moon in its phases varies from a sliver to a circle, in color from luminous white to the bronzed hunter's moon. Sheldon (1950) collected a series of photographs of the same individual over a period of 15 years, the person standing in the same position against a uniform background. The photographs span the period from early boyhood to full manhood. As one riffles through the stack, there is a strong and dramatic impression of the identical person in the process of growth. Yet the pictures go through a drastic metamorphosis. Because such identity responses are ubiquitous and because they are learned very early in life, we tend to regard them somehow as a different process from other forms of categorizing —the recognition of two different people as both being people. Yet both depend upon what Michotte (1950) speaks of as the presence of a *cachet spécifique* or essential quality. They are both forms of categorizing. What differs is the nature of the inference: in the one case we infer "identity" from the presence of the *cachet,* in the other case "equivalence."

How one comes to learn to categorize in terms of identity categories is, as we have said, little understood. Too often we have succumbed to the Kantian heritage and taken identity categories as given. Piaget's recent work (1953) and the work of Michotte (1946) leave the question open. Piaget speaks of the learning of identity as corresponding to the mastery of a principle of conservation as in the conservation of energy in physics. At certain stages of development, an object passed behind a screen is not judged by the child to be the same object when it emerges on the other side. Hebb (1949) proposes that certain forms of neural growth must precede the capacity for the maintenance of identity. Whether the capacity is "innate" and then developed by being extended to new ranges of events or whether the capacity to recognize identity is itself learned is not our concern here. It suffices to note that its development depends notably upon learning.

That there is confusion remaining in the adult world about what constitutes an identity class is testified to by such diverse proverbs as *plus ça change, plus la même chose* and the Heraclitan dictum that we never enter the same river twice. Indeed, in severe psychotic turmoil one sometimes notes an uncertainty about the identity category that is the "self" in states of depersonalization, and a rather poignant reminder that the identity of self is even equivocal in normal states is provided by the sign behind a bar in the Southwest:

I ain't what I've been.
I ain't what I'm going to be.
I am what I am.

We speak of an equivalence class when an individual responds to a set of discriminably different things as the *same kind of thing or as amounting to the same thing.* Again we depend for our knowledge of the existence of a category upon the presence of a common response. While there is a striking phenomenological difference between identity and equivalence, both depend upon the acceptance of certain properties of objects as being criterial or relevant—again Michotte's *cachet spécifique*—and others as being irrelevant. One may distinguish three broad classes of equivalence categories, each distinguished by the kind of defining response involved. They may be called *affective, functional,* and *formal* categories.

Certain forms of grouping appear to depend very heavily upon whether or not the things placed in the same class evoke a common affective response. A group of people, books, weather of a certain kind, and certain states of mind are all grouped together as "alike," the "same kind of thing." Further inquiry may reveal that all of them were experienced during a particularly poignant summer of childhood. What holds them together and what leads one to say that some new experience "reminds one of such and such weather, people, and states" is the evocation of a defining affective response.

Characteristically, categories marked by an affective defining response are not amenable to ready description in terms of the properties of the objects comprising them. The difficulty appears to lie in the lack of correspondence between affective and linguistic categories. As Schachtel (1947) and McClelland (1951) have suggested, categories bound together by a common affective response frequently go back to early childhood and may resist conscious verbal insight by virtue of having been established before the full development of language. For categorizing activity at the preverbal stage appears to be predominantly nonrepresentational, depending not so much on the common external properties of objects as on the relation of things encountered to internal needs, to follow Piaget's argument (1951), or, to follow Schachtel's, on idiosyncratic and highly personalized impressions. Dollard and Miller (1950) argue persuasively that much of psychotherapy consists of the verbal labelling and resorting of such preverbal categories, so that they may become more accessible to the forms of symbolic or linguistic manipulation characteristic of adult problem-solving. Indeed, it is not difficult to imagine that the effectiveness of poetry often rests on its ability to cut across our conventional linguistic categories in a way evocative of more affective categorizations. Archibald MacLeish (1939) catches well this esthetic need for freedom from conventional verbal categories in his lines,

> A poem should be palpable and mute
> As a globed fruit
> Dumb
> As old medallions to the thumb
> Silent as the sleeve-worn stone
> Of casement ledges where the moss has grown—
> A poem should be wordless
> As the flight of birds.

The problems of specifying the properties of objects that mediate a common categorizing response become less arduous when the category is a functional or utilitarian one. Rather than an internal state rendering a group of things equivalent, now equivalence is based on an external function. The objects of a functional category fulfill a concrete and specific task requirement—"things large enough and strong enough to plug this hole in the dike." Such forms of defining response almost always have, as Bartlett (1951) suggests, a specific interpolative function ("gap filling") or a specific extrapolative function ("how to take the next step"). The experiments by Maier (1930, 1931, 1945) represent an outstanding instance of research on the conditions which facilitate and inhibit the recognition of "requirements" necessary for correct identification of an object as fulfilling specific functions in a particular task situation, such situations, for example, as how to bridge a gap between two objects given certain limits and certain properties in the materials provided.

Formal categories are constructed by the act of specifying the intrinsic attribute properties required by the members of a class. Such categories have the characteristic that one can state reliably the diacritica of a class of objects or events short of describing their use. The formal properties of science are a case in point. Oftentimes the careful specification of defining properties even requires the constructions of special "artificial" languages to indicate that common-sense functional categories are not being used. The concept "force" in physics and the word standing for the functional class of events called "force" in common sense do not have the same kind of definition. What is accomplished in effect by formal categories is that one is able to devise classes whose defining properties are not determined by the suitability of objects to a specific task. The emphasis of definition is placed more and more on the attribute properties of class members and less and less on "utilitanda properties," to borrow a term from Tolman (1932). The development of formalization is gradual. From "things I can drive this tent stake with" we move to the concept "hammer" and from there to "mechanical force," each step being freer of definition by specific use than the former.

The development of formal categories is, of course, tantamount to science-making and we need not pause here to discuss this rather impenetrable problem. It suffices to note that formal categories and formal category systems appear to develop concurrently with methods for representing and manipulating them symbolically. What impels one to formalization we cannot say. That the urge is strong is unquestionable. Indeed, it is characteristic of highly elaborated cultures that symbolic representations of formal categories and formal category systems are eventually developed without reference to the classes of environmental events that the formal categories "stand for." Geometry provides a case in point, and while it is true that its original development was contingent upon the utilitarian triangulation systems used for redividing plots after floods in the Nile Valley, it is now the case that geometers proceed without regard for the fit of their formal categories to specific empirical problems.

It is obvious that there are close relationships between affective, functional, and formal categories and that they are often convertible one into the other. About the conversion of functional categories into formal ones—finally rendering the category of "things good for postpartum mothers" such as ground bone and certain chalks into the formal class "calcium"—we have already taken some notice. It is interesting that the gifted mathematician often speaks of certain formal categories in terms that are also affective in nature. G. H. Hardy in his delightful "apology" (1940) speaks of the class of things known as "elegant solutions" and while these may have formal properties they are also marked by the fact that they evoke a commmon affective response. The distinction between the three types is, we would suggest, a useful one and it may well be that the process whereby they are learned is informatively different. It is suggestive, for example, that the brain-injured patients described by writers like Goldstein (1940) and Head (1926) seem quite capable of utilizing functional categories but are precipitated into a crisis when faced with the need of locating or forming or using categories divorced from the immediate function to be served by their exemplars.

The Invention of Categories

To one raised in Western culture, things that are treated as if they were equivalent seem not like man-made classes but like the products of nature. To be sure, the defining criteria in terms of which equivalence classes are formed exist in nature as potentially discriminable. Rocks have properties that permit us to classify them as rocks, and some human beings have the features that permit us to categorize them as handsome. But there exists a near infinitude of ways of grouping events in terms of discriminable properties, and we avail ourselves of only a few of these.

Our intellectual history is marked by a heritage of naive realism. For Newton, science was a voyage of discovery on an uncharted sea. The objective of the voyage was to discover the islands of truth. The truths existed in nature. Contemporary science has been hard put to shake the yoke of this dogma. Science and common-sense inquiry alike do not discover the ways in which events are grouped in the world; they invent ways of grouping. The test of the invention is the predictive benefits that result from the use of invented categories. The revolution of modern physics is as much as anything a revolution against naturalistic realism in the name of a new nominalism. Do such categories as tomatoes, lions, snobs, atoms, and mammalia exist?In so far as they have been invented and found applicable to instances of nature, they do.[1] They exist as inventions, not as discoveries.

Stevens (1936) sums up the contemporary nominalism in these terms: "Nowadays we concede that the purpose of science is to invent workable descriptions of the universe. Workable by whom? By us. We invent logical systems such as logic and mathematics whose terms are used to denote discriminable aspects of nature and with these systems we formulate descriptions of the world as we see it and according to our convenience. We work in this fashion because there is no other way for us to work" (p. 93). Because the study of these acts of invention is within the competence of the psychologist, Stevens calls psychology "the propadeutic science."

The recognition of the constructive or invented status of categories changes drastically the nature of the equivalence problem as a topic for psychological research. The study of equivalence becomes, essentially, a study of coding and recoding processes employed by organisms who have past histories and present requirements to be met. The implicit assumption that psychological equivalence was somehow determined by the "similarity" or "distinctive similarity" of environmental events is replaced by the view that psychological equivalence is only limited by and not determined by stimulus similarity. The number of ways in which an array of events can be differentiated into classes will vary with the ability of an organism to abstract features which some of the events share and others do not. The features available on which to base such categorial differentiation, taken singly and in combination, are very numerous indeed. As Klüver (1933) so well put it more than two decades ago, the stimulus similarity that serves as a basis for grouping is a selected or abstracted similarity. There is an act of rendering similar by a coding operation rather than a forcing of equivalence on the organism by the nature of stimulation.

Two consequences immediately become apparent. One may ask first what are the preconditions—situational and in the past history of the organism—that lead to one kind of grouping rather than another. The characteristic forms of coding, if you will, now become a dependent variable worthy of study in their own right. It now becomes a matter of interest to inquire what affects the formation of equivalence classes or systems of equivalence coding. The second consequence is that one is now more tempted to ask about systematic individual and cultural difference in categorizing behavior. In so far as each individual's milieu and each culture has its own vicissitudes and problems, might one not expect that this would reflect itself in the characteristic ways in which members of a culture will group the events of their physical and social environment? And, moreover, since different cultures have different languages, and since these languages code or categorize the world into different classes, might it not be reasonable to expect some conformance between the categories normally employed by speakers and those contained in the language they use?

Consider now the scope of the problem, the generality of categorizing, and the benefit to be derived from studying its various manifestations.

The Generality of Categorizing

The first benefit to be derived from a closer study of categorizing behavior is a gain in generality for psychological theory. Categorizing is so ubiquitous that an understanding of its psychological nature cannot help but shed light on a wide range of problems within psychology. Most of the examples we have given thus far have, perhaps for simplicity's sake, been drawn from the field of perception. This is misleading. For the act of categorizing, operationally defined in the manner discussed in the foregoing, may occur in a perceptual situation or one not involving the presence of stimulus objects. Logically speaking, there is no distinction between them save in the sense that the materials categorized differ. Categorization at the perceptual level consists of the process of identification, literally an act of placing a stimulus input by virtue of its defining attributes into a certain class. An object of a certain color, size, shape, and texture is seen as an apple. The act of identification involves a "fit" between the properties of a stimulus input and the specifications of a category. Categorization of "conceptual objects" also involves the fit of a set of objects or instances to the specifications of a category. We categorize, say, Whig and Tory statesmen of the first half of the nineteenth century in terms of whether each instance of the class had certain characteristics of allegiance, belief, etc. Or we class together all prime numbers by virtue of whether they meet the criterion of nondivisibility.

One of the principal differences between the two forms of categorization —the "perceptual" on the one hand and the "conceptual" on the other—is the immediacy to experience of the attributes by which their fitness to a category is determined. In the perceptual case, the relevant attributes are more immediately given by which we judge the categorial identity of an object, at least in simple perceptual situations. At the other end, the attainment of knowledge about the attributes that are relevant may require a difficult strategy of search as, for example, in the field of art history when one seeks to identify a painting as, say, a Massaccio or a product of one of his students, or as in science when by the use of the Ascheim-Zondek test one seeks to classify a woman two weeks after her last menstruation as pregnant or not. There are, of course, steps in between the two extremes where the relevant cues to categorization are only "moderately immediate" and in which some strategy of search behavior is required of the subject, a striking experimental example being the behavior of subjects attempting to identify tachistoscopically presented material or material presented peripherally or at low illumination or with a high noise background.

We have lingered on the continuity of categorization at the perceptual and conceptual levels not so much to insist upon the identity of all categorization behavior—for there are striking differences in the behavior of subjects operating with conceptual and perceptual categories as we can see in examining the experimental literature—but rather to urge the importance of the economy gained by treating the underlying process as common in the two activities and in the phenomena that lie between. Undoubtedly some people show preferences for the extreme of utilizing perceptually immediate attributes in their categorizing while others are more "conceptual" or "abstract," which we know from the important work of Hanfmann and Kasanin (1937, 1942), Goldstein and Scheerer (1941), and others who have studied sorting behavior systematically. Our objective is to show that the basic processes of categorization are the same, even though operating under different conditions of attribute immediacy and under different conditions of life history in the organism.

One final point on the relationship between conceptual and perceptual categorization is worth attention. It is frequently the case that people develop means of altering conceptual categories into categories that can be utilized with more immediate perceptual cues. One example will suffice, one that is fairly common in the act of differential diagnosis in medicine. It is the pride of the good diagnostician that with practice he no longer needs elaborate laboratory tests to determine the nature of a patient's syndrome, that frequently he can "spot" the case by the time the patient has walked across the consultation room and taken his seat by the physician. Immediate features of gait, complexion, posture, and the like come to serve for the act of categorization that had formerly to depend upon highly mediate cues gleaned from laboratory tests.

In the most general sense, then, any cognitive operation involving the grouping and regrouping of materials into equivalence classes is rendered more comprehensible once one has a better grasp of the nature of categorizing. Judgment, memory, problem-solving, inventive thinking, and esthetics—not to mention the more conventional areas of perception and concept formation—all involve such operations.

There is a more extended sense in which categorizing is ubiquitous. To this we turn next.

Language, Culture, and Categorizing

The categories in terms of which man sorts out and responds to the world around him reflect deeply the culture into which he is born. The language, the way of life, the religion and science of a people: all of these mold the way in which a man experiences the events out of which his own history is fashioned. In this sense, his personal history comes to reflect the traditions and thought-ways of his culture, for the events that make it up are filtered through the categorial systems he has learned. The typologies into which kinds of people are sorted, as, for example, witches and non-witches among the Navaho; the manner in which kin are categorized in societies with and without primogeniture rules; the classification of women into "sisters" and "eligibles" described by Hallowell (1951); the categorization of certain acts as friendly and others as hostile: all of these are projections of deep cultural trends into the experience of individuals. The principal defining attribute of an "intelligent man" for the Navaho is, according to one informant, a man who has seen a great many different things and traveled much. The word *yaigeh* which denotes this type of intelligent man does not include a man who, say, is noted for his domestic wisdom. It is difficult to determine whether there is a unitary category for "general intelligence" in Navaho. The first category used by our informant in specifying intelligence is especially interesting. The Navaho were historically a nomadic people who, though geographically no longer mobile, continue to show a great interest in distant things and events.[2]

The example just cited immediately suggests the controversial theories of Benjamin Lee Whorf (1940) and brings into question the relation between the lexical categories of a language and the customary cognitive categories in terms of which the speakers of a language sort their worlds. We shall not pause here to attempt a resolution of the two extreme views, the "cloak theories" and the "mold theories," the one holding that language is a cloak conforming to the customary categories of thought of its speakers, the other that it is a mold in terms of which thought categories are cast. The resolution will obviously have great bearing on theories of categorizing and on the issues involved in understanding the relation between culture and personality. These are problems the reader will find discussed in the appendix to [our] book prepared by Dr. Roger W. Brown.

In fine, we would note only that problems of how categories are formed and used are relevant not only to classical problems within psychology, but also to the sciences of culture, notably anthropology and linguistics.

The Achievements of Categorizing

What does the act of rendering things equivalent achieve for the organism? It is a good preliminary question, like the functional query of the biologist: "What is accomplished by digestion?" The answer provides only a prolegomenon to further inquiry, for if we reply, "Digestion serves to convert external substances into assimilable materials that can then enter into the metabolic process," the next question is bound to be "How is this accomplished?" But the functional question is clearly important, for unless it is fruitfully posed, the later questions about "how" must surely miscarry. So long as the nervous system was conceived of as something that cooled the humors, it served little purpose to ask how this was accomplished.

A first achievement of categorizing has already been discussed. By categorizing as equivalent discriminably different events, the organism *reduces the complexity of its environment.* It is reasonably clear "how" this is accomplished. It involves the abstraction and use of defining properties in terms of which groupings can be made and much will be said of these things later.

A second achievement has also been mentioned: categorizing is the *means by which the objects of the world about us are identified.* The act of identifying some thing or some event is an act of "placing" it in a class. Identification implies that we are able to say either "There is thingumbob again" or "There is another thingumbob." While these identifications may vary in the richness of their elaboration, they are never absent. A certain sound may be heard simply as "that sound which comes from outdoors late at night." Or it may be heard as "those porcupines chewing on that old tree stump." When an event cannot be thus categorized and identified, we experience terror in the face of the uncanny. And indeed, "the uncanny" is itself a category, even if only a residual one.

A third achievement, a consequence of the first, is that the establishment of a category based on a set of defining attributes *reduces the necessity of constant learning.* For the abstraction of defining properties makes possible future acts of categorizing without benefit of further learning. We do not have to be taught *de novo* at each encounter that the object before us is or is not a tree. If it exhibits the appropriate defining properties, it "is" a tree. It is in this crucial aspect, as we mentioned earlier, that categorizing differs from the learning of fiat classes. Learning by rote that a miscellany of objects all go by the nonsense name BLIX has no extrapolative value to new members of the class.

A fourth achievement inherent in the act of categorizing is the *direction it provides for instrumental activity.* To know by virtue of discriminable defining attributes and without need for further direct test that a man is "honest" or that a substance is "poison" is to know *in advance* about appropriate and inappropriate actions to be taken. Such direction is even provided when we come up against an object or event which we cannot place with finality. To the degree the new object has discriminable properties and these properties have been found in the past to be relevant to certain categories, we can make a start on the problem by a procedure of "categorial bracketing." The object appears to be animate; what does it do if it is poked? It stands on two legs like a man; does it speak? Much of problem-solving involves such repeated regrouping of an object until a pragmatically appropriate grouping has been found. In short, such successive categorizing is a principal form of instrumental activity.

A fifth achievement of categorizing is the opportunity it permits for *ordering and relating classes of events.* For we operate, as noted before, with category *systems*—classes of events that are related to each other in various kinds of superordinate systems. We map and give meaning to our world by relating classes of events rather than by relating individual events. "Matches," the child learns, will "cause" a set of events called "fires." The meaning of each class of things placed in quotation marks—matches, causes, and fires—is given by the imbeddedness of each class in such relationship maps. The moment an object is placed in a category, we have opened up a whole vista of possibilities for "going beyond" the category by virtue of the superordinate and causal relationships linking this category to others.

In speaking of achievements we have not, perhaps, placed enough stress on the anticipatory and exploratory nature of much of our categorizing. In the case of most categorizing, we attempt to find those defining signs that are as *sure* as possible as *early* as possible to give identity to an event. At the barest level of necessity, this is essential to life. We cannot test the edibility of food by eating it and checking the consequence. We must learn ways of anticipating ultimate consequences by the use of prior signs. In simpler organisms than man, one often finds that there is a built-in mechanism for response to such anticipatory signs. The greylag gosling, observed by Tinbergen (1948), responds with a flight reaction to a hawk-like silhouette drawn on a wire across its pen. The young of the black-headed gull responds to a red spot on the side of its mother's bill with a "begging response" for food and the mother responds to the open bill of the young by inserting food. Lashley's description (1938) of the response of cyclostoma to anticipatory danger signs by the mobilization of stinging nettles provides an example at an even simpler phyletic level. Anticipatory categorizing, then, provides "lead time" for adjusting one's response to objects with which one must cope.

It is this future-oriented aspect of categorizing behavior in all organisms that impresses us most. It is not simply that organisms code the events of their environment into equivalence classes, but that they utilize cues for doing so that allow an opportunity for prior adjustment to the event identified. We are especially impressed with the anticipatory nature of categorizing when we consider the phenomenon of the "empty category."

This is the process whereby defining attributes are combined to create fictive categories: classes of objects that have not been encountered or are clearly of a nature contrary to expectancy. The empty category is a means whereby we go beyond the conventional groupings we impose on the segments of nature we have encountered. It is a way of going beyond the range of events one encounters to the sphere of the possible or even, in the phrase of the philosopher Nelson Goodman (1947), to the "counterfactual conditional"—events that could be but which are contrary to experience. This surely is one of the principal functions of categorizing.

Two cases may be given to illustrate the uses of such categories in the cognitive economy of man. One is the class of creatures known as centaurs, half man, half horse. The other is the class of "female Presidents of the United States, past, present, and future." The first example illustrates the use of the empty category as the currency of art, fantasy, and dream; perhaps it is a vehicle for exploring the ambiguous interstices of experience. The second example of an empty category is from the sphere of problem-solving and thinking. Hypotheses in problem-solving often take the form of creating new categories by the combining of potential defining attributes.

The physicist says, "Consider the possibility of a nuclear particle whose orbit is a spiral." Indeed, the neutrino in nuclear physics was postulated first as an empty category on logical grounds, and only when appropriate measures became available was it "found." So too Neptune. Working from data on the perturbation of Uranus, Bessel reached the conclusion that a trans-Uranian planet must exist. Adams and LeVerrier computed possible orbits for the as yet undiscovered planet. It was only then that the planet was "found" by observation at the Berlin Observatory in 1846, 23 years after Bessel's conclusion.

To a certain extent, the foregoing dicussion of the achievements of categorial activity almost precludes the necessity for discussing the problem of "cognitive motivation." What is served by postulating categorizing motives beyond saying such things as "The person strives to reduce the complexity of his environment," or "There is a drive to group things in terms of instrumental relevance?" We would argue that the postulation of motives to correspond to achievements of functioning is an empty procedure. But there are problems of motivation involved in categorizing behavior over and beyond this level of discourse, and to these we turn next.

The Motive to Categorize

There are three ways in which cognitive motives in general may be conceived. The first is to postulate need processes assumed to be at the basis of cognitive activities. Bartlett (1932), for example, speaks of "effort after meaning" and Tolman (1951) of a "placing need" to account for the push that impels people to categorize, identify, and place things. Hilgard (1951) postulates two goals of perception: the goal of stability and the goal of clarity or definiteness. These take on the function of guiding and impelling perceptual and cognitive behavior. One can justify the positing of such needs or goal strivings only on the ground that they are frustratable, satiable, and to a certain degree specific with respect both to appropriate initiators and gratifiers. The difficulty with all such conceptions to date, whether in the general forms of "cognitive need" or in the more restricted form of Woodworth's will to perceive (1947), is that they have no specifications about the conditions that arouse the need, gratify it, frustrate it, or satiate it. To the extent that this is true, such theories serve no purpose save to equate cognitive achievements with a motive to achieve.

We believe, however, that there are clear signs now present in the psychological literature whereby it is possible to construct a theory of cognitive needs that goes beyond this general form. Experiments by Wyatt and Campbell (1951) and Postman and Bruner (1948) indicate that the presentation of objects to be recognized under difficult or stressful conditions of viewing leads to categorizing or identification behavior that varies in a systematic way from the behavior prevailing under normal perceptual conditions. The latter experiments show that, when the completion of categorizing is blocked by the introduction of almost impossible viewing conditions, the effect is to produce "reckless" identification behavior on subsequent opportunities for perceiving, reckless in the sense that abortive identification occurs in the absence of adequate cues. The result, as Wyatt and Campbell point out, is to "saddle" the perceiver with an inappropriate categorization which must then be disconfirmed by subsequent stimulation before pragmatically adequate, "correct" recognition can occur. Here then is a first step toward specifying some of the effects of frustration of a "placing need." The McGill studies of perceptual deprivation (Bexton, Heron, and Scott, 1954) provide another example of systematic study of the "placing need." Deprivation in the form of being barred from perceptual commerce with the normally rich world of objects appears to have the temporary effect of disrupting the smooth sequential flow of cognitive activities normally involved in problem-solving and may indeed even disrupt the normal constancy processes so basic to object perception and object recognition. In so far as studies establish the nature of antecedent conditions affecting the operation of cognitive needs, to that extent do notions about "needs for clarity and stability" become theoretically viable. Short of this the postulation of cognitive needs is little more than a restatement of the fact that cognitive activity achieves something for the organism.

Undoubtedly one of the conditions affecting the manner in which we categorize the objects around us is the need-state of the organism. For cognition is also instrumental activity geared to other forms of goal striving. This is not to say that, were it not for "primary" needs like hunger or "secondary" needs like the desire for prestige, cognitive processes would be as idle as a lawn mower when the grass is not in need of cutting. Perhaps the most thoroughgoing exposition of cognition as instrumental activity is to be found in McDougall's general theory (1926), but he too had to postulate a primary need or "propensity" called curiosity to keep his organism from falling into a vegetative state in the absence of other needs. Such "directive state" theories of cognition, to use F. H. Allport's term (1955), have recently come much into vogue in the implicit assumptions underlying much of the "New Look" work in perception and have clearly proved to be fruitful in stimulating research on the relationship between need-states in general and perceptual selectivity. But it is quite apparent that cognitive activity is not entirely a handmaiden of other drives. There is some process of "decentration," to use Piaget's term (1951), that frees our cognitive activity from such domination and makes it possible for us eventually to play chess or be abstractly curious without being driven to do so by hunger, anger, etc.

One characteristic of cognitive activity, whether at the level of instrumental activity or in the playful realms of chess, is that it has associated with it some rather unique affective states. The sense of tension that occurs when we cannot "place" somebody, the frustation we have been able to induce in subjects serving in tachistoscopic experiments when exposure levels were too low, the malaise of the trained mind faced with a seemingly causeless effect—all of these are as characteristic of frustrated cognitive activity as desire is of blocked sexual activity. There is also the phenomenology of the Eureka experience: the "Aha, *Erlêbnis*," or the "That's it!" feeling. Reports of such experiences have, of course, been used as a basis for inferring the presence of a generalized cognitive need, be it called "effort after meaning" or what not.

We have seen our subjects going through agonies of frustration with difficult problems and experiencing "Eureka!" when they thought (often wrongly) that they had found a solution, and we have wondered what function was served by such an affect. Perhaps none, or perhaps even our question is meaningless. We have the impression that such an affect provides a kind of feedback which regulates the flow of problem-solving behavior. Cognitive frustration, within tolerable limits, helps keep search-behavior going. The "insight" experience leads to new bursts of testing activity. We are completely without evidence for such assertions or even without proposals as to how one might gather evidence.

On the Validation of Categorizing

Categorizing an event as a member of a class and thereby giving it identity involves, as we have said, an act of inference. Whether one is deciding what the blob was that appeared for a few milliseconds in a tachistoscope or what species of bird it is that we have our binoculars trained on or what Pueblo period this potsherd belongs to, the basic task is not only to make an inference but to make the "right" inference. Is the blob a face, the bird a scissor-tailed flycatcher, the potsherd from Pueblo II? How can we be sure? Let it be clear that we are not asking philosophical questions. We want to know, simply, how people make sure (or make sur*er*) that they have placed an event in its proper identity niche.

There appear to be four general procedures by which people reassure themselves that their categorizations are "valid." The first is *by recourse to an ultimate criterion,* the second is *test by consistency;* the third, *test by consensus* and the fourth, *test by affective congruence.* Consider each in turn.

Recourse to an Ultimate Criterion

A simple functional category provides an example. By means of such defining properties as color, size, and shape, mushrooms are divisible into a class of edible mushrooms and a class of inedible ones. A mushroom fancier, out in the woods picking mushrooms, must decide whether a particular mushroom is or is not edible. To the extent that the defining properties are not masked, he is able to make a preliminary categorization: he calls it inedible. If you should ask him how he can be sure, he would doubtless tell you that the way to be absolutely sure is to eat it. If it makes you sick or kills you, then his categorization was "right" or "valid."

The example chosen is perhaps too simple. For there are many categories where it is difficult to specify *the* ultimate criterion against which to check the adequacy of the defining attributes. But the simplification will serve us for the while.

When recourse to an ultimate criterion for defining a category is of grave consequence, the culture may take it upon itself to invent labels or signs by which examplars of the category can be spotted in sufficient time for appropriate avoidance. The custom of putting a red skull and crossbones on bottles of poison, the use of red color on dangerous industrial machinery, stop signs at dangerous intersections—all of these are examples of the artificial creation of anticipatory defining attributes that in effect save one an encounter with a dangerous ultimate criterion.

Test by Consistency

Perhaps the simplest example one can give of such testing is the perception of speech. One is "surer" that one identified a word correctly if the word fits the context of what has gone before. Since the categorization of events usually takes place in a context which imposes constraints on what a particular event can be, there is more often than not the possibility of validation by consistency.

Some listeners to the famous Orson Welles broadcast of *The War of the Worlds*, faced with the choice of deciding whether the Martian invasion was "real" or "theatrical," used a consistency criterion determined by the set of beliefs that had already been established in their past lives. "We have found that many of the persons who did not even try to check the broadcast had preexisting mental sets that made the stimulus so understandable to them that they immediately accepted it as true. Highly religious people who believed that God willed and controlled the destinies of man were already furnished with a particular standard of judgment that would make an invasion of our planet and a destruction of its members an 'act of God.' This was particularly true if the religious frame of reference was of the eschatological variety providing the individual with definite attitudes or beliefs regarding the end of the world. Other people we found had been so influenced by the recent war scare that they believed an attack by a foreign power was imminent and an invasion—whether it was due to the Japanese, Hitler, or Martians—was not unlikely" (Cantril, 1940, p. 191).

Validation by consistency is perhaps nowhere better illustrated than in modern taxonomic research. At the lowest level, so-called alpha taxonomy, one seeks to differentiate as many species as possible in terms of whatever defining properties are visible. Such a technique leads to vast multiplication of categories. There are now about a third of a million species of plants, and each year about 5,000 are added. There are about 2 million species and subspecies of animals and it is estimated that new ones are being added at the rate of 10,000 per year. Some estimates of the number of insect species run as high as three million (Silvestri, 1929), and given new radiological methods of producing mutations, the possible number of virus types seems almost unlimited. As far as identification is concerned, the modern taxonomist readily agrees (Mayr, 1952) that species are not "discovered" but "invented." The principal problem of "validation" at this level is to establish the "existence" of a category, which means, essentially, that other investigators can distinguish the same grouping if they follow directions for finding it.

It is at the next level of taxonomy, beta taxonomy, that the criterion of consistency becomes critical, for now the task is to order the bewildering array of species into a *system* of classification. Whether or not one's grouping of a series of species into genera and then into a phylum is "valid" or not depends upon whether the properties of the grouped species are consistent with one's conception of evolution. The correctness of the grouping "elasmobranches" as distinguished from "teleostean fishes" depends upon whether the defining morphological properties of the two classes fit a consistent pattern of development as formulated in evolutionary theory. Teleostean fishes are more "evolved" or "higher than" sharks because of the consistent differences in skeletal system, renal system, circulatory system, etc. What makes the classification valid is that it is explicable in terms of a more general theory about the changes in morphology and physiology that characterize the evolution of animal life. If one would seek to establish the validity of considering a certain group of animals as constituting a phylum, the test would be by consistency with the requirements of the theory governing classification not only of this new phylum but of phyla generally.

Test by Consensus

Such categories as "good citizen" or "decent person" are often in effect consensually validated. Because the defining properties are vague and disjunctive, there is often uncertainty about the status of instances. In consequence, to validate our categorization of a man as a "decent fellow" we may turn to the categorizations made by people with whose values we identify—what a number of sociologists call a *reference group* (cf. Merton and Kitt, 1950). Under other circumstances, we may turn simply to those individuals who happen to be in the immediate vicinity when a categorial decision must be made. We see two men fighting on the street: "Who started it?" we ask a man on the edge of the crowd that has collected, in an attempt to categorize the guilty member. In deciding whether the Welles broadcast was "real" or a play, many victims were determined in their categorization by the fact that others were treating the broadcast as "news" rather than "entertainment."

Where the placement process has marked consequences for the society and when the criteria to be used are ambiguous in nature, virtually every culture has devised a process whereby an official decision can be provided. In our own society, the courts and the judicial process provide this means. Whether or not a man is a felon is decided by specialists in such matters, working with the guide of official definitions embodied in a legal code. Due process of law involves a careful inspection of the degree to which an individual and his acts "fit" the defining properties of a thief or an embezzler. We also create official definitions of a more positive type. Working with a highly ambiguous set of standards, the French Academy makes the decision whether or not a given Frenchman is "an immortal"; or a special body weighs the scientific products of a man and decides whether he should be "starred" in *American Men of Science* or be entitled to the distinction of wearing the initials "F.R.S." after his name. Establishment of consensus by official action is effective to the degree that people will give precedence to the official decisions made. If validation by either direct test, consistency, or unofficial consensus is given precedence, then official methods of categorizing may be at odds with what generally prevails as categorization in a society.

Test by Affective Congruence

While this is a special case of test by consistency, it merits treatment on its own. It is best described as an act of categorizing or identifying an event that carries with it a feeling of subjective certainty or even necessity. Such subjective certainty may also characterize an act whose validation rests on other forms of validating test. But we refer here to the pure case: the unjustifiable intuitive leap buttressed by a sense of conviction. One infers the existence of God, for example, from the overwhelming beauty of a mountain scene: "Such beauty could be produced neither by man nor by the random force of nature." God's presence is thereafter inferred from the experience of beauty. There is buttressing both by consistency and by consensus, but what provides the basic validating criterion is the affective component in the act of categorizing.

Such acts, because they are particularly inaccessible to disproof, are of special interest to the student of nonrational behavior. What seems especially interesting about acts of categorization of this sort is that they seem to be inaccessible in proportion to the strength of certain inner need systems whose fulfillment they serve. "The more basic the confirmation of a hypothesis is to the carrying out of goal striving activity, the greater will be its strength. It will be more readily aroused, more easily confirmed, less readily infirmed," (Bruner, 1951, p. 127). In its most extreme pathological form, validation by affective congruence makes it possible for the paranoid to construct a pseudoenvironment in which the random noises about him are categorized as words being spoken against him. At the level of normal functioning, it permits the acceptance of such unknowable absolutes as God, the Dignity of Man, or Hell.

Learning to Categorize

Much of our concern in subsequent chapters will be with the "attainment of concepts," the behavior involved in using the discriminable attributes of objects and events as a basis of anticipating their significant identity. We can take as a paradigm the behavior of a young gourmet who is determined to gather his own mushrooms in the conviction that the wild varieties are far more worthy of his cooking skills that the cultivated types available in the market. His first aim is to discriminate between edible and nonedible mushrooms. If he were really starting from scratch, he would have two sources of information. On the one hand, he would be able to note the characteristics of each mushroom or toadstool he picked. He could note its color, shape, size, habitat, stalk height, etc. He would also know whether each mushroom, fully described as we have noted, made him ill or not when eaten. For the sake of the inquiry, we endow our man with considerable enthusiasm and sufficient sense so that he eats only a small enough portion of each mushroom to allow him to determine edibility without being killed by the adventure. His task is to determine which discriminable attributes of the mushrooms he tries out lead with maximum certainty to the inference that the type is edible.

Note that our man already knows of the existence of the two classes of mushroom in terms of the ultimate criterion of edibility. He is seeking defining attributes that will distinguish exemplars of these two classes. In this sense, we speak of his task as one of concept *attainment* rather than concept *formation.* If his task were that of attempting to sort mushrooms into some meaningful set of classes, *any* meaningful set of classes in the interest of ordering their diversity, then we might more properly refer to the task as concept formation. Concept formation is essentially the first step en route to attainment. In the case of mushrooms, the formation of the hypothesis that *some* mushrooms are edible and *others* are not is the act of forming a concept. *Attainment refers to the process of finding predictive defining attributes that distinguish exemplars from nonexemplars of the class one seeks to discriminate.*

There are two ways of asking questions about the searcher in this example of concept attainment. The first asks, "What is the best, the most rational way for him to proceed?" At this level, we are dealing with the analysis of ideal strategies, a topic that will concern us centrally in subsequent chapters. A second question is, "How does he in fact proceed?" The first question is, if you will, a question of the logic of science or of "operations research" and its answer will be based on a consideration of how the searcher for defining attributes can most rapidly or most safely or most stylishly or most joyfully learn which attributes to trust. We shall ask both questions, for our interest lies in the relation between ideal performance and actual performance. How one proceeds in this way will presently be told.

Notes

1. See Burma and Mayr (1949) for an enlightening discussion of the "reality" of the species concept in systematic zoology.

2. We are greatly indebted to Professors Evon Vogt and John Roberts, both of whom have discussed with us at length the cognitive characteristics of Navaho and Zuni society. Professor Vogt also made it possible for one of the authors (J.S.B.) to get some sense of the cross-cultural importance of categorizing phenomena on an all-too-brief visit to New Mexico in the summer of 1954.

Literature Cited

ALLPORT, F. H.: 1955. *Theories of perception and the concept of structure.* New York: Wiley.

BARTLETT, F. C.: 1932. *Remembering.* Cambridge, Eng.: Cambridge U. Pr.

———: 1951. *Thinking.* Memoirs and Proceedings of Manchester Literary and Philosophical Soc. 93:31–44.

BEXTON, W. H., HERON, W., & SCOTT, T. H.: 1954. "Effects of decreased variation in the sensory environment." *Canad. J. Psychol.* 8:70–76.

BRUNER, J. S.: 1951. "Personality dynamics and the process of perceiving," In R. R. Blake & G. V. Ramsey, eds., *Perception: An approach to personality.* New York: Ronald, pp. 121–147.

BURMA, B. H., & MAYR, E.: 1949. "The species concept: a discussion." *Evolut.* II, 4, 369–373.

CANTRILL, H.: 1940. *The invasion from Mars.* Princeton: Princeton U. Pr.

DOLLARD, J., & MILLER, N. E.: 1950. *Personality and psychotherapy.* New York: McGraw.

GOLDSTEIN, K.: 1940. *Human nature in the light of psychopathology.* Cambridge, Mass.: Harvard U. Pr.

——— & SCHEERER, M.: 1941. "Abstract and concrete behavior; an experimental study with special tests." Psychol. Monogr. 53, No. 2 (Whole No. 239).

GOODMAN, N.: 1947. "The problem of counterfactual conditionals." *J. Phil.* 44:113–128.

HALLOWELL, A. I.: 1951. "Cultural factors in the structuralization of perception." In J. H. Rohrer & M. Sherif, eds., *Social psychology at the crossroads.* New York: Harper, pp. 164–195.

HANFMANN, E. & KANSANIN, J.: 1937. "A method for the study of concept formation." *J. Psychol.* 3: 521–540.

———: 1942. "Conceptual thinking in schizophrenia." *Nerv. Ment. Dis. Monogr. Ser.* No. 67.

HARDY, G. H.: 1940. *A mathematician's apology.* Cambridge, Eng.: Cambridge U. Pr.

HEAD, H.: 1926. *Aphasia and kindred disorders of speech.* New York: Macmillan.

HEBB, D. O.: 1949. *The organization of behavior.* New York: Wiley.

HILGARD, E. R.: 1951. "The role of learning in perception." In R. R. Blake & G. V. Ramsey, eds., *Perception: an approach to personality.* New York: Ronald, pp. 95–120.

KLUVER, H.: 1933. *Behavior mechanisms in monkeys.* Chicago: U. of Chicago Pr.

LASHLEY, K. S.: 1938. "Experimental analysis of instinctive behavior." *Psychol. Rev.* 45:445–472.

MCCLELLAND, D. C.: 1951. *Personality.* New York: Scribner.

MACLEISH, A.: 1926. "Ars Poetica," In *Collected Poems, 1917–1952.* Boston: Houghton Mifflin, pp. 40–41.

MAIER, N. R. F.: 1930. "Reasoning in humans, I. On direction." *J. comp. Psychol.* 10: 115–143.

———: 1931. "Reasoning in humans. II. The solution of a problem and its appearance in consciousness." *J. comp. Psychol.* 12:181–194.

———: 1945. "Reasoning in humans. III. The mechanism of equivalent stimuli and of reasoning." *J. exp. Psychol.* 35:349–360.

MAYR, E.: 1952. "Concepts of classification and nomenclature in higher organisms and microorganisms." *Ann. N.Y. Acad. Sc.* 56:391–397.

MERTON, R. K., & KITT, A. S.: 1950. "Contributions to the theory of reference group behavior." In R. K. Merton, & P. F. Lazarsfeld, eds., *Continuities in social research.* New York: Free Press, pp. 40–105.

MICHOTTE, A.: 1946. *La perception de la causalite.* (1st Ed.) Paris: Vrin.

MICHOTTE, A.: 1950. "A propos de la permanence phenomenale: Faits et theories." *Acta Psychol.* 298–322.

PIAGET, J.: 1951. *Play, dreams and imitations in childhood.* New York: Norton.

———: 1953. "Experimental epistemology." Unpublished lecture at Harvard University.

POSTMAN, L., & BRUNER, J. S.: 1948. "Perception under stress." *Psychol. Rev.* 55: 314–323.

SCHACHTEL, E. G.: 1947. "On memory and childhood amnesia." *Psychiatry* 10: 1–26.

SHELDON, W. H.: 1950. Personal communication.

SILVESTRI, F.: 1929. "The relation of taxonomy to other branches of entomology." *Fourth Interntl. Congr. Entomology* 2: 52–54.

STEVENS, S. S.: 1936. "Psychology: the propaedeutic science." *Phil. Sci.* 3:90–103

TINBERGEN, N.: 1948. "Social releasers and the experimental method required for their study." *Wilson Bull.* 60: 6–51.

TOLMAN, E. C.: 1932. *Purposive behavior in animals and men.* New York: Century.

———: 1951. "A psychological model." In T. Parson, & E. A. Shils, eds., *Toward a general theory of action.* Cambridge, Mass.: Harvard U. Press, pp. 279–361.

WHORF, B. L.: 1940. "Linguistics as an exact science." *Technol. Rev.* 43: 61–63.

WOODWORTH, R. S.: 1947. "Reenforcement of perception." *Amer. J. Psychol.* 60: 119–124.

WYATT, D. F. & CAMPBELL, D. T.: 1951. "On the liability of sterotype or hypothesis." *J. abnorm. soc. Psychol.* 46: 496–500.

10 THE ETHNOGRAPHIC STUDY OF COGNITIVE SYSTEMS

Charles O. Frake

Chapter 9 discussed the general nature and function of categories from a psychological viewpoint. This chapter shifts to a methodological perspective: "How does the anthropologist study the category systems of a culture?" Most people do not stop to consider that they are continuously using categories as they think and talk. Much of their knowledge about the classification of experience and the attributes that are used for this purpose are outside of awareness. They believe that it is natural for the world to be divided up and structured in the way they have learned it to be. When they speak, each utterance is a stream of sounds which label categories and relate them in a variety of ways. The ethnographer interested in cognition seeks to describe this tacit knowledge of categories, their labels, and the relationships among them. Here, Charles O. Frake develops an explicit methodology for doing this. And in Chapter 13 I discuss the specific discovery procedures I used in studying urban tramps.

The best way to learn the principles of ethnoscience is through a research project using these methods. For example, each student might find a friend to act as an informant for several interviews. It is relatively simple to identify several nouns which an informant uses to classify objects in his experience. A child in school knows about *games*; a ski enthusiast has learned about *skis* and *turns*; a dean knows the different *departments* in his school; and many informants could talk about kinds of *animals*, *TV programs*, or *professors*. By asking for the *kinds* of these objects, one can construct a taxonomy which represents the way his informant organizes a category system. The discovery of attributes used by an informant is more difficult, but it can be done by following the suggestions here and in Chapter 13. After this kind of research is well under way, the student will probably want to reread Frake's discussion.—EDITOR'S NOTE

Reproduced by permission of the author and the Anthropological Society of Washington from *Anthropology and Human Behavior*, pp. 72–85, 1962.

Words for Things[1]

A relatively simple task commonly performed by ethnographers is that of getting names for things. The ethnographer typically performs this task by pointing to or holding up the apparent constituent objects of an event he is describing, eliciting the native names for the objects, and then matching each native name with the investigator's own word for the object. The logic of the operation is: if the informant calls object X a *mbubu* and I call object X a *rock*, then *mbubu* means *rock*. In this way are compiled the ordinary ethnobotanical monographs with their lists of matched native and scientific names for plant specimens. This operation probably also accounts for a good share of the native names parenthetically inserted in so many monograph texts: "Among the grasses (*sigbet*) whose grains (*bunga nen*) are used for beads (*bitekel*) none is more highly prized than Job's tears (*glias*)." Unless the reader is a comparative linguist of the languages concerned he may well ask what interest these parenthetical insertions contain other than demonstrating that the ethnographer has discharged a minimal obligation toward collecting linguistic data. This procedure for obtaining words for things, as well as the "so-what" response it so often evokes, assumes the objective identifiability of discrete "things" apart from a particular culture. It construes the name-getting task as one of simply matching verbal labels for "things" in two languages. Accordingly, the "problem-oriented" anthropologist, with a broad, cross-cultural perspective, may disclaim any interest in these labels; all that concerns him is the presence or absence of a particular "thing" in a given culture.

If, however, instead of "getting words for things," we redefine the task as one of finding the "things" that go with the words, the eliciting of terminologies acquires a more general interest. In actuality not even the most concrete, objectively apparent physical object can be identified apart from some culturally defined system of concepts (Boas 1911:24–25; Bruner *et al.*, 1956; Goodenough 1957). An ethnographer should strive to define objects[2] according to the conceptual system of the people he is studying. Let me suggest, then, that one look upon the task of getting names for things not as an exercise in linguistic recording; but as a way of finding out what are in fact the "things" in the environment of the people being studied. This paper consists of some suggestions toward the formulation of an operationally-explicit methodology for discerning how people construe their world of experience from the way they talk about it. Specifically these suggestions concern the analysis of terminological systems in a way which reveals the conceptual principles that generate them.

In a few fields, notably in kinship studies, anthropologists have already successfully pushed an interest in terminological systems beyond a matching of translation labels. Since Morgan's day no competent student of kinship has looked upon his task as one of simply finding a tribe's words for "uncle," "nephew," or "cousin." The recognition that the denotative range of kinship categories must be determined empirically in each case, that the categories form a system, and that the semantic contrasts underlying the system are amenable to formal analysis, has imparted to kinship studies a methodological rigor and theoretical productivity rare among ethnographic endeavors. Yet all peoples are vitally concerned with kinds of phenomena other than genealogical relations; consequently there is no reason why the study of a people's concepts of these other phenomena should not offer a theoretical interest comparable to that of kinship studies.

Even with reference to quite obvious kinds of material objects, it has long been noted that many people do not see "things" quite the way we do. However, anthropologists in spite of their now well-established psychological interests have notably ignored the cognition of their subjects. Consequently other investigators still rely on stock anecdotes of "primitive thinking" handed down by explorers, philologists, and psychologists since the nineteenth century (Brown 1958:256; Hill 1952; Jespersen 1934:429; Ullman 1957:95, 308). Commonly these anecdotes have been cited as examples of early stages in the evolution of human thought—which, depending on the anecdote selected, may be either from blindly concrete to profoundly abstract or from hopelessly vague to scientifically precise. A typical citation, purporting to illustrate the primitive's deficient abstractive ability, concerns a Brazilian Indian tribe which allegedly has no word for "parrot" but only words for "kinds of parrots" (Jespersen 1934:429ff.). The people of such a tribe undoubtedly classify the birds of their environment in some fashion; certainly they do not bestow a unique personal name on each individual bird specimen they encounter. Classification means that individual bird specimens must be matched against the defining attributes of conceptual categories and thereby judged to be equivalent for certain purposes to some other specimens but different from still others. Since no two birds are alike in every discernable feature, any grouping into sets implies a selection of only a limited number of features as significant for contrasting kinds of birds. A person learns which features are significant from his fellows as part of his cultural equipment. He does not receive this information from the birds. Consequently there is no necessary reason that a Brazilian Indian should heed those particular attributes which, for the English-speaker, make equivalent all the diverse individual organisms he labels "parrots." Some of this Indian's categories may seem quite specific, and others quite general, when compared to our grouping of the same specimens. But learning that it takes the Indian many words to name the objects we happen to group together in one set is trivial information compared to knowing how the Indian himself groups these objects and which attributes he selects as dimensions to generate a taxonomy of avifauna. With the latter knowledge we learn what these people regard as significant about birds. If we can arrive at comparable knowledge about their concepts of land animals, plants, soils, weather, social relations, personalities, and supernaturals, we have at least a sketch map of the world in the image of the tribe.

The analysis of a culture's terminological systems will not, of course, exhaustively reveal the cognitive world of its members, but it will certainly tap a central portion of it. Culturally significant cognitive features must be communicable between persons in one of the standard symbolic systems of the culture. A major share of these features will undoubtedly be codable in a society's most flexible and productive communication device, its language. Evidence also seems to indicate that those cognitive features requiring most frequent communication will tend to have standard and relatively short linguistic labels (Brown 1958:235–241; Brown and Lenneberg 1954). Accordingly, a commonly distinguished category of trees is more likely to be called something like "elm" by almost all speakers rather than labelled with an ad hoc, non-standardized construction like, "You know, those tall trees with asymmetrical, serrated-edged leaves." To the extent that cognitive coding tends to be linguistic and tends to be efficient, the study of the referential use of standard, readily elicitable linguistic responses—or *terms*—should provide a fruitful beginning point for mapping a cognitive system. And with verbal behavior we know how to begin.

The beginning of an ethnographic task is the recording of what is seen and heard, the segmenting of the behavior stream in such a way that culturally significant noises and movements are coded while the irrelevant is discarded. Descriptive linguistics provides a methodology for segmenting the stream of speech into units relevant to the structure of the speaker's language. I assume that any verbal response which conforms to the phonology and grammar of a language is necessarily a culturally significant unit of behavior. Methodologies for the structural description of non-verbal behavior are not correspondingly adequate in spite of important contributions in this direction by such persons as Pike and Barker and Wright (Barker and Wright 1955; Pike 1954; cf. Miller *et al.* 1960:14–15). By pushing forward the analysis of units we know to be culturally relevant, we can, I think, more satisfactorily arrive at procedures for isolating the significant constituents of analogous and interrelated structures. The basic methodological concept advocated here—the determination of the set of contrasting responses appropriate to a given, culturally valid, eliciting context—should ultimately be applicable to the "semantic" analysis of any culturally meaningful behavior.

Segregates

A terminologically distinguished array of objects is a *segregate* (Conklin 1954, 1962; cf. Lounsbury 1956). Segregates are categories, but not all categories known or knowable to an individual are segregates by this definition. Operationally, this definition of a segregate leaves a problem: how do we recognize a "term" when we hear one? How do we segment the stream of speech into category-designating units?

The segmentation of speech into the grammatically functioning units revealed by linguistic analysis is a necessary, but not sufficient, condition for terminological analysis. Clearly no speech segment smaller than the minimal grammatical unit, the morpheme, need be considered. However, the task requires more than simply a search for the meanings of morphemes or other grammatical units. The items and arrangements of a structural description of the language code need not be isomorphic with the categories and propositions of the message. Linguistic forms, whether morphemes or larger constructions, are not each tied to unique chunks of semantic reference like baggage tags; rather it is the use of speech, the selection of one statement over another in a particular socio-linguistic context, that points to the category boundaries on a culture's cognitive map (Chomsky 1955; Haugen 1957; Hymes 1961; Joos 1958; Lounsbury 1956; Nida 1951).

Suppose we have been studying the verbal behavior accompanying the selection and ordering of items at an American lunch counter.[3] The following text might be typical of those overheard and recorded:

> "What ya going to have, Mac? Something to eat?"
> "Yeah. What kind of sandwiches ya got besides hamburgers and hot dogs?"
> "How about a ham 'n cheese sandwich?"
> "Nah . . . I guess I'll take a hamburger again."
> "Hey, that's no hamburger; that's a cheeseburger!"

The problem is to isolate and relate these speech forms according to their use in naming objects. Some, but apparently not all, orderable items at a lunch counter are distinguished by the term *something to eat*. A possibility within the range of 'something to eat' seems to be a set of objects labeled *sandwiches*. The forms *hamburger, hot dog, ham 'n cheese sandwich*, and *cheeseburger* clearly designate alternative choices in lunch-counter contexts. A customer determined to have a 'sandwich' must select one of these alternatives when he orders, and upon receipt of the order, he must satisfy himself that the object thrust before him—which he has never seen before—meets the criteria for membership in the segregate he designated. The counterman must decide on actions that will produce an object acceptable to the customer as a member of the designated segregate. The terminological status of these forms can be confirmed by analysis of further speech situations, by eliciting utterances with question frames suggested to the investigator by the data, and by observing non-verbal features of the situation, especially correlations between terms used in ordering and objects received.

In isolating these terms no appeal has been made to analysis of their linguistic structure or their signification. *Sandwich* is a single morpheme. Some linguists, at any rate, would analyze *hot dog* and even *hamburger* as each containing two morphemes, but, since the meaning of the constructions cannot be predicted from a knowledge of the meaning of their morphological constituents, they are single "lexemes" (Goodenough 1956) or "idioms" (Hockett 1958:303–318). *Ham 'n cheese sandwich* would not, I think, qualify as a single lexeme; nevertheless it is a standard segregate label whose function in naming objects cannot be distinguished from that of forms like *hot dog*. Suppose further utterances from lunch-counter speech show that the lexically complex term *something to eat* distinguishes the same array of objects as do the single morphemes *food* and *chow*. In such a case, a choice among these three terms would perhaps say something about the social status of the lunch counter and its patrons, but it says nothing distinctive about the objects designated. As segregate labels, these three frequently-heard terms would be equivalent.

Although not operationally relevant at this point, the lexemic status of terms bears on later analysis of the productivity of a terminological system. In contrast, say, to our kinship terminology, American lunch-counter terminology is highly productive. The existence of productive, polylexemic models such as *ham 'n cheese sandwich* permits the generation and labeling of new segregates to accommodate the latest lunch-counter creations. However, the non-intuitive determination of the lexemic status of a term requires a thorough analysis of the distinctive features of meaning of the term and its constituents (Goodenough 1956; Lounsbury 1956). Such an analysis of the criteria for placing objects into categories can come only after the term, together with those contrasting terms relevant to its use, has been isolated as a segregate label.

Contrast Sets

In a situation in which a person is making a public decision about the category membership of an object by giving the object a verbal label, he is selecting a term out of a set of alternatives, each with classificatory import. When he asserts "This is an *X*," he is also stating that it is *not* specific other things, these other things being not everything else conceivable, but only the alternatives among which a decision was made (Kelly 1955). In lunch-counter ordering, 'hamburger,' 'hot dog,' 'cheeseburger,' and 'ham and cheese sandwich' are such alternatives. Any object placed in one of these segregates cannot at the same time belong to another. Those culturally appropriate responses which are distinctive alternatives in the same kinds of situations—or, in linguistic parlance, which occur in the same "environment"—can be said to *contrast.* A series of terminologically contrasted segregates forms a *contrast set.*

Note that the cognitive relation of contrast is not equivalent to the relation of class exclusion in formal logic and set theory. The three categories 'hamburger,' 'hot dog,' and 'rainbow' are mutually exclusive in membership. But in writing rules for classifying hamburgers I must say something about hot dogs, whereas I can ignore rainbows. Two categories contrast only when the difference between them is significant for defining their use. The segregates 'hamburger' and 'rainbow,' even though they have no members in common, do not function as distinctive alternatives in any uncontrived classifying context familiar to me.

Taxonomies

The notion of contrast cannot account for all the significant relations among these lunch-counter segregates. Although no object can be both a hamburger and a hot dog, an object can very well be both a hot dog and a sandwich or a hamburger and a sandwich. By recording complementary names applied to the same objects (and eliminating referential synonyms such as *something to eat* and *food*), the following series might result:

Object A is named: *something to eat, sandwich, hamburger*
Object B is named: *something to eat, sandwich, ham sandwich*
Object C is named: *something to eat, pie, apple pie*
Object D is named: *something to eat, pie, cherry pie*
Object E is named: *something to eat, ice-cream bar, Eskimo pie.*

Some segregates include a wider range of objects than others and are sub-partitioned by a contrast set. The segregate 'pie' *includes* the contrast set 'apple pie,' 'cherry pie,' etc. For me, the segregate 'apple pie' is, in turn, sub-partitioned by 'French apple pie' and 'plain (or 'ordinary') apple pie' Figure 1 diagrams the sub-partitioning of the segregate 'something to eat' as revealed by naming responses to objects A–E.[4]

Again it is the use of terms, not their linguistic structure, that provides evidence of inclusion. We cannot consider 'Eskimo pie' to be included in the category 'pie,' for we cannot discover a natural situation in which an

	something to eat				
	sandwich		pie		ice-cream bar
	hamburger	ham sandwich	apple pie	cherry pie	Eskimo pie
Objects:	A	B	C	D	E

Figure 10:1. Subpartitioning of the segregate 'something to eat,' as revealed by naming responses to objects A–E.

object labelled *Eskimo pie* can be labelled simply *pie*. Thus the utterance, "That's not a sandwich; that's a pie," cannot refer to an Eskimo pie. Similar examples are common in English. The utterance, "Look at that oak," may refer to a 'white oak' but never to a 'poison oak.' A 'blackbird' is a kind of 'bird,' but a 'redcap' is not a kind of 'cap.' For many English speakers, the unqualified use of *American* invariably designates a resident or citizen of the United States; consequently, for such speakers, an 'American is a kind of 'North American' rather than the converse. One cannot depend on a particular grammatical construction, such as one of the English phrasal compounds, to differentiate consistently a single cognitive relation, such as that of inclusion (cf. Hockett 1958:316–317). Because English is not unique in this respect (Frake 1961), the practice of arguing from morphological and syntactic analysis directly to cognitive relations must be considered methodologically unsound.

Segregates in different contrast sets, then, may be related by inclusion. A system of contrast sets so related is a *taxonomy* (Conklin 1962; Gregg 1954; Woodger 1952). This definition does not require a taxonomy to have a unique beginner, i.e., a segregate which includes all other segregates in the system. It requires only that the segregates at the most inclusive level form a demonstrable contrast set.

Taxonomies make possible a regulation of the amount of information communicated about an object in a given situation (compare: "Give me something to eat" with "Give me a French apple pie a la mode"), and they provide a hierarchal ordering of categories, allowing an efficient program for the identification, filing, and retrieving of significant information (Herdan 1960:210–211). The use of taxonomic systems is not confined to librarians and biologists; it is a fundamental principle of human thinking. The elaboration of taxonomies along vertical dimensions of generalization and horizontal dimensions of discrimination probably depends on factors such as the variety of cultural settings within which one talks about the objects being classified (Frake 1961: 121–122), the importance of the objects to the way of life of the classifiers (Brown 1958; Nida 1958), and general properties of human thinking with regard to the number of items that the mind can cope with at a given time (Miller 1956; Yngve 1960).[5] Determining the precise correlates of variations in taxonomic structure, both intraculturally and cross-culturally, is, of course, one of the objectives of this methodology.

In order to describe the use of taxonomic systems and to work out their behavioral correlates, evidence of complementary naming must be supplemented by observations on the socio-linguistic contexts that call for contrasts at particular levels. One could, for example, present a choice between objects whose segregates appear to contrast at different levels and ask an informant to complete the frame: "Pick up that——." Suppose we have an apple pie on the counter next to a ham sandwich. The frame would probably be completed as "Pick up that pie." If, however, we substitute a cherry pie for the ham sandwich, we would expect to hear "Pick up that apple pie." Variations on this device of having informants contrast particular objects can be worked out depending on the kind of phenomena being classified. Some objects, such as pies and plants, are easier to bring together for visual comparison than others, such as diseases and deities.

Another device for eliciting taxonomic structures is simply to ask directly about relations of inclusion: "Is *X* a kind of *Y*?" Since in many speech situations even a native fails to elicit a term at the level of specification he requires, most, if not all, languages probably provide explicit methods for moving up and down a taxonomic hierarchy:

"Give me some of that pie." "What kind of pie d'ya want, Mac?"

"What's this 'submarine' thing on the menu?" "That's a kind of sandwich."

Once a taxonomic partitioning has been worked out it can be tested systematically for terminological contrast with frames such as "Is that an X?" with an expectation of a negative reply. For example, we could point to an apple pie and ask a counterman:

1. "Is that something to drink?"
2. "Is that a sandwich?"
3. "Is that a cherry pie?"

We would expect the respective replies to reflect the taxonomy of lunch-counter foods:

1. "No, it's something to eat."
2. "No, it's a pie."
3. "No, it's an apple pie."

(Admittedly it is easier to do this kind of questioning in a culture where one can assume the role of a naive learner.)

In employing these various operations for exploring taxonomic structures, the investigator must be prepared for cases when the same linguistic form designates segregates at different levels of contrast within the same system ('man' vs. 'animal,' 'man' vs. 'woman,' 'man' vs. 'boy') (Frake 1961:119); when a single unpartitioned segregate contrasts with two or more other segregates which are themselves at different levels of contrast ("That's not a coin; it's a token." "That's not a dime; it's a token."); and when incongruities occur in the results of the several operations (terminological contrasts may cut across sub-hierarchies revealed by complementary naming; explicit statements of inclusion may be less consistent than complementary naming).

Attributes

Our task up to this point has been to reveal the structure of the system from which a selection is made when categorizing an object. When you hand a Navajo a plant specimen, or an American a sandwich, what is the available range of culturally defined arrays into which this object can be categorized? Methodological notions of contrast and inclusion have enabled us to discern some structure in this domain of cognitive choices, but we still have not faced the problem of how a person decides which out of a set of alternative categorizations is the correct one in a given instance. How does one in fact distinguish a hamburger from a cheeseburger, a chair from a stool, a tree from a shrub, an uncle from a cousin, a jerk from a slob?

A mere list of known members of a category—however an investigator identifies these objects cross-culturally—does not answer this question. Categorization, in essence, is a device for treating new experience as though it were equivalent to something already familiar (Brown 1958; Bruner 1957; Bruner *et al.* 1956; Sapir 1949). The hamburger I get tomorrow may be a quite different object in terms of size, kind of bun, and lack of tomatoes from the hamburger I had today. But it will still be a hamburger—unless it has a slice of cheese in it! To define 'hamburger' one must know, not just what objects it includes, but with what it contrasts. In this way we learn that a slice of cheese makes a difference, whereas a slice of tomato does not. In the context of different cultures the task is to state what one must know in order to categorize objects correctly. A definition of a Navajo plant category is not given by a list of botanical species it contains but by a rule for distinguishing newly encountered specimens of that category from contrasting alternatives.

Ideally the criterial attributes which generate a contrast set fall along a limited number of dimensions of contrast, each with two or more contrasting values or "components." Each segregate can be defined as a distinctive bundle of components. For example, the plant taxonomy of the Eastern Subanun, a Philippine people, has as its beginner a contrast set of three segregates which together include almost all of the more than 1,400 segregates at the most specific level of contrast within the taxonomy. This three-member contrast set can be generated by binary contrasts along two dimensions pertaining to habit of stem growth (see Table 10:1). Applications of

TABLE 10:1. *Defining Attributes of the Contrast Set of Stem Habit in the Subanun Plant Taxonomy*

CONTRAST SET	DIMENSIONS OF CONTRAST	
	Woodiness	Rigidity
gayu 'woody plants'	W	R
sigbet 'herbaceous plants'	$\overline{W}$	R
belagen 'vines'		$\overline{R}$

componential analysis to pronominal systems and kinship terminologies have made this method of definition familiar (Austerlitz 1959; Conklin 1962; Goodenough 1956; Lounsbury 1956; McKaughan 1959; Thomas 1955; Wallace and Atkins 1960). The problem remains of demonstrating the cognitive saliency of componential solutions—to what extent are they models of how a person decides which term to use?—and of relating terminological attributes to actual perceptual discriminations (Frake 1961; Wallace and Atkins 1960). As a case of the latter problem, suppose we learn that informants distinguish two contrasting plant segregates by calling the fruit of one 'red' and that of the other 'green.' We set up 'color' as a dimension of contrast with values of 'red' and 'green.' But the terminology of 'color' is itself a system of segregates whose contrastive structure must be analysed before color terms can serve as useful defining attributes of other segregates. Ultimately one is faced with defining color categories by referring to the actual perceptual dimensions along which informants make differential categorizations. These dimensions must be determined empirically and not prescribed by the investigator using stimulus materials from his own culture. By careful observation one might discover that visual evaluation of an object's succulence, or other unexpected dimensions, as well as the traditional dimensions of hue, brightness, and saturation, are criterial to the use of "color" terms in a particular culture (Conklin 1955).

Whether aimed directly at perceptual qualities of phenomena or at informants' descriptions of pertinent attributes (Frake 1961:122–125), any method for determining the distinctive and probabililistic attributes of a segregate must depend, first, on knowing the contrast set within which the segregate is participating, and, second, on careful observations of verbal and non-verbal features of the cultural situations to which this contrast set provides an appropriate response.

This formulation has important implications for the role of eliciting in ethnography. The distinctive "situations," or "eliciting frames," or "stimuli," which evoke and define a set of contrasting responses are cultural data to be discovered, not prescribed, by the ethnographer. This stricture does not limit the use of preconceived eliciting devices to prod an informant into action or speech without any intent of defining the response by what evoked it in this instance. But the formulation—prior to observation—of response-defining eliciting devices is ruled out by the logic of this methodology which insists that any eliciting conditions not themselves part of the cultural-ecological system being investigated cannot be used to define categories purporting to be those of the people under study. It is those elements of *our informants'* experience, which *they* heed in selecting appropriate actions and utterances, that this methodology seeks to discover.

Objectives

The methodological suggestions proposed in this paper, as they stand, are clearly awkward and incomplete. They must be made more rigorous and expanded to include analyses of longer utterance sequences, to consider non-verbal behavior systematically, and to explore the other types of cognitive relations, such as sequential stage relations (Frake 1961) and part-whole relations, that may pertain between contrast sets. Focussing on the linguistic code, clearer operational procedures are needed for delimiting semantically exocentric units ("lexemes" or "idioms") (Goodenough 1956; Nida 1951), for discerning synonomy, homonymy, and polysemy (Ullman 1957:63), and for distinguishing between utterance grammaticalness (correctly constructed code) and utterance congruence (meaningfully constructed message) (Chomsky 1957; Joos 1958). In their present form, however, these suggestions have come out of efforts to describe behavior in the field, and their further development can come only from continuing efforts to apply and test them in ethnographic field situations.

The intended objective of these efforts is eventually to provide the ethnographer with public, non-intuitive procedures for ordering his presentation of observed and elicited events according to the principles of classification of the people he is studying. To order ethnographic observations solely according to an investigator's preconceived categories obscures the real content of culture: how people organize their experience conceptually so that it can be transmitted as knowledge from person to person and from generation to generation. As Goodenough advocates in a classic paper, culture "does not consist of things, people, behavior, or emotions," but the forms or organization of these things in the minds of people (Goodenough 1957). The principles by which people in a culture construe their world reveal how they segregate the pertinent from the insignificant, how they code and retrieve information, how they anticipate events (Kelly 1955), how they define alternative courses of action and make decisions among them. Consequently a strategy of ethnographic description that gives a central place to the cognitive processes of the actors involved will contribute reliable cultural data to problems of the relations between language, cognition, and behavior; it will point up critical dimensions for meaningful cross-cultural comparison; and, finally, it will give us productive descriptions of cultural behavior, descriptions which, like the linguists' grammar, succinctly state what one must know in order to generate culturally acceptable acts and utterances appropriate to a given socio-ecological context (Goodenough 1957).

Notes

1. In preparing this paper I have especially benefited from suggestions by Harold C. Conklin, Thomas Gladwin, Volney Stefflre, and William C. Sturtevant.

2. In this paper the term *object* designates anything construed as a member of a category (Bruner *et al.* 1956:231), whether perceptible or not.

3. Because this is a short, orally presented paper, suggested procedures are illustrated with rather simple examples from a familiar language and culture. A serious analysis would require much larger quantities of speech data presented in phonemic transcription. For a more complex example, intended as an ethnographic statement, see Frake 1961.

4. This example is, of course, considerably over-simplified. If the reader does not relate these segregates in the same way as our hypothetical lunch-counter speakers, he is not alone. Shortly after I completed the manuscript of this paper, a small boy approached me in a park and, without any eliciting remark whatsoever on my part, announced: "Hamburgers are more gooder than sandwiches." One could not ask for better evidence of contrast.

5. At least in formal, highly partitioned taxonomic systems an ordering of superordinates according to the number of their subordinates appears to yield a stable statistical distribution (the Willis distribution) regardless of what is being classified or who is doing the classifying (Herdan 1960:211–225; Mandelbrot 1956).

References Cited

AUSTERLITZ, ROBERT. 1959, Semantic components of pronoun systems: Gilyak. Word 15(1):102–109.

BARKER, ROGER G. and HERBERT F. WRIGHT. 1955, Midwest and its children, the psychological ecology of an American town. New York, Harper & Row.

BOAS, FRANZ. 1911, Introduction. *In* Handbook of American Indian languages, Bureau of American Ethnology Bulletin 40, Pt. 1, 1–83.

BROWN, ROGER. 1958, Words and things. New York, Free Press.

BROWN, ROGER AND ERIC H. LENNEBERG. 1954, A study in language and cognition. Journal of Abnormal and Social Psychology 49(3):454–462.

BRUNER, JEROME S., 1957, Going beyond the information given. *In* Contemporary approaches to cognition; a symposium held at the University of Colorado. Cambridge, Harvard University Press, 41–70.

BRUNER, JEROME S., J. J. GOODNOW, AND G. A. AUSTIN, 1956, A study of thinking. With an appendix on language by Roger W. Brown. New York, Wiley.

CHOMSKY, NOAM, 1955, Semantic considerations in grammar. Georgetown University Monograph Series on Language and Linguistics, No. 8, 141–150.

______, 1957, Syntactic structures. The Hague, Mouton.

CONKLIN, HAROLD C., 1954, The relation of Hanunóo culture to the plant world. Unpublished Ph.D. dissertation. New Haven, Yale University.

______, 1955, Hanunóo color categories. Southwestern Journal of Anthropology 11(4):339–344.

______, 1962, Lexicographical treatment of folk taxonomies. Work paper for Conference on Lexicography, Indiana University, Nov. 11–12, 1960. *In* Fred W. Householder and Sol Saporta, eds., Problems in lexicography. Supplement to International Journal of American Linguistics, Vol. 28, No. 2—Indiana University Research Center in Anthropology, Folklore and Linguistics, Publication 21. Bloomington.

FRAKE, CHARLES O., 1961, The diagnosis of disease among the Subanun of Mindanao. American Anthropologist 63(1):113–132.

GOODENOUGH, WARD H., 1956, Componential analysis and the study of meaning. Language 32(1):195–216.

______, 1957, Cultural anthropology and linguistics. Georgetown University Monograph Series on Language and Linguistics, No. 9, 167–173.

GREGG, JOHN R., 1954, The language of taxonomy, an application of symbolic logic to the study of classificatory systems. New York, Columbia University Press.

HAUGEN, EINAR, 1957, The semantics of Icelandic orientation. Word 13(3):447–459.

HERDAN, GUSTAV, 1960, Type-token mathematics, a textbook of mathematical linguistics. The Hague, Mouton.

HILL, A. A., 1952, A note on primitive languages. International Journal of American Linguistics 18(3):172–177.

HOCKETT, CHARLES F., 1958, A course in modern linguistics. New York, Macmillan.

HYMES, DELL H., 1961, On typology of cognitive styles in language (with examples from Chinookan). Anthropological Linguistics 3(1):22–54.

JESPERSON, OTTO, 1934, Language: its nature, development, and origin. London, Allen & Unwin.

JOOS, MARTIN, 1958, Semology: a linguistic theory of meaning. Studies in Linguistics 13(3):53–70.

KELLY, GEORGE, 1955, The psychology of personal constructs. New York, Norton.

LOUNSBURY, FLOYD G., 1956, A semantic analysis of the Pawnee kinship usage. Language 32(1):158–194.

MANDELBROT, BENOIT, 1956, On the language of taxonomy. *In* Colin Cherry, ed., Information theory. New York, Academic Press 135–145.

MCKAUGHAN, HOWARD, 1959, Semantic components of pronoun systems: Maranao. Word 15(1):101–102.

MILLER, GEORGE. 1956, Human memory and the storage of information. IRE transactions on information theory IT, 2:129–137. New York, Institute of Radio Engineers.

MILLER, GEORGE, EUGENE GALANTER AND KARL PRIBRAM, 1960, Plans and structure of behavior. New York, Holt, Rinehart and Winston.

NIDA, EUGENE. 1951, A system for the description of semantic elements. Word 7(1):1–14.

——. 1958, Analysis of meaning and dictionary making. International Journal of American Linguistics 24(4):279–292.

PIKE, KENNETH. 1954, Language in relation to a unified theory of the structure of human behavior. Part 1. Glendale, Summer Institute of Linguistics.

SAPIR, EDWARD. 1949, The psychological reality of phonemes. *In* David G. Mandelbaum, ed., Selected writings of Edward Sapir in Language, culture, and personality. Berkeley, University of California Press 46–60.

THOMAS, DAVID. 1955, Three analyses of the Ilocano pronoun system. Word 11(2):204–208.

ULLMAN, STEPHEN. 1957, The principles of semantics. New York, Philosophical Library.

WALLACE, ANTHONY AND J. ATKINS. 1960, The meaning of kinship terms. American Anthropologist 62(1):58–80.

WOODGER, J. H. 1952, Biology and language, an introduction to the methodology of the biological sciences including medicine. Cambridge, The University Press.

YNGVE, VICTOR H. 1960, A model and an hypothesis for language structure. Proceedings of the American Philosophical Society 104(5):444–466.

11 ETHNOSCIENCE AND ETHNOMETHODOLOGY

George Psathas

Ethnoscience research has often focused upon very limited aspects of everyday experience—some have suggested that it is microethnography. A set of kinship terms, the names for diseases, the terms for beer, a nomenclature for kinds of firewood, the places in a jail—these and other domains have been studied. In somewhat the same way, a recent development in sociology known as ethnomethodology has also stressed the importance of common, everyday activities. In this chapter George Psathas contrasts the two approaches and discusses their relationship to the philosophical position called phenomenology. While his critique of ethnoscience is accurate for much of the work done, recent developments are beginning to invalidate it. For instance, he feels that ethnoscience is concerned only with emic units and therefore is not cross-cultural in its approach. In their study of basic color terminology, Brent Berlin and Paul Kay (*Basic Color Terms.* Berkeley and Los Angeles: University of California Press, 1969.) have demonstrated how ethnoscience involves testing general hypotheses cross-culturally. The criticism that ethnoscience has been a static approach is well taken. At the same time, with more attention being given to the concept of *plans* (see Chapters 14 and 15), the dynamic aspects of human interaction are being accounted for with increasing rigor. Psathas's study does much to open the way for more communication between these two approaches. —EDITOR'S NOTE

There are two approaches in the social sciences which have developed in recent years, one in anthropology called ethnoscience, the other in sociology called ethnomethodology. Both have the potential for making a great impact on research in anthropology and sociology. In this paper, I would like to examine these approaches, show some of the similarities and differences between them, comment on their significance, and indicate their relation to phenomenological approaches.

Reprinted from "Ethnomethods and Phenomenology," *Social Research* 35 (1968): 500–520 by permission of the author and the publisher.

Ethnoscience

Ethnoscience has been defined by Sturtevant[1] as "the system of knowledge and cognition typical of a given culture." He says that, from this point of view, "a culture amounts to the sum of a given society's folk classifications, all of that society's ethnoscience, its particular ways of classifying its material and social universe."

Following this approach, the task of the social scientist is to discover how members of a culture perceive, define and classify, how they actually perform their activities and what meanings they assign to acts occurring in the context of their culture.

Despite the fact that ethnoscience has been called the New Ethnography,[2] there is much in it that is old. Malinowski, some years ago, stated that the aim of the ethnographer is "to grasp the native's point of view, his relation to life, to realize his vision of the world."[3] Anthropologists would agree that this has been a central task of anthropology. Ethnoscience may simply be providing a more recent statement of that aim within a framework of new methodology and reasearch techniques.

With reference to the method for determining what the native has "in mind," Malinowski stated:

> . . . we cannot expect to obtain a definite, precise and abstract statement from a philosopher, belonging to the community itself. The native takes his fundamental assumptions for granted, and if he reasons or inquires into matters of belief, it would be always in regard to details and concrete applications. Any attempts on the part of the ethnographer to induce his informant to formulate such a general statement would have to be in the form of leading questions of the worst type because in these leading questions he would have to introduce words and concepts essentially foreign to the native. Once the informant grasped their meaning, his outlook would be warped by our own ideas having been poured into it. Thus, the ethnographer must draw the generalizations for himself, must formulate the abstract statement without the direct help of a native informant.[4]

The ethnoscientist would agree that the phrasing of questions must be carefully done so as not to introduce ideas to the native which were not part of *his* cognitive system. Borrowing from methods in linguistics, he would attempt more systematic (and possibly replicable) questioning procedures to elicit data adequate to the development of a more complete analysis of that aspect of the culture which he is studying. Frake[5] offers examples of question frames for accomplishing such purposes. However, critics of ethnoscience have noted that little attention has been given to the determination of how the questioning process and the relation between the researcher and his native informant affect the responses given. Marvin Harris[6] has also noted that there is little indication of the range or variety of responses given but rather that most reports are phrased in terms of "usually" or "rarely" whenever any indication of frequency is made. (I think this matter needs attention though in my estimation it is not a statistical problem but rather one of determining typifications and, more broadly, essences.)

Goodenough, in a more recent statement of the aim of the New Ethnography, repeats that the aim is to grasp the native's view:

> A society's culture consists of whatever it is one has to *know* or believe in order to operate in a manner acceptable to its members, and to do so in any role that they accept for any one of themselves. . . . It is the forms of things that people have in mind, their models for perceiving, and otherwise interpreting them . . . Ethnographic description, then, requires methods of processing observed phenomena such that we can inductively construct a theory of how our informants have organized the same phenomena. It is the theory, not the phenomena alone, which ethnographic descriptions aim to present.[7]

As this last quotation indicates, the task of the ethnographer is not merely to describe events as he might see them from his observer's perspective, but also to get "inside" those events to see what kind of theory it is that the natives themselves inductively use to organize phenomena in their daily lives. In terms used in phenomenology, the task is to discover how natives "constitute" the phenomena which exist for them in their lives. From a slightly different perspective, the task of the social scientist is to construct a theory of natives' theories, or as Schutz has put it, "a typification of their typifications." (I think that Goodenough's use of the term "theory" can be interpreted in the sense of Schutz's notion of typification.)

Developments in ethnoscience are not being influenced to any great extent by phenomenology. The mainstream of contemporary influence in ethnoscience is coming from linguistics. The influence of linguistics can be seen particularly in research involving the method of componential analysis. This method is stimulating considerable discussion and controversy among anthropologists.[8] Componential analysis is concerned with the relation between the categories of language and objects, concepts or events in the real world, i.e., the "things." The components or conceptual principles which underlie the process by which a name is used to classify things are sought by the investigator. If these principles are discovered, the investigator can then reproduce culturally appropriate behavior since he will have grasped the native's perspective. He will also have discovered what components are significant or relevant to members of the culture being studied.[9]

Typically, componential analyses are made of cognitive systems, i.e., phenomena, which are related to one another categorically, e.g., color systems, kinship systems, botanical taxonomies, etc. Opposed to the cognitive side of the semantic or sign-object relationship is the terminological system of the spoken language. In essence, the relationship between the terminological system (the way he talks about his world) and the cognitive system (the way he experiences it) is studied by having the informant make discriminations between a variety of stimuli presented to him and having him name the "things" that he has discriminated, thus presenting the investigator with evidence of how the informant interprets and classifies the world around him. The first phase of an analysis consists of *generating* the terminological system by presenting native informants with a "substitution frame" which can be filled by many possible responses, e.g., "the color of this is called —," at the same time that the informants are presented with a stimulus, e.g., a color sample. In this phase, a list is obtained of names used by the informant in categorizing the stimuli presented to him.

The next phase consists of *classifying* the names into a taxonomy of sub-categories. Taxonomies are composed of "segregates" and "contrast sets." A segregate is a terminologically distinguished array of objects and a contrast set is a series of terminologically contrasted segregates. For example, any color name such as "light red" or "reddish orange" is a segregate because each is a category which can include several particular "light reds" or "reddish oranges." The contrast sets, however, may be named red, green, blue, etc., with each containing a series of segregates composed of particular color stimuli that are named and responded to in the same way. The taxonomy is also generated by substitution frames. One useful frame is a question that asks directly about inclusive relationships, e.g., "is X a kind of Y?", "is reddish-orange a kind of orange?"

The final and most difficult phase involves determining the components or rules that informants use in placing different stimuli within particular segregates or contrast sets. Since not only taxonomies but components differ between cultures, it is necessary that the components be ascertained from the subject's perspective, especially because it is the aim of the method to discover the informant's experience and not to impose or prescribe any schema which the investigator may have.

An example of components drawn from an analysis of the use of English personal pronouns reveals gender, person, number and grammatical function in the components used to generate personal pronouns. From such rules accurate predictions can be made of the word that native speakers will use, e.g., when "I" rather than "me" will be used. The analysis is not considered complete until rules can be formulated that can predict almost any naming response in the cognitive system.[10]

One criticism which can be made of componential analysis is the fact that it narrows the focus of research to the study of classification systems and the use of terms, or linguistic categories, by native speakers. If research focuses only on problems that can be studied with available methods, then significance may be sacrificed for precision and there exists a danger that techniques will determine the selection of problems for study. For example, much work has been and is being done using componential analysis for the analysis of kinship terms.[11] The kinship system continues, thus, to remain the anthropologists' "white rat," a handy little "subject" that he can study in a variety of ways.

There is a danger that componential analysis will be regarded as *the* method of ethnoscience. Sturtevant notes that "ethnoscientific work has thus far concentrated on the sorts of cognitive structure involved in selection classes: the interrelations of categories considered as sets of possible alternatives under varying environmental conditions. Little attention has yet been paid to the methods required for the investigation of the sort of structures involved in rules of combination, the temporal or spatial ordering of co-occurring categories from different selection classes."[12] There is an obvious need for ethnoscientific work to range more broadly and to develop methods which permit the study of larger structures. The necessity for apprehending essential relationships among the elements of the phenomena being analyzed,[13] as phenomenologists have termed it, remains important. It is not enough to discover and describe the components; rules regarding their possible combinations must also be defined. Further, the analysis of the combinations of "categories from different selection classes," as Sturtevant has put it, will allow for the determination of essential relationships among such elements as they combine to form new phenomena, e.g., sentences, or broader conceptual categories.

In contrast to the work traditionally done in anthropological linguistics, workers in ethnoscience are more willing to enter into semantic analysis, to try to discover the meanings of terms. Further, the meanings they are concerned with are the meanings-in-use, i.e., the everyday meanings used in the present situation, rather than dictionary meanings or etymologically analyzed meanings. In this sense, they have adopted one important attitude or perspective found in phenomenology, namely, that man's cognitive world is "shot through with meaning,"[14] and that it is these meanings which must be understood in order to grasp the life-world of particular others.

The application of componential analysis to native classification systems and the discovery of the components which underlie the native speaker's use, i.e., the criteria he uses in assigning a term to an object or event,[15] seem to me to lead to an outcome which phenomenology also seeks, namely, how "things" are constituted. The components are the criteria used by the native speaker to constitute, in an active manner, the phenomena. By discovering the irreducible components which natives use, it is possible to arrive at a complete account which then enables the investigator to generate the constituted phenomena in a form of appearance which is recognizable to the native. This is stated in terms of "accurate prediction of naming responses" by ethnoscientists. In my opinion, it represents an aspect of phenomenological method not explicitly recognized by workers in ethnoscience.

For those more interested in longer utterances or interaction sequences than in particular terms, componential analysis seems cumbersome and perhaps even inappropriate. At least, it has not yet been applied to data of this kind. Because of this lack, it is not yet possible to determine to what extent the method has a built-in limitation. If this limitation exists, then it should be clearly pointed out so that the problems and data will not be "forced" into the framework required by the methodology.

Here is one contrast between the work being done in ethnoscience and that being done in ethnomethodology. The ethnomethodologists, since they are interested in discovering the units of meaning that are operational in the on-going social world, are willing to study more complex social phenomena and not limit themselves to cognitive structures for which linguistic terms exist.[16]

At this point several critical remarks must be made. It is I who have interpreted some aspects of the ethnoscientists' orientation in terms of phenomenology. There is, as yet, no explicit recognition of phenomenology in the work of ethnoscientists. Their work, furthermore, is so heavily influenced by linguistics that they "equate semantic features with cognitive distinctions."[17] Too much of man's behavior is assigned to the cognitive mode and too little to emotions. There is an implicit disdain for the emotional aspect of man's behavior and a tendency to equate the "experience of the world" with the cognitive categories used to describe it.

There is an assumption that communication and language form the basis for cultural life. The significant cognitive features of the shared symbolic system of the culture are presumed to be codifiable into language. Language can therefore be analyzed to determine the shared code or set of rules that members have and use in constructing and interpreting messages about their world. Their understanding of the code need not be explicit but the ethnoscientist assumes that there is such a code and that it can be discerned. Once it is discovered, he will have arrived at a description of the world as viewed by the native, i.e., an insight into his categories and conceptualizations. This reliance on an analysis of how members of the society talk *about* their world as a means of understanding it does not allow the ethnoscientist to examine non-verbal but nevertheless experienced aspects of the real world. Thus, he is not faithful to the phenomenological concern with *all* of man's experience and not solely his categorized, linguistically organized experience.

This is, therefore, a fundamental criticism of the ethnoscientist: he is not faithful to the phenomena of the social world which constitute themselves in a variety of ways.

Ethnomethodology

Ethnomethodology is the term coined by Garfinkel and his students[18] to refer to their work. Garfinkel has defined ethnomethodology as: "the investigation of the rational properties of indexical expressions and other practical actions as contingent ongoing accomplishments of organized artful practices of everyday life."[19] An elaboration of the particular meanings of these terms, as Garfinkel defines them, is beyond the scope of this paper. We shall only note that he is concerned with the practical, everyday activities of men in society as they make accountable, to themselves and others, their everyday affairs, and with the methods they use for producing and managing those same affairs. He sees similarity in the activities of producing and making accountable. His concern with the everyday, routine and commonplace activities as phenomena in their own right, deserving of detailed study, is certainly consistent with the views of phenomenology.[20]

The ethnomethodologist seeks to discover the "methods" that persons use in their everyday life in society in constructing social reality and also to discover the nature of the realities they have constructed. In studying, for example, the way that jurors recognize the "correctness" of a verdict, he would focus on how the jurors make their activities "normal," on how the moral order of their world is created. They are seen as creating, through their activities, familiar scenes and procedures which are recognizable to them as the world they know in common and take for granted, by which and within which "correctness" of a verdict is determined. Only by examining their procedures and discovering what they consist of, can one fully understand what they mean by correctness, as *correctness is decided by those who construct it.* Further, as Garfinkel shows, some understanding of decision-making in daily life, i.e., in situations other than the jury-room, is also achieved.

In common with ethnoscience is the ethnomethodologist's effort to understand the world as it is interpreted by men in daily life. For example, Natanson, in his introduction to Schutz's collected papers, states "the social scientist's task is the reconstruction of the way in which men in daily life interpret their own world."[21] This is a basic position in the work of ethnomethodologists and in Schutz's own work.

The distinction between natural science and social science, as Natanson, Schutz and others clearly point out, is based on the fact that men are not only objects existing in the natural world to be observed by the scientist, but they are creators of a world, a cultural world, of their own. In creating this world, they interpret their own activities. Their overt behavior is only a fragment of their total behavior. Any social scientist who insists that he can understand all of man's behavior by focusing only on that part which is overt and manifested in concrete, directly observable acts is naive, to say the least. The challenge to the social scientist who seeks to understand social reality, then, is to understand the meaning that the actor's act has for him. If the observer applies only his own categories or theories concerning the meanings of acts, he may never discover the meanings these same acts have for the actors themselves. Nor can he ever discover how social reality is "created" and how subsequent acts by human actors are performed in the context of *their* understandings.

This, it seems to me, is similar to the problem of bracketing in phenomenological analysis. The scientist must bracket his own pre-suppositions concerning the phenomena and seek to discover the suppositions which human actors, *in situ*, adopt and use. Further, he must also bracket these suppositions in an effort to analyze the phenomena themselves.[22]

Both ethnoscience and ethnomethodology are involved in the problem of cultural relativism, but ethnomethodology, in my estimation, may come closer to escaping the bounds of the particular culture that is studied because of the phenomenological sophistication which aids it. For example, the ethnoscientist in studying one culture's classification system has no reason to expect that another culture's classification system will be the same. His emic analysis refers to one society's culture, i.e., he may discover how the Subanun classify disease but he does not claim that any other culture will have the same system of classification. Certainly he can do cross-cultural comparisons to see if emic systems of different cultures share common elements. But he does not take the position that an emic analysis will produce a system which is universally true or valid. Similarly, the ethnomethodologist studying particular actors in particular groupings in a particular society cannot claim that what he discovers will be true generally for all men. Some aspects of decision-making by jurors, for example, may change depending on changes in legal rules and procedures at a later historical point, may differ from one culture to another depending on how the legal system is structured, etc.

However, the grounding of ethnomethodology in phenomenology implies that research problems will be defined and approached in such a way as to result in the discovery of the essential features of the social phenomena being studied. This may appear to be a contradiction. In one sense it is, but at another level it may not be. For example, if one looks at the problem of jurors making decisions as a study of the general phenomenon of decision-making, an analysis of their procedures has implications for the understanding of the essence of the process of decision-making, of how groups, in contrast to individuals, make decisions, and of the rules of decision-making in everyday life. By taking a phenomenological position in which one tries to discover the basic essence of the process, it is possible for the ethnomethodologist to discover that which is more generally true and not be limited to culturally and temporally relative conclusions. As an example from what is more clearly a phenomenological analysis, the "natural attitude" and the "inter-subjective world of everyday life"[23] are presented as being characteristic not only of Western man, but probably of all men living in society. They are part of the basic human condition, so to speak. For example, that men assume, and assume that others assume, that if "I change places with the other, so that his 'here' becomes mine, I shall be at the same distance from things and see them with the same typicality that he does; moreover, the same things would be in my reach which are actually in his (and that the reverse is also true)" (*Ibid.* p. 12); that the world is taken for granted to be an intersubjective world; that the world existed yesterday and will exist tomorrow; that my actions are based on my believing that others can interpret those actions as intelligible, given their understanding of what we know in our culture, etc. If we take the position that the basic features of the "natural attitude" and of the "inter-subjective world of everyday life" may represent essences of the human condition which are universally true—and there is certainly much to indicate in Schutz's analysis that the natural attitude is a taken-for-granted aspect of everyday life—then it is on this background or within this frame that men perform meaningful acts in their everyday activities. The meanings which are then added to behavior are based on the pre-suppositions of the natural attitude. If this is so, then it is possible to look for those common elements in a variety of cultures, based on the natural attitude and the inter-subjectivity of knowledge, that may affect the meanings assigned to activities. What I am saying here is that it is possible that, given this background, some restrictions are placed on how men can perceive and interact. The use of drugs to "escape" the taken-for-granted aspects of everyday life and throw these into sharp question is some indication that men are somehow tied down, bound by, the "facts" of human existence. It is only with some effort, such as the taking of drugs, that one can escape the bounds of the world of everyday life and enter other realities.

Given this grounding in phenomenology (of Schutz and others), the ethnomethodologist's approach to problems, it seems to me, is somewhat different from that of the ethnoscientist's. One contrast is that the former is directed more towards problems of *meaning* in everyday life situations. But even more basic is his concern with discovering those basic features (essences, perhaps) of everyday interaction so that the problem of how meanings are constructed and how social reality is created out of the interlocked activity of human actors becomes an important and critical topic for examination.[24]

Starting from the taken-for-granted, everyday world analyzed by the phenomenologist, the ethnomethodologist takes the position that this is the basis for all other strata of man's reality. This is the ground on which all other realities are constructed. If so, it is important to know what it is that is basic, since one is concerned with the reality of everyday-life-as-seen-by-men-in-society, and one wants to learn how men perceive, experience, and construct the social reality in which they live.[25] This represents, in a real sense, I believe, a phenomenological position of "going to the things themselves," to the social phenomena rather than to previously developed theories to be tested by the formulation of deductive hypotheses.

Both approaches emphasize the importance of investigating the taken-for-granted aspects of man's existence in the world. The ethnoscientists investigate what they call components and the ethnomethodologists what they call background expectancies. Both are concerned with the "methods" which men use to make their world meaningful. The difference between the two approaches is that ethnoscience tends to emphasize the static thingness of the phenomena being studied, whereas ethnomethodology is concerned with the active processes whereby things (mainly activities) are constituted in the world of social action.[26]

It is important to note, in this connection, the effort by Garfinkel in his article "Studies in the Routine Grounds of Everyday Activities"[27] to demonstrate the existence of the natural attitude and the intersubjectivity of knowledge drawing from Schutz's analysis. In what Garfinkel calls "demonstration experiments," the technique used was that of disturbing or introducing a "nasty surprise" in interacting with others in order to demonstrate the presence of much that was taken for granted. The technique is simple though limited, and if imaginative variation were used,[28] would possibly not be necessary. Garfinkel disturbed others by simply not performing those acts which they expected—or by performing acts which others did not have any "reason" to expect. For example, his students were instructed to treat their parents at home as though they, the students, were guests in the home rather than the sons or daughters of the parents. The politeness and small acts of kindness they performed were then taken by their parents to be signs of hostility, antagonism or fatigue. For example, to ask one's parents if one may be allowed to look in the refrigerator or the pantry for something to eat—or to ask permission to eat in the first place—was greeted with perplexity, confusion and surprise.

Garfinkel reports going up to a customer standing in line in a restaurant and treating him as though he were the waiter, or revealing to a friend during a conversation that he, Garfinkel, had a tape recorder and was recording the entire conversation. What can be learned from such demonstrations? A great deal, though I would not wish to recommend these procedures to others since I do not feel that these are necessarily the only, or even the best, ways of obtaining data concerning the taken-for-granted assumptions of the common sense world of everyday life. They may certainly reveal the variety and complexity of the pre-suppositions or taken-for-granteds that exist in everyday life. The grounds of man's social existence can be discovered. Such discovery can have tremendous possibilities not only for understanding particular social worlds but also for changing or even destroying them altogether.

From my own work,[29] I would like to refer to the study of how cab drivers locate addresses. In order to understand this activity, it is necessary to understand not only the cab driver and his world but also the phenomenon of an address or, even more basic, the phenomenon of a location in space. A phenomenological analysis would lead us to the essence of "location" on which are imposed, in layers of meaning, so to speak, the more unique and specific elements and relationships among elements that constitute locations for the cab driver in a particular kind of socio-cultural space, e.g., the urban environment.

In this research we have thus far studied the constitution of addresses in radio-dispatched orders transmitted to the driver. The order represents a constitution of a location made by the radio dispatcher and understood by the cab driver. There is thus a shared system of relevances. Following the model of componential analysis, we sought to discover the components underlying particular orders. For example, a place that is a frequent source of passengers, that can have more than one potential passenger waiting at the same time, which has more than one point within it at which a passenger may be waiting, and which can be identified by a proper name will be referred to by messages that contain the name of the place, possible information concerning the location of the passenger (to find him within the location) and, as a further possibility, the name of the passenger (to differentiate him from others). For example, "Hanley and Olive, The A&P, for Bush." In contrast, a complete order which consists of a street name and number (e.g., 6604 Pershing) can be used to indicate single or small multi-family residences, where no ambiguity concerning entrances and exits exists and where no more than one potential passenger is likely to be waiting.

We thus found, in examining a large number of radio-dispatched orders, that for places lacking the criteria mentioned but whose location is unambiguous and well-known, name of place alone is sufficient. If the place is distinguished by the regularity of the customer who uses it, the customer's name alone may be sufficient. If the place is a residence or otherwise poses no problems concerning the location of the passenger within it, then descriptions of the passenger or where to find him are not needed. We can then arrive at the meaning of "complexity" or "difficulty" in locating a place and passenger *as complexity is defined within the cab driver's world.* Further, a phenomenological analysis would reveal the essential relationships among the elements of the phenomenon, i.e., an address, and from this, what essential possibilities exist for referring to addresses. That is, by determining the essential properties of an address, we can then understand how these make possible particular ways of referring to it. For example, its location *on* one side of a street *between* other structures gives it a position with reference to other streets and with reference to other buildings that makes it locatable in terms of a number (if discrete numbers are assigned to buildings) and a street name (if names are assigned to streets). If such numbers and names are not assigned, it can still be located in terms of those features which distinguish it from other structures (size, color, shape, texture, etc.) and which distinguish its street from other streets (width, compass direction, right or left from some other street, etc.).

I do not claim to have completed the analysis, but this brief description may serve to illustrate what is possible.

The last point I want to make concerns the importance of understanding subjective reality. It is indeed significant that the problem of understanding the *manner* by which men understand other men's minds has not been solved in social science. It is a basic fact of everyday life, however, that men claim to and act as though they can and do understand others, i.e., that they can "know others' minds." They can, at least, know that which is relevant to be known, given the interaction in which they are engaged. Men in everyday society do not doubt that they can know others' minds. They further assume that other men can know their minds, as well.

For the social scientist, a major task in any study is to discover the understandings that the actor and the other have of *one another.*[30] His task is to explicate those understandings. It is not his concern to analyze, in all their detail, the subjective aspects of the actor's behavior, nor of his own (the scientist's) perceptions. His task is to form objective, ideal constructs relating to the understandings and the typifications that men have of one another. (Ethnomethodology, more than ethnoscience, is involved in this task.) In so doing he need not elaborate all of the variations that are involved in some of these typifications. Rather, it is his task to make typifications; to make abstractions, to make constructs, and to determine the essences of the typifications which actors make. It is significant that phenomenologists are also undertaking the analysis of some of these problems and have discussed methods whereby men can determine how other men perceive. For example, Spiegelberg[31] shows that "imaginative self transposal" can occur, and sets out some of the elements of this process. One of these elements is what he calls "imaginative projection in thought"[32] in which one begins to "construct the other in his world on the basis of the clues which we find in the situation into which we have put ourselves imaginatively . . . and try to build, from these elements, his self and the world as he is likely to see it." The aim, as stated by Spiegelberg, is one which could not have been stated better by sociologists or anthropologists. It is to "see the world through another person's eyes" and consider the "whole 'frame' of existence which the other occupies."[33]

The other method, that of cooperative encounter or cooperative exploration, involves exploring the other's world with his helpful cooperation in a prolonged and extended dialogue involving the sympathetic probing, exploring and interrogation of the other. Anthropologists who have used native informants for long periods of time have experienced the phenomenon of coming to see the world through the other's eyes aided by the checks and qualifications introduced by the other in response to questions and comments. A better example, though it is a model which has not been extensively used for the development of scientific or phenomenological accounts of the other's world, is that of the patient-therapist relationship. Here the psychiatrist can achieve an encounter in which he comes to understand the other "in his entirety."

The method of participant observation in the social sciences has some of these possibilities also.[34] The extension of this method into *disguised* participant observation, in which the observer actually becomes a member of the group and performs a role within the group which others take to be his real identity rather than a role "put on" for the sake of collecting data, enables the observer-researcher to experience the role from within. That is, by having to perform *in that world*, he must develop and adopt the perspective that goes with that world. An example from my own experience is that of being a person who was asking others for directions in order to experience the receiving of directions; also vice versa—offering others directions in order to experience the giving of directions. This could be extended to many roles which I as a sociologist could take, even to that of being a sociologist presenting a paper to a sociological convention. By then examining my own feelings, ideas, behavior, etc., I can construct possible typifications of the social role and the perspective which it provides for *me.* I can then use myself as a model of what others who perform this role are like, i.e., what the world is as seen by typical others from this perspective.

It is to be hoped that ethnomethodologists will turn their attention to methods whereby it is possible to "know other men's minds." It is often taken for granted in research done by those in the symbolic interactionist tradition in social psychology (influenced by G.H. Mead, C.H. Cooley, W. I. Thomas and others) and ethnomethodologists that it is possible for the researcher to "know the mind" of the subjects studied. A necessary extension is the determination of how members of society know other members' minds. What ethnoscientists are doing is calling our attention to the possibility of devising strict and rigorous procedures for the determination of the other's "mind" and furthermore making possible the replication of results. However, their methodology may have built-in limitations stemming from the assumption that linguistic categories and their underlying components can provide adequate understanding of men in society. It remains to be seen whether more "imaginative," "introspective" and "subjective" approaches to the understanding of others can produce *replicable* results in a manner similar to the methods used in linguistic and semantic analysis.[35]

There is much to be expected from these approaches. Phenomenology has a great deal to offer the social scientist. We may hope that attention now being directed to phenomenology by the ethnomethodologists will stimulate the selection of those aspects of phenomenological methods and insights which are most relevant and significant for the social scientist's endeavor.

Both approaches promise to affect the course of research by focusing attention on the world of everyday life. Since the world is so vast and complex, they virtually guarantee that scientific activity will never end. More important, however, than guaranteeing us jobs forever is that they guarantee a better understanding of human behavior-in-society, which I take to be the main aim of social science, that is, not an understanding of behavior-in-the-laboratory, or behavior-in-the-sociologists' society, but rather behavior where it occurs, in everyday life.

Notes

AUTHOR'S NOTE: This paper was presented at the meetings of the American Sociological Association, San Francisco, 1967. I am grateful to Marvin Cummins, Lindsey Churchill, Murray L. Wax and William J. Chambliss for their critical comments on an earlier draft of this paper, and to Martin Kozloff for the many discussions we have had as it has been successively revised. I also wish to express my gratitude to Herbert Spiegelberg for the opportunity to present it to his Workshop on Phenomenology at Washington University, June, 1967.

1. W. C. Sturtevant, "Studies in Ethnoscience," *American Anthropologist*, Special Publication, 66, Part 2; Romney, A. K., and D'Andrade, R. G. (eds.), "Transcultural Studies in Cognition," Report of a Conference sponsored by the Social Sciences Research Council, 1964.
2. Sturtevant, *ibid*, p. 99.
3. B. Malinowski, *Argonauts of the Western Pacific*, New York: E. P. Dutton and Company, 1950, p. 396.
4. *Ibid.*, p. 396.
5. C. O. Frake, "Notes on Queries in Ethnography," *American Anthropologist*, 66, Part 2, 1964, pp. 132–145. Of added significance is the fact that Frake undertakes a self-conscious analysis of methodological issues in data collection by anthropologists. The work of the ethnoscientists has stimulated attention to methodological issues, sometimes lacking in anthropology, in contrast to sociology (where sometimes there is more method than data).
6. M. Harris, "Emics, Etics and the New Ethnography," unpublished paper.
7. W. Goodenough, "Cultural Anthropology and Linguistics," in Garvin, P. L. (ed.), *Monograph Series on Languages and Linguistics* No. 9, Institute of Languages and Linguistics, Washington: Georgetown University, 1957, pp. 167–173.
8. For example, see the critical comment by Burling and the rejoinder by Hymes (R. Burling, "Cognition and Componential Analysis: God's Truth or Hocus Pocus?" *American Anthropologist*, 66, 1964, pp. 20–28. D. H. Hymes, "Discussion of Burling's Paper," *American Anthropologist*, 66, 1964, pp. 116–119).
9. I am grateful to Martin Kozloff for the following summary of the method of componential analysis.
10. Frake, "The Ethnographic Study of Cognitive Systems" in T. Gladwin and W. C. Sturtevant, (eds.) *Anthropology and Human Behavior*, Washington: The Anthropological Society of Washington, 1962.
11. A. F. C. Wallace and J. Atkins, "The Meaning of Kinship Terms," *American Anthropologist*, 62, 1960, pp. 58–80.
12. Sturtevant, "Studies in Ethnoscience," p. 124. For an exception in which combinations of terms used to refer to different environmental conditions are analyzed, see G. Psathas and J. Henslin, "Dispatched Orders and the Cab Driver: A Study of Locating Activities," *Social Problems*, 14, 1967, pp. 424–443. In this study, radio dispatched messages instructing the cab driver as to the location of a passenger are analyzed.
13. H. Spiegelberg, *The Phenomenological Movement*, II, The Hague: Martinus Nijhoff, 1965, ch. 14, p. 680.
14. Spiegelberg, *ibid.*, p. 695.
15. Whether this analysis is getting at the criteria actually used by the native ("psychological reality") in contrast to the imposition of the researcher's own criteria ("structural reality") is discussed in A. F. C. Wallace, "The Problems of the Psychological Validity of Componential Analysis," *American Anthropologist*, 67, Part 2, 1965.

16. The studies in ethnoscience which have been concerned with classification systems, e.g., C. O. Frake, "The Diagnosis of Disease among the Subanun of Mindanao," *American Anthropologist*, 63, 1961, pp. 113–132; A. F. C. Wallace and J. Atkins, "The Meaning of Kinship Terms," *American Anthropologist*, 62, 1960, pp. 58–80, can be contrasted with Garfinkel's analysis of how jurors decide the correctness of a verdict or how suicides are classified. See H. Garfinkel, *Studies in Ethnomethodology*, Englewood Cliffs, N.J.: Prentice Hall, 1967.

17. R. G. D'Andrade, Introduction in *American Anthropologist*, Special Publication, 66, Part 2, 1964.

18. For representative works see the following: H. Garfinkel, "Studies of the Routine Grounds of Everyday Activities," *Social Problems*, 11, 1964, pp. 225–250; Garfinkel, "Studies in Ethnomethodology," *op. cit;* E. Bittner, "The Police on Skid-Row," *American Sociological Review*, 32, 1967, pp. 669–715; A. Cicourel, *Method and Measurement in Sociology*, New York: The Free Press, 1964; D. Sudnow, "Normal Crimes," *Social Problems*, 12, 1965, pp. 255–276; L. Churchill, "Everyday Quantitative Practices," paper presented to meetings of the American Sociological Association, August, 1966. For critical reviews of Garfinkel, see "The Review Symposium on *Studies in Ethnomethodology*," *American Sociological Review*, 33, 1968, pp. 122–130. It is not clear whether ethnomethodology is to be regarded as a special field within sociology, as a method for "doing" sociology or as a school or movement which may remake the field. There are elements of each of these, so far as I can determine.

19. Garfinkel, "Studies of the Routine Grounds," p. 11.

20. For an elaboration of the notion of accounts, see M. Scott and S.M.Lyman, "Accounts," *American Sociological Review*, 33, 1968, pp. 46–62.

21. M. Natanson, in A. Schutz, *Collected Papers*, Vol. 1, The Hague: Martinus Nijhoff, 1962, Editor's Introduction, p. lxvi. Schutz is the phenomenologist most frequently cited by ethnomethodologists though Garfinkel is also familiar with the work of Husserl. There is no question that Schutz's work is most relevant for the student of social life. Much of his work has now been translated, the third volume of his collected papers having appeared in 1966; a translation of his *Der Sinnhafte Aufbau der Sozialen Welt* has now been published under the title *The Phenomenology of the Social World*, Northwestern University Press, Evanston, Illinois, 1967. P. L. Berger and T. Luckmann have drawn extensively from Schutz's and Luckmann's work, *Die Strukturen der Lebenswelt*, also being prepared for publication, in their recent book, *The Social Construction of Reality*, New York: Doubleday, 1966.

22. Spiegelberg, *The Phenomenological Movement*, II, p. 690.

23. A. Schutz, *Collected Papers*, Vol I, The Hague: Martinus Nijhoff, 1962.

24. Another expression of this view in the sociological literature, again drawing heavily from Schutz, is that of P. L. Berger and T. Luckmann, *The Social Construction of Reality*. Although they subtitle their book a treatise on the sociology of knowledge, they are concerned with knowledge in the same sense that Garfinkel is, i.e., the everyday, ordinary knowledge that men have about themselves and their social world and with how the knowledge that men have comes to be established as reality for them.

25. It is possible to go into an analysis of the convergences between symbolic interaction theory, ethnomethodology and phenomenology, but this is beyond the scope of the present paper. There is without doubt much overlap in the work of W. I. Thomas, Cooley, Mead, William James, and more recent symbolic interactionist theorists such as Strauss, Shibutani, Goffman, Lindesmith, Becker and Garfinkel and his students.

26. I am grateful to Martin Kozloff for the recognition of this distinction.

27. Garfinkel, "*Studies of the Routine Grounds.*"

28. Spiegelberg, *The Phenomenological Movement*, II, p. 680.

29. Psathas and Henslin, "Dispatched Orders."

30. It is this meaning of *verstehen* which, as Wax argues, is the meaning which is of greatest relevance to the actual work of the sociologist. M. L. Wax, "On Misunderstanding *Verstehen*: A Reply to Abel," *Sociology and Social Research*, 51, 1967, pp. 323–333. Wax calls it "intra-cultural" *verstehen* involving "socialization into the meanings of the members of the culture."

31. H. Spiegelberg, "Phenomenology Through Vicarious Experience," in E. Strauss, *Phenomenology: Pure and Applied*, Pittsburgh: Duquesne University Press, 1964.

32. This concept is drawn by Spiegelberg from Hans Kunz, who termed it *phantasierend-denkendes Entwerfen. Ibid*, p. 122.

33. H. Spiegelberg, "Toward a Phenomenology of Imaginative Understanding of Others," *Proceedings of XIIth International Congress of Philosophy*, Brussels, 1953, p. 237.

34. For a recent analysis of the methodology of participant observation which makes explicit reference to its relation to phenomenology, see S. Bruyn, *The Human Perspective: The Methodology of Participant Observation*, Englewood Cliffs, N.J.: Prentice-Hall, 1966.

35. In the study of cab drivers, Psathas and Henslin, "Dispatched Orders," I try to show how this might be possible.

12 IS ETHNOSCIENCE RELEVANT?

Gerald D. Berreman

Ethnoscience has probably raised more academic hackles than any other subfield of anthropology, and the hostility and criticism has not been entirely undeserved. Some of its practitioners have made claims which are pretentious. Ethnoscientists have developed a new language for talking about *ethnography*, a discipline belonging to all of anthropology, which some believe is merely jargon. The theoretical nature of many of the writings and the use of abstract notational systems have added to the misunderstanding. Some professionals have responded in much the same way one of my students did after she read a particularly difficult article: She wrote, "Is it possible that the author is the leader of an esoteric cult based on the divination of the inner meaning of his published writings?" Gerald D. Berreman expresses many of the questions asked by anthropologists in this brilliantly written article. He suggests that the goals of ethnography demand insight into human behavior, as well as rigor in our descriptions of that behavior. Berreman's questions arise, in part, from the conflict over a long-standing debate as to whether anthropology is to be a humanistic or scientific field. The student may wish to evaluate the studies presented in Part 4 of this book on the basis of the questions raised in this chapter.—EDITOR'S NOTE

I

At the conclusion of my paper on "Caste in Cross-Cultural Perspective," delivered before the Southwestern Anthropological Association meetings, spring 1965, a gentleman came to me and suggested helpfully that I might use a framework for the comparative study of caste which would be based on *emic*, *etic* and *allo* concepts. This experience, on brief reflection, inspired me to the title and topic of this essay, which I presented orally before the Kroeber Anthropological Society's ninth annual meeting at Berkeley, on May 9, 1965.

Reproduced from "Anemic and Emetic Analyses in Social Anthropology," *American Anthropologist*, vol. 68, no. 2 (1966), pp. 346–354, by permission of the author and the American Anthropological Association.

On scarcely more reflection, I though of the spate of recent and announced journal articles, special issues, and other works by "ethnoscientists" or "componential analysts" who treat culture in a linguistic idiom in the avowed hope of discovering structure and enhancing rigor in ethnology. I especially recalled those in a special edition of this journal entitled *Transcultural Studies of Cognition* (American Anthropologist, 1964).

I then recalled a statement, whose author shall remain anonymous, in which that edition was described as "an attempt to understand the mood and temper of man through empty words. Vacuous, sterile, inconclusive, programmatic, hyper-professionalized, and the product of apolitical, asexual, amoral, asocial anthropology."

A major aim of the ethnoscientists is cogently and readably put by Frake (1962) in an article which should be required reading for all commentators on componential analysis: that by utilizing the linguistic analogy and seeking "contrast sets" of "cultural segregates" we can derive superior ethnography.

Superior ethnography is a concern of mine too. I see the concern of those advocating a linguistic analogy to achieve this end, and my own concern to achieve this end, as deriving from a common source: the problem of how to treat human situations scientifically. It can be phrased, and has often been treated, as a dilemma: how to be scientific and at the same time retain the humanistic insights—the human relevance—without which no account of human beings makes sense.

There are two extreme but common reactions to this dilemma, namely, to ignore one or the other of its two horns. That is, to be scientific at the expense of insight, or to be insightful at the expense of being unscientific. The first is what I would term the "scientistic" refuge. It involves a retreat to, or preoccupation with, such things as quantification, abstract models, simulation, and highly formal methods of data collection and analysis. It rejects intuitive insights. The second refuge I would call "humanist." It rejects any serious attempt at scientific method, relying entirely upon intuitive insights and the qualitative, empathetic ethnographic result thereof. The first approach results most often in descriptions and interpretations which are reliable but whose validity is questionable; the latter results in accounts which may be valid, but whose reliability is undemonstrated.

I believe that the dilemma can be resolved if we take as the relevant question not *whether* to be rigorous or insightful, scientific, or humanistic, but rather, how to be *both*—how to develop a methodology which is at once subject to verification and conducive to perceptive insights in the study of men.

II

Thomas Gladwin (1964) has written a brilliant article contrasting the method by which the Trukese navigate the open sea, with that by which Europeans navigate. He points out that the European navigator begins with a plan—a course—which he has charted according to certain universal principles, and he carries out his voyage by relating his every move to that plan. His effort throughout his voyage is directed to remaining "on course." If unexpected events occur, he must first alter the plan, then respond accordingly. The Trukese navigator begins with an objective rather than a plan. He sets off toward the objective and responds to conditions as they arise in an *ad hoc* fashion. He utilizes information provided by the wind, the waves, the tides and current, the fauna, the stars, the clouds, the sound of the water on the side of the boat, and he steers accordingly. His effort is directed to doing whatever is necessary to reach the objective. If asked, he can point to his objective at any moment, but he cannot describe his course. The European may not know where his objective is relative to himself at a given moment, but he knows his course and can quickly compute his location on the course.

Gladwin points out that the European can verbalize his navigational techniques whereas the Trukese cannot. The European's system is based on a few general principles applied to any given case. The Trukese' system is based on a great many cues, interpreted as they arise. Presumably, the European can relatively easily teach his navigational techniques to others, whereas the Trukese cannot—it takes apprenticeship to learn them. This does not mean that the Trukese does not *have* techniques; it means, rather, that they are subtle and complex. That they work is evidenced by the fact that Trukese get where they are going just as do the Europeans. Conceivably neither method is superior to the other as a method of getting there. They reflect different styles of thought rather than more or less good ones. For some purposes each is doubtless superior. Also, of course, there are good navigators and bad navigators among both Europeans and Trukese.

I think there is a lesson here for ethnographers. I think scientistic ethnographers are the intellectual brethren of the European navigators. They know how they are going, but often are not sure where. The humanistic ones are spiritual kinsmen of the Trukese. They know where they are going but are not sure how. To extend the parallel, let me quote two paragraphs of Gladwin's analysis:

(1) . . . Once the European navigator has developed his operating plan and has available the appropriate technical resources, the implementation and monitoring of his navigation can be accomplished with a minimum of thought. He has simply

to perform almost mechanically the steps dictated by his training and by his initial planning synthesis (Gladwin 1964:175).

(2) This total process [of Trukese navigation] goes forward without reference to any explicit principles and without any planning, unless the intention to proceed to a particular island can be considered a plan. It is nonverbal and does not follow a coherent set of logical steps. As such it does not represent what we tend to value in our culture as "intelligent" behavior. . . . We might refer to this kind of ability as a "knack,". . . . Yet it is undeniable that the process of navigating from one tiny island to another, when this is accomplished entirely through the mental activity of the navigator, must reflect a high order of mental functioning (Gladwin 1964: 175).

I hope the parallel is obvious. But there is an important difference between navigation and ethnography. Navigators can prove the validity of their methods by the pragmatic test of whether or not they get where they are going. Ethnographers, when their trip is over, do not know for sure, or cannot agree upon, whether they got where they were going or not. There have been no agreed-upon tests of whether an ethnography is right or not, no standardized measurements of how right it is, though suggestions have been made. Conklin (1964:26), for example, advocates "productivity" (by which he means anticipation of events in a culture), "replicability," and "economy" as criteria of ethnographic adequacy. In his own words, "An adequate ethnography is here considered to include the culturally significant arrangement of productive statements about the relevant relationships obtaining among locally defined categories and contexts [of objects and events] within a given social matrix" (Conklin 1964:25).

The experience of Tepoztlan, of the analyses of Pueblo culture, and several others have made the lack of a standard of ethnographic accuracy and relevance clear. Redfield and Lewis obviously got to different places in their ethnographic voyage through Tepoztlan, as did Benedict and Goldfrank in navigating Pueblo cultures (cf. Bennett 1946). But neither is clearly right or wrong. The scientistic anthropologist offers no help on this matter since the difference between the analyses of Lewis and Redfield, of Goldfrank and Benedict he defines as unscientific questions and hence out of his purview. I believe that they are also the *crucial* questions in the understanding of human behavior. The humanistic anthropologist offers no help on this matter either, because he has no criterion by which to judge two different interpretations of the same data except by how convincing they are.

Under these circumstances, an explicit methodology would be an advantage, for it would enable one to chart a course and to communicate to others the route you intend to follow. Afterwards, you could show how you got where you got to, and even if you didn't know where that was, others could get there too, presumably, if they followed the same course. Since one of our functions as ethnographers and teachers is to train others, this is the most expeditious way it can be done. Since ours is a science, replicability and communicability are obviously essential.

III

Frake has called for "an explicit methodology" (1964a:236), for "public . . . procedures" (1962:85), for "ethnographic statements that can be demonstrated to be *wrong*, and not simply judged to be unpersuasively written" (1964b:142–43). With this I clearly agree. Humanistic anthropologists tend to ignore the fact that findings are only as good as the theories and methods by which they are derived, and are only convincing if they can be verified. But I think that much of the current effort at providing verifiable statements (and here Frake is among the *least* culpable) has the effect of sacrificing the insight into the nature of human behavior which is the ultimate aim of all ethnography. It results in astoundingly pallid, sterile, and fragmentary ethnography. It is effectively a retreat to method without sufficient reference to goals. The goals I have in mind are understanding how people relate to one another and to their environment, what is the nature of their social interaction and how it relates to their values, emotions, attitudes, and self-conceptions; their hopes and fears. Without knowing these things we cannot claim to understand a society or the culture its members share. Obviously a technique *need* not preclude other techniques and need not obscure goals, a fact to which Frake's own work is testimony. But it is empirically demonstrable that those who become enamored of a technique often lose sight of what their technique is for, and the work of many scientistic anthropologists is ample testimony to this. Peter Berger (1963) has compared those who become preoccupied with methods, to the magician who worked so long and hard to find the secret of how to get the mighty jinn out of the bottle that when he finally got him out he couldn't remember what it was he wanted to ask him. He has also stated, in what must become a classic aphorism, that "in science as in love, an overemphasis on technique is quite likely to lead to impotence" (Berger 1963:13).

Frake has called for "non-intuitive" procedures in ethnography. I think in this term, if not in his usage, lies the fundamental fallacy of the scientistic anthropologists. That is, the assumption that intuition is somehow indefinable and therefore invalid, indefensible, and reprehensible. I submit that intuition is nothing more nor less than inference that is unanalyzed because it is based on complex cues, subliminal cues, or subtle reasoning. In the last analysis, intuition is inference and as such it is the basis for all science. By insisting upon "non-intuitive" procedures, naively defined, one reduces insight by focusing on gross facts and interpretations or on a very narrow range of facts and interpretations. Those who insist upon this, confuse verification with discovery and assume that science is comprised of the former, whereas, in fact, the former is only an adjunct of the latter.

What is called for, I think, is a methodology which *combines* rigor and insight, verification and discovery, accuracy and empathy, replicability and human relevance. This, I think, can be achieved through defining—making explicit—the bases for the inferences that lead to insights; that is, by defining the constituents and cultural contexts of intuition. Componential analysis and other linguistic analogies may be one way to do this. But they are by no means the only way nor have they been demonstrated to be a superior or even a particularly effective way. They tend, I think, to oversimplify. This is inevitable, for language, I believe, is far simpler and more rigidly structured than most aspects of culture. Techniques applicable to it, while theoretically applicable elsewhere, may be practically inadequate. One evidence of this is the fact that analyses on the linguistic model have been applied almost entirely to terminological systems—i.e., to linguistic materials. Little effort, and less success, has been manifest in other spheres (see Frake 1964a, describing religious behavior, for a noble effort which he modestly describes as "deficient in detail and rigor" as an ethnographic statement).

I would suggest that extensive, explicit, and perceptive field notes, self-analytical reporting of research procedures and research contexts, documentation of sources, documentation of the bases for inferences, and documentation of the ethnographer's theories of society and his biases, are steps which work toward the same end and with greater promise. What I would call for, in short, if verification is to be enhanced, is a *sociology of ethnographic knowledge;* an *ethnography of ethnography.* Nothing less will achieve the basis for scientific rigor—for verifiability—without sacrificing the significant insights which are equally crucial to science.

My objection to the linguistic analogies is not that they are useless, but that they are too often productive of lifeless descriptions of human life; that they are too often uncritically applied and especially that they characteristically are grimly and unconscionably pretentious. Their advocates often behave like the methodological pixies of whom Everett Hughes has spoken, who have a method and flit about eagerly looking for something to which to apply it, manifesting what C. Wright Mills has described as a kind of "empty ingenuity," and what Berger has termed "humorless scientism." Such efforts are not worthless, but they are unlikely to go far toward contributing to social science unless supplemented by other methods and disciplined by clearly defined goals. Fortunately the most accomplished of their advocates are not totally deficient in this respect, just as their detractors are not totally deficient in rigor. But they *are* pretentious. Sturtevant (1964:101) says, for example, that "ethnoscience shows promise as the New Ethnography required to advance the whole of cultural anthropology." He says that it "raises the standards of reliability, validity, and exhaustiveness of ethnography." Whether or not one agrees with that, the next sentence seems unexceptionable: "One result is that the ideal goal of a complete ethnography is farther removed from practical attainment. The full ethnoscientific description of a single culture would require many thousands of pages published after many years of intensive fieldwork based on ethnographic methods more complete and more advanced than are now available" (Sturtevant 1964:123). This is exhaustion, if not exhaustiveness. I doubt that an ethnoscientific ethnography will ever be written. If it is, I doubt that it will lead to better understanding than extant ethnographies, or that it will be more valid or more reliable. I doubt that it will be more convincing or more comprehensive. It will be at best a skeleton to which only less formal techniques can supply the flesh. Without such techniques, it cannot be expected to accomplish more than accuracy at the expense of relevance. Perhaps a full ethnography is unattainable by any method. Certainly not all anthropologists need seek it. But it is an ideal worth attempting to approximate, for human behavior occurs in total cultural context, no part of which is entirely independent of any other.

Frake notes that in ethnoscience the focus has been, of necessity, on particular domains rather than on general accounts of the cultures studied. The scope of the accomplishments can be indicated by quoting Frake's summary (1964a:143; cf. Sturtevant 1964:113–122): "Metzger and Williams, for example, emerged from one field session with descriptions of firewood . . . , terms of personal reference . . . , curers . . . , and weddings . . . . Conklin has described ethnobotanical systems, agriculture, betel chewing, pottery, verbal play, color, kinship and water. . . . None of these descriptions, whatever the faults, can be called superficial. . . ."

I would say, none of these descriptions, whatever the virtues, can in themselves be called very significant. They sound like ethnoscientific trait lists. They remind me of Mill's warning that many sociologists have gotten to the point where they overlook what is important in their search for what is verifiable, and that some of them break down the units of analysis so minutely that truth and falsity are no longer distinguishable. Many have worked so hard on what is trivial that it comes to appear important—or at least triviality and importance become indistinguishable when fitted into the molds of formal analysis.

I agree with Frake and others that one goal in ethnography, if it is to result in scientific statements, must be verifiability and replicability. I agree that the way to accomplish this is by utilizing an explicit methodology. I do not think, however, that the most promising way is to substitute for our present methods a more formal, hence less flexible and creative methodology. Actually, I would be prepared to argue that componential analysts remain as intuitive, and obscure in the *crucial* steps of their research, as anyone else, and that their explicitness is largely illusory. This they share with the quantifiers in sociology—those Mills has called the "abstract empericists." I would also maintain that their method is actually, except for its jargon and pretention, not nearly as novel as they think or hope. They still base their work on selective inquiry, selective observation, selective recording, inference, implicit theories and *ex post facto* analysis, and these are where the research stands or falls. But I have not space to go into these portentious and perhaps pretentious assertions. I think the way to scientific ethnography is to explicate our theories and methodologies, adding to, deleting from, or altering them as this seems useful.

Some ethnoscientists *have* made notable (if to me unconvincing) efforts at explicating their field methods (Frake, 1962; Conklin, 1964). Frake (1962), for example, describes "eliciting frames" or as he calls them synonymously, "situations" or "stimuli" for evoking and defining responses to ethnographic inquiries. This is a step toward replicability. My own innate drive for terminological parsimony leads me to suggest that these three synonymous terms—stimuli, situations, eliciting—be combined, and I would suggest the term "soliciting" as apropos, combining as it does the first phoneme of two of the synonyms with the third synonym. I considered, in fact, subtitling this communication: "Soliciting in Ethnoscience." (One might even define, then, illicit soliciting and licit soliciting in ethnoscience, depending upon the putative validity of the results, or the ethics of the inquiry.) In any event, Frake makes the point that ethnographic inquiries—"discovery procedures"—need to be made problematic. I would carry it further and say that *all* aspects of ethnographic method (including how one selects his informants, how he decides to whom to talk, what to ask, whom to believe, whose information to ignore, what to observe, what to record, etc.) must be made problematic—be made the subject of inquiry, definition, and analysis—if scientific criteria are to be applied to ethnography. Ethnoscience, I think, does this for only limited phases of research, thereby giving the appearance without the fact of rigor.

IV

Even if the Trukese ethnographers were absolutely correct and could be demonstrated to be so, I doubt that it would be possible to convert the errant Europeans. If the Trukese ethnographers were absolutely wrong and could be demonstrated to be so, I doubt that it would be possible to convert *them.* For an indication of why this is so, I can only refer the reader to an ingenious little study, *When Prophecy Fails*, by Leon Festinger, *et al.* (1956). I will quote a paragraph from the first chapter thereof:

Suppose an individual believes something with his whole heart; suppose further that he has a commitment to this belief, that he has taken irrevocable actions [such as publication] because of it; finally, suppose that he is presented with evidence, unequivocal and undeniable evidence, that his belief is wrong: what will happen? The individual will frequently emerge, not only unshaken, but even more convinced of the truth of his beliefs than ever before. Indeed, he may even show a new fervor about convincing and converting other people to his view (Festinger *et al.* 1956:3).

The authors go on to show why this is so: "If more and more people can be persuaded that the system of belief is correct, then clearly it must, after all, be correct" (Festinger *et al.* 1956:28). The adherents to one or the other of the extreme positions, the scientistic and the humanistic ethnographers, in fact, often resemble in their commitment and singleness of purpose the cultists studied by Festinger and his associates.

I would prefer that we Trukese ethnographers not give up our Trukese methodology, but that instead we define, explicate and thereby improve it. For I think it is possible to demonstrate that it works—that it gets us there—when well and properly done. What we have to do is find out how one goes about doing it well and properly. And there may be many ways of doing it; or a few principles which can be applied in different ways, or many techniques which work in various combinations. Perhaps some new techniques need to be added—Trukese navigators, after all, have by now acquired compasses for use in emergencies. European ethnographers, meanwhile, might unbend a bit—try coming out of the chartroom and observe more of the world around them. Each approach has something to say to the other. Time will tell what is useful and what is not.

Europeans need not become Trukese, but Trukese need not be dazzled by the European technology to the point of hastily and self-consciously giving up their own ways. Europeans may even be, after all, a flash in the pan and the eternal verities just possibly lie with the Trukese. In any case, let us try pluralism in preference to succumbing to colonialism. Reciprocal acculturation and accommodation is more likely to result in a viable synthesis than is precipitous assimilation; selective advantage should be given an opportunity to manifest itself.

Lest the title of this article mislead, let me say that I think linguistics has much to offer the rest of anthropology. I may even *try* using emic, etic, and allo concepts in comparing caste systems cross culturally, for I think some such concepts are essential for comparative studies and I think comparative studies are crucial in anthropology. I just do not see linguistics as the one true science of man, nor its methods as curative for all of the ills of ethnography.

I hasten to add that some of my best friends, after all, are ethnoscientists or componential analysts. I empathize even where I don't sympathize. I too yearn for rigor in my research. I just urge that in my colleagues' search for scientific rigor, they not inadvertently succumb to scientific *rigor mortis*.

REFERENCES CITED

ROMNEY, A. K. and R. G. D'ANDRADE, eds.
1964 Transcultural studies in cognition, A. K. Romney and R. G. D'Andrade, eds. American Anthropologist 66, No. 3, Part 2.

BENNETT, JOHN W.
1946 The interpretation of Pueblo Culture: A question of values. Southwestern Journal of Anthropology 2:361–374.

BERGER, PETER L.
1963 Invitation to sociology: A humanistic perspective. Garden City, N.Y., Doubleday.

CONKLIN, HAROLD C.
1964 Ethnogenealogical method. *In* Explorations in cultural anthropology: Essays presented to George Peter Murdock. Ward H. Goodenough, ed. New York, McGraw-Hill.

FESTINGER, LEON, H. W. RIECKEN, and STANLEY SCHACHTER
1956 When prophecy fails. Minneapolis, The University of Minnesota Press.

FRAKE, CHARLES O.
1962 The ethnographic study of cognitive systems. *In* Anthropology and human behavior. T. Gladwin and W. D. Sturtevant, eds. Washington, D.C. Anthropological Society of Washington, pp. 72–93.
1964a A structural description of Subanun religious behavior. *In* Explorations in cultural anthropology: Essays presented to George Peter Murdock. Ward H. Goodenough, ed. New York, McGraw-Hill, pp. 111–129.
1964b Notes on queries in ethnography. American Anthropologist 66, No. 3, Part 2, pp. 99–131.

GLADWIN, THOMAS
1964 Culture and logical process. *In* Explorations in cultural anthropology: Essays presented to George Peter Murdock. Ward H. Goodenough, ed. New York, McGraw-Hill.

STURTEVANT, WILLIAM C.
1964 Studies in ethnoscience. American Anthropologist 66, No. 3, Part 2, pp. 99–131.

PART 4 STUDIES IN CULTURE AND COGNITION

Cities

Law

Technology

Kinship

Acculturation

Religion

Cities

13 ADAPTIVE STRATEGIES OF URBAN NOMADS

James P. Spradley

The study of urban subcultures in his own society presents the researcher with many difficulties, not the least of which is the tendency to impose his meaning on the behavior of informants. It is a truism in anthropology that even the most objective physical phenomena do not imply their own meaning. Yet, it is all too easy to believe that what one observes himself must be much the same thing seen by those he studies—the features of a city are open for all to see, so why is it necessary to discover how members of a particular subculture define them? This assumption often creeps into the best-designed research. In this article I show how the methods of ethnoscience are especially suited to overcoming this problem. I set forth an explicit series of steps which lead to a description that reflects the insider's point of view—in this case, the tramps who inhabit the deteriorating sections of large American cities. In addition, I raise several of the important questions about urban ethnography and then show how they are at least partly resolved by a cognitive approach.—EDITOR'S NOTE

I. Introduction[1]

Urban anthropology includes a variety of approaches. Nearly every subfield of anthropology can bring its methods, techniques, and theories to bear upon human life in the urban setting. At the same time, there are certain unique contributions which anthropologists may be able to make by virtue of their cross-cultural and non-Western orientation. In fact, it is argued here that we may be in danger of selling our birthright for orientations developed by others who have been studying the city for decades. Research in non-Western societies has helped us lay aside our cultural blinders, a prerequisite for discovering the behavioral environment

This paper, which received the 1969 Stirling Award in Culture and Personality from the American Anthropological Association, is reproduced by the permission of the Society for Applied Anthropology from the *Anthropological Study of Urban Environments*, Thomas Weaver and Douglas White, eds. Monograph no. 11, 1972.

or socially constructed reality of those we study. This is not an easy task in any society but for the urban anthropologist there are additional problems. Urban groups do not live in the "city" but in their own socially constructed definition of the city. This paper begins with a discussion of five interrelated problems faced by the researcher: (a) cultural pluralism, (b) ethnocentrism, (c) subcultural interpreters, (d) similar cultural forms, and (e) relevant social units. An ethnographic approach to an urban subculture will then be presented as an effective strategy for urban research. Five major steps in the research will be discussed along with data from the subculture under consideration. Finally, I shall raise a number of issues which need further exploration by urban anthropologists.

II. Urban Research Problems

(a) *Cultural pluralism.* When the ethnographer studies his own urban society, attempting to discover the meaning of objects and events according to the conceptual systems of city dwellers, he is confronted with a complex multicultural situation. In addition to the thousands of different roles in the city, resulting from specialization, there are many distinct life styles in a myriad of subcultural groups. Considerable strain is placed upon the holistic bias of the anthropologist in conceptualizing the city as a cultural phenomenon. Concepts such as "rural-urban," "primitive-civilized," and "ecological zone" have been used to understand cities as a whole, but they often obscure the cultural pluralism of the urban situation. If we are to understand the city as a functioning whole, we must begin by looking at the different units of that whole. Only then will we be in a position to fruitfully develop conceptual models of the city as a unit to be compared with other cities as well as peasant villages and nomadic tribes. After the various parts of an urban culture have been described and compared, even wider comparisons will be more valid; in fact, we may find that the minority group described here has more in common with nomadic tribes than it does with other urban subcultures. It is of utmost importance then for anthropologists to recognize, identify, and describe the various subcultures within the city, for, as A. F. C. Wallace (1962:351) has pointed out, "All of the comparative and theoretical work of cultural anthropology depends upon thorough and precise ethnographic description."

(b) *Ethnocentrism.* The belief that one's own traditions, values, and ways of life are better than those which exist in other societies is probably universal. Anthropologists have long championed the need to recognize the validity and dignity of diverse cultural traditions while not abandoning a commitment to one's own heritage. The contemporary urban scene throughout the world is heavily influenced by Western culture, and the researcher has learned values and definitions about urban life which will profoundly influence the questions he asks and the research he undertakes. The use of hallucinogenic drugs by students in American cities is evaluated differently from their use by an isolated Indian tribe living in the Amazon basin. The drinking behavior of men in the Skid Road district of the city is similar to that of the Camba Indians, but Westerners define and evaluate them quite differently.[2] It may not be easy for one studying a remote tribe in New Guinea to overcome his feelings that their way of life is inferior to his own, but that difficulty is even greater when one studies the culture of those who live in his own society but have a very different style of life. Much of the research on the urban population considered here has been criticized for such an ethnocentric bias.

> When the sociologist arrives on skid row with pre-coded, pre-tested, survey questionnaire in hand, every one of his questions implicitly assumes the person is a failure and asks why. Even though this question remains unstated, both questioner and questioned perceive its fundamental reality (Wallace, S. E., 1965: 159).

It is naive for the researcher to believe that he can study urban subcultures without being influenced by his own culture. While "value free" research is impossible, the problems in approaching this ideal are much greater in the study of urban subcultures for which the researcher's own socialization has provided him with traditional definitions.

(c) *Subcultural interpreters.* Isolated tribesmen or villagers have little knowledge of the anthropologist's culture, and informants have no basis for responding to questions based upon that culture. The field worker does not expect them to translate their way of life into the categories and terms which have significance in his way of life. Instead, he immerses himself in the field situation, learns the native language, discerns not only the answers to questions but also which questions to ask, and finally describes the culture in a way which his colleagues and students will understand. The ethnographer's job is one of translating and interpreting the culture he studies into terms which can be understood by the outsider. Urban anthropologists are faced with a different situation. Literacy, communication, and interaction among members of different subcultures have provided informants with a knowledge of the researcher's culture. This is especially true among the groups which are deprived of status and power within the city, for their very survival requires that they know the life styles of members of superordinate status groups. They are keenly aware of attitudes, values, and individual differences among the power holders. As a result the anthropologist who studies an urban population encounters many informants with the ability to translate their way of life into his language and culture. Informants act as subcultural interpreters; their translation competence may lead the anthropologist to describe another subculture in terms of his own without realizing he is doing so. Questions are formulated in the researcher's dialect of English and based on the categories of his culture. When they are put to an informant, they are quickly translated and thus "understood." Then the informant responds to questions he has imperfectly understood with answers phrased in the idiom of the researcher's culture. The ethnographer may thus guide his informants to conceptualize their culture from the perspective of the outsider. Such interpreters may provide a wealth of data which can be analyzed, but the investigator has been effectively prevented from discovering the meaning and definition of experience from the insider's point of view.

(d) *Similar cultural forms.* Urban communities contain distinct subcultural groups which share many similar cultural forms and appear to live in the same environment. They live in the same geographic area and climatic zone, often sharing transportation systems, law-enforcement agencies, educational insititutions, and many other facets of city life. It would be easy to conclude that different groups actually have the same culture and that a description of these aspects of urban life for one group would be an accurate description for all groups. This appearance of sharing similar forms may even be empirically verified if culture is treated as a statistical description of behavior. But if culture involves the forms people have in mind, the fact that people share the "same" urban environment and institutions may obscure important cultural differences. "In actuality not even the most concrete, objectively apparent physical object can be identified apart from some culturally defined system of concepts" (Frake 1962b:74). Men who live on Skid Road participate in many of the major institutions of the city. They visit missions, work in jail, go to the theater, walk the streets, get into bathtubs, visit cemeteries, and go to junk yards. Other city dwellers also engage in these activities but *define* them differently. The underlying attributes, values, and meanings which each group assigns to urban life must be discovered if we are to do justice to the pluralistic nature of the city. This paper is based on the premise that:

> The great problem for a science of man is how to get from the objective world of materiality, with its infinite variability, to the subjective world of form as it exists in what for lack of a better term, we must call the minds of our fellow men (Goodenough 1957:173).

(e) *Relevant social units.* All behavioral science is faced with the task of specifying the units and classes of behavior to be described and explained. This has always been a thorny problem for anthropologists and may be seen in such controversies as what is meant by a "tribe." The task has been easier in studying nonurban societies by the coincidence of geographical and social unit boundaries, less mobility, limited communication among social units, and greater linguistic variation. If the city is not a homogeneous sociocultural unit, how are we to identify the unit we are studying and establish its boundaries? Some scholars have studied "Skid Road" using geographical criteria to identify the subculture reported on here. Some even determine the boundaries of this area by asking professionals who attempt to help those who live on Skid Road. Are such professionals to be considered as part of this social unit? Is every individual in such a locale to be treated as part of that subculture? If the city is multicultural in nature, then the identification of units which make up this pluralistic phenomenon is of utmost importance. The criteria for treating minority groups, black ghettos, urban Indians, and other units as relevant for research must be explicitly stated in order to make replication and comparison possible. All too often urban research has been carried out with an implicit mixture of biological, social, geographical, historical, and cultural criteria which leads to confusing results. Even more crucial is the *arbitrariness* involved in the selection of criteria for identification of a subculture. Conklin (1964:29) has pointed to two aspects of this problem:

> We should like especially to avoid the pitfalls of (1) *translation-labeling analysis*, wherein the *units* are provided not by the culture studied but by the metalanguage given before the investigation begins; (2) *translation-domain analysis*, wherein the boundaries and establishment of larger contexts are similarly provided by prior agreement instead of by ethnographic investigation.

Different approaches or models have been used in many studies of the urban population which will be considered in this article. A brief consideration of these models may highlight some of the research problems discussed above for this particular group. The social units which appear to be similar have been referred to variously as "Skid Road alcoholics," "homeless men," "vagrants," "hoboes," "tramps," "indigent public intoxicants," etc. The *folk model* is the stereotype of this population held by the majority of urban society. They are seen as people who fail abysmally, are dependent on society, lack self-control, drink too much, are unpredictable, and often end up in jail for criminal behavior. In a word, they are *bums*. The *medical model* defines this social unit in terms of their primary illness: alcoholism. The concept of being an alcoholic is hardly better defined among medical professionals than the idea of being a bum among others in society. Skid Road alcoholics in particular are sometimes considered to be like "burned-out, backward schizophrenic" (Solomon 1966: 165) patients who are almost without culturally organized behavior. The *legal model* defines these people as criminals, guilty of many minor crimes, but especially public drunkenness. The criminal court in the city studied had a special file for keeping track of this population and they were officially designated as *common drunkards*. The *sociological model* defines this unit in terms of a variety of criteria including homelessness, age, sex, race, income, drinking behavior, and geographic location. Each of these four models tends to predefine the social unit in terms which are considered relevant to the outsider, using criteria determined by folk, medical, legal, or sociological standards. The folk model in particular has heavily influenced the criteria used by the others. The focus upon drinking behavior and homelessness, for instance, reflects the American cultural values of sobriety, self-control, and the home. All of these approaches are, in different ways and to different degrees, outsider models. The *ethnographic model* to be presented here avoids the predefinition of what is to be considered relevant and aims at discovering the insider's view of his social world. While all of these models are useful for certain purposes, it is argued here that, because of their training and experience, anthropologists can make a unique contribution by discovering the insider's model for any particular urban subculture.

III. An Ethnoscientific Approach to the Study of Urban Areas

The methods of ethnoscience hold promise of partially overcoming some of the problems of urban research. I consider the task of ethnography to be the discovery of the characteristic ways in which members of a society categorize, code, and define their experience. Ethnographic descriptions based on techniques of ethnoscience have been largely limited to a few selected domains in non-Western societies, such as kinship, color categories, and plant taxonomies.[3] The application of these techniques to an urban subculture is based on the premise that "the units by which the data of observation are segmented, ordered, and interrelated be delimited and defined according to contrasts inherent in the data themselves and not according to *a priori* notions of pertinent descriptive categories" (Frake 1962a:54).

The various ethnic and social groups within the city have developed different strategies of adaptation. Each subculture provides such strategies in the form of cognitive maps which are learned through socialization. These cognitive maps categorize the world of experience into equivalence classes which eliminate the necessity of responding to every unique event in the environment. This is one of the most important ways that culture enables human beings to survive. Following Bruner and his associates (1956:2), it is maintained that,

> The learning and utilization of categories represent one of the most elementary and general forms of cognition by which man adjusts to his environment.

If we are to discover different strategies of adaptation among urban groups we must discover the different category systems they use to reduce the complexity of their environment and organize their behavior. Category systems enable the individual to identify those aspects of the environment which are significant for adaptation, provide direction for instrumental activity, and permit the anticipation of future events (Bruner *et al.* 1956: 11–14). Thus, an important avenue to understanding both the *strategies of adaptation* and the *environment* to which urban groups are adjusting is in the study of category systems through ethnoscientific techniques. An ethnographic description of an urban subculture,

> must tap the cognitive world of one's informants. It must discover those features of objects and events which they regard as significant for defining concepts, formulating propositions, and making decisions (Frake 1962a:54).

How shall we approach this goal? The present study was begun by means of participant observation at an alcoholism treatment center, on Skid Road, and in a municipal criminal court. The first few months were spent in observation and recording casual conversations among informants in order to discover which questions were relevant to them. This was followed by more formal ethnographic interviews using a number of different discovery and testing procedures. Although these procedures will be discussed in more detail later in this paper, we may note five major steps in the research at this point. After some familiarity had been established with this population and several informants had been selected, I began by (1) *hypothesizing* that certain areas were culturally significant, and then (2) recording a corpus of relevant statements in the language of informants. It was then possible to (3) examine the corpus of statements for possible domains, question frames, and substitution frames and go on to (4) elicit the categories of culturally relevant domains. This last step resulted in a folk taxonomy or native category system for identifying significant objects in the subculture. Finally, a number of eliciting techniques were used to (5) discover the semantic principles of a number of domains.

IV. The Subculture of Urban Nomads

Tramps and Their Domains

The category of men considered in this paper *could* be characterized in many different ways depending upon the criteria selected. They live part of their lives on Skid Road (geographic criteria); join small groups for drinking (behavioral criteria); violate city ordinances which prohibit public drunkenness, begging, urinating in public, and drinking in public (legal criteria); and are characterized by low income and homelessness (sociological criteria). Table 13:1 provides a summary of several characteristics for a group of 216 men who had been arrested and committed to an alcoholism treatment center. While most of the social characteristics given in Table 13:1, as well as those noted above, are useful for some purposes, few go very far toward an ethnographic identification of the urban population under consideration. The data which are gathered in any research are determined, to a large part, by the questions asked. With the ethnoscience approach, questions are derived, not from previous research studies, theories, or one's own research interest, but primarily from informants. This approach involves "a search for sets of questions that the people of a society are responding to when they behave in systematic ways, and for the relations existing among these questions and responses" (Black and Metzger 1965:141). Thus the first task was to discover how these men identified themselves and to formulate appropriate questions. Using the methods discussed in Section II, above, it was found that informants identified their subcultural membership with the lexeme *tramp*. There were at least eight major categories of tramps recognized by informants: *working stiffs*, *mission stiffs*, *bindle stiffs*, *airedales*, *rubber tramps*, *home guard tramps*, *box car tramps*, and *dings*. This category system constitutes one of the major social-identity domains in this subculture. The significance of these findings is that the identity of this subculture has most often been based on *external* criteria. External definitions of the primary social identity of any group profoundly influence the kinds of questions asked and data gathered by the researcher. It may be important for some purposes to identify this population as "homeless men" or "chronic alcoholics," but it does not necessarily reflect the insider's conception of his own social identity. It may even preclude discoveries of great cultural significance.

A semantic analysis of this domain revealed that the underlying criteria in statements elicited from informants were *mobility-related*. The different kinds of tramps were differentiated in terms of their degree of mobility, mode of travel, type of home base, and economic survival

strategies. For example, *home guard tramps* travel very little, while the other kinds of tramps travel extensively. *Box car tramps* customarily travel by freight train in large continental circuits which cover most of the United States. *Rubber tramps* travel in their own car while *working stiffs* may ride freight trains or use commercial vehicles. The criteria of *homelessness* was not significant to these men in defining their social identity but rather the *type of home base they had.* The *airedale* and *bindle stiff* both carry their "homes" with them in the form of a pack and bedroll. *Rubber tramps* live in their cars, *mission stiffs* at the mission, and *dings* who are professional beggars have no home base. While many tramps drink and drunkenness is institutionalized in their world, drinking behavior was not a defining criteria for their social identity. Once it was established that informants conceived their primary social identity to be anchored to a mobile, nomadic life style, the importance of other facts which might have appeared trivial came to light.

Tramps are arrested often and taken to jail, where they move through a series of *inmate* identities. Initially they are *drunks*, whether their crime has been public drunkenness, begging, shoplifting, or urinating in public. After a period of waiting in a drunk tank they are taken to a criminal court for arraignment where over 90% of them plead guilty and are sentenced for their crimes. Most courts follow a sentencing procedure which is graduated so that on each successive conviction, especially for public drunkenness, a man's sentence is increased. Sentences for this crime may begin with two to five days in jail and increase to as much as one year in jail where a man will work as a *trusty*, remain confined to a time tank as a *lockup*, and finally become a *kickout* just prior to his release. The judges often believe that this approach curbs the drinking behavior in the constant repeater. The validity of this belief need not concern us here, but graduated sentences act as a strong reinforcement for a nomadic way of life and the individual's identity as a tramp. After several arrests in one city he is motivated to move on to another in order to escape the longer sentences. Even a suspended sentence often induces a man to increased mobility since, if he stays in town and is arrested too soon, it will mean serving time on the earlier suspended sentence in addition to the current charge. Evidence of mobility is seen in some of the social characteristics presented in Table 13:1. The number of jobs, times moved, and time in jail for this population all show a high degree of mobility. Even sleeping behavior is influenced by the nomadic quality of their lives as we shall see later in this paper. While observations, interview data, and life histories all support the contention that the dominant life style of these men is nomadic, most important is the fact that these reflect their cognitive world. These men are *tramps*, members of a subculture which is present in most large American cities, the subculture of *urban nomads*.

The problems and vicissitudes of urban nomads are different from those encountered by members of other urban groups. As socialization occurs in this subculture a variety of strategies are learned for satisfying biological needs, achieving subcultural goals, and adjusting to the environment. In each of the major scenes in the world of the tramp there are specialized modes of action for solving common problems. These scenes include *buckets* (jails), *farms* (treatment centers), *jungles* (encampments), *skids* (Skid Roads), and *freights* (railroad cars). Tramps learn to solve certain problems in the bucket, for example, as they acquire the categories and rules of this subculture. In jail there are the common problems of restricted freedom, restricted communication, and lack of resources such as food, cigarettes, and clothing. The specialized modes of action for alleviating these perceived deprivations are referred to as *hustling*. Hustling is a cover term for a large number of specific actions which tramps group into the following equivalence classes: *conning*, *peddling*, *kissing ass*, *making a run*, *taking a rake-off*, *playing cards*, *bumming*, *running a game*, *making a pay-off*, *beating*, *making a phone call.*[5] These adaptive strategies used in jail are very important to this group of men who often find themselves in a new jail with no other way to meet their needs. Many have actually spent years in jail on short sentences. One tramp had been sentenced to a total of fourteen years in one city alone on convictions for public drunkenness. As one informant stated, "you aren't a tramp if you don't make the bucket." While "hustling in the bucket" is important, tramps have a large number of adaptive strategies which may be employed in almost any scene. In the remainder of this paper we shall consider those related to satisfying their need for sleep in the wider urban environment.

Making a Flop

The ethnographic description which follows has resulted from a variety of research methods and techniques. Previous studies in ethnoscience and cognitive psychology have been especially valuable in this regard.[6] Some aspects of this research are difficult to make explicit, such as the values of the researcher, intuitive insights, and the complex relationship between researcher and informant. While these factors can never be eliminated, a major goal in ethnography is to increase the degree to which all operations may be explicitly stated. This will provide the possibility for replication, an important criterion for evaluating the adequacy of ethnographic descriptions (Conklin 1964:26). It is for this reason that the following description includes a statement of the procedures used in gathering and analyzing the data presented. While interviewing, recording, observing, and analyzing often occurred simultaneously, the data will be presented here in terms of several research steps. These data represent a partial description of the cognitive map for some members of the population studied. The extent to which other members of the population share this map is an empirical problem. It is assumed that systematic differences will occur depending on social identity, length of socialization into this subculture, geographical area of major socialization experiences, and other characteristics of each informant. Some of these have been examined, and all are important areas for further research.[7] It is beyond the scope and purpose of this paper to deal with many of these theoretical and methodological problems in detail.

1. *Hypothesizing the area as culturally significant*. The researcher's cultural background precluded the prediction that sleeping and places to sleep would be culturally revealing or significant. The popular image of the "bum" or "derelict" in American culture portrays these men as sleeping in cheap hotels or passing out in an alcoholic stupor from too much alcohol. Although very little review of previous studies on this population was done prior to beginning the study, subsequent research has shown that, with a few exceptions, sleeping has not been considered very important in the published works. Participant observation, carried out among the population at the alcoholism treatment center, revealed the importance of "making a flop." Conversations among tramps at informal gatherings, meals, card-playing groups, and "bull sessions" were recorded. As these men related their experiences to one another there were many references to "making a flop." Friends were identified as someone you would "make a flop with." Comments about making a flop were often linked to other important behavior such as being arrested, drinking, and traveling. Informants made such statements as "The most important thing is something to eat and a place to flop." One recent study (Wallace, S.E., 1965:29) of Skid Road in a Midwestern city emphasized the importance of this aspect of behavior:

> A place to sleep is, in some ways, more important to the men who live on skid row than food to eat or something to drink. This is so for two reasons. First, a man sleeping in the open is an easy victim for the weather, as well as for assailants be they jack rollers or police. Secondly, the law uniformly requires that "everyone must have a bedroom" if he is not to be charged with vagrancy . . . .

This author then discusses the different places where these men sleep, giving the following list: single room hotels, cubicle hotels, mission hotels, dormitories, transportation depots, busses, subways, movie houses, flop houses, box cars, hobo jungles. Thus, in discovering which questions to ask and by examining other studies, it was *hypothesized* that making a flop was a significant aspect of this subculture.

2. *Recording a corpus of relevant statements.* At this stage, conversations were recorded and statements gathered which all related to the general focus of sleeping. Earlier field notes on other subjects were combed for verbatim statements made by informants about this domain. The tramps' membership at some time in the dominant American society enables them to translate their concepts into those of the researcher. Because of this, very few questions were asked at this stage of the research. One approach that helped overcome their bias in interpreting similar cultural forms was to ask a *group* of informants to discuss their "experiences of making a flop." In such situations the individuals often talked among themselves rather than to the researcher. The following examples are drawn from these tape recorded sessions:

I took a nose dive (laughter by all) in the Bread of Life when it was real cold because they just pick out certain ones you know (laughter). If you're not sitting in the right position there, why, they'll liable not to give you a ticket. And I just walked back in that little room (laughter). But it was cold! Had to take a nose dive to get it (flop).

A lot of guys make them halls over at the Puget Sound. Either they sleep in the hallway or they sleep in the bathtub over at the Puget Sound (laughter). I've gone up and sleep in the bathroom. You know where they got those trash cans, up on the 4th floor. No one ever looks up there. That Jap says, "I got 300 rooms," he says, "and twelve hundred tramps come out every morning" (laughter).

You know where they got this little private club, down at the end of the block, towards Alaska Way from the Bread of Life, that little dock back there? (Others: yea.) There's garbage cans back there, but they're paper cans, not garbage. They're clean. And many a night, you know, in the summer time, I'd go in there, turn the barrels over, and put a pasteboard box there, and turn that barrel and stick my feet in it, and maybe I'd stick my head and shoulders in this damn pasteboard box, well I was out of sight. I'd lay there with half my body in a garbage can and the upper half in a pasteboard box. Until someone kicks that can or tries to load it and you better get out! (laughter) (Another informant: I never corked out like that!) Well, that way no one knows.

You know where I used to flop when I went out there to Interbay? I knew those Great Northern switchmen there. I'd go into those crummies, those cabooses. The guy would tell me to come down there and go ahead and build a fire in one of those stoves.

I usually hit a car lot, I'd either get in the back row, or go right up by the office. They're gonna look for you in the dark. But you pick out the best lighted place and they ain't looking for you in the light, but you get in a dark place and they come looking for you with a flashlight, right by the office, crawl in a car, 'cause they ain't looking for you in the light.

Statements made by one member of this subculture to another member and those which could be placed within a larger verbal context were most valuable. At the same time, written statements, statements made to the researcher, and fragmentary statements were extremely useful. The following examples indicate the variety and range of such data: "I got my flop for the night." "Where you gonna bed down for the night?" "I flopped out in the weeds." "In a stairway you got to sleep with one eye open or someone will bang you on the head or start taking your shoes off." "I'm not bothered if I flop in a broom closet." "I paid for my banner." "In a flophouse you can cop a heel, double up, hit the deck." "The Sally is a one night flop." "I robbed a whole clothesline to make a bed." "Head for the weeds." "You lay down there and . . ." "Got me ten or twelve newspapers back in the Frye Hotel . . . . had a bed that thick." While most of these statements could easily be judged relevant because they were elicited in the defined context of "sleeping," this was not true for others which were provisionally accepted. The first two steps were important in reducing the degree to which categories were imposed on the data from outside. As Metzger and Williams (1963:1077) have pointed out, the purpose of recording verbal interaction is "to arrive at a description that parallels the discriminations of the people under study."

3. *Examining the corpus of statements for possible domains, question frames, and substitution frames*. For this study a domain was considered to be a category system which was labeled with a cover term or a set of terms which all occurred in some restricted environment. There are a number of domains or category systems within the general focus of making a flop which could be analyzed. These include but are not limited to the following: (1) kinds of "flops"; (2) ways to "make a flop"; (3) ways to "make your own flop"; (4) kinds of "people who bother you when you flop"; (5) ways to "make a bed"; and (6) kinds of "beds." Some of these domains are sets of terms referring to objects; others refer to modes of action. This does not exhaust the possible domains and subdomains within this area, nor does it consider "covert categories" (Berlin, Breedlove and Raven 1968) which tramps utilize but which do not have cover terms. While several of these domains will be discussed, the focus of this study is primarily on kinds of "flops." Question frames were derived primarily from the cover terms for the various domains. The questions, "What kinds of flops are there?" "What are the different ways to make your own flop?" "What kinds of persons can bother you when you sleep?" and many others were developed. Substitution frames were discovered by inspecting the statements related to making a flop for those with terms that appeared to be replaceable by other terms. The following examples show several frames which were utilized: "(*The sally*) is a one night flop." "I'm not bothered if I flop in (*a broom closet*)." "I flopped in a bathtub in (*a flophouse*)."

4. *Eliciting the categories of the domain.* The most important question frame for eliciting the categories of the domain labeled "flop" was, "What kinds of flops are there?" This resulted in a large number of terms which are ordered on the principle of inclusion and form a folk taxonomy (Table 13:2). Some of the terms were discovered through examination of previously recorded texts and others overheard in informal conversations. While the taxonomy appears to be clear-cut, and one might assume that the persistent application of the above question frame with different informants led to unambiguous results, such was not the case. The final taxonomy given in Table 13:2 is a result of informant responses, intuitive insights, and some ordering of categories during analysis to satisfy the aesthetic values of the researcher! There are no doubt alternative ways to structure some aspects of this taxonomy as well as the componential definition to follow. I do not feel that such facts appreciably limit the possibility of replication and I would maintain that this analysis is still more rigorous than other approaches to this kind of material. In order to avoid the impression that all indeterminacy was ruled out and to identify the choices which I made, a number of factors may be examined in relation to this taxonomy.

First, there were a number of terms which were excluded from the taxonomy because they were extremely rare or very little information could be gathered on them for further analysis. One informant indicated that one kind of flop was a *mortar box*. He recalled: "My wife and I were hitchhiking to Chattanooga and we slept in an old filling station that was closed, in an old mortar box. We picked up some grass they had just cut along the highway and used it for a bed." Further investigation may reveal that there is a category of flops called *boxes* which would include *mortar box* and *trash box*, but the latter was the only box included here as a kind of flop. Another informant reported that a friend had flopped in a *junky cart*. Tramps have a variety of "ways of making it," modes of action which bring some kind of economic gain. One of these is *junking*. In this case, two tramps in Chicago had acquired a junky cart and were traveling the streets of the city picking up bottles, metal, and any object of value to sell to the junk dealer. Their *junky cart* was large enough to sleep in, so one man would crawl in and cover himself with an overcoat to keep out of sight while he slept and the other man pushed the cart along. I was unable to discover how common such a practice was nor any other information which would enable me to define the junky cart from the tramp's point of view. There is reason to believe that further research would validate such terms, and undoubtedly other categories would be discovered.

Second, there were a variety of places "in buildings" which informants identified that were not included, and the taxonomic status of those which were included is problematical. In most urban environments there are many public buildings which are accessible to tramps. Within these buildings there

TABLE 13:2. *Taxonomic Definition of Flops*

Term	Subcategory	Category	Top
truck		*Car Flop*	FLOP
used car lot		*Car Flop*	FLOP
junk yard		*Car Flop*	FLOP
transit bus		*Car Flop*	FLOP
harvest bus		*Car Flop*	FLOP
car on street		*Car Flop*	FLOP
own car		*Car Flop*	FLOP
lobby		*"Places in Paid Flop"*	FLOP
toilet floor		*"Places in Paid Flop"*	FLOP
hallway		*"Places in Paid Flop"*	FLOP
bathtub		*"Places in Paid Flop"*	FLOP
broom	*Closet*	*"Places in Paid Flop"*	FLOP
clothes	*Closet*	*"Places in Paid Flop"*	FLOP
window well			FLOP
under building			FLOP
all night laundromat			FLOP
all night bar			FLOP
all night restaurant			FLOP
all night show			FLOP
paddy wagon			FLOP
cotton wagon			FLOP
hay barn			FLOP
furnace room			FLOP
newspaper building			FLOP
bar room			FLOP
night club			FLOP
bus depot			FLOP
brick yard			FLOP
scale house			FLOP
harvest shack			FLOP
bucket			FLOP
tool house			FLOP
stairwell			FLOP
park bench			FLOP
penny arcade			FLOP
church			FLOP
trash box			FLOP
doorway			FLOP
apple bin			FLOP
haystack			FLOP
loading dock			FLOP
motel		*Paid Flop*	FLOP
hotel		*Paid Flop*	FLOP
apartment		*Paid Flop*	FLOP
dormitory	*Fleabag (flophouse)*	*Paid Flop*	FLOP
wire cage	*Fleabag (flophouse)*	*Paid Flop*	FLOP
flophouse	*Fleabag (flophouse)*	*Paid Flop*	FLOP
motel		*Empty Building*	FLOP
hotel		*Empty Building*	FLOP
house		*Empty Building*	FLOP
apartment		*Empty Building*	FLOP
abandoned		*Empty Building*	FLOP
under construction		*Empty Building*	FLOP
being torn down		*Empty Building*	FLOP
pasture		*Weed Patch*	FLOP
cemetery		*Weed Patch*	FLOP
viaduct		*Weed Patch*	FLOP
bridge		*Weed Patch*	FLOP
riverbank		*Weed Patch*	FLOP
field		*Weed Patch*	FLOP
orchard		*Weed Patch*	FLOP
between buildings		*Weed Patch*	FLOP
park		*Weed Patch*	FLOP
sidewalk		*Weed Patch*	FLOP
town	*Jungle*	*Weed Patch*	FLOP
railroad	*Jungle*	*Weed Patch*	FLOP
railroad track		*Weed Patch*	FLOP
alley		*Weed Patch*	FLOP
dump		*Weed Patch*	FLOP
switchman's shanty		*Railroad Flop*	FLOP
conductor's quarters		*Railroad Flop*	FLOP
coal car		*Railroad Flop*	FLOP
box car		*Railroad Flop*	FLOP
flat car		*Railroad Flop*	FLOP
reefer		*Railroad Flop*	FLOP
piggyback		*Railroad Flop*	FLOP
station		*Railroad Flop*	FLOP
gondola		*Railroad Flop*	FLOP
passenger car		*Railroad Flop*	FLOP
sand house		*Railroad Flop*	FLOP
crummy		*Railroad Flop*	FLOP
mission flop			FLOP

are public places which make good sleeping quarters because they are heated. These include depots, hotels, business buildings, police stations, etc. Many men reported that one kind of flop was a *toilet floor*. Further inquiry revealed that there were many different places where *toilet floors* could be found. For instance, informants reported: "I slept in jail in Mississippi. We went into the jail toilet and slept all night." "I've slept in a railroad station toilet and a bus depot toilet." "I have no trouble walking in a second floor, second rate hotel upstairs and curling up and going to sleep in the men's room. If it's very late at night I know there's a very poor possibility of anyone wanting to take a bath, so I just sleep in the bathtub." These places are not considered kinds of "paid flops," yet very often they are in hotels or flophouses. One arrangement that might have been used was to consider *toilet floor* a cover term for a great many location concepts such as *in jails, in hotels*, and *in buildings*. Since most informants reported that they usually found these places in *flophouses*, it was decided to consider "places in flophouses" as a category which included *toilet floors, lobbies, hallways*, etc., and exclude the other locations from the present analysis.

Third, the discovery of some middle level terms in the taxonomy presented certain difficulties. Informants responded freely with the most generic term, *flop*. They also responded freely with specific instances of places where they had flopped, such as "I slept in a crummy," or "We slept in a big truck that was loaded with cotton from seats of old cars." Initially the taxonomy appeared to be primarily made up of a generic and specific level. In order to discover the middle levels, the question frame "What kind of a flop is that?" was used with the specific terms elicited. Through this process it was possible to discover that a *crummy* (a caboose on a train) was a railroad flop and the big truck noted above was a *junk yard truck* which is a kind of *junk yard car flop*. When informants indicated that a certain term was to be included in a higher level term, it was possible to elicit other specific terms or place those already discovered by using substitution frames. For example, the substitution frame "A *crummy* is a railroad flop" led to expanding the list of kinds of railroad flops.

Fourth, there was a tendency to assume taxonomic relationships by confusing the form and function, as well as different functions, of an object. It will be noted by examining the taxonomy given in Table 13:2 that the terms categorize objects, not according to their physical form, but according to the function they serve for tramps and not other members of urban society. While this phenomenon has long been recognized by anthropologists, urban anthropologists face greater problems because they often share similar forms with those they study but the functions are defined differently. One cannot assume similarity of taxonomic relationships but must test all such relationships empirically. For instance, at first it appeared that *paddy wagon* and *cotton wagon* might be included in the term *wagon flop*, but informants denied this relationship. There are several terms which include the phrase "all night," such as *all night laundromat*. When asked to sort these into similar categories, or asked if they were to be considered as similar kinds of flops, informants refused to include them in any more generic term than flop. The discovery of taxonomic relationships for similar terms which exist in two or more urban subcultures is one way of demonstrating that such terms are or are not homonyms. Many terms in the domain of flops would be classed only as *vehicles* by this researcher. Informants classified some objects which were vehicles separately and some objects which were not vehicles, such as *sand house*, together with vehicles.

Fifth, it was necessary to constantly check those terms which might be homonyms or synonyms. The problem of intercultural homonyms has already been noted in the preceding paragraph. I shared the term *cemetery* with my informants, yet it was included in the terms *weed patch* and *flop* for them but not for me. This type of intercultural homonym contrasts with intracultural homonyms such as informants' dual use of the term *hotel.* One refers to a kind of *paid flop* and the other a kind of *empty building flop*. There were many synonyms used by informants such as *flea bag/flop house*. Some men referred to all kinds of cheap Skid Road hotels as *flea bags*; others used the term *flop houses*. There was some confusion over this since in the city studied there were no *dormitory flops* or *wire cage flops*, so informants could use the cover term *flophouse* without specifying the level of contrast, i.e., what terms it contrasted with, since there were only specific flophouses in that city.[8] Some other synonyms encountered were the following: *crummy-caboose, mission-sally*, and *jail-bucket-can*. When a choice was to be made between terms which informants reported "meant the same thing," preference was given to terms used by those who had been members of this subculture for a longer period of time and also reflected the predominant usage of the geographical location of the research. Dialectal variation among tramps was encountered frequently, especially among those who had been socialized into this subculture in the southern part of the United States.

It should be noted that the lower level terms in the taxonomy do not refer to specific objects, but classes of objects judged as equivalent. For some of these terms it was possible to elicit more specific named objects which were members of the class. For instance, *park* is a kind of *weed patch flop*, but there were many different parks where informants had slept. Some different kinds of parks were elicited which are not included here, such as *hobo park*. The discovery of more specific terms was carried out in some cases with the question frame, "What are the different kinds of ——?" or "Can you tell me the names for the different—— where tramps flop?" Some category terms such as *box car* refer to a large number of different objects, but these are not named. Instead, informants would distinguish between members of a set by such statements as "I slept in a box car outside of Omaha on a rip track where I was bothered by the railroad bulls." While *empty buildings, weed patches*, and *railroad flops* are not generally named at a very specific level, other subdomains such as *flophouse* and *mission* have many specific named members, reflecting the importance of these subdomains for this population.

We may now ask what this taxonomy says about the subculture of urban nomads. How culturally revealing is it to elicit the categories which this group uses to order their environment in relationship to sleeping behavior? While this category system is not exhaustive it contains nearly one hundred *categories* of sleeping places. Furthermore this taxonomy has five levels and could have been extended to at least six by including more specific terms. Several tentative conclusions may be drawn from these facts. First, the importance of nondrinking behavior such as sleeping appears to have been underestimated by most researchers in this field. Even the study quoted earlier which stressed the importance of finding a place to sleep lists only eleven categories of places to sleep. While the initial participant observations led to the *impression* that "making a flop" was important and would be culturally revealing, we now have a basis for comparison with other domains, both intraculturally and interculturally. While I would not contend that a simple count of the number of terms or the levels of a taxonomy are conclusive evidence of importance, they cannot be easily dismissed. Preliminary work with other domains in this subculture have not revealed any other category system which organizes so much of the environment or in such a detailed fashion. There are many different kinds of *bars, bulls, time,* and *ways of making it,* but none of these domains are as elaborate as the different kinds of *flops*. The domain which comes closest to being as elaborate is the kinds of *people in the bucket,* or social roles in jail. Further research is necessary to make a more complete intracultural comparison.

Only superficial intercultural comparisons are possible at this time, since, to my knowledge, similar domains in other cultures have not been studied by this means. Sleeping places do not appear to be culturally revealing in the rest of American culture. In fact, the eleven categories of sleeping places noted above from other research are probably more than most Americans use. It is interesting to compare the usage of the two terms *flop* and *sleep*. *Flopping* is used by tramps to refer to the activity which other Americans refer to as *sleeping*, although most tramps will also use *sleeping*. When we consider the use of these two terms in their noun form an interesting difference appears. The noun *flop* refers to a place in the environment where the activity takes place while the noun *sleep* refers to the bodily state of rest or to the occasion of sleeping. Thus the verbs may be considered translations of each other but this is not so for the nouns. Tramps, in their language, stress the place where sleeping occurs, while other Americans do not. Frake (1961:121–122) has proposed the following hypothesis related to taxonomic differences between cultures:

> The greater the number of distinct social contexts in which information about a particular phenomenon must be communicated, the greater the number of different levels of contrast into which phenomenon is categorized. . . . If the botanical taxonomy of tribe A has more levels of contrast than that of tribe B, it means the members of tribe A communicate botanical information in a wider variety of sociocultural settings.

It seems apparent that tramps communicate information regarding places to sleep in a wider variety of sociocultural settings than do members of the larger American society. One is not surprised that sleeping behavior has been largely overlooked by those who have studied this group. The social scientist in his own culture has learned that there are relatively few places to sleep, that places to sleep do not enter into a wide variety of sociocultural settings, and probably holds the implicit assumption that places to sleep are not culturally relevant. While the major basis for designating these men as urban nomads was their own definition of social identity, this taxonomy strongly supports such a designation. Although a nomadic way of life does not necessarily require a large number of categories for places to sleep, we are not surprised to find that this is so for these men. We might well be surprised to discover a group which is sedentary and also had such an elaborate category system for places to sleep.

A taxonomic definition is culturally revealing but it does not take us far enough in understanding this group of men. It tells us that tramps have many places to sleep but it does not tell us very much about what they consider significant about each place for sleeping purposes. It does not tell us much about how they choose one place to sleep instead of another. There are a very large, if not infinite, number of criteria which could be used to define such objects as *cemeteries*, *box cars*, *bridges*, and *bathtubs*. All of these items have at least one feature of meaning in common for the population under consideration: they are all *flops*, places to sleep. If we are to understand what meaning these places hold for tramps, we must discover the underlying semantic principles by means of which tramps differentiate one kind of flop from another. This leads us to the next step in the research.

5. *Discovering the semantic principles of the domain.* The procedures used to discover the underlying semantic principles of a domain have been referred to as componential analysis (Goodenough 1956). A set of objects or events which are identified as equivalent and labeled with a category

term are not necessarily identical. All of the objects referred to by the terms in Table 13:2 are classed as equivalent. They all share at least one feature of meaning, but there are many differences among them. Each term *contrasts* with the other terms and those at the same level of contrast make up a *contrast set*. The dimensions of meaning which are important in differentiating among members of a contrast set are the *dimensions of contrast*. Each dimension of contrast has two or more values. The differences in meaning among members of a contrast set are indicated in terms of the values on each dimension of meaning. By specifying how each term included in the *flop* domain contrasts with every other term we would be stating, in part, the underlying semantic principles which organize the domain. If the dimensions of contrast reflect the cognitive world of our informants we would also be stating, in part, the significant criteria which they use in selecting one place to sleep over another. This study was aimed at a description which approximated the psychological reality of informants. Wallace and Atkins (1960:75) have distinguished between analyses which are psychologically real and those which are structurally real:

> The psychological reality of an individual is the world as he perceives and knows it, in his own terms; it is his world of meanings. A "psychologically real" description of a culture thus is a description which approximately reproduces in an observer the world of meanings of the native users of that culture. "Structural reality," on the other hand, is a world of meanings, as applied to a given society or individual, which is real to the ethnographer, but it is not *necessarily* the world which constitutes the mazeway of any other individual or individuals.

It is assumed here that any componential analysis of a category system will fall somewhere between an exact replica of the cognitions of informants and one which is completely divorced from how they perceive the world. As the above authors note, "A problem for research, then, must be to develop techniques for stating and identifying those definitions which are most proximate to psychological reality" (1960:78).

Several techniques were used to elicit the dimensions of contrast employed by tramps and to avoid imposing dimensions relevant only to the investigator. The underlying goal of all these techniques was to elicit from informants those differences in meaning which they felt existed among members of the set. Probably the most useful approach was the triadic sorting task (Kelly 1955; Romney and D'Andrade 1964). Informants were presented with three terms for different categories of *flops* and asked to indicate which two were most alike and/or which one was different. *After* a selection was made they were queried regarding the basis of their choice. Substitution frames were formulated from these responses or from other textual material. For example, an informant would be presented with the frame, "If you flop in the (*main jungle*) you may be bothered by other

TABLE 13:3. *Dimensions of Contrast for Flop Domain* (highest level of contrast)

1.0 *Monetary resources*
- 1.1 Not required
- 1.2 Required to pay for the flop
- 1.3 Required to pay for something else

2.0 *Atmospheric conditions* (weather)
- 2.1 Almost no protection
- 2.2 Out of the rain/snow
- 2.3 Out of the wind
- 2.4 Out of the wind, possibly out of the cold
- 2.5 Out of the wind and rain/snow
- 2.6 Out of the wind and rain/snow, possibly out of the cold
- 2.7 Out of the wind, rain/snow and cold

3.0 *Body position*
- 3.1 May lie down
- 3.2 Must sit up
- 3.3 Should sit up but may lie down

4.0 *Intoxication*
- 4.1 Must be sober
- 4.2 Must be drunk
- 4.3 Any state of intoxication

5.0 *Drinking restrictions*
- 5.1 Low risk drinking
- 5.2 High risk drinking
- 5.3 Purchase drinks

6.0 *Civilian interference*
- 6.1 Waitress
- 6.2 Night watchman
- 6.3 Bartender
- 6.4 Manager
- 6.5 Owner
- 6.6 Farmer
- 6.7 Engineer
- 6.8 Tramps
- 6.9 Anybody
- 6.10 Minister or priest
- 6.11 Truck driver
- 6.12 Probably no civilian

7.0 *Police interference*
- 7.1 Police check and may also be called
- 7.2 Police check
- 7.3 Police must be called
- 7.4 Police do not interfere

8.0 *Security*
- 8.1 Public/Concealed/Protected
- 8.2 Public/Concealed/Unprotected
- 8.3 Public/Unconcealed/Protected
- 8.4 Public/Unconcealed/Unprotected
- 8.5 Non-public/Concealed/Protected
- 8.6 Non-public/Concealed/Unprotected
- 8.7 Non-public/Unconcealed/Unprotected

TABLE 13:4. *Componential Definition of Flops* (highest level of contrast)

Flops	*Dimensions of Contrast*							
	1.0	2.0	3.0	4.0	5.0	6.0	7.0	8.0
Paid Flop	1.2	2.7	3.1	4.3	X	X	7.4	X
Empty Building	1.1	2.6	3.1	4.1	5.1	6.2,6.8	7.1	8.6
Weed Patch	1.1	X	3.1	X	5.1	X	X	X
Railroad Flop	1.1	X	X	X	X	X	X	X
Mission Flop	1.1	2.7	3.1	4.1	5.2	6.8	7.4	8.4?
Car Flop	X	X	3.1	X	5.1	X	X	X
"Places in Paid Flop"	1.1	2.7	X	X	X	X	7.3	X
Window Well	1.1	2.4	3.1	4.3	5.1	6.8	7.2	8.7
Under Building	1.1	2.6	3.1	4.3	5.1	6.8	7.2	8.6
All Night Laundromat	1.1	2.7	3.3	4.3	5.2	6.5	7.2	8.4
All Night Bar	1.3	2.7	3.2	4.3	5.3	6.1,3,4	7.1	8.4
All Night Restaurant	1.3	2.7	3.2	4.3	5.2	6.1	7.1	8.4
All Night Show	1.3	2.7	3.3	4.3	5.1	6.8	7.4	8.2
Paddy Wagon	1.1	2.5	3.1	4.2	5.2	6.12	7.2	8.7
Cotton Wagon	1.1	2.5	3.1	4.3	5.1	6.12	7.4	8.6
Hay Barn	1.1	2.6	3.1	4.3	5.1	6.6	7.4	8.6
Furnace Room	1.1	2.7	3.1	4.3	5.1	6.2,7	7.3	8.6
Newspaper Building	1.1	2.7	3.1	4.3	5.2	6.4	7.3	8.6
Bar Room	1.3	2.7	3.2	4.3	5.3	6.1,3,4	7.1	8.4
Night Club	1.3	2.7	3.2	4.3	5.3	6.1,3,4	7.1	8.4
Bus Depot	1.1	2.7	3.2	4.3	5.2	6.9	7.1	8.4
Brick Yard	1.1	2.7	3.1	4.3	5.1	6.4	7.3	8.6
Scale House	1.1	2.6	3.1	4.3	5.1	6.8	7.3?	8.6
Harvest Shack	1.1	2.7	3.1	4.3	5.1	6.8	7.4	8.1
Bucket	1.1	2.7	3.1	4.3	5.2	6.8	7.4	8.4
Tool House	1.1	2.5	3.1	4.3	5.1	6.12	7.3	8.6
Stairwell	1.1	2.4	3.1	4.2	5.1	6.5,8	7.1	8.7
Park Bench	1.1	2.1	3.1	4.3	5.2	6.8	7.2	8.7
Penny Arcade	1.1	2.7	3.2	4.3	5.2	6.12	7.2	8.4
Church	1.1	2.6	3.1	4.3	5.2	6.2,10	7.1	8.6
Trash Box	1.1	2.5	3.1	4.3	5.1	6.12	7.2	8.6
Doorway	1.1	2.1	3.1	4.2	5.1	6.8,9	7.1	8.7
Apple Bin	1.1	2.5	3.1	4.3	5.1	6.12	7.4	8.6
Haystack	1.1	2.7?	3.1	4.3	5.1	6.12	7.4	8.6
Loading Dock	1.1	2.1	3.1	4.2	5.1	6.2,11,8	7.1	8.7

NOTE: See Table 13:3 for the meaning of each numerical symbol. A question mark indicates lack of information, while an X indicates variability among the terms at the next lowest level. In Column 1.0 *car flop* has an X because some kinds require money and others do not.

(*tramps*)," and asked to indicate what other terms would appropriately go together in the two spaces. This approach is very similar to the "grid method" discussed by Bannister and Mair in a recent work based on Kelly's personal construct theory of personality (Bannister and Mair 1968). Another approach was to ask informants to sort the terms into two or more groups in any way they desired. Then they would be asked to indicate why they had grouped the terms in a particular way. These techniques led to the discovery of the dimensions of contrast for this domain. Those which are used for defining the terms at the highest level of contrast are listed in Table 13:3 and a componential definition of these terms is provided in Table 13:4. A more complete discussion of these dimensions of contrast as well as those used in analyzing several other subdomains has been provided by Spradley (1970).

A componential definition does not tell us everything there is to know about a domain. The definition in Table 13:4 does provide us with the information which some tramps use to identify objects they consider places to sleep with the appropriate label. It also enables us to see how most terms are distinguished from one another. Sleeping *under a building* is both similar to and different from sleeping in a *window well,* and this componential definition shows us how these places are alike and different from the tramp's perspective. They are similar kinds of flops because they require no money, permit lying down, allow any state of intoxication, involve low risk of arrest for drinking, are relatively free from civilian interference, and are checked occasionally by the police. They differ in that when a man sleeps *under a building* he has more protection from rain and snow as well as concealment from other people. At this level of contrast there are two sets of terms with identical values for each dimension of contrast and thus it is not possible to discriminate among them by means of elicited criteria. A *bar room, all night bar,* and *night club* have the same values, a fact which suggests that there may be a covert category which includes these three sleeping places. *Apple bin* and *cotton wagon* are not distinguished; they are both rather concealed places in the vicinity of farms or orchards. Further research would probably yield more criteria which would distinguish among these terms.

Another problem with this analysis involves the criterion of economy which has been suggested for evaluating the adequacy of ethnographic statements (Conklin 1964:26). Are all the dimensions of contrast *necessary* to define this contrast set? Except for the terms noted above which are not distinguished at the first level of contrast, only the first seven dimensions of contrast are necessary to discriminate among all the other terms. This means that the dimension of *security* (8.0) does not add anything to the goal of economy, although I would suggest that it is culturally revealing and thus should be included. In any componential analysis one may choose the criteria of economy or exhaustiveness. The analysis presented here does not measure up to either of these criteria completely. In some cases it *could* be more exhaustive and in other cases more economical. It seems likely that there are often *more* dimensions of contrast than are necessary to economically define a particular set of terms. The following hypothesis is proposed to account for this: *The semantic criteria used to identify events and objects in the environment are determined by situational variables.* These variables may be external to the organism such as time of year, climate, and presence of other people. They may be within the organism in the form of need states. For example, a tramp with a few dollars may contemplate going to a *paid flop* or selecting some other place to sleep. An *empty building, church,* and *stairwell* are all nearby and since the weather is warm all seem to be possible flops which will not cost him anything. Then he remembers that his arrest record is such that another conviction will mean several months in jail and since these three flops are all checked by the police they are ruled out. A paid flop would protect him from the police and provide the greatest security, but he would like to use his money to purchase something to drink. He recalls that nearby there is an *all night show* which would cost less than a *paid flop*, leave him enough money for his drink and where he would escape detection by the police. As he decides on the *all night show* he notes that he is tired enough to sleep sitting up, he may even be able to lie on the floor, especially after he has finished off the bottle he can now purchase. He has taken account of a variety of situational variables and finally made a selection based on his definition of flops. The definition of situational variables and their relationships to the semantic criteria for this domain remains an important research task.

Does this analysis provide insight into broader aspects of the culture of tramps or is it merely an exercise in analyzing trivial "ethnoscientific trait lists" (Berreman 1966:351)? Although a more complete discussion of this domain and its relationship to other important features of the culture of urban nomads is presented elsewhere (Spradley 1970), we may note several important themes which have emerged from this analysis. Tramps define sleeping places in terms of some of the most important concerns in their lives: they experience poverty (1.0); as nomads they must be aware of changing weather conditions (2.0); drinking groups and drunkenness are institutionalized (4.0, 5.0); they experience the rejection and harassment from the dominant society which is common to many minority groups (6.0); many do life sentences on the installment plan as a result of their encounter with the police (7.0); and they survive, in part, by reducing their visibility and thus increasing their security (8.0). The ethnographic approach not only led to the discovery that "making a flop" was one of the most important features of life for tramps but through an analysis of this domain many other significant aspects of their culture were revealed.

V. Conclusion

This paper presented a study of the adaptive strategies of urban nomads by means of an ethnoscientific analysis of one domain in their culture. This approach, based on a recognition of the multicultural nature of urban life, allowed informants to identify the relevant social units and the criteria for membership in these categories. The methods used were designed to reduce the influence of that form of ethnocentrism which not only prejudges the value of tramp culture but also predifines the categories and meanings of that culture. Native terminological systems were studied in ways which avoided the tendency of informants to act as subcultural interpreters, translating their way of life into terms which are acceptable to members of the dominant culture. It was shown that, while tramps share such objects as cars, missions, jails, brick yards, cemeteries, and bathtubs with other urban dwellers, the meaning of such objects varies greatly from one subculture to another. Those who live in cities may share the same locality but they are actually cultural worlds apart. One important part of *urban* anthropology must be the careful ethnographic description of these cultural worlds.

Ethnography is only a beginning and this study raises many questions for further research. How do those living by different subcultures within the city interact in predictable ways, i.e., how do urban societies manage to "organize diversity" (A.F.C. Wallace 1961)? Can the methods of ethnoscience enable us to map the equivalence structures of the interaction between tramps and the police, bar tenders, or social workers? Would it be possible to correlate certain features of tramp culture, as viewed from the inside, with the categories of behavior which are the focus of the medical and sociological approaches? How is mobility related to alcoholism, homelessness, and criminal behavior? What are the inherent limitations of the ethnographic approach outlined here in studying urban cultures? Ethnoscience and similar approaches to ethnography cannot begin to answer all the questions which must be asked to increase our understanding of urban man. They can, however, make us sensitive to the culture-bound nature of human existence whether, as social scientists we are investigating other cultures or as tramps we are looking for a place to flop.

Notes

1. This paper is a revised and expanded version of "Ethnoscientific Study of a Tramp Sub-Culture," a paper presented to the 67th Annual Meeting of the American Anthropological Association, November 21–24, 1968, Seattle, Washington. Some of the material used to illustrate the methods of research are drawn from Spradley 1970, where they receive much fuller treatment along with many other domains in the culture of urban nomads. The research for this paper was carried out in Seattle, Washington, during 1967/1968. I wish to express my thanks to Paul Kay, Michael Lieber, and Lydia Kotchek for their comments on earlier drafts and to Per Hage for suggestions regarding many aspects of the method and data discussed here.

2. "Skid Road" is used here in preference to "skid row," which appears in much of the literature. *Skid Road* is a term which originated in Seattle to describe the road down which logs were skidded to the sawmill and where bars, flophouses, and gambling houses were prevalent. There is an extensive literature on Skid Road and the men described in this paper. Those who are interested may consult Wallace, S. E., 1965, which contains an extensive bibliography.

3. Since there are many studies which have not been published, it is difficult to estimate the degree to which ethnoscience techniques have actually been used in the study of urban groups. There are a number of reports on American kinship terms (Goodenough 1965; Romney and D'Andrade 1964), one on American law terms (Black and Metzger 1965), and one on German beer terms (Hage 1972) which have to do with urban populations.

4. Since all the men in this sample did not answer every question, some of the percentages do not total 100 percent. The remainder represents those who did not respond.

5. A more detailed analysis of *hustling* may be found in two other publications on tramp culture (Spradley 1968, 1970).

6. The work of George Kelly (1955) provides one of the closest links between psychology and ethnoscience. Anthropologists whose work has been especially helpful include Conklin 1962, 1964; Frake 1961, 1962a, 1962b; Goodenough 1956; Kay 1966; Metzger and Williams 1963, 1966; and Black and Metzger 1965.

7. Some differences among informants regarding different kinds of tramps have been investigated. A sample of about sixty-five men were asked to respond to a questionnaire based on the criteria used by informants to define the domain of "tramps." Relationships between a self-image adjective check-list, social identity as a kind of tramp, and knowledge of this particular taxonomy are being analyzed.

8. See Frake's discussion of the use of the same linguistic form at different levels of contrast for further discussion of this kind of problem (1961:119).

Bibliography

BANNISTER, D. and J. M. M. MAIR. 1968. *Evaluation of Personal Constructs*. London: Academic Press.

BERLIN, BRENT, DENNIS E. BREEDLOVE, and PETER H. RAVEN. 1968. "Covert Categories and Folk Taxonomies." *American Anthropologist* 70:290–299.

BERREMAN, GERALD D. 1966. "Anemic and Emetic Analyses in Social Anthropology." *American Anthropologist* 68:346–354.

BLACK, MARY and DUANE METZGER. 1965. "Ethnographic Description and the Study of Law," in The Ethnography of Law, Laura Nader, ed. *American Anthropologist* 67(6) 2:141–165.

BRUNER, JEROME S., J. J. GOODNOW, and G. A. AUSTIN. 1956. *A Study of Thinking.* New York: John Wiley and Sons.

CONKLIN, HAROLD C. 1962. "Lexicographical treatment of folk taxonomies," in Problems in Lexicography, F. W. Householder and Sol Saporta, eds. *International Journal of American Linguistics* 28.2 Part IV:119–141.

———. 1964. "Ethnogenealogical Method," in *Exploration in Cultural Anthropology,* Ward H. Goodenough, ed. New York: McGraw-Hill, pp. 25–55.

FRAKE, CHARLES O. 1961. "The Diagnosis of Disease Among the Subanun of Mindanao." *American Anthropologist* 63:113–132.

———. 1962a. "Cultural Ecology and Ethnography." *American Anthropologist* 64:53–59.

———. 1962b. "The Ethnographic Study of Cognitive Systems," in *Anthropology and Human Behavior,* Thomas Gladwin and W. C. Sturtevant, eds. Washington, D.C: Anthropological Society of Washington.

GOODENOUGH, WARD. 1956. "Componential Analysis and the Study of Meaning." *Language* 32:195–216.

———. 1957. "Cultural Anthropology and Linguistics." *Georgetown University Monograph Series on Language and Linguistics.* No. 9:167–173.

———. 1965. "Yankee Kinship Terminology: A Problem in Componential Analysis," in Formal Semantic Analysis, E. A. Hammel, ed. *American Anthropologist* 67(2):259–287.

HAGE, PER. 1972. *Münchner Beer Categories.* Chapter 14, this volume.

KAY, PAUL. 1966. "Comment." *Current Anthropology* 7:20–23.

KELLY, GEORGE. 1955. *The Psychology of Personal Constructs.* New York: W. W. Norton.

METZGER, DUANE and GERALD E. WILLIAMS. 1963. "A Formal Ethnographic Analysis of Tenejapa Ladino Weddings. *American Anthropologist* 65:1076–1101.

———. 1966. "Some Procedures and Results in the Study of Native Categories: Tzeltal "firewood." *American Anthropologist* 68:389–407.

ROMNEY, A. K. and R. G. D'ANDRADE. 1964. "Cognitive Aspects of English Kin Terms," in Transcultural Studies in Cognition, S. K. Romney and R. G. D'Andrade, eds. *American Anthropologist* 66(3), 2:146–170.

SPRADLEY, JAMES P. 1968. "A Cognitive Analysis of Tramp Behavior." *Proceedings of the 8th International Congress of Anthropological and Ethnological Sciences,* Japan, 1968.

———. 1970 *You Owe Yourself A Drunk: An Ethnography of Urban Nomads.* Boston: Little, Brown and Company.

SOLOMAN, PHILIP. 1966. "Psychiatric Treatment of the Alcoholic Patient." in *Alcoholism*, Jack H. Mendelson, ed. Boston: Little, Brown and Company.

WALLACE, ANTHONY F. C. 1961. *Culture and Personality.* New York: Random House.

———. 1962. "Culture and Cognition." *Science* 135:351–357.

WALLACE, A. F. C. and JOHN ATKINS. 1960. "The Meaning of Kinship Terms." *American Anthropologist* 62:58–80.

WALLACE, SAMUEL E. 1965. *Skid Row As A Way of Life.* Totowa, New Jersey: The Bedminster Press.

Cities

14 MÜNCHNER BEER CATEGORIES

Per Hage

In every culture some domains are more important than others. Hunting techniques among the Bushmen, sleeping places for tramps, the automobile for Americans, potlatch displays among the Kwakiutl—the list could be extended indefinitely. These domains become linked to many other aspects of a culture. In this article Per Hage presents an elegant analysis of one such domain among the population of a European city. Beer is a special symbol, and drinking it has a variety of cultural meanings. Like all other phenomena, beer is culturally defined, and the author examines these meanings in detail with the tools of ethnoscience. The attributes of different beers, motives for their consumption, stages of intoxication, and the social values of drinking are all discussed. Furthermore, the author suggests some implications for the study of folk taxonomies in general and the evolution of category systems.—EDITOR'S NOTE

I. Introduction

München is one of those cultures in which beer is, to borrow Mandelbaum's (1965) phrase, "essential and blessed." It is consumed by all ages and classes, by both sexes, at many times during the day, in a large number of cultural scenes, for a variety of motives. It has a venerable tradition going back to the monks who many centuries ago began brewing it and thereby changed München from a "wine city" to a "beer city." Its origin is still reflected in the names of two of the breweries and in their advertisements, which picture roly-poly, smiling, beer-drinking monks. It has its own patron saint, *Gambrinus der Bierheilige.* It is symbolic of social solidarity and is a culturally recognized means for achieving it. It is the focus for an annual festival—the *Oktoberfest*—during which Münchner[1] reaffirm their collective sentiments and values. It is, in effect, the Münchner totem. The domain of beer categories is extensive, and beer and its consumption con-

This article was written for this volume and has never before been published.

stitute, to use a very subjective term, a cultural focus. Knowledge of the properties of beer, its uses, effects, and symbolism would certainly constitute a first step in getting to know the Münchner.

The aim of this paper is to describe some Münchner attitudes toward beer and beer drinking and to formally define the beer categories and show certain of their behavioral and cognitive correlates. More specifically, the aims are to show the taxonomic and semantic structure of these categories and to relate the dimensions by which informants define the set of beer categories to the culturally defined set of motives for the consumption of beer and to some Münchner concepts of space, time, and identity.

II. Münchner Beer Categories

Determining the universe. Theoretically there are, according to Goodenough (1956), two ways of doing this: by a cover term or by complementation on *n* dimensions. Each method has its difficulties. The first can lead to inclusion of homonyms, the second to inclusion of terms which, while complementary on some dimensions, would not be regarded as belonging to the same universe as the other terms. In the present case, for example, *Sprudel,* a kind of soda water could be defined on some of the same dimensions as beer, but, according to informants, it clearly belongs to another domain. The usual practice is the use of a cover term, the method followed here.

"Core" terms. After determining that there was a category, *Münchner Biere,* the various types were elicited with the frame: 'What kinds of Munich beer are there?' (*'Was fur Münchner Biere gibt es?'*).

Wiesnbier: Literally, 'meadow beer', but *Wiesn* refers here to the *Theresienwiese,* the site of the annual October Festival where this beer is dispensed.
Märzenbier: 'March beer.'
Heller Bock: 'Light, strong beer.'
Salvator: The Paulaner brewery's name for dark, strong beer. Each of the seven major breweries has its own name for this category of beer, but *Salvator* is often used generically, probably because it was one of the first of this kind to be brewed.
Helles: 'light beer.'
Dunkles: 'dark beer.'
Weisses: 'white beer.'
Russ: 'white beer mixed with *limo*' ('sweet lemon-flavored soda water').
Radlermass: 'dark beer mixed with *limo,*' (*Radler* = bicyclist, *Mass* = short for *Masskrug,* a liter-sized beer container). The name, according to some informants, derives from its supposed invention by bicyclists' clubs.
Nährbier: from *nähren* 'to nourish,' thus, 'nourishing beer.'

Paradigmatic relationships. These categories are paradigmatically related (a paradigm being defined as "any set of linguistic forms, whatever their shape, which signify complementary sememes . . ." Goodenough 1956, p. 197) on the following dimensions. These were found by asking informants, 'What is the difference between——*and*——?' ('*Was ist der Unterschied zwischen* —— und —— ?'), using all pair combinations:

STÄRKE ('strength'); *stark* ('strong') = S; *normal* ('normal') = N; *schwach* ('weak') = W; *alkoholfrei* ('alcohol-free') or *olkoholarm*, ('negligible alcoholic content') = O.
FARBE ('color'): *hell* ('light') = L; *dunkel* ('dark') = D; *braunlich* ('brownish') = B.
SPRITZIGKEIT ('fizziness'): *spritzig* (fizzy') = F; *nicht spritzig* ('nonfizzy') = NF.
GELAGERT VS UNGELAGERT ('aged *vs* unaged') = A *vs* U.

The individual beers are defined in Table 14.1.

TABLE 14:1. *The Componential Definition of Munich Core Beers*

Type of Beer	Strength	Color	Fizziness	Ageing
Wiesnbier	S	B	NF	A
Märzenbier	S	B	NF	U
Heller Bock	S	L	NF	A
Salvator	S	D	NF	A
Helles	N	L	NF	U
Dunkles	N	D	NF	U
Weisses	N	L	F	U
Russ	W	L	F	U
Radlermass	W	D	F	U
Nährbier	O	D	NF	U

"Kenner" terms. Table 14:1 can be expanded by distinguishing subtypes and by the addition of other types: *Vol-Helles:* 'Full light beer'; *Export-Helles:* 'Export light beer'; *Voll-Dunkles:* 'Full dark beer'; *Export-Dunkles:* 'Export dark beer'; *Champagner-Weisses:* 'Champagne white beer'; *Normal-Weisses:* 'Normal white beer'; *Export-Weisses:* 'Export white beer'; *Aventinus* or *Weisser Bock:* 'White bock'; *Lunchbier:* 'Lunch beer'; and *Nährweizenbier:* 'Nourishing wheat beer.'

The distinction between what may be conveniently labeled *Kenner* ('connoisseur') and core terms has both a cognitive and a behavioral basis. On the behavioral side, the distinctions between *Export* and *Voll-Helles* and *-Dunkles*, and *Normal-* and *Champagner-Weisses*, are common knowledge, but most informants consider them irrelevant with respect to choosing a beer. Which of these subtypes one gets is a matter of where one drinks or buys beer. The distinctions are also not very salient, in that they are often omitted from a list or else are given near the end of it. Of the remaining types, on the other hand, some are not well known. In the case of

TABLE 14:2. *The Componential Definition of Munich Beers Including Kenner Categories*

Type of Beer	Strength	Color	Fizziness	Ageing	Clear/Cloudy
Weisnbier	S	B	NF	A	
Märzenbier	S	B	NF	U	
Heller Bock	S	L	NF	A	
Salvator	S	D	NF	A	
Aventinus	N+	L	F	U	
Export-Helles	N+	L	NF	U	
Voll-Helles	N	L	NF	U	
Export-Dunkles	N+	D	NF	U	
Voll-Dunkles	N	D	NF	U	
Export-Weisses	N+	L	F	U	C
Champagner-Weisses	N	L	F	U	K
Normal-Weisses	N	L	F	U	C
Russ	W	L	F	U	
Radlermass	W	D	F–	U	
Lunchbier	W	L	NF	U	
Nährbier	O	D	NF	U	
Nährweizenbier	O	L	F	U	

KEY:

S: strong
N: normal
N+: stronger than normal
W: weak
O: alcohol-free

L: light
B: brownish
D: dark
F: fizzy
F–: less fizzy
NF: nonfizzy

A: aged
U: unaged
C: clear
K: cloudy

Lunchbier, a weak, light beer designed especially for motorists, this is because it is a recent invention.[2]

The taxonomy including Kenner terms is:

(MÜNCHNER) BIER
- MÄRZENBIER
- WIESENBIER
- HELLER BOCK
- SALVATOR
- AVENTINUS
- HELLES
  - *Export-Helles*
  - *Voll-Helles*
- DUNKLES
  - *Export-Dunkles*
  - *Voll-Dunkles*

WEISSES
Export-Weisses
Champagner-Weisses
Normal-Weisses
LUNCHBIER
RUSS
RADLERMASS
NÄHRBIER
NÄHRWEIZENBIER

When *Kenner* categories are included, the componential definition of Munich beers requires a few modifications: the addition of one dimension, *blank/trüb* ('clear/cloudy'), and the addition of another value to the dimensions of both 'strength and 'fizziness,' as in Table 14:2.

Finally, a complete taxonomy specifies the products of individual breweries:[3]

(MÜNCHNER) BIER
MÄRZENBIER
Hackerbräu Märzenbier
Augustinerbräu Märzenbier
Hofbräu Märzenbier
Paulaner-Thomasbräu Märzenbier
Pschorrbräu Märzenbier
Spatenbräu Märzenbier
Löwenbräu Märzenbier
WIESNBIER
Hackerbräu Wiesnbier
Augustinerbräu Wiesnbier
Hofbräu Wiesnbier
Paulaner-Thomasbräu Wiesnbier
Pschorrbräu Wiesnbier
Spatenbräu Wiesnbier
Löwenbräu Wiesnbier
HELLER BOCK
Hackerbräu Heller Bock
Augustinerbräu Heller Bock
Hofbräu Heller Bock
Paulaner-Thomasbräu Heller Bock
Pschorrbräu Heller Bock
Spatenbräu Heller Bock
Löwenbräu Heller Bock
SALVATOR
Patronator
Maximator
Delikator
Salvator
Animator
Optimator
Triumphator

AVENTINUS
HELLES
Export-Helles
Hackerbräu Export-Helles
Augustinerbräu Export-Helles
Hofbräu Export-Helles
Paulaner-Thomasbräu Export-Helles
Pschorrbräu Export-Helles
Spatenbräu Export-Helles
Löwenbräu Export-Helles
Vol-Helles
Hackerbräu Voll-Helles
Augustinerbräu Voll-Helles
Hofbräu Voll-Helles
Paulaner-Thomasbräu Voll-Helles
Pschorrbräu Voll-Helles
Spatenbräu Voll-Helles
Löwenbräu Voll-Helles
DUNKLES
Export-Dunkles
Hackerbräu Export-Dunkles
Augustinerbräu Export-Dunkles
Hofbräu Export-Dunkles
Paulaner-Thomasbräu Export-Dunkles
Pschorrbräu Export-Dunkles
Spatenbräu Export-Dunkles
Löwenbräu Export-Dunkles
Voll-Dunkles
Augustinerbräu Voll-Dunkles
Hofbräu Voll-Dunkles
Paulaner-Thomasbräu Voll-Dunkles
Pschorrbräu Voll-Dunkles
WEISSES
Export-Weisses (Löwenbräu)
Normal Weisses
Hackerbräu Weisses
Hofbräu Weisses
Paulaner-Thomasbräu Weisses
Pschorrbräu Weisses
G. Schneider & Sohn Weisses
Champagner-Weisses
Spatenbräu Champagner-Weisses
Löwenbräu Champagner-Weisses
RUSS
RADLERMASS
LUNCHBIER (*Hackerbräu*)
NÄHRBIER
Löwenbräu Malzbier
Hackerbräu Nährbier
Hofbräu Malzbier

Paulaner-Thomasbräu Malzbier
Pschorrbräu Malzbier
Spatenbräu Malzbier
NAHRWEIZENBIER (*Löwenbräu*)

At this level individual knowledge is fragmented, and discrimination breaks down. Few, if any, individuals have the entire taxonomy in their heads. Attempts to elicit it revealed not only gaps but also some error and guesswork. At most, everyone knows only that each of the seven major breweries produces *Wiesnbier, Märzenbier,* and *Salvator* and some form of *Helles* and *Dunkles*. Beyond this, knowledge is limited to a few specific products of some of the breweries. The cognitive map of the beer world therefore varies somewhat from individual to individual. As for discrimination, most informants stated that it was not possible at this level. Those who maintained that it was, were often unable to verbalize the differences, or, if they could, were able to do so for only a few of the products of a few of the breweries. There is much dispute about such ability.

III. Behavioral and cognitive implications of the dimensions of discrimination.

An analysis of the culturally defined, nonlinguistic contexts in which beer is consumed, of informants' responses to questions about why and when they drink one type rather than another, and of various unsolicited statements about Munich beer and beer drinking, reveals that four of the dimensions above have important implications for the culturally defined contrastive set of motives for the consumption of beer and for such cognitive items as the Münchner concepts of space, time, and identity. The relationships between these variables can be shown by using the kind of model developed by Romney and Epling (1958) for the analysis of Kariera kinship, as in Table 14:3.

Motivation

As can be seen from the model, each of the dimensions of discrimination breaks down the set of beers into subsets which, while not uniquely, are ideally suited for certain purposes. For example, if the aim is refreshment, the fizzy beers are an especially apt choice. If the aim is refreshment and avoidance of intoxication, the weak, fizzy beers are ideal.

The facilitation of social interaction and integration. Beer drinking in Munich is preeminently a social activity. The expectation is that it will facilitate social interaction by producing an atmosphere of *Gemütlichkeit*

TABLE 14:3. *The Behavioral and Cognitive Implications of the Dimensions of Discrimination*

		BEHAVIORAL AND COGNITIVE IMPLICATIONS		
Dimensions of Discrimination	*Semantic Implications*	*The culturally defined set of motives*	*Spatio-temporal*	*Status*
1. The domain *beer*	beer *vs* other beverage domains	facilitation of social interaction, integration and:	defining value for Munich and Bavaria	
2. Strength	subset of strong beers	strong beers for (rapid) intoxication, for meals	strong beers constitute the Munich *Bier Kalender* historical origin as a food substitute	for normal adults
	subset of normal beers	normal beers for meals, for intoxication		for normal adults
	subset of weak beers	weak beers to avoid intoxication or keep it minimal		
	subset of nonalcoholic beers	nonalcoholic beers for the avoidance of intoxication		for children, the aged, ill, pregnant
3. Color	light *vs* dark subsets of beer	dark beers stimulate growth and health	Münchner see displacement of dark by light beers as index of culture change	
4. Fizziness	fizzy *vs* nonfizzy	fizzy beers for refreshment		
5. Aging	aged *vs* unaged subsets of beer		aged beers have festive significance	for normal adults

and that it has the power to unite people of different status and origin. Consider, for example, a description of life at the *Hofbräuhaus*, the largest and most famous beer hall in Munich and in some respects the very incarnation of the good life:

> . . . no one can forget the atmosphere which pervades the taproom of this brewery. The thick air consists of spilled hops and malt, of pork sausage, radish juice, roast sauce and tobacco smoke. No science is able to analyze the chemistry of this mixture, nor can the hodgepodge of the guests be reduced to a common denominator. The local inhabitant sits next to the foreigner, the master locksmith from a side street opposite the Privy Counsellor from Tokyo, the vendor from the public market next to the film star from Florida. A Babylonian confusion of tongues enlivens the talk for the reason that one person doesn't understand the other. A circuit of feeling is closed and former enemies become friends. Fraternization increases with each beer until an entire table drinks from the same mug and eats white sausage with their fingers. Even Kaiser Wilhelm II participated in this ritual when he visited the Hofbräuhaus in full-dress uniform (Hoferichter and Moll 1964).[4]

This is hyperbole, to be sure, but it is not far from the Münchner ideal. In addition to expectations concerning the style and effects of beer drinking, its communal and integrative character is expressed: *spatially* in the vastness of the beer halls, tents, and gardens and in the large tables in such places which make it difficult to drink alone or remain aloof from one's fellows; *linguistically* in the morphology of some of the terms for various types of beer drinkers—*Bierbruder, Saufbruder,* and *Stammtischbruder; literarily*, for example, in Ludwig Thoma's famous short story, *Ein Münchner im Himmel (A Münchner in Heaven)* in which the archetypal Münchner longs not only for his *Mass* of beer instead of the tasteless manna but also for the companionship of his *Stammitsch* (a table always reserved for the same group of beer drinkers); *in the beer festivals*, where, as the travel literature puts it, der *Durst völkervereiningend gelöscht ist*, ('thirst is quenched in a people-uniting way'); and *ritually* in the drinking of brotherhood ('*Bruderschaft trinken*') in which two or more persons in the course of drinking together agree to change their status from the formal term of address, *Sie*, to the intimate *Du*, the change symbolized by drinking beer together with arms intertwined.

Intoxication. In addition to this rather general ethnosociological motive, which is present in many beer drinking situations, there are a number of more specific motives. For intoxication, any of the strong or normal beers is especially appropriate. Münchner terminologically distinguish three stages of intoxication and a number of different kinds of intoxication, which contrast in terms of emotional disposition, amount consumed, and the degree of self-control the drinker shows:

TABLE 14:4. *Categories of Intoxication*

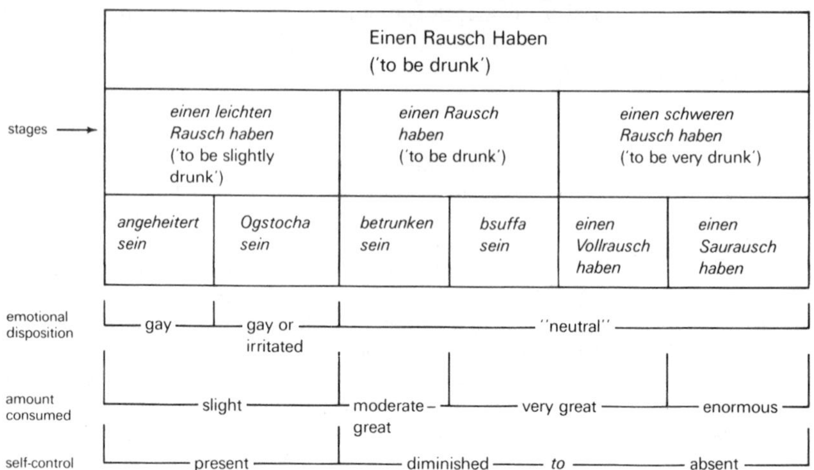

	Einen Rausch Haben ('to be drunk')					
stages →	*einen leichten Rausch haben* ('to be slightly drunk')		*einen Rausch haben* ('to be drunk')		*einen schweren Rausch haben* ('to be very drunk')	
	angeheitert sein	*Ogstocha sein*	*betrunken sein*	*bsuffa sein*	*einen Vollrausch haben*	*einen Saurausch haben*
emotional disposition	gay	gay or irritated	"neutral"			
amount consumed	slight		moderate–great	very great		enormous
self-control	present		diminished *to* absent			

NOTE: The dimensions of contrast for categories of intoxication (and categories of drinkers, below) were inferred from informants descriptive statements about them. The formulations presented here were checked by using them to formulate definitions of the various categories and asking informants whether they were correct, and by inventing hypothetical situations concerning intoxication and drinking style and asking informants to label them.

A few of the terms require explanation: *Angeheitert*, which comes from *heiter* ('cheerful,' 'gay'), means to be gaily drunk. *Ogstocha* is Münchner dialect for High German *angestochen* ('stung'). *Bsuffa* is Münchner dialect for *besoffen*, from *saufen*, the verb applied to the drinking activity of animals, as opposed to people (compare *essen/fressen*, 'to eat'). It suggests intoxication as a result of uninhibited and uncontrolled drinking. A more extreme form is referred to as *einen Saurausch haben*, *Sau* meaning female pig. Social disapproval attaches to these categories under the following circumstances: (1) in many situations if the drinker is female and intoxication has progressed beyond the first stage; (2) if an individual is regularly in any of these categories; and (3) if intoxication occurs in an inappropriate context.

There are, of course, other reasons for getting high besides the promotion of *Gemütlichkeit* and solidarity. An individual can get drunk not only to relieve tension, expressed in such phrases as *sich aus Ärger vollaufen lassen* ('to get drunk out of anger') but out of happiness as well, for example, *sich aus Freude an saubern Rausch zulegen* ('to get drunk out of happiness'). From a Münchner point of view, beer can intoxicate, but whether it does, how quickly, and to what extent depend on a number of factors—the context, the type of beer, the amount consumed, and the type of drinker. A feeling of euphoria depends largely on context. It is absent or minimal in such scenes as meals or work breaks. For example, an engineer, construction worker, or secretary does not, after a glass or liter of beer with lunch, return to work drunk. On the other hand, the same size glass may make him very high, and often almost immediately, at such socially effervescent events as the *Oktoberfest*. Strong beers are thought to lead to more rapid intoxication and thus may be avoided when slight, moderate, or gradual intoxication is sought.

The extent and nature of intoxication also depends on the drinker. Most physically and socially normal Münchner drink beer. It is an essential component of their identity. In addition to the general category *beer drinker*, there are terminologically distinguished subtypes, which contrast in terms of the usual extent of intoxication, drinking style, the presence or absence of addiction, and social approval or disapproval, as indicated in Table 14:5.

TABLE 14:5. *Categories of Munich Beer Drinkers*

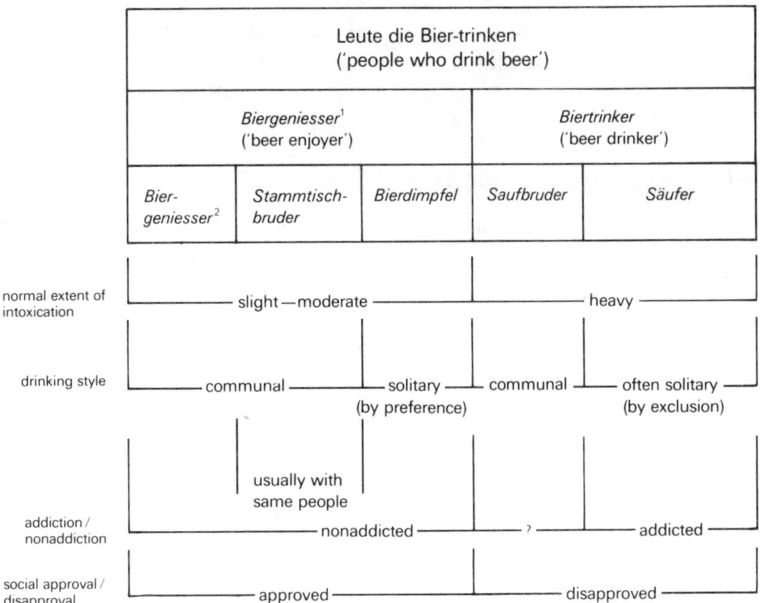

Here again the contrast between the animalistic, or uncontrolled, and the social, or controlled, aspect of drinking emerges. The *Säufer* (from *saufen*, see above) in his lack of restraint and complete loss of self-control behaves like an animal and is thus not fit to drink with other people.

Accompaniment for meals. The normal beers are especially suitable for ordinary meals.

Avoidance of intoxication. Since beer is consumed in such a wide variety of contexts, since it can intoxicate, and since there are individual differences with respect to tolerance, an individual may, in situations such as while driving and in very hot weather, wish to avoid intoxication or keep it minimal. For this purpose the weak or alcohol-free beers are ideal, with the qualification that *Nährbier* is usually reserved for the young, the aged, the ill, and the pregnant.

Stimulation of growth and health. The dark beers stimulate growth and health. This value is especially apparent for *Nährbier*, which may be given to one before and several years after leaving the womb and later as an adult during times of illness and convalescence. Its beneficial effects are common knowledge and have the official blessing of doctors. *Nährbier* also has the explicit function of enabling children to feel a part of the group in many beer-drinking situations. While originally only dark beers were brewed, their popularity is said to be declining. For some Münchner, their fattening effects contradict a change in emphasis on body-image from a robust to a more streamlined shape. The motive is hygienic and/or aesthetic.

Spatio-temporal implications.

Germans sometimes identify regions of their country by their most popular alcoholic beverages—Prussia is the land of *Schnaps*, the Rhineland, that of wine, and Bavaria (of which Munich is the capital), that of beer. Collectively and spatially a Münchner is therefore a member of a beer-drinking group. Individually he is a particular kind of beer drinker.

Beer also has spatial significance at a level other than that of the domain as a whole: the exact center of the old city is marked by the *Höfbrauhaus* (the most salient point of the city). The highest natural point, the *Nockerberg* (the site of a minor beer festival) is associated with *Salvator*. The southwestern boundary connects with the site of the October Festival, where *Wiesnbier* is dispensed.

With respect to time, the decline of the dark beers is regarded as an important index of the gradual disappearance of the old Münchner way of life. The traditional[5] seasonal appearance of the strong beers constitutes a *Bier Kalender—Wiesnbier* in September and October, *Märzenbier* and *Salvator* in March, and *Heller Bock* in May. From a Münchner point of view, the most important of these is *Wiesnbier*, the occasion for and focus of the *Oktoberfest*. Any account of the meaning of beer would have to include a description of this celebration. This can be most easily and naturally done by contrasting it to *Fasching*, or Carnival. These two events are the high points of the Munich social year. Together they bisect it into Maussian halves of greater and lesser social effervescence:

The Oktoberfest	Fasching
Bavarian national festival	pan(Catholic)-German festival
fall	winter
national costume	masquerade
familial	adults[6]
localized	dispersed
entire population	specific social groups
drinking, eating	drinking, dancing, erotic encounters
beer (*Wiesnbier*)	wine, champagne[7]

The *Oktoberfest* originated in 1810 with the celebration of the marriage of the Crown Price of Bavaria to the Archduchess Therese—thus, the *Theresienwiese*, the meadow where it is held. To put it in Durkheimian terms, it is the annual occasion for the collective reaffirmation of the sentiments of being Münchner and Bavarians. The collective symbol is beer (thus, the totem is drunk rather than eaten), and the image that is reaffirmed is that of a highly sociable and accessible beer drinker. The *Oktoberfest* begins on the penultimate Saturday in September and ends on the second Sunday in October. The national costume (which includes knee stockings, *Lederhosen*, and Tyrolian hat for men, and *Dirndl* dress or Bavarian suit for women—the Bavarians of the travel posters) is optional, although most *echte Münchner* wear it. It is an event for the entire family and population, and the principal activities are orgiastic eating, drinking, and singing. Given the fundamental importance of beer in *das Münchner Leben*, the *Oktoberfest* is significantly a mere intensification of everyday life.

IV. Discussion

The primary aim of this chapter has been to articulate some features of semantic structure with certain behavioral and cognitive correlates. It may be worth remarking on some respects in which the Munich beer categories may be typical of folk taxonomies in general. Taxonomically, the structure is not particularly deep, and the levels are irregular. Semantically, if the terms are mapped on a class-product space, its structure is non-orthogonal, a property which one author has postulated is generally true of folk domains.[8] There are also some matters pertaining to sampling which are of a kind that may frequently be found in ethnosemantic studies.

First, as mentioned above, few individuals know the entire taxonomy, nor beyond the level of "core" terms do they all share the same portion of it. Second, some lower-level discriminations, although known, have no behavioral significance for some individuals. Third, at the lowest taxonomic level categories are named but not discriminated to any extent. Fourth, although the categories above the lowest level are highly terminologized—that is, there is high consensus on defining attributes—the consensus is *not* complete. Disagreement is particularly apparent for two dimensions which were not analytically necessary but which are sometimes used—sweet/bitter (*suss/bitter*) and thick/thin (*dick/dünn*). Finally, a fair amount of variability is produced by synonymy for some of the beer categories and particularly for some states of intoxication. All of these are problems which deserve to be studied in a systematic way, particularly those concerning sampling.

Another problem worthy of investigation has to do with the evolution of lexical domains. In his paper on Trukese kin terms Goodenough states:

> A theoretically possible combination such as $AB_1E_2H_1$ is not an active part of the Trukese conceptual repertoire. But such combinations are latent in Trukese culture, because the necessary components are represented in other combinations forming native concepts. Should $AB_1E_2H_1$ ever be activated as a category of Trukese thought, it will represent a change in culture less basic than the development of an entirely new conceptual component (Goodenough 1956:211).

There are some good examples of such activation in the Münchner beer domain. For example:

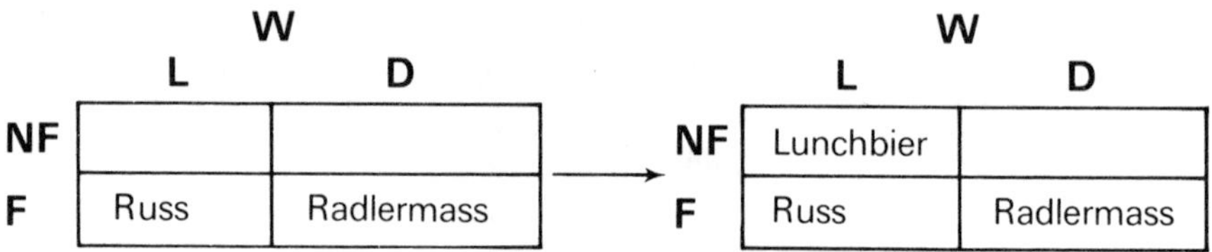

Figure 14:1.

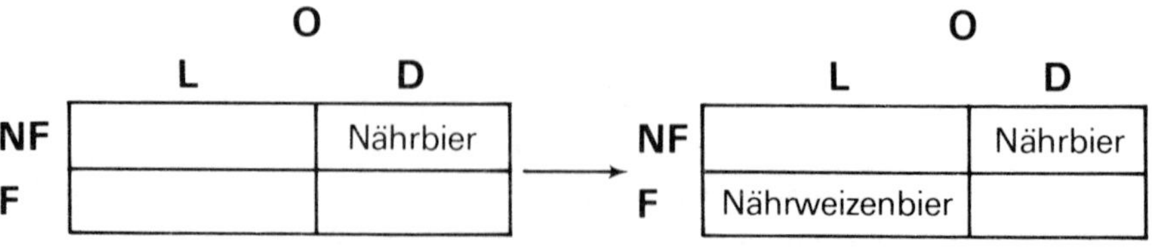

Figure 14:2.

In contrast to these innovations, which meant nothing more than the realization of concepts that were implicitly present, there were others of a more radical nature, such as the introduction of the first fizzy beer. In a culture like that of München having abundant historical records, it should be relatively easy to document these processes and trace the evolution of the entire domain over a period of several centuries.

Notes

1. The *Münchner* are a Germanic, Catholic people inhabiting the city of Munich in the Free State of Bavaria. They distinguish three categories of inhabitants: *echte Münchner* ('real Münchner'), those born in the city; *WahlMünchner* ('Münchner by choice'); and *Zuag'raste* (=High German *Zugereiste*, meaning simply those who have come to live in the city). The third term, in contrast to the second, is used contemptuously, connoting a lack of familiarity with and appreciation of the *Münchner* way of life. The description of beer drinking in this paper applies primarily to the first category. Fieldwork was done in 1963/1964. This paper was written with the support of Public Health Service Research Grant # 5 RO1 MH11245-03 from the National Institute of Mental Health, administered by Lewis Langness and Robert Rhodes. I wish to thank Josef Stadler of Munich for his hospitality and his efforts on my behalf, Kristen Hawkes for comments on an earlier draft of this paper, and John Atkins for some conceptual suggestions.

2. I understand that *Lunchbier* is no longer brewed. Non-Münchner beers such as *Pils* have been excluded here. *Diätbier* ('diet beer'), a beer brewed especially for diabetics, has also been omitted because of the lack of diabetic informants from whom to elicit its properties.

3. NOTE: The breweries themselves may use somewhat different names for their products. For example, only Hackerbräu can use the name *Nährbier* for this type of beer, while the others use *Malzbier; Löwenbräu* calls its *Voll-Helles "Hell-Quell"* and its *Champagner-Weisses "Champagner-Weizenbier,"* etc. I have ignored such differences because the natives usually do so.

4. The fact that Wilhelm II, the arch-Prussian and antithesis of the Münchner and Bavarian (arrogant, stiff, and ambitious *vs* modest, relaxed, and easy-going) accommodated himself to the atmosphere of the *Hofbräuhaus*, attests to the integrative power of beer.

5. The strong beers have now become available throughout the year.

6. This is not to say that children play no role in *Fasching* but rather that the most intensively celebrated events—the costumed balls—are for adults or the sexually mature.

7. Beer may be drunk at *Fashing*, but the ideal drink is wine or champagne.

8. See Wallace (1962).

References Cited

GOODENOUGH, W. H.
1956 "Componential Analysis and the Study of Meaning." *Language* 32: 195–216.

HOFERICHTER, E. AND P. MOLL
1964 *München, Bilder einer Fröhlichen Stadt.* Munich: F. A. Ackermann Kunstverlag.

MANDELBAUM, D. G.
1958 "Alcohol and Culture." *Current Anthropology* 7:281–293.

ROMNEY, A. K. AND J. P. EPLING
1958 "A Simplified Model of Kariera Kinship." *American Anthropologist* 60:59–74.
WALLACE, A. F. C.
1962 Culture and Cognition." *Science* 135:351–357.

15 STRUCK BY SPEECH

Charles O. Frake

It is possible to study non-Western legal systems using the concepts of Western law. When such data have been encapsulated into our concepts, one could then contrast the result with our own system of law. The distortion which would occur could be obscured by focusing attention on the content of the legal systems under consideration. Ethnographic studies often fall into this trap, but Charles O. Frake has avoided this by allowing informants to define those activities which appeared to be "law." What something is always depends upon what it contrasts with in its own culture. Before making any comparison with other cultures, the author carefully contrasts those interactions which informants have labeled as litigation with other kinds of talk. Just as physical objects have attributes which are used for classifying them into sets, so speech behavior also has attributes which are used to distinguish one kind of talk from another. After a careful analysis of Yakan concepts of legal matters, the author makes a brief comparison with another Philippine society.—EDITOR'S NOTE

> *tiyaq ku tawwaq bissah*
> Here I am struck by speech
> (Remark of an accused in a trial)

The Yakan legal system is manifest almost exclusively through one kind of behavior: talk. Consequently the ethnographer's record of observations of litigation is largely a linguistic record, and the legal system is a code for talking, a linguistic code. In this paper we focus initially on a small part of this talk, that representing the concept of litigation. We subsequently attempt to illustrate how a definition of this concept guides a description of the legal system and, finally, points the way toward meaningful comparisons with legal systems of other cultures.

The Yakan are Philippine Moslems inhabiting the island of Basilan located off the southern tip of Zamboanga Peninsula, a western extension

Reprinted from Laura Nader, editor, *Law in Culture and Society* (Chicago: Aldine Publishing Company, 1969):

of the island of Mindanao.[1] Southwest of Basilan stretches the Sulu archipelago, a chain of small islands extending some 200 miles to within a few miles of the northeast coast of Borneo. Some 60,000 Yakan share Basilan's 1,282 square kilometers with Christian Filipinos concentrated along the north coast and with Taw Sug and Samal Moslems living mostly in coastal villages all around the island.[2] The Yakan are close linguistic kin of the sea-faring Samal but, unlike them, practice an exclusively land-oriented economy: diversified grain, root, and tree-crop agriculture on plowed fields and swiddens, commercial copra production, and cattle raising. Supplementary economic activities include plantation labor, distribution of cigarettes smuggled from Borneo by their Moslem brothers, and banditry. These economic activities bring the Yakan into close contact with the Philippine economy, political system, and army. Having been given this much information, the anthropological reader has probably already classed the Yakan as "peasants," which is appropriate as long as the concept does not bring to mind a downtrodden, economically exploited, culturally deprived people submerged by the weight of some "great tradition."

Houses, mosques, and graveyards dot the Yakan countryside, rarely revealing any obvious patterns of spatial clustering. Each, however, represents the focus of a pattern of social alignment. Houses are occupied by nuclear families, independent units of production and consumption. The family is the unit of membership in a parish, a religious and political unit under the titular leadership of a mosque priest (*qimam*). Parishes are alliances of independent families; affiliation is by choice, not by residence or kinship ties. Parishes comprise only several dozen families, and any family has a network of social relations with kin and neighbors extending beyond the parish. Ancestors, buried in conspicuously decorated graves, define networks of cognatic kinship ties among the living. Although these networks are unsegmented by discrete, corporate groups of any kind, the Yakan talk about groupings of kin in ways that would do credit to a social anthropologist. Note, for example, the contrast between *paŋkat baqirah*, "the unrestricted, nonunilineal descent group defined by an ancestor (female) named Baira," and *qusba baqirah*, "the kindred centered around an ego named Baira." Like the legal expressions we are about to discuss, this talk about social groups must be understood to be a part of social behavior as well as a description of it.

Defining Litigation

A description of a culture derives from an ethnographer's observations of the stream of activities performed by the people he is studying. As a first step toward producing an ethnographic statement, the investigator must segment and classify the events of this behavior stream so that he can say, for example, of two successive events that one is "different" from the other, and of two nonsuccessive events that they are repetitions of the "same" activity. If the ethnographer claims his people do X three times a week, verification of his statement requires not simply counting occurrences of X, but also assessing the criteria for distinguishing X from all the other things people do during the week and for deciding that all the different events construed as instances of X in fact represent the "same" activity. Information about what is the "same" and what is "different" can only come from the interpretations of events made by the people being studied.

Within the stream of behavior observable in Yakan society, there are some events that are difficult to characterize initially except as "a group of people talking together." There seems to be no focus of activity other than talk—no distinctive settings, apparel, or paraphernalia. We might postulate that all such events are manifestations of the same category of cultural activities, that all are repetitions of the same scene. At a very general level we could justify this decision. All these activities can be labeled *magbissāh*, 'talking to each other' in response to a query such as *magqine siyeh*, 'what are they doing?'[3] But, as the English glosses indicate, this categorization is not particularly informative, especially to an observer of the scene. To discover a more refined categorization we must attend to the way the Yakan talk about talking.

Yakan, like English, provides a large number of linguistic expressions for talking about a great variety of aspects of speech behavior. Of these, we sort out for consideration the following set of semantically related expressions, all possible responses to the query "What are they doing?" (Only the variable portion of the response is shown.[4] Some of these forms, especially *hukum*, have different, but related meanings in different contexts. Etymological information is given for later discussion):

1. *mitiŋ* (from English), 'discussion';
2. *qisun*, 'conference';
3. *mawpakkat* (from Arabic), 'negotiation';
4. *hukum* (from Arabic), 'litigation.'

The structure of inclusion and contrast relations manifest in the use of these terms to denote events is shown in Figure 15:1. Let A, B, C, D represent situations that can be labeled as *mitiŋ*, *qisun*, *mawpakkat*, and *hukum*, respectively. Then it is the case that *mitiŋ* can label the set of situations {ABCD}, *qisun* the set of situations {BCD}, *mawpakkat* the set {CD}, [whereas] *hukum* can label only {D}. Thus these expressions form an ordered series, the situations labelable by a given term including all those labelable by each succeeding term. However, it is also the case

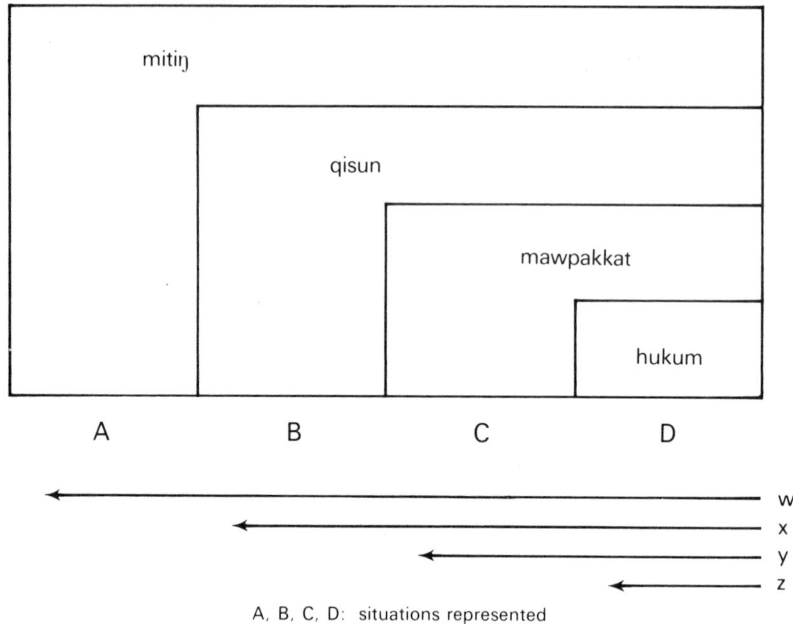

Figure 15:1. Semantic structure.

that *mitiŋ* can be used to contrast situation A with each of the other situations (A not B, C, or D) as in the exchange: *magqisuŋ qenteq siyeh*, 'They seem to be conferring.' *Dumaqin, magmitiŋ hadja qiyan*, 'No, they're just discussing.' The form *hadja*, 'just, merely,' specifies that *mitiŋ* is to be construed in its minimal sense, but its use is not obligatory to convey this sense. Similarly, *qisun, mawpakkat*, and *hukum* can be used to contrast B, C, D respectively with each of the other situations. We have, then, a case of the use of the same form at different levels of contrast, a situation common in semantic representation (Frake 1961), and one that has caused some controversy over interpretation (Bright and Bright 1965:258).

In the use of the same expression at different levels of contrast, there is in Yakan a distinction between those cases, such as the present example, in which use at the less inclusive level is specifiable by a de-emphatic particle (for example, *hadja*, 'just, merely') and those in which it is specifiable by an emphatic particle (such as *teqed*, 'very, true, real').

Contrast *magmitiŋ hadja qiyan*, 'They're just discussing' (and not 'conferring,' 'negotiating,' and the like), with *magpoŋtinaqi teqed qiyan*, 'They're real siblings' (and not 'half-siblings,' 'cousins,' and so on). The use of the same term at different levels of contrast results, in the former case, from a *specification* of the basic general sense of an expression. In the latter case it results from an *extension* of the basic specific sense of an expression. Cases of specification, such as the present example, can be interpreted as manifestations of "marking," a phenomenon widespread in linguistic representation in phonology and morphology as well as in semantics (Jakobson 1957, Greenberg 1966).

Semantic marking means that given two expressions, A and B sharing some feature of meaning x but differeing with respect to some feature y and in that sense contrasting, the difference is not

term A represents the meaning: $x\ y$
term B represents the meaning: $x\ \bar{y}$

but rather

term A represents the meaning: x
term B represents the meaning: $x\ y$.

The use of term B necessarily implies feature y, but the use of term A does not necessarily say anything about the presence or absence of y. Term B is marked for y. In our series each term is marked for a feature (or features) not necessarily implied by its predecessor:

mitiŋ, 'discussion': w
qisun, 'conference': $w\ x$
mawpakkat, 'negotiation': $w\ x\ y$
hukum, 'litigation': $w\ x\ y\ z$

The next task is to characterize the features of meaning represented above as w, x, y, z; w being what the set has in common and x, y, z being successive increments to this common meaning.

At the outset we should be clear about just what linguistic and cognitive operations of our informants we are trying to account for. It is not simply a case of determining the perceptual cues for distinguishing one object from another. If a Yakan sees some people engaged in mutual speech behavior (that categorization he can make perceptually) and wants to know what they are doing, he will in all probability ask them. In this case the object of categorization, a group of people engaged in some activity, is aware of what it is doing. This awareness is, in itself, an attribute—a necessary one—of the category. Just as in classifying a plant one might apply a test of taste or smell to determine a criterial property, in classifying these speech events one applies a test of eliciting a linguistic response from the performers of the activity. It is impossible for people engaged in 'litigation' or in 'conference' not to be aware of what they are doing and not to be able to communicate their awareness. For people engaged, say, in 'litigation' to be able to state that they are 'litigating' is a necessary condition for the activity to be 'litigation,' but it is not a sufficient condition. They might be lying or, more probably in Yakan life, they might be joking. Being funny is a prominent goal of Yakan speech behavior, and semantic incongruity is a standard way of adding humor to speech—but the effect is dependent on the hearer's ability to recognize the incongruity. What we are trying to formulate, then, are the conditions under which it is congruous, neither humorous nor deceitful, to state that one is engaged in 'litigation.' These conditions are the semantic features of the concepts in question. Our evidence for semantic features does not come from informants' statements about the linguistic representations of these concepts (though such explicit definitions of terms are often useful guides for preliminary formulations), but from informants' interpretations of the situations that the concepts represent. Our aim is not to give an elegant formulation of minimal contrastive features, but a statement that reflects the various dimensions of speech behavior revealed in the use and interpretation of these expressions.

Let us consider first the features common to the whole set, those that distinguish all events construable as *mitiŋ*, 'discussion,' from other things Yakan do. This set of events includes the events labeled by the other expressions. Then we will consider what each successive term adds to these common features. Four dimensions of speech behavior appear to be involved in contrasting 'discussion' with other activities.

1. Focus. The focus of 'discussion' is on the topic of messages. There is a subject of discussion. Excluded are speech events in which the focus is on message form: storytelling, riddling, exchanging verses, joking, prayer (which, being in Arabic, has no semantic content for the Yakan).

2. Purpose. The purpose of the gathering is to talk. Excluded are activities in which the intent to accomplish something other than talking is responsible for the gathering of participants.

3. Roles. Speaking time is distributed among the participants. Each role in the scene, whatever its other characteristics, is both a speaking and a listening role. Excluded are monologues, in which speaking time is monopolized by one person.[5]

4. Integrity. Integrity refers to the extent to which the activity is construed as an integral unit as opposed to being a part of some other activity. A 'discussion' must have sufficient integrity not to be construable as incident to or accompanying some other activity. A 'discussion' can occur within the context of another kind of event, but only as a recognizably bounded interruption, as when participants disengage from some other activity to talk something over. (This dimension will sound less fuzzy when we consider its relevance to the contrast between 'litigation' and other kinds of 'discussion.')

The expression *mitiŋ*, 'discussion,' necessarily implies only these features. Each of the succeeding expressions in the series adds some necessary implications along one or more of these dimensions (Table 15:1):

TABLE 15:1. *Semantic Features*

	Topic	*Purpose*	*Role Structure*	*Integrity*
'discussion'	subject	talk	undifferentiated	minimal
'conference'	issue	decision	undifferentiated	minimal
'negotiation'	disagreement	settlement	opposing sides	moderate
'litigation'	dispute	ruling	court	maximal

Qisun, 'Conference'

1. Focus. The subject of discussion is an *issue* , some topic that presents a problem to be decided: when to plant rice, when to go on a trip, what price to pay in a transaction.

2. Purpose. A 'conference' has an expected outcome, a *decision* about the issue. Participants meet in order to reach a decision, and, if a decision is made, the conference is concluded.

3. Roles. No added implications.

4. Integrity. No added implications.

Mawpakkat 'Negotiation'

1. Focus. The issue in 'negotiation' is a disagreement, a topic over which participants have conflicting interests.

2. Purpose. The decision is a *settlement*, a legally binding resolution of the disagreement.

3. Roles. Participants are divided into two protagonistic sides. Witnesses may be present.

4. Integrity. No clear added implications. Although *mawpakkat* is more likely to refer to an integral event than *qisun*, and *qisun* than *mitiŋ*, these are not necessary implications.

Hukum, 'Litigation'

1. Focus. The disagreement is a *dispute*, a disagreement that arises from a charge that an *offense* has been committed. A dispute can also be handled by negotiation, but the topic of litigation is necessarily a dispute. A dispute handled by litigation is a *case*.

2. Purpose. The settlement takes the form of a legal *ruling* based on precedent and having special sanctions.

3. Roles. In addition to protagonists and optional witnesses, 'litigation' requires a *court*, a set of neutral judges who control the proceedings and attempt to effect a ruling.

4. Integrity. 'Litigation' is always an integral activity. If it is interrupted by a different kind of activity—eating, for example—there is a new instance of litigation, a different court session. "Discussion," "conference," and "negotiation," in their minimal senses, can occur as parts of "litigation," but "litigation" cannot occur as a part of these other activities.

Each expression in our series except the terminal one has a maximal and minimal sense, depending on whether the speaker intends to include or exclude the meanings marked by succeeding expressions. 'Mere discussion' (*mitiŋ hadja*), the minimal sense of *mitiŋ*, implies the features listed as common to the whole set, but the topic is simply a subject to discuss, not an issue to be decided, a disagreement to be settled, or a case to be ruled on. The purpose is to talk, but there is no expected outcome that terminates the event, no decision to be reached, no settlement to be negotiated, no ruling to be handed down. Role structure is undifferentiated and integrity minimal, although it is still greater than that implied by *magbissāh*, 'talking to each other.' A *mitiŋ* in its minimal sense more closely resembles an American "bull session" than what we would call a "meeting."

"Mere conference" applies to situations in which the issue is not a dispute, the decision not a settlement, and role structure remains undifferentiated. 'Mere negotiation' applies to situations in which, though the disagreement may be a dispute, the intended outcome is a settlement that is not a legal ruling and that is reached without the aid of judges.

The flexibility of reference afforded by this semantic structure, the ability to be ambiguous about whether a general or specific sense is intended, reflects the fact that not only are these expressions used to talk about speech behavior, but their use is also a part of the behavior they describe. A Yakan uses terms like *mawpakkat* and *hukum* not simply to give serious answers to probes for information, but also to further his own objectives in speech situations by advancing a particular—perhaps ostensibly incongruous—interpretation of an event and by representing this conceptualization linguistically in an effective way. He can, for example, call for a 'conference' without immediately committing himself to an interpretation of the divisiveness of the issue; he can call for a 'discussion' without implying that there is an issue at stake.

For these reasons, stylistic features of expression—selections among alternative linguistic representations of a given conceptual distinction—figure importantly in their use and affect their semantic properties. In our set, *mawpakkat* is considered more learned than the other terms, all of which are ordinary, everyday words. Although the word is widely known, it occurs most often during 'litigation' when 'negotiations' are being talked about. In other contexts the notion of 'mere negotiation' is more likely to be referred to as *qisun*, using 'conference' in its general sense. It is probably a consequence of this stylistic difference that the semantic contrast between *mawpakkat* and *qisun* seems less sharply drawn than that between the other pairs of expressions. In direct questioning about the meaning of these terms, many informants have stated offhand that *mawpakkat* and *qisun* have the same meaning. No one has said that of *hukum* and any other term in the set. The same informants will still agree that if, for example, several guests at a festivity get together to decide when to leave, that this is a case of *qisun* but not of *mawpakkat*. The two expressions are not synonymous but the difference between them is somewhat harder to uncover than is the difference between the other terms. The concept of "negotiation" can also be represented by expressions referring to the distinctive aspects of the event, for example: *pagsulutan*, 'agreement, settlement'—not including legal rulings (*hukuman*); *qalegdah* (from Spanish), 'to settle a dispute by any means'; *janjiqan* (from Malay), 'negotiated contractual promise.'

Any citation of Yakan legal terms illustrates another property of these expressions—that is, the large percentage of forms that are loan words from the languages of both of the "great traditions" impinging on the Yakan: Arabic and Malay of the Malaysian-Moslem tradition, English and Spanish of the Filipino-Western tradition.[6] These loans have been acquired through contact with intermediary languages (Taw Sug and Zamboangueño), and their prevalence is not a reflection of a crushing impact of either Moslem or Western legal concepts upon Yakan law, but of the stylistic coups a speaker of Yakan scores by displaying a knowledge of foreign words. This process apparently has a long history. Many loans, such as *hukum* (from Arabic), are now completely assimilated and are not now recognized as foreign. The term *mitiŋ*, currently much more popular than alternative designations of 'discussion,' seems to be on the verge of losing its loan-word aura. English loans used in current litigation include: *wantid, holdap, kidnap, wadan* ('warrant'), *supenah, pospon, pendiŋ, qokeh* ("approval"), and *qistodok* ('strategy,' from "stroke").

Describing Litigation

Our formulation states that litigation is a kind of topic-focused mutual speech behavior, the distinctive attributes of which pertain to the content and role structure of talking. An observer of Yakan litigation would have difficulty finding any other element that sets it apart from other activities. There are no distinctive settings, no courtrooms in which litigation takes place. A site for a trial should be neutral and should require no one to play a host role—a role that requires the offering of food. A typical result of these considerations is convocation on the porch of the house of one of the judges (in Yakan terms, "on" the house but not "within" it). But a wide variety of other activities takes place here as well. There are no distinctive paraphernalia associated with litigation: no law books, no gavel, no judges' bench, no witness stand. There is no provisioning of participants. They may smoke and chew betel, but the rules for soliciting and proffering smoking and chewing makings are the same as for other informal gatherings. There is no distinctive dress associated with litigation—no judges' robes—and participants do not dress up to go to court as they do to go to ceremonies. If one were to make distinction in Yakan activities between festive and nonfestive, formal and informal, litigation would clearly fall on the nonfestive, informal side. As speech-focused activity, litigation is outside the domain of ceremonies, feasts, technological tasks, and other object-focused activities. We must therefore organize a discription of litigation along those dimensions of speech behavior found to be significant.

Cases

The topic of litigation is a 'case' (*pākalaq*, from Malay from Sanskrit), a 'dispute' brought to court. A 'dispute' arises when an identified party is 'charged' with an 'offense' and the accused counters the charge. To make a charge is to publicly proclaim a particular interpretation of an act. To counter a charge is to advance another interpretation. Clearly the key descriptive problem is to state the rules for interpreting an act as an offense. Equally clear is that these rules cannot be perfectly consistent in their formulation or straightforward in their application. There must be room for argument if there is to be litigation.

Offenses. 'Offenses' (*salaq*) are a subset of 'wrongs' (*duseh*)—those wrongs against persons that can lead to a dispute. There are also wrongs against God (*tuhan*), such as desecrating a Koran; wrongs against this-world supernaturals (*saytan*, from Arabic), such as cutting down a tree they inhabit; and wrongs against ancestors (*kapapuqan*) now in the other world (*qahilat*, from Arabic), such as selling an heirloom. But these beings need not rely on courts to seek redress.

The Yakan employ a large number of linguistic expressions for talking about different kinds of offenses, along a variety of semantic dimensions dealing with the nature and consequences of acts as well as with the social relationships between offender and victim. The saliency of dimensions with respect to one another can vary in different portions of the domain. For example, physical assault with intent to kill (*bonoq*) and sexual assault (*hilap*, from Arabic, and many other expressions) are terminologically distinguished unless the offense is also a wrong against God, as is the case if the victim and offender are primary kin or primary affines. There is one term, *sumbaŋ*, to cover these grievous sins against both man and God. One might say that the contrast "sex versus killing" is neutralized when an expression is marked for "interference by God." (It might be noted that sexual relations are often designated euphemistically or facetiously by metaphors based on expressions for killing or fighting. "To make a killing" in Yakan does not refer to business success.) We will state here only a few general inferences about the nature of the concept of 'offense,' which have been drawn from Yakan talk about particular kinds of offenses.

At the most general level, for an act to be interpretable as an offense it must be a threat to a *dapuq* relationship. The term *dapuq* occurs together with a possessive attribute in response to the same query that elicits kinship terms and other relationship expressions. Unlike kinship relations, however, a person may be *dapuq* of an object as well as of another person. Being someone's or something's *dapuq* implies having an economic interest in him (it) and a responsibility for him (it). The notion includes, but is broader than, that of ownership. To be a *dapuq* of a person in no way implies that the person is one's slave. One is *dapuq* to his children, his legal wards, his spouse, and himself. To be a *dapuq* of an object does not necessarily imply that one has rights of use, possession, or sale, but only that one has a legitimate interest in its use or disposal. A water source, for example, has its *dapuq* (*dapuq boheq*)—those who use it and who would suffer economic loss if it were destroyed—but it has no owner. The *dapuq* of a mosque (*dapuq laŋgal*) is not its owner—there is such a person—but the entire congregation. The *dapuq* of an inheritance (*dapuq pusakaq*) is a potential heir. Any threat to a *dapuq* relationship can be interpreted as an economic threat, a threat whose gravity is expressible in pesos and centavos. All offenses, including murder, can be compensated for by money. The purpose of Yakan litigation is not to mete out punishment, but to award compensation for injury.

There are two ways in which an act can be an offense. First, it can challenge a person's status as a *dapuq*, usually in the form of a claim that some other person is properly the *dapuq* of a given object or person. Second, an act can damage an object or person in such a way as to reduce its economic value to its *dapuq* (including, in the case of persons, the victim himself). Since a given object or person is likely to have more than one *dapuq*, an offense generally produces several plaintiffs. A sexual assault, for example, is an offense against the victim (*dapuq badannen*, '*dapuq* of one's body'), her parents (*dapuq qanakin*, '*dapuq* of the child'), and if she is married, her husband (*dapuq qandahin*, '*dapuq* of the wife').

Charges. It is up to a victim of an offense to make a charge (*tuntut*); all Yakan law is civil law. He must, furthermore, determine the identity of the offender and assume responsibility for the identification. Offenses in which victim and offender do not meet face to face or in which the victim does not survive are difficult to prosecute. Even though theft, ambush shootings, and murder are among the more common—and certainly the most complained about—offenses in Yakan life, they rarely reach the courts. It is largely sex and, to a lesser extent, fights and property disputes that keep court agenda full.

An initial charge can be made in the form of a complaint (*diklamuh*, from Spanish) to a court or even by directly confronting the accused. More often an accuser will utilize gossip channels to make his charge known to the accused. In this way he can feel out the response of his opponent before being irrevocably committed. A way out is left open through denying the truth or serious intent of the gossip. One of the dangers of Yakan life is *limorok* (literally, 'slip through'): 'inadvertently instigating a dispute by incautious gossip in the presence of someone who is likely to relay the accusation to the accused.'

There are three strategies available for countering a charge:

1. One can deny the validity of the accuser's definition of the offense in question, disputing the meaning of a concept. Does, for example, the notion of sexual offense include all acts in which a male makes unnecessary physical contact with a female not his spouse, or only those acts in which a male has sexual designs on the woman?

2. One can deny that the act in question has the properties to qualify it as an instance of an offense, disputing what really happened. For example, granted any physical contact as described above is an offense, did any such contact actually occur in the particular instance?

3. One can deny responsibility for the act because (a) someone else committed it; (b) the accused was provoked by the accuser; (c) the accused was incited by some third party (a much stronger excuse for wrongdoing among the Yakan than among ourselves); (d) the act was unintentional.

To deny a charge is at the same time to make a charge against one's accuser, for a false charge is in itself an offense: it threatens the economic interests of the accused. The set of arguments propounded by one side in a dispute to counter the charges of the other is their *daqawah* (from Arabic) or "case" in the sense of "the defense rests its case."

Disputes. Once a charge has been made and countered, a dispute exists. Disputants may simply decide to live with the dispute, they may attempt to dispose of each other, or they may seek a settlement. If they decide on the last course of action, they may either 'negotiate' or 'litigate.' In 'negotiation' two opposing parties meet to settle a disagreement by mutual agreement. The disagreement need not be a dispute (that is, the outcome of a charge). Negotiating a contract, property settlements, marriage (which involves all of the preceding) are cases to point. Negotiations are often sufficient to handle minor disputes and are necessary for major disputes difficult to place under the jurisdiction of any Yakan court. An agreement is specific to the negotiating parties and need not derive from legal precedents; the breaking of an agreement, however, is an offense and can result in a dispute taken to court. Marriages are made by negotiation but dissolved by litigation. To settle a dispute by litigation requires that it be reported to a court, at which point the dispute becomes a legal case. The party that considers itself offended against should report first, but often by the time a case reaches court, there is such a complex of charges and countercharges that any distinction between plaintiff and defendant becomes obscure.

Courts

What distinguishes litigation from other methods of settling disputes is the presence of a court (*saraq*, from Arabic)—a set of persons, performing the role of judge, who are ostensibly neutral on the issue and whose task it is to formulate a settlement. The Yakan court has few of the tangible manifestations of its Western counterpart: professional judges holding an office, court houses, explicit and continuous schedules, and well-defined jurisdictions. On the other hand, a set of judges is not recruited ad hoc to try each case that appears. Particular sets of judges meet more than once and may try more than one case in a single session. Furthermore, there is a fundamental difference between a single case appearing again in a subsequent session of the same court—a continuation of a single trial—and a case appearing again in a different court—a retrial of the same case. One may also report to a court when the court is not in session—to file a charge, for example, or to seek asylum. The crucial problems in a description of Yakan courts are those of legal authority and of jurisdiction. How are persons recruited to the role of judge? How are cases assigned to particular courts?

Judges. To act as a judge, a person must be a parish leader with the ability and knowledge to perform the role and with sufficient political power at the jurisdictional level of the court to make his voice effective. Parish leadership is not a political office with formal rules of recruitment, but a position achieved by accumulating influence and prestige by a variety of means: religious learning, economic success, military prowess, forensic ability, acquisition of a title, pilgrimage to Mecca, election to a local office in the Philippine political system (councilor or barrio captain), or simply growing older. (The most common expression for a leader is *bahiq*, 'elder.') Typically, parish leadership is vested in a small group of close kinsmen, each specializing in one or more of these routes to power. One man may be the priest and litigator, another the entrepreneur, another the fighter. Larger political groupings are informal and unstable alliances of parishes. To exert leadership at this wider level, one must also be a leader at the parish level. One does not rise to higher positions; one merely extends the range of his influence. An exceptional position is that of titular tribal chief (*datuq*) of all the Yakan, a hereditary office now held by the Westernized son of a Christian Filipino escaped convict, who, during the latter part of the Spanish regime, fled to Basilan. There he assumed political leadership over the Yakan and achieved formal recognition of his position by both the Spaniards and the Sultan of Sulu.

Jurisdiction. The jurisdiction of a court is a function of the social distance between the judges who comprise it and the disputants before it. This distance, in turn, is a response to the need to preserve neutrality with respect to the cases brought before it. The rule for assignment of a case to a court is to maintain minimal social distance between court and protagonists consistent with preserving neutrality. This rule has the effect that the greater the social distance between protagonists and the more serious the case, the higher the jurisdiction of the court that can try the case. If both protagonists belong to the same parish, then one or more of their own parish leaders may be found who, by kinship and other dimensions of social affiliation, are equidistant from both sides. If, however, the protagonists belong to different parishes, the court must comprise representatives of both parishes. The seriousness of a case is measured by the number of active supporters recruited by each disputant. As the number of active supporters surrounding each disputant increases—that is, as each party of protagonists grows larger—the further afield one must go to find judges who are not involved on one side or another. Because of these considerations, there is a certain ad hoc nature to the formation of courts as adjustments are made to handle particular cases. Nevertheless, three basic jurisdictional levels can be distinguished: parish, community, and tribal.

The tribal court, composed of leaders appointed by the tribal chief, meets in the yard of the chief's Western-style house in the town of Lamitan. Although in theory it is a sort of supreme court for all the Yakan, handling cases local courts have failed to settle, in practice its jurisdiction and its composition is geographically limited to the side of the island where the court meets. Parish courts are generally formed ad hoc to try relatively trivial disputes—fights among young men, for example—among parish members. Occasionally a parish trial will be conducted with the absolute minimum personnel: two disputants and one judge. The bulk of litigation occurs at what might be called the community level. In most areas there are regular court sessions about once a week. Adjustments are made in these courts to handle particular cases. Any court intermediate between a regular community court and the tribal court is an ad hoc formation to handle a special case. Before reaching the tribal level, however, there is a limit beyond which jurisdiction cannot be stretched, where judges who are neutral and at the same time sufficiently close socially to act together cannot be found. Disputes at this level may be referred to the tribal court or to government courts, or a settlement by negotiation may be attempted. Frequently, however, disputants resort to violence at this point.

Other roles. Added to the basic role structure of litigation—a court and two opposing sides—there is a further differentiation of roles within each party of protagonists: (a) the principal, the one primarily involved in the original dispute, the person who, as the Yakan say was 'struck' by speech (*tawwaq bissāh*) or who 'collided' with litigation (*lumaŋgal si hukum*); (b) his guardian, the one who assumes responsibility for accepting or rejecting a ruling and complying with it. The guardian may be the principal himself, a parent or parental surrogate, or a spouse; (c) senior and peer supporters.

The Yakan speak about this role structure in the language of kinship, using an ideal model in which the principal is a child, the court his elders, the guardian his parent, and his supporters his senior and peer kin. A final role is that of witnesses, who may be called by either side or by the court.

Rulings

The intended outcome of litigation is a ruling (*hukuman*) on a case handed down by the court. The crucial fact shaping Yakan legal rulings is that the court has no powers of coercion to force compliance with a ruling. It must resort to persuasion. What distinguishes a ruling from an agreement arrived at by negotiation consists largely of the elaborate verbal trappings that go along with a ruling and lend it a sacrosanct aura. The ideology expressed in talking about rulings during the process of proclaiming them should not be taken as an expression of the manner in which rulings are actually derived, but as part of the behavior of making a ruling in the most effective way. The basic principle for actually arriving at successful rulings seems to be the same as those for agreements, namely to give each side somewhat less than full satisfaction but something better than the worst they might expect—in other words, to effect a compromise. The basic objective of both litigation and negotiation is to eliminate a dispute, to re-establish normal social relations between the disputants. It is not to do justice whatever the cost.

A ruling may call for one or more of three acts: payment of a fine (*multah*, from Spanish; *qātaq*, from Malay from Sanskrit), listening to an admonition (*nasihat*, from Arabic; *pituwah*, from Arabic; *tōqan*) from the court, and performing a prayer (*duwaqah*, from Arabic) of reconciliation. A fine, in turn, has one or more of three components: a compensation for the offense, an amount serving to "wipe away" any sin against God associated with the offense (which the court collects), and a payment to the court, the *baytalmāl* (from Arabic 'treasury'). Fines are calculated in ten-peso units (*laksaq*) and paid in Philippine currency (₱1 = $.25). In proposing a ruling, the court must explain in detail how the amount was arrived at, relating it to traditional fines for the offense and to the particular exigencies of the case at hand. In one case involving two youths who had been in a fight, one side claimed damages for bodily injury and presented a medical bill for the amount of ₱180.25 from a Christian Filipino physician. The court suggested a fine of ₱100 to the injured party, explaining its decision as follows:

₱120 for paying the medical bill (principle: never give full satisfaction);
−50 in recognition of the countercharge of collusion between the plaintiff and the physician. The court was careful to state that it did not necessarily believe the countercharge, but since there were no witnesses, account must be taken of the possibility.
+50 for the offense against the plaintiff.
−20 for the plaintiff's responsibility in instigating the fight.
₱100

If an admonition is part of the ruling, it is given in the form of a lecture by the court to both sides at the end of the trial. It is designed to make both parties feel their share of responsibility for the dispute, to smooth ruffled feelings, and to warn of the grave consequences of repeating the offense. Admonitions are especially common in rulings over marital disputes and fights among youths.

If a prayer of reconciliation is called for, it is performed at a later time in the form of a different scene, a religious ceremony. Its performance involves expenses, instructions for the payment of which is an important aspect of the ruling. The prayer unites the former disputants in a divinely sanctioned ritual-sibling tie. A call for prayer is especially common in cases of violence.

Upon suggesting a ruling, the court argues for compliance, not only by carefully justifying the form of the decision, but also by pointing out the dire consequences of refusal to comply. God and the ancestors may mete out sickness upon the offender and his kin. Opponents may resort to violence against the offender and his kin. The offender's kin, under threat from these sanctioning agents, may withdraw support or even disown the offender. Judges threaten to wash their hands of the case and withdraw political support, and finally the case may be referred to Philippine government legal system with its expensive lawyers and prisons. Figure 15:2 diagrams these sanctioning forces converging on an offender.

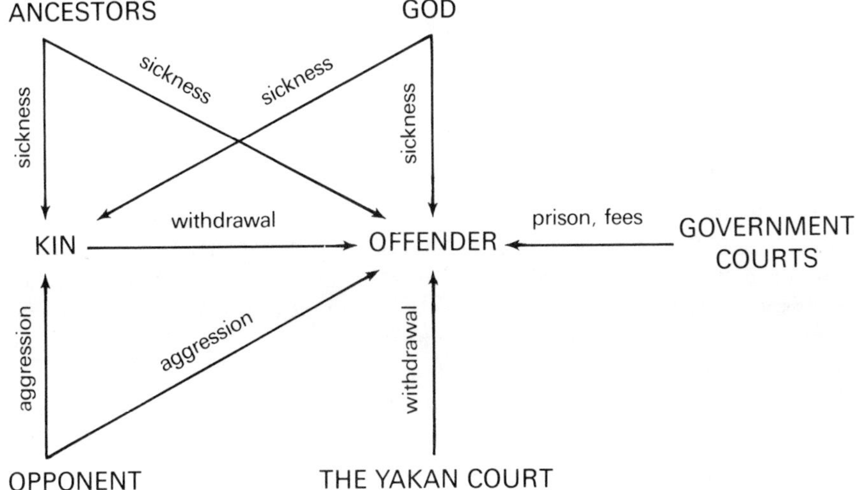

Figure 15:2. Sanctions and sanctioning agents.

If the litigants agree to the ruling, those who are called upon to hand over money almost never pay in full on demand, this being a rule in all monetary transactions. They ask for *tanguh*, a deferment of part of the payment until a specified later date. As might be expected, failure to pay *tanguh* when due is itself a major cause of disputes.

If a court fails to formulate an acceptable ruling, the litigants may attempt to take the case to another Yakan court, seek redress in a government court, or drop attempts to settle the dispute by litigation. Another alternative is to turn the decision over to God. In a religious ceremony each disputant swears (*sapah*) on the Koran to the validity of his arguments in the case. God decides who is right and announces his decision by inflicting fatal illness (*kasapahan*) upon the person who swore a false oath or upon his kin. Swearing is a serious matter, rarely resorted to in fact. The threat of it, however, figures prominently in legal debate. One can protect himself from false charges by challenging his opponent to participate in a swearing ritual. In several recorded cases young men saved themselves from conviction on charges of sexual assault by this tactic. The fact that God may punish not only the offender but also his kin may seem capricious to Western moralists; yet it greatly increases the effectiveness of the punishment. Support of one's kin is crucial in a dispute, but they will be extremely reluctant to carry this support to the point of swearing unless they are firmly convinced of their kinsmen's innocence. Furthermore, if the disputants are in any way related to each other, as they often are, this relationship tie must be dissolved before swearing. Consanguineal kinship ties can be formally broken in a religious ceremony. The term for the ritual payments required to disown a kinsman is *tallak*, from the Arabic word for the formula spoken by a husband to divorce his wife (Yakan divorce is not that simple).

Procedures and Schedules

Our formulation of the concept of litigation states that litigation is an integral activity never performed as part of another scene. It is a maximal unit of planning and scheduling. The description of the manifestations of this aspect of the concept requires a statement of the constituent structure of the scene—the sequence of parts that make up the whole—and of the scheduling of litigation with respect to other scenes in the society.

Procedures. Unlike mere negotiation or conference, litigation is conducted according to definite procedural rules. Although these rules are much looser than those of Western courts, they are, by Yakan standards, fairly strict and explicit. During proceedings judges frequently make reference to the following general rules governing the conduct of court sessions.

1. Speaking time is a free good, available in unlimited quantity to any person present as long as what he says is relevant to the case.

2. A speaker has the right to finish before being interrupted.

3. Judges have the right to call on a person to speak, but one may speak without being called upon.[7]

4. Litigants should address all their arguments to the court.

5. Overt expression of anger, and especially any violence, must be avoided. Allowance should be made for the necessity, in litigation, for people to say unkind things about one another. Disputants must be allowed to accuse, judges to admonish.

6. Each party of protagonists, as well as the judges, has the right to confer in private whenever necessary.

7. A continuous period of time should be allotted to each case during a single court session.

Although there is some variation by type of case, the usual sequence of events is as follows:

1. Presentation of the case by the person to whom it is reported.
2. Taking testimony from each side and from witnesses.
3. Arguments from each side presented together (one side does not present its complete case and then defer to the other side).
4. Private conference of the judges.
5. Presentation of a ruling.
6. Further argument (optional but inevitable).
7. Private conference of each side (optional).
8. Expression of acceptance or refusal by each side.
9. Final decision for disposition of case.
10. Payment of fines, listening to courts admonition (if required).
11. Ritual handshaking (*salam*, from Arabic) with the judges signaling the termination of a trial session.

Steps 2 and 3 often occur simultaneously; steps 4–8 may be repeated several times.

Schedules. Fixed timing is not an attribute of litigation, as it is, say, of some calendrical religious ceremonies and agricultural activities. Court sessions are fitted into vacancies left by the schedules of other scenes. As a matter of convenience, community courts generally have regular scheduled meetings (Friday afternoon after mosque service is a favorite time), but these are easily accommodated if schedules conflict. The tribal court meets two afternoons a week. Court sessions must be scheduled between meals, with allowance made for participants to return home to eat. The five daily prayers of Islam, performed in most localities only by a few religiously inclined individuals, cause no problem. If someone wants to say a prayer, he can always go off and do so.

Comparisons

In this section we make a few summary comparisons with another Philippine legal system. The purpose is not to offer an explanation of these differences, but to demonstrate that the ethnographic approach argued for here, rather than hampering cross-cultural comparison as some critics seem to fear, provides a basis for determining which units are comparable and points up significant dimensions of comparison.

The Eastern Subanun are pagan swidden agriculturists inhabiting the interior of Zamboanga Peninsula on the island of Mindanao.[8] The Yakan and Subanun are not in direct contact, but they speak related languages and, along with other central Malaysian peoples, share many basic technological and social-organizational features. Subanun communities are much smaller and more scattered, although the basic principles of settlement pattern are the same: nuclear family household dispersed in individual fields. The difference is that the Yakan practice continual exploitation of privately owned fields and groves. Both groups have long been subject first to Moslem, then to Christian cultural influence, political authority, and economic exploitation. The Yakan accommodated where necessary and resisted where possible. They became Moslems, they participate in Philippine politics; and they market copra. At the same time, they have retained a marked cultural distinctiveness and some freedom to run their own affairs and, above all, their land. The Subanun, on the other hand, retreated or succumbed entirely. They have remained pagan and retained temporary economic and political independence at the price of increased isolation and loss of land. Perhaps not unrelated to this difference in adaptation to external pressures is a marked difference in the behavior of the two peoples today: the Subanun drink, whereas the Yakan fight.

There is among the Subanun a set of activities that, in contrast to other Subanun activities, can be defined in much the same terms as Yakan litigation: an integral speech event concerned with settling disputes by means of a ruling formulated by neutral judges. A brief description of litigation in one Subanun community appears elsewhere (Frake 1963). Here we will restrict ourselves to a few comparisons along the dimensions of topic, outcome, role structure, and integrity.

Topic

Subanun legal cases arise in much the same way as Yakan ones, except that they need not be initiated by a plaintiff. A judge can try someone for an offense even if no complaint has been made. It seems ridiculous, however, to call this criminal law, since the offenses in question are generally slanderous or flirtatious remarks made by an incautious drinker, often not at all resented by the victim. Otherwise the definitions of particular kinds of offenses are similar. (A major difference is that the Yakan consider sexual relations with an affine as incestuous, whereas the Subanun practice levirate and sororate marriage and sororal polygyny.) There are great differences, however, in the kinds of offenses that occur (violence is almost unknown among the Subanun) and the types of cases that reach court. Adultery, for example, fills the agendas of Yakan courts, whereas it is rarely the overt basis of a Subanun legal case. This fact is not a comment on Subanun virtue but on the weakness of Subanun legal sanctions.

Outcome

The rulings of a Subanun court, like those of the Yakan, generally demand financial compensation (but fines are calculated in units of twenty centavos rather than of ten pesos) and may call for admonitions and rituals of reconciliation. But not only does the Subanun court have no legal sanctions of force to back up a decision, there is also little realistic threat of illegal force it can bring to bear. The Subanun offender may fear a certain amount of social censure—a real enough sanction, to be sure—but he need not fear a shotgun blast interrupting his evening meal, the outcome of more than one Yakan dispute. The Subanun also lack an Almighty God to mete out justice when litigation fails. For this reason, "A large share, if not the majority, of legal cases deal with offenses so minor that only the fertile imagination of a Subanun legal authority can magnify them into a serious threat to some person or to society in general" (Frake 1963:221). Yakan courts, too, cannot cope with the full range of offenses committed, but the Yakan, by absolute standards, commit much more serious crimes. A Parkinsonian cynic viewing Yakan and Subanun life and law might conclude that the severity of crime increases with the ability of a legal system to cope with it.

Role Structure

Subanun courts are always formed ad hoc to try a particular case. There are no court schedules or regular meeting places. The role of judge is open to any adult male with the ability to formulate successful decisions, and performance in the role is largely a route to community leadership, rather than a result of it. Unlike the Yakan, where a parish priest is generally a political leader as well, Subanun roles of legal and religious authority are quite distinct and typically filled by separate individuals. Subanun litigation less often musters bodies of kin in support of disputants, partly because there is usually less of common interest at stake and kin do not share collective responsibility under mortal and divine sanctioning agents.

Integrity

The striking difference between Subanun and Yakan litigation, and one that does not derive from differences in socio-economic complexity in any obvious way, is the place of the activity in the over-all structure of cultural scenes. Subanun activities are sharply divisible into festive and nonfestive scenes, the former always involving feasting and drinking (Frake 1964b). Subanun litigation is festive behavior, performed as part of a larger scene and accompanied by eating, drinking, and merrymaking. In this respect it is the same kind of behavior as the performance of religious offerings; the two activities, in fact, often occur together as parts of the same festivity. Subanun litigation, then, is less of an integral unit of performance and scheduling than is the comparable Yakan activity. Subanun legal arguments, as they develop in the course of drinking, exhibit more obvious attention to message form. Litigants and judges employ esoteric legal language, often arranged into verse and sung to the tune of drinking songs (Frake 1964a). Thus, whereas the Yakan try relatively serious cases in scenes of informal discussion, the Subanun devote themselves to trivial disputes in scenes of formal festivities. This difference is crucial to any functional interpretations of litigation in the two societies. Participation in litigation has different meanings and different consequences in the two societies because of it.

Notes

1. Fieldwork among the Yakan in 1962, 1963–1964, and 1965–1966 was supported by a United States Public Health Service Grant under the National Institute of Mental Health and by an auxiliary research award from the Social Science Research Council. The statements in this paper are at a level of generality applicable to the Basilan Yakan as a whole and represent knowledge that any adult Yakan could be expected to have. Yakan expressions are represented by a linguistically motivated orthography, but certain canons of traditional phonemic analysis are ignored ("*a*," for example, represents both /a/ and /e/ where this contrast is neutralized). This practice enables dialect differences to be accounted for by special rules applicable to a uniform orthography. /q/ is a glottal catch, /e/ a mid-front vowel, /j/ a voiced, palatal affricative. The ethnographic record upon which this description is based includes the investigator's observations of court sessions, transcriptions of forty-three tape-recorded trial sessions at all jurisdictional levels, and informants' interpretations of the content of these observations and texts. In addition, by living in Yakan households during the entire field period, the investigator was continually exposed to conversations related to litigation. Special acknowledgment is due to Samuel Pajarito and Reuben Muzarin for assistance in recording and transcribing court sessions and to Hadji Umar of Giyung for many long discussions about Yakan law.

2. There are also Yakan speakers on Sakol, Malanipa, and Tumalutab islands just east of Zamboanga City. These communities are beyond the scope of this paper.

3. Single quotes enclose English glosses. These are to be assigned the meaning given to the Yakan expressions for which they substitute.

4. In response to *magqine* (<N, 'active,' + *pag*, 'mutuality,' + *qine*, 'what'), 'What is the mutual activity or relationship?' the forms cited, all unanalyzable morphemes, replace *qine*, 'what': *magqine siyeh*, 'What are they doing?' *magqisun*, 'Conferring with each other.' Note also: *magqine siyah*, 'How are they related to each other?' *magpoɲtinaqih*, 'As siblings.'

5. The mutuality of the behavior is represented by the prefix *pag* in the sequence N + *pag* > *mag*. See Note 4.

6. The source of etymological information on Malay and Arabic loans is Wilkinson (1932).

Yakan expressions are marked as Malay loans only when there are phonological grounds for distinguishing loans from inherited cognates.

7. The question of someone's refusing to testify never seems to arise.

8. Reference is to the Eastern Subanun of the Lipay area of Zamboanga del Norte, studied in the field in 1953–1954 and 1957–1958.

Bibliography

BRIGHT, J. O., AND W. BRIGHT. 1965 "Semantic structures in Northwestern California and the Sapir-Whorf hypothesis." *American Anthropologist* 67(5)2:249–258.

FRAKE, C. O. 1961 "The diagnosis of disease among the Subanun of Mindanao." *American Anthropologist* 63(1):113–132.

1963 "Litigation in Lipay: a study of Subanun law." Bangkok: *The proceedings of the Ninth Pacific Science Congress*, Volume 3.

1964a "How to ask for a drink in Subanun." *American Anthropologist* 66(6):2:127–132.

1964b "A structural description of Subanun religious behavior." In *Explorations in Cultural Anthropology: Essays in Honor of George Peter Murdock*, W. H. Goodenough, ed. New York: McGraw-Hill, pp. 111–130.

GREENBERG, J. H. 1966 "Language universals." In *Current Trends in Linguistics*, Volume 3, T. A. Seboek, ed. The Hague: Mouton, pp. 61–112.

JAKOBSON, R. 1957 *Shifters, verbal categories and the Russian verb.* Cambridge, Massachusetts: Harvard University Russian Language Project.

WILKINSON, R. J. 1932 *A Malay-English dictionary* (romanized). Mytilene, Greece: Salavopoulos and Kinderlis.

16 BEATING THE DRUNK CHARGE

James P. Spradley

One of the greatest problems described by tramps is finding ways to stay out of jail. This fact emerged from the earlier analysis in Chapter 13 of the attributes employed by these men in defining places to "make a flop." In spite of precautions, many men end up in jail, and then, after a few hours to dry out, they are arraigned in court. In the urban American court studied, nearly 12,000 men are charged each year with public drunkenness. While some post bail and go free, most of the poor appear in court and place themselves at the mercy of the judge. They are not entirely destitute, however, for they have learned an elaborate set of strategies for "beating the drunk charge." These were discovered by the author through observation and interviews. A semantic analysis of their meaning shows how tramps define each strategy in terms of the risks involved. Whereas this study begins with the symbolic system of one minority group, it leads to an analysis of certain broad American cultural values and shows how these adversely affect those outside the mainstream of our society.—EDITOR'S NOTE

It could be Miami, New York, Chicago, Minneapolis, Denver, Los Angeles, Seattle, or any other American city. The criminal court may be in the basement of a massive public building constructed at the turn of the century, or high above the city in a modern skyscraper. The judges who hear the never-ending list of cases may be veterans of the bench or men whose memories of law school are fresh and clear. But one scene does not change. Each weekday morning a group of unshaven men file into court with crestfallen faces, wrinkled clothing, and bloodshot eyes. They stand before the prosecuting attorney and hear him say, "You have been charged with public drunkenness, how do you plead?"

The most staggering problem of law and order in America today is public drunkenness. In 1968 the F.B.I. reported that one and a half million arrests for this crime made up nearly one-third of all arrests. This means that

Reprinted from *Conformity and Conflict: Readings in Cultural Anthropology*, James P. Spradley and David W. McCurdy, editors, by permission of the publisher.

every twenty seconds another person is arrested and charged with being drunk in public. During 1967, in Seattle, Washington, 51 percent of all arrests and 65 percent of all cases that appeared in the criminal court were for intoxication. In that same year the chief of police stated, "As a public official I have no choice. Whether alcoholism is a disease or not would not affect my official position. Drunkenness is a crime. So we must enforce the law by arresting people. We know in the Police Department that probably right at this moment there are more than two hundred men in the city jail serving sentences for drunkenness who have never posed any threat to the community in any fashion at all."

Who are these men that are repeatedly arrested for drunkenness? Who are the ones who spend much of their lives in jail for their public behavior? The first task in this study was to discover how these men identified themselves. This was necessary because the police, courts, social scientists, and most citizens see them as criminals, homeless men, derelicts, and bums who have lost the ability to organize their behavior in the pursuit of goals. The word these men used to identify their subcultural membership was the term *tramp*. There were several different kinds of tramps recognized by informants; for example, a "mission stiff" is a tramp who frequents the skid-road missions, while a "rubber tramp" travels about in his own car. This category system constitutes one of the major social identity domains in the subculture.

Tramps have other ways to conceptualize their identity when they "make the bucket," or are incarcerated. As an inmate in jail one is either a *drunk*, a *trusty*, a *lockup*, a *kickout*, or a *rabbit*. In the particular jail studied there are over sixty different kinds of trusties. This fact led some tramps to believe they were arrested to provide cheap labor for the police department. In their capacity as trusties, nearly 125 men provide janitorial service for the city hall, outlying police precincts, and the jail. They assist in the preparation of food, maintain the firing range, care for police vehicles, and do numerous other tasks. Most men soon learn that doing time on a drunk charge is not a desirable occupation, so they use many strategies to escape the confines of the jail or to reduce the length of their sentence. When a man is arrested he is placed in the drunk tank, where he awaits his arraignment in court. Those sentenced to do time will spend it in close association with other tramps. If a man is not experienced in the ways of this culture, he will learn them while he is in jail, for it is a veritable storehouse of invaluable information for those who are repeatedly arrested for public intoxication. He will learn to think of himself as a tramp and to survive on the street by employing more than a dozen "ways of making it." More important, as he discovers that the jailhouse has a revolving door for drunks, he will do his best to "beat the drunk charge." The casual observer in court may find the arraignment and sentencing of drunk cases to be a cut-and-dried process. From the perspective of these men, however, it is more like a game of skill and chance being played by the tramp and law-enforcement agencies. In this article we shall examine the rules of this game, the strategies employed by tramps, and the underlying American cultural values that make it intelligible to the outsider.

Plans for Beating the Drunk Charge

Every culture contains one type of shared knowledge called *plans*. These are related to the achievement of goals. A plan is a set of rules that specifies a goal, conditions under which the goal will be chosen, techniques for the attainment of the goal, and conditions under which a particular technique will be used to attain the goal. The methods of ethnoscience are designed to map culturally shared systems of knowledge, and were used in this study to discover the plans tramps employ in their relationship to law-enforcement agencies.

The goal: Maximize freedom—minimize incarceration. There are many goals which tramps pursue. Most aims are referred to in a specific manner, such as "making a flop," "making a jug," "getting a dime," or "bailing out." Freedom is a general objective that includes such specific goals as rabbiting from jail, concealing one's identity, making a pay-off to a bull, leaving town, avoiding the police, and beating a drunk charge. Men do not always select one of these goals in order to maximize freedom—they sometimes even choose paths leading to *incarceration*. In a sample of a hundred men, 10 percent reported they had gone to jail and asked to be locked up in order to stop drinking. At other times a tramp will go to jail on his own to request a place to sleep or something to eat. Such cases are rare, and most tramps abhor imprisonment because they have learned a life style of mobility and the restrictions in the bucket lead to intense frustration. A testimonial to the fact that men do not seek imprisonment, as some outsiders believe, is the large number of strategies this culture has for avoiding incarceration. Almost every experience in the tramp world is defined, in part, by noting the degree of risk it entails for being jailed.

Techniques for the attainment of the goal. Because of the public nature of their life style, sooner or later most of these men end up in jail. Their specific objective at that time is to "beat the drunk charge." If successful, this could mean freedom in a few hours or at least a sentence of shorter duration than they would otherwise have received. The techniques for reaching this goal were discovered during interviews in which informants were asked: "Are there different ways to beat a drunk charge?" They responded with many specific instances in which they had taken action to beat the charge. These were classified as follows:

1. Bail out.
2. Bond out.
3. Request a continuance.
4. Have a good record.
5. Use an alias.
6. Plead guilty.
7. Hire a defense attorney.
8. Plead not guilty.
9. Submit a writ of habeas corpus.
10. Make a statement:
    a. Talk of family ties.
    b. Talk of present job.
    c. Talk of intent to work.
    d. Tell of extenuating circumstances.
    e. Offer to leave town.
11. Request the treatment center (alcoholic).

Each of these techniques labels a *category* of many different acts that are considered equivalent. For example, a man may bail out by using money he had with him when arrested, by borrowing from another man in jail, by contacting an employer who loans or gives him the money, and so on. There are several ways to "have a good record": a man must stay out of jail for at least six months for his record to begin to affect the length of his jail sentence. In order to do this a man may travel, quit drinking, stay off skid road, or go to an alcoholism treatment center for a long stay. Each kind of statement includes specific instances, varying from one man to another and from one time to the next. This category system is extremely important to tramps. Once they have learned these techniques, they practice them until their skill increases. Judges may consider an old-time tramp as a "con artist," but in this culture he is a man with expertise in carrying out these culturally shared techniques.

Conditions influencing selection. When a man is arrested he must process a great deal of information before he makes a decision to employ one or more of these techniques. He must assess his own resources, the probabilities of success, the risk of doing more time, etc. He needs to know the sentencing practices of the judge, the population of the jail, and the weather conditions. The most important factors that influence his decision are shown in Table 16:1.

American Cultural Values

Every society is based upon shared values—conceptions of the desirable in human experience. They are the basis for rewards and punishments. It

TABLE 16:1. *Conditions Influencing Selection of a Way to Beat a Drunk Charge*

Strategy	*Risk of outcome?*	*Risk offending bulls?*	*Risk getting more time?*	*Risk doing dead time?*	*Money needed?*
Bail out	No	No	No	No	$20
Bond out	No	No	No	No	$20+
Request a continuance	Yes	Yes	No	Yes	Yes
Have a good record	No	No	No	No	No
Use an alias	Yes	Yes	Yes	No	No
Plead guilty	Yes	No	No	No	No
Hire a defense attorney	Yes	Yes	No	Yes	Yes
Plead not guilty	Yes	Yes	Yes	Yes	No
Submit a writ of habeas corpus	Yes	Yes	Yes	Yes	No
Make a statement	Yes	No	Yes	No	No
Request a treatment center	Yes	Yes	Yes	Yes	No

is not surprising to most Americans that our culture, like most others, has rules about the undesirability of certain behavior *in public*. We have outlawed nudity, begging, drinking, elimination of wastes, and intoxication in public places. We are offended by many other acts—if they occur in public. Tramps are booked for public intoxication, but they are often arrested because they urinate, sleep, or drink in some public place. Poverty has made it impossible for them to conceal their behavior behind the walls of a home. The extent of these restrictions upon *public* acts are in contrast to many non-Western societies where there is a wider range of acceptable public behavior. Because public drunkenness, which covers a multitiude of other public sins, involves more arrests each year than any other crime, we may conclude that *privacy* is an important value in our culture.

Above the judge's bench in the criminal court where this study took place, there is a large wooden plaque inscribed "Equal Justice for All Under the Law." Given the laws prohibiting public behavior of various kinds, we might still expect that the punishment for violation would be distributed *equally*. Thus, if two men with the same criminal record are found guilty of the same crime, they should receive the same punishment. If two men are found drunk in public for the first time, it would be unfair to fine one a few dollars and require the other to pay several hundred dollars. Upon examining the penalties given for public drunkenness, we discover a rather startling fact: *the less a man conforms to other American values, the more severe his punishment*—not because he violates other laws, but because he does not conform to the values of *materialism, mor-*

alism, and *work.* These values are the basis for a set of implicit "punishment rules." Although they are unwritten, those who administer justice in our society have learned to punish the drunk offender on the basis of these rules.

Rule 1: *When guilty of public drunkenness, a man deserves greater punishment if he is poor.* In every society, when individuals violate legal norms they are punished. Physical torture, public humiliation, incarceration, and banishment from the society are some of the forms this punishment takes. It is not surprising that in our society, with its emphasis upon the value of material goods, violators are punished by making them give up some form of property. An individual may be fined after he has been convicted of public drunkenness. Most offenders pay money in the form of a "bail" prior to conviction. A few hours after being arrested, most men are able to be released from jail in a sober condition. They are still innocent before the law and an arraignment is scheduled at which time they may plead guilty or not guilty. If they enter the later plea, they must appear in court at another time for a trial. In order to insure that a man returns for his arraignment he is asked to deposit bail money with the court, which will be returned to him when he is sentenced or acquitted. In most courts a man may choose to ignore the arraignment and thereby "forfeit" his bail. It is still within the power of the court to issue a warrant for his arrest in this case and compel him to appear in court, but this is seldom done. Instead, much like bail for a traffic violation, forfeiture of the drunk bail is considered as a just recompense to society for appearing drunk in public.

When arrested, tramps are eager to post bail since it means an immediate release from jail. They do not need to wait for the arraignment which may not occur for several days. The bail is $20 and is almost always forfeited. This system of punishment treats offenders equally—*unless a man does not have $20.*

Those who are caught in the grip of poverty are usually convicted, and their punishment is "doing time" instead of "paying money." In America, the rich have money, the poor have time. It might be possible to punish men equitably using these two different commodities but such is not the case. If a man is poor he must be unwilling to expend his energies in the pursuit of materialism, and therefore his punishment should be more severe than that given to those with money. How does this occur? Each time a man is arrested his bail is always twenty dollars, but if he is indigent, his sentences become longer with each conviction. A man can be arrested hundreds of times and bail out for only twenty dollars, but not if he is poor. Consider the case of one man who was arrested in Seattle over one hundred times during a twenty-one-year period. On many arrests he bailed out, but for about seventy convictions he was sentenced to jail, and gradually his sentenced grew to the maximum of six months for a single arrest. During this period he was sentenced to nearly fourteen years in jail—a punishment he could have avoided for only a hundred dollars for each of those years. This man was given a life sentence on the installment plan, not for being drunk but for being poor. There are many cases where a rich man and a poor man are arrested and booked for drunkenness on the same night. The rich man is released in a few hours because he had twenty dollars. The poor man is released in a few months because he did not have twenty dollars. One way then to beat a drunk charge is to bail out. If you do not have money, it is still possible to use this strategy by bonding out or asking for a continuance. A bond requires some collateral or assurance that the twenty dollars *plus* a fee to the bondsman will be paid. A continuance enables you to wait a few more days before being sentenced, and during that time, it may be possible to get money from a friend or an employer. Whether he can use these ways to beat a drunk charge or not, the tramp who is repeatedly arrested soon learns he is being punished because he does not conform to the value of materialism.

Rule 2: *When guilty of public drunkenness, a man deserves greater punishment if he has a bad reputation.* Most cultures have a moralistic quality that often leads to stereotyping and generalizing about the quality of a man's character. In our society once a person has been convicted of a crime, he is viewed by others with suspicion. He may never violate legal norms again, but for all practical purposes he is morally reprehensible. Since judges increase the length of a man's sentence with each arrest, he must engage in behavior designed to give him a "good record" if he is to beat the drunk charge. One way to do this is by travelling. For example, if a man stayed out of jail in Seattle for six months, subsequent convictions would begin again with short sentences; thus, when arrested several times, he often decided it would be better if he went to another town. When his arrest record began to grow in this new place, he would move on; after a period of time he would return to Seattle. Men learn to calculate the number of "days hanging" for each city where they are arrested, and their mobility is determined by the magnitude of the next sentence. Some men use an alias when arrested in an attempt to obscure the fact that they have a long record. If this ploy is successful, a man who, because of his record, deserves a sentence of six months, may only be given two or three days. Another way to beat a drunk charge is to volunteer to go to an alcoholism treatment center. A man may not believe that he is an alcoholic or even that he has a "drinking problem," but if he will agree with society's judgment—that his long record of arrests shows he is morally debased—and ask to be helped, his incarceration will be reduced. But not all men are candidates for treatment. Those with the worst records are rejected and must do their time in jail. A man with a bad reputation thus will be given a more severe punishment for the same crime than one with a good reputation.

Rule 3: *When guilty of public drunkenness, a man deserves greater punishment if he does not have a steady job.* American culture places great value on work as an end in itself. Resistance to hippies and welfare programs alike is based, in part, on the value of work. Tramps know that judges punish more severely those who do not have steady employment. If a man cannot beat a drunk charge in some other way, he will make a statement telling the judge that he will find a job, return to a former job, or provide evidence that he is currently employed in a respectable occupation. Tramps often earn a living by "junking" to find things to sell, "spot jobbing," or "panhandling" (begging on the street)—but all these "occupations" are not admired in our society and cannot be used as evidence that one is conforming to the value of work. When a man appears in court with evidence that he is working, the judge will often suspend or shorten his sentence.

Tramps who have been unable to beat the drunk charge before being sentenced may capitalize on this value in another way. One man reported that he had written a letter to himself while in jail. The letter appeared to have been written by an employer in another city offering the man a steady job. The inmate asked another man who was being released from jail to carry the letter to that city and mail it from there. When it arrived, he used it to convince the judge that he sould receive an early release in order to accept steady employment. Another inmate, when released from jail, went personally to the judge and pretended to be a contractor; he told him that a man who had worked for him was in jail and he would employ him if he were released. The judge complied with the request, and the two tramps left town together—proud of their achievement, surer than ever that one of the best ways to beat a drunk charge was to understand the value of work in American culture.

The values our culture places upon privacy, materialism, moralism, and work are not the only ones affecting the lives of tramps. These are men who live in a society that holds no place for them. Their life style is offensive to most Americans, and for this reason they are arrested, jailed, and punished by standards that do not apply to the rest of society. In response to these practices they have learned a culture with well-developed plans for survival. They have adopted a nomadic style of life—moving from one urban center to another to maximize their freedom. In spite of their efforts, sooner or later, most tramps find themselves arrested, and it is then that the techniques for beating a drunk charge will be found most useful.

Technology

17 DRIVING TO WORK

Anthony F. C. Wallace

The study of cultural knowledge leads to more than static, structural descriptions of what someone has learned. In Chapter 16 it was shown how information was used to organize behavior to achieve particular goals. In this chapter, Anthony F. C. Wallace discusses more fully the dynamic aspects of cognitive systems. He selects one technical task from our culture and examines the rules, maps, and plans used to accomplish it. Every culture includes a set of recipes or plans for carrying out such technical activities as hunting, fishing, harvesting crops, building houses, navigating rivers, constructing bridges, and cooking meals. A description of any of these activities could be made using the methods which are discussed in this chapter.

Introduction

It was A. I. Hallowell who pointed out to me, when I was a student of his, that cognitive maps were an interesting object of study for an anthropologist. He spoke of "the self" as an object of human awareness, developing along with man's moral capacity in the long reaches of human evolution, and of the unique "behavioral environment" that in each culture man has created for himself by a process of selective attention to his total environment. These ideas were of importance to me in developing the concept of "mazeway," by which I mean the sum of all the cognitive maps which at any moment a person maintains, of self, of behavioral environment, and of those valued experiences or states of being which attract or repel him.

This paper is devoted to an effort to describe in some detail one segment of the mazeway of one individual in one culture. The technical background for the train of thought represented here may be found in several of the

Reprinted with permission of the author and The Macmillan Company from *Context and Meaning in Cultural Anthropology*, Melford E. Spiro, editor. Copyright © 1965 by The Free Press, a Division of The Macmillan Company.

writer's publications (*vide* Wallace: 1961a, 1961b, 1962). But for the documentation of the empirical data to be presented, no informant, no authority can be cited beyond the writer himself. This paper is simply an introspective account in which the anthropologist used himself as his own informant. In it, the informant-anthropologist seeks to describe the cognitive operations he carries out in performing a task which, in a sense, is "required" by the culture in which he lives: driving an automobile from home to work.

For the anthropologist to act as his own informant presents some interesting methodological problems. At first glance, it would appear that the issue is simply one of "introspection" versus objective description of behavior by an "outsider" observer. Introspection, indeed, has little or no value as a source of information about certain sorts of psychological processes, or even about the finer details of processes for which it has some value as an initial method of observation. But, nonetheless, it is unavoidable, and the anthropologist derives a large proportion of his information by the simple procedure of asking an informant to introspect: to say, or write, what he is thinking about a certain subject. Thus for the anthropologist to record, by writing or by dictating, his own throughts about his own culturally relevant behavior involves only a minor difference in method from standard procedure. And, as in this case, when the technique is used as a means of approach to certain theoretical problems, it has the advantage of permitting a high degree of thoroughness of inquiry and of directness of approach to "psychological reality."

But, one may legitimately inquire, would not the faithfulness of recall of a task like driving to work be improved by lessening the time span between actual behavior and introspective recall of that behavior? Would it not be better, for instance, to have the informant dictate to a portable tape recorder while he is carrying out the task? There are two strong reasons why this would be, in balance, positively undesirable. First of all, the purpose of the investigation is not to describe one day's experience, but the mental pattern, the cognitive map, or mazeway, which is the ever-changing product of many days' experiences. Since not all of that mazeway will be evoked by the circumstances of one day, it is evident that only an introspective process can approach the complexity of the mazeway as it exists even on a single day. And second, requiring the informant to "inform" while he is carrying out the task would change the very psychological processes which are the object of description. Memory, for all its well-known fallibility, is at least *a* record of the actual experience; requiring the informant to record data while he is supposedly doing something else would change the experience itself. We have here another instance of the awkward principle of behavioral complementarity, akin to the principle of complementarity in physics, which may be more serious for the behavioral sciences than for the physical.

Thus, the description of the process of driving to work will depend upon the introspective consultation of memory by an anthropologist-informant, sitting at his writing table, recalling patterns of experience in specific activity which he has personally experienced approximately five hundred times.

The Route

The route to work—or at least certain features of it—is displayed in brief in Figure 17:1. The map shows the general compass orientation of the roadway, the turns at intersections or choice points (but not all intersections where the route continues straight ahead), the location of all stop signs and traffic lights, certain environmental landmarks (including origin and destination), and the names of several major roads and highways which

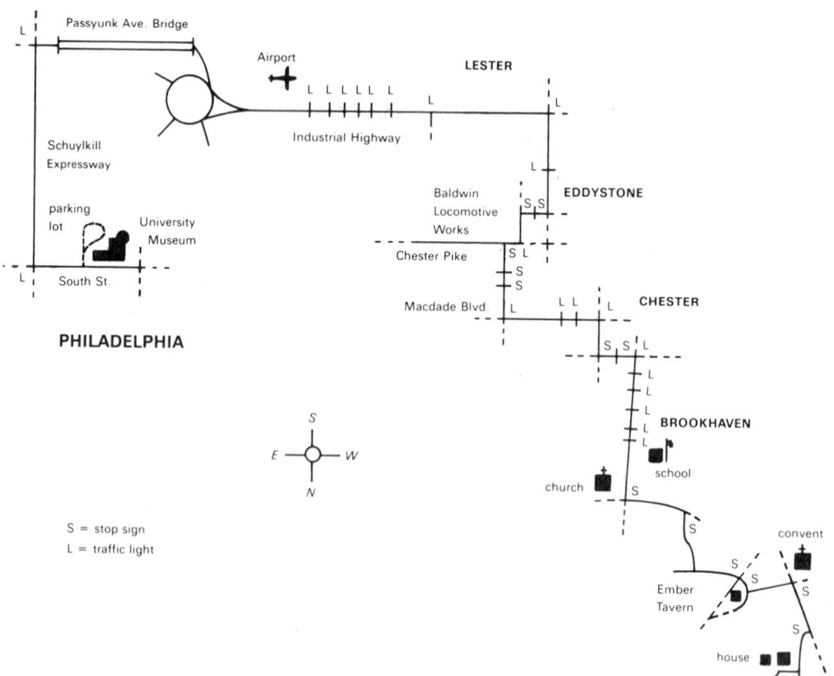

Figure 17:1. Route plan.

are followed for part of the way. The map was drawn from memory on September 15, 1963.[1] The total driving distance is about 17 miles. Any section of it (i.e., any stretch between any pair of turns, stop signs, lights, or landmarks) can be "blown up," in memory, into sufficient detail to characterize the major type of construction, minor landmarks, road surface, and miscellaneous features of approximately 100-foot units of distance. Thus, for instance, the stretch between the first and second traffic lights is a distance of about 300 yards (see Figure 17:2). Although from memory it is not possible for me to list and describe in order every building and every intersecting alley or road, nevertheless the character of the area, its major type of construction, its traffic and parking pattern, and the pedestrian activity to be expected are generally available to recall. Effort to recall this detail mobilizes dozens of specific memories of particular incidents: stopping at the drug store (on the way home) to ask for directions; parking along the highway to let a child off at the school; visiting the shoe store and the bowling alley; stopping for gas at the second gas station; being held up in traffic at the second light behind a car with a torn fan belt, and so on to less vivid, more selective images of past impressions. The possible maximum speed

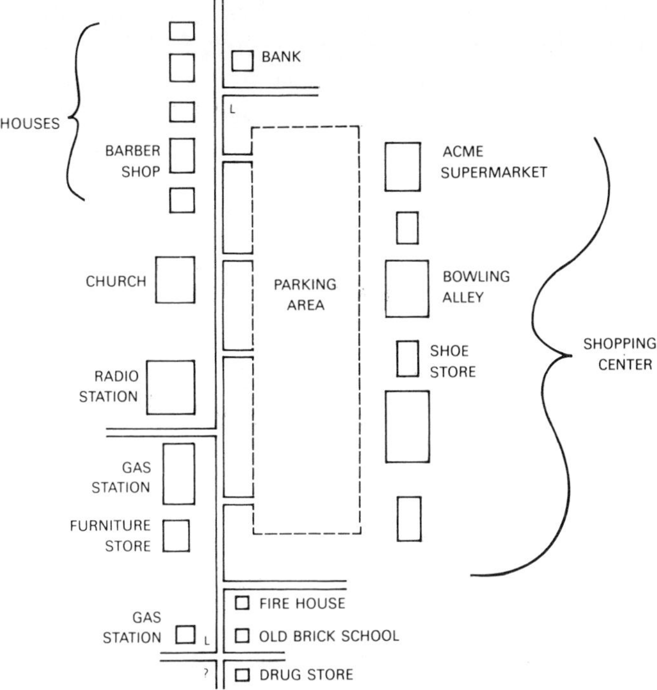

Figure 17:2. Route plan section between first and second traffic lights.

in this area is about 40 miles per hour; the legal limit is 35; one must watch out for children at the drug store and the school, and for cars entering and leaving the shopping area. The pavement is concrete, traffic markings are apt to be arbitrary (cross-walks are now painted Kelly green, for instance, no doubt by an overly zealous police department), and the surface may be slippery when wet—it is an old, smooth, concrete road. Traffic is single lane, although the pavement is wide enough for two lanes in each direction, because of cars and trucks parking or stopping on the right, and because the highway has not been painted for two-lane traffic, thus encouraging drivers to wander slowly between the curb and the center line. This strip is somewhat over-patrolled by police: I was arrested once (going the other way) for passing on the right, but discharged by the magistrate because the traffic markings and signs were misleading; foot-police control traffic at market rush hours. The town has a curfew for teenagers. In general, the atmosphere is one of disorganization in the face of suburban inundation by a neighboring industrial city, with local authorities attempting to control the tide, including traffic, by heavy police coverage. All this dictates cautious driving.

The number of times I have driven this route is on the order of five hundred, spread out over a three-year period. The length of time varies between forty-five minutes, as a minimum, and an hour (barring unusual mishaps, such as car trouble or a traffic jam), as a maximum. Usually the drive is made in the morning, leaving the house between eight-thirty and nine-o'clock, and arriving at work between nine-thirty and ten. Earlier travel tends to run into heavy traffic on the industrial highway when it is crowded by workmen hurrying to get to their plants by eight or eight-thirty. By now, I feel, as the saying goes, that I could drive this road in my sleep.

Driving Rules

There are a number of standard driving rules (what in military jargon used to be called "standard operating procedure" or "SOP") which constitutes a set of instructions for what to do under various circumstances. The rules to which I refer are *my* rules, which may or may not conform to the legal regulations for driving; in general, however, these rules are intended to effect a reasonable compromise between, on the one hand, considerations intended to maximize speed and comfort while driving and, on the other hand, considerations intended to minimize the likelihood of accident or arrest by police. These rules govern the following major matters: the pattern of spatial distance between my car and other objects;

speed; and response to signals and written instructions on, or at the side of the road. The rules are as follows:

Rule 1: Aim car along route, keeping to right side of road and changing direction as required by Route Plan in order to keep car moving along route toward goal, and go as fast as possible consistent with Rule 2.

Rule 2: Do not exceed posted legal speed limits by more than ten miles per hour except in an emergency (e.g., in order to avoid collision, or in order to get a sick person to a hospital).

Rule 3: Obey all traffic signals and written instructions (e.g., traffic lights, stop signs, painted guide lines on road surface, instructions to slow down, emergency slowdown blinkers at obstructions, etc.).

Rule 4: Reduce speed when visibility is poor, road surface is slippery, traffic is heavy, road bends, or in general whenever current speed is greater than that permitting safe driving.

Rule 5: Maintain visual pattern characterized by safe distance between own car and cars proceeding and following, and equal distance between own car and the lane (especially opposing traffic lane) on left and road shoulders (or lane marker) on right.

Rule 6: Pass vehicles proceeding ahead in same direction as own car but more slowly than own car by turning out to left of these vehicles and accelerating; return to original lane when passing is complete.

Rule 7: Use turn signals to indicate major changes in direction of own car.

Rule 8: At all times be able to control the vehicle and to monitor relevant information; if control and information monitoring functions are seen to be nearing a limit of minimal adequacy, slow down and if necessary stop.

Rule 9: Under all circumstances and by any means, including means which violate any of the other rules except Rule 8, avoid collision between own car and other cars, pedestrians, and large objects or obstructions; this implies automatically giving other vehicles the right of way whenever a collision is liable to occur if both own and other vehicle continue in present course.

While each of the terms included in these nine rules can be given further definition, to spell out the meaning of all terms would be a long and tedious task and will not be attempted here. Suffice it to say that there are criteria for judging whether or not visibility is "poor," traffic is "heavy," etc. (Rule 4); whether a distance is "safe" (Rule 5); whether, because of speed, the condition of the car, or whatever, one is approaching a point of no control of the vehicle (Rule 8); whether, in general, a specific operation must be performed in order to follow the route plan and to remain in compliance with the rules.

Operations

In order to travel along the route from home to work, and to follow the driving rules, I must perform various operations. These involve, in general, two kinds of activity: moving various parts of the car in order to control its motion; and moving various parts of the car, or my own position in the car, in order to maintain myself in a comfortable condition for driving.

Control of Direction and Speed of the Automobile—The automobile which I am describing is a 1962 Volkswagen. It has twelve mechanical controls which must be adjusted in order to direct the car safely, legally, and efficiently in a given direction, at the appropriate acceleration, and at the optimal velocity, in conformity with the Driving Rules. These controls are: the ignition switch; the steering wheel; the clutch pedal; the brake pedal; the accelerator pedal; the gearshift; the horn; the emergency brake; the headlight switch; the headlight beam control; the turn signal; and the windshield wiper. The ignition switch starts and stops the motor. It is managed by the left hand and turns "on" clockwise a quarter turn; if the car stalls, the switch must be turned counterclockwise first, and then clockwise, in order to start again. The steering wheel, which faces the seated driver at chest height, is normally grasped by both hands; turning it clockwise turns the car right, turning it counterclockwise turns the car to the left; in a central position the car moves straight ahead. It can normally be turned, or held steady, by one hand. The "settings" are not marked and the correct position must be judged by the directional movement of the car. The steering wheel must be held in the correct position by one or both hands at all times, and minor adjustments in its position must be made almost continuously—at least once every second or two on the average—in order to correct drift caused by wind, irregularities in the road surface, or slight error in the previous wheel setting. Major movements, involving turns of the wheel of 90% amplitude or more, in order to avoid obstacles and follow turns in the route, generally require the use of both hands. The accelerator pedal is pressed down with the right foot in order to make the motor go faster; when the foot is off the pedal, or resting so lightly that the pedal is not depressed, the motor idles at a minimum speed. The speed of the car can be increased by stepping on the accelerator pedal; it can be decreased, at a low negative acceleration, by reducing the pressure on the accelerator pedal. The brake pedal is also controlled by the right foot; it slows down the car, when in motion, and prevents it from moving when it is stopped. Because both the accelerator and the brake are managed by the right foot, it is not possible (without an awkward movement of the left foot) to operate so as to increase motor speed and to brake the car at the same time. The clutch pedal is managed by the left foot; when it is depressed, it is possible to operate the gear shift so as to connect the rear wheels with the motor in one or another gear position. The gear shift is operated by the right hand. There are six positions: neutral, in which the motor does not drive the wheels; reverse, in which the motor drives the car backward; and four forward-driving postions, within approximate velocity ranges: respectively, 0–20, 10–30, 20–50, and 30 to the maximum speed of about 85 miles per hour. The gear shift can be moved from any position to any other, provided the clutch pedal is depressed and the velocity of the car is within shifting range. The horn ring is located inside the circumference of the steering wheel and sounds when pressed by either hand. The emergency brake, for use when the foot brake fails or (more usually) to hold the car when it is stopped or parked, is operated by the right hand; pulling up the lever from a horizontal position sets the brake, letting it drop releases the brake. In order to let the lever drop, a button in the end must be pressed by the thumb. A switch on the instrument panel controls the outside lights. It is managed by the right hand; pulling it out one notch lights the front and rear parking lights (used, actually, most often for driving in twilight); the second notch sets the headlights on, for driving at night; and rotating the knob brightens or dims the light on the instrument panel. The button on the floor near the left foot sets the headlights to high-beam or low-beam; stepping on it shifts the beam from high to low or low to high, depending on where the beam is set at the moment. The outside turn signals are turned on to indicate a right or left turn by moving a lever on the steering column, below the wheel, with the left hand; clockwise a few degrees for a right turn, counterclockwise for a left turn. Finally, the windshield wiper, for driving in rain, snow, or mist, is located on the instrument panel and is operated by pulling by the right hand.

The twelve major controls are thus managed by four limbs. The steering wheel and the horn are managed by both hands, or either one. Of the other nine, two are managed by the left foot (clutch and headlight beam button); two by the right foot (accelerator and brake); two by the left hand (ignition switch and turn signal); and four by the right hand (gearshift, lights, windshield wiper, emergency brake). Evidently the right limbs are given both more, and more responsible, assignments than the left; the three controls of critical importance to safety are all handled, optionally or exclusively, by the right side of the body (steering wheel, brake, and accelerator).

Control of Comfort and Convenience—In addition to the twelve critical direction-and-speed control devices, there are thirteen others (or rather, thirteen classes of others) which the driver operates to maximize his comfort and convenience while driving. These do not require the continuous high-priority attention given to the first twelve; they are apt to be adjusted before, or in the early part of the trip, and then are given occasional attention during relaxed stretches when critical decisions are occurring with minimal frequency. These comfort-and-convenience devices are: the sun visors (two); the rear-view mirrors (two: one inside and one outside); the window open-shut controls (four); seat position levers (two); dome light switch (one switch with three positions); the heater valve handle (a wheel); the ventilator controls (four); cigarette lighter; radio (six); clock (one wheel control); and antifogging cloth. Of these twenty-five discrete devices, nineteen can be managed by the driver while driving: one by the left foot; five by the left hand; and thirteen by the right hand. These controls in general can be said to be important, without being critical, because they enable the driver to maintain an uninterrupted flow of information via windows, mirrors, sun visors, and antifogging cloth; keep him from being too hot or too cold (ventilators and heat valve); permit him to select the least fatiguing posture (seat position); and make it easier and safer to light cigarettes (electric lighter).

The controls in both groups, with a few exceptions, operate by simple motions: pushing, pulling, releasing, and rotating. The electric controls tend to be of a binary, on-off type; the mechanical controls tend to have continuous settings, so that the precise position has to be selected by estimation and corrected from feed-back information. Nine permit, or require, heavy muscular effort except, occasionally, the brakes. And no more than three, in addition to the steering wheel, can be manipulated at the same time.

Monitoring

I make decisions as to which control to operate, and how, in order to follow the Route Plan in conformity with the Driving Rules, on the basis of a continuous influx of information. This information is gathered via many sensory modalities: sight, sound, smell, temperature, pressure (measuring acceleration and deceleration), equilibrium (measuring angular momentum and slope), internal situations of various kinds. In general, for routine decisions, sight is the principal modality and sound a somewhat distant second; but in extreme emergency, or in case of trouble with the car itself, sound and the other modalities may become as important as sight. We may classify the data monitored into three regions of origin: the space outside the car; the car itself; and the driver.

The Space outside the Car—From outside the car, by sight and sound, I acquire a great deal of information which is relevant to decisions concerning the operation of the vehicle. Most obviously, of course, I keep my eye on the road almost all of the time, matching its course with the configurations of the cognitive map of the route, and turning, slowing down, speeding up, and so forth, as I recognize successive points for which standard instructions are provided by the map itself. I constantly check the road for vehicles: vehicles ahead, vehicles behind, vehicles approaching on the other lane, vehicles which may be entering my traffic lane, vehicles parked beside the lane. I check for bicyclists, for pedestrians, for animals, and for obstructions like slow-moving vehicles, excavations, accidents, and so on; for traffic lights, official instructions in signs, flares, and painted road markings. I monitor the state of the road with respect to its width, the condition of the surface (dry, wet, snow, ice, leaves), its physical smoothness (ripples, pot-holes, etc.), the condition of the shoulders, its composition (concrete, asphalt of various kinds, gravel, wind, etc.), its grade. I note the wind conditions and I monitor the efficiency of the monitoring itself, noting the lighting conditions outside (dawn, dark, bright, cloudy, foggy, rainy, snowy), the clearness of vision through the windows, the noise level from wind, air turbulence, machinery, and other sources.

The Car Itself—Within the car, there are certain instruments which must be checked from time to time, changes in the reading of which indicate the need for control operation. These include the speedometer, the gasoline gauge, the oil pressure light (which shines green when pressure is low), the generator light (which shines red when the generator is not charging the battery), the clock, and the odometer (mileage indicator). Any variation in the sound of the motor from the expected pattern; the smell of gasoline, of burning rubber, of burning electrical insulation or cloth; unusual vibration in the body; a constant pulling or swaying of the car unaccountable by wind or road conditions: all of these indicate probable trouble with motor, gasoline supply, brakes, or tires. And, of course, I must monitor the current setting of the control devices in order to know what action to take in response to information.

The Driver—I, the driver, must also monitor my own state. I must recognize sleepiness, undue fatigue, slow reaction time, distracting pain or discomfort, any difficulty with any of my own sensory equipment, and any motivational state which is prompting me to such behavior as excessive speed, excessive caution, irritability, competitiveness with other drivers, or inattention, any one of which may interfere with efficient driving.

Attention Control

The nature of the monitoring activity in general seems to me to involve several principles in the control of attention which are, insofar as they are applied to driving, the product of experience rather than of explicit instruction. One of these principles is the control of the angle of the cone of visual attention. When driving routinely, the attention is scattered over a wide visual field, shaped like a cone with perhaps 120° of arc from side to side, and covering a considerable distance ahead of the car—where visibility is unhampered, perhaps a quarter of a mile. When, however, data are available to indicate that a decision has to be made on the basis of further information as the situation develops, an "alert" instruction is invoked and the cone of attention is narrowed to an acute angle of perhaps 10° of arc, so that the other data are relegated to the periphery of consciousness. Such a condition will occur if, for instance, a car suddenly appears at a side street, a hundred yards ahead. Will it stop? Attention focuses on that car, in order to glean all possible data relevant to the decision on whether or not to slow down, turn, stop, or sound horn.

Another feature of attention control is the way in which it is distributed over the various control devices inside the car, and over the various regions and types of data monitored. Some parts of the system function almost autonomously and will continue to function satisfactorily even when conscious attention is directed elsewhere. This is particularly true with respect to the subsystem of visual extravehicular data, responsive control of the steering wheel, and maintenance of all other controls at "steady." This system can, as it were, be forgotten and, as long as no disturbance of routine driving occurs, be left to operate by itself while attention is devoted to other monitoring data and controls, or to thinking about other matters: a paper one is writing, a problem at home or at the office, or whatever. Furthermore, most of the stream of monitored data, although it is being received and processed, leads to no executive action at all; the process of sensory intake and semantic evaluation of the data occurs without consciousness. Only when its nature suddenly invokes an executive responsibility does one become conscious of it. Thus the sound of the motor is constantly being funneled into the ear; but only when the motor begins to miss, or clank, or whine, or whatever, does conscious attention suddenly focus on it. The process is similar to that in the well-trained radio operator who can sleep soundly beside his open receiver, ignoring all the radio traffic until his own call letters are transmitted; he wakes up suddenly and completely as soon as these come over the air.

A third feature of attention control might be referred to as a cyclical ranging of conscious attention. "Every so often" I check the speed by glancing at the speedometer rather than by simply assessing the revolutions per second of the motor from its sound; I check the rear-view mirror for following traffic, and look to the left for cars on the left, particularly in the blind spot over the left shoulder; I note the time; check the gasoline gauge. This flickering passage of conscious attention over various types of monitored data supplements the nonconscious readiness to respond to certain cues by directing attention to these sources of data which cannot be judged accurately without conscious attention, which require additional data, or which fall outside the cone of visual observation. The rate of this ranging would be difficult to estimate; I would guess that every second or two, for a fraction of a second, conscious attention shifts from a stream of conscious thinking or talking about nondriving matters to monitor some datum or other, and among these flickers of attention, every twenty or thirty seconds, the ranging process turns on.

Organization

The simplest model of how this total process operates is to consider the driver as a cybernetic machine. Diagrammatically, one might represent the system as follows (see Fig. 17:3):

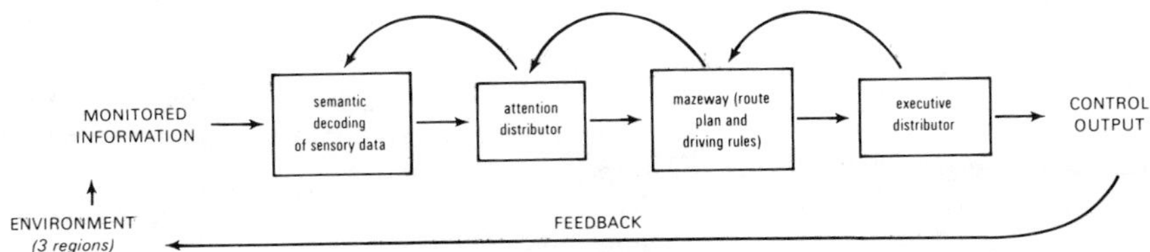

Figure 17:3. Mazeway functions in information-and-control system for driving.

This diagram does not, of course, adequately reflect the complexity of the system of information and control. Some minimum estimate of this complexity is implicit in the simple enumeration of the classes of monitored data which must be meshed with the classes of control responses. At any choice point in the route—such as a traffic light—data from all three regions of information must be screened. The observed combination defines the current situation as one of several types, corresponding to which is one combination of the several possible control responses. That one response combination must be the out-put. The control responses, which are fewer in number, may be analyzed first.

Let us assume that at route choice points, only major responses involving one or more of the twelve primary controls are allowed. The recognition that the situation involves a route choice point may be regarded as Phase 1. The initial response to this recognition is an alerting function, in which Mazeway instructs Attention Distributor to scan for data relevant to major response. Phase 2 involves the selective scanning of the monitored data, according to a setting of the Attention Distributor; the recognition of the situation as belonging to situation type such-and-such (defined according to criteria selected for attention) by Mazeway; and the selection of response type so-and-so, onto which the situation type maps according to instructions from Mazeway.

With respect to route choice points, data concerning the interior state of the car and the condition of the driver must be considered temporarily irrelevant. Certain aspects of the space outside the car are relevant, however. Let us say that the immediate dimension of importance, and the one which alerted the driver, is approach to a traffic light. The outside-of-car dimensions and values listed in Table 17:1 are relevant and must be scanned consciously:

TABLE 17:1. *Outside-of-Car Dimensions*

	Dimension	*Values*
A.	Traffic light	a_1 red; a_2 yellow; a_3 green
B.	Route direction	b_1 turns right; b_2 straight; b_3 turns left
C.	Traffic (preceding)	c_1 no car in front; c_2 car in front too close; c_3 car in front distance safe
D.	Traffic (following)	d_1 no car following; d_2 car following too close; d_3 car following distance safe
E.	Road surface	e_1 slippery; e_2 normal
F.	Cross traffic	f_1 object entering from right; f_2 no object entering from right
G.	Closeness of light	g_1 within stopping distance at current speed; g_2 not within stopping distance at current speed

The matrix of possible states of the system resulting from the combination of these criteria contains 3×3×3×2×2, or 216 cells. The possible combinations of action at such a choice point, however, are more limited. Ignition switch, clutch pedal, gearshift, emergency brake, headlight switch, turn signal, and windshield wiper may be considered temporarily irrelevant. The control operations listed in Table 17:2—again defined as dimensions and values—are relevant:

TABLE 17:2. *Control Operations*

	Dimension	*Values*
V.	Steering wheel	v_1 turn left; v_2 hold steady; v_3 turn right
W.	Accelerator	w_1 press; w_2 release
X.	Brake	x_1 press; x_2 release
Y.	Horn	y_1 press; y_2 do not press
Z.	Clutch	z_1 press; z_2 do not press

There are, thus, no more than $3 \times 2 \times 2 \times 2 \times 2$ or 48 combinations of actions each to be considered as a unitary response. But, as a matter of fact, there are fewer than this, because the combination $w_1\ x_2$ is impossible (not absolutely impossible, but nearly so, for the left foot has standing instructions not to touch the brake) so that the number reduces to 24.

Now we can see that the large matrix of situations, under the alerting rubric *traffic light,* which is on the order of 216, is mapped onto a much smaller matrix of outputs, on the order of 24. But we also must recognize that the defining of the situation must be performed repeatedly, at intervals of time considerably less than a second, because the situation changes as a result of the motion of the car, the (possibly) changing setting of the traffic light, movement of traffic and the action of the driver on the controls.

Now a sequence of events comparable to the one just illustrated is initiated whenever the monitoring system receives a signal which means "choice to be made." The map of route (Figure 17:1) illustrates major classes of choice points: traffic lights; stop signs; turns from one road or street onto another; start of journey; end of journey. The foregoing list of classes of data to be monitored includes as a minimum some 29 dimensions of relevance to the 24-cell accelerate-slow-down-stop matrix previously listed. But the complexity of the whole system—whose measure reaches very large numbers indeed, when one includes all the second-order dimensions relevant to comfort, convenience, and the maintenance of the car itself—is made manageable by two factors: first, its division into a hierarchical, branching taxonomy of situations and responses, governed by the Driving Rules; and second, by the serial invocation of parts of the taxonomy according to the actual situation revealed by the monitoring process. Thus the actual behavior sequence, following the general TOTE model of Miller, Galanter, and Pribram (1960) (where T represents the information input selected by the attention distributor and O the control response output), must resemble the following (in which we add the symbol A for the Alert Signal to invoke a particular subsection of the monitoring matrix):

A_1	O_1					T_2						
a_1	v_2	w_2	x_2	y_1	z_2	a_1	b_2	c_1	d_2	e_2	f_2	g_1
T_2							O_3					
a_1	b_2	c_1	d_2	e_2	f_2	g_1	v_2	w_2	x_1	y_1	z_1	
T_n							O_n					A_2
a_1	b_2	c_1	d_2	e_2	f_2	g_1	v_2	w_2	x_1	y_1	z_1	a_3

From this standpoint, indeed, it would appear that what I have been referring to as "The Mazeway" can in part be regarded as an extremely large system of related monitoring and operation taxonomies, matching portions of which are invoked serially (and to a lesser extent simultaneously, where several systems are operating at the same time) at fraction-of-a-second intervals. Higher order codings, such as the alerting and motivational or value signals, are contained in the Route Plan and Driving Rules, and serve to "switch on" or "alert" the portion of the taxonomy relevant to the task at hand. The magnitude of the total logical net is, of course, very large indeed; but the size of the monitoring and operational segments in use at any one time is very much smaller.

The possibility, of course, does exist that situations can develop whose relevant defining matrices are extremely large, too large for convenient and rapid matching with the appropriate response matrices, and the result in such cases should be confusion, indecision, and possibly disaster. As we all know, such disasters do occur.

Conclusion

In the foregoing passages, I have attempted to delineate in some detail the system of cognitive maps—or portion of mazeway—which I, as one informant, use in driving to work. It is a minimal description, in the sense that not only are there, probably, additional categories to be added at the level of analysis which I have been using, but also other categories, both more abstract cover categories and less abstract subordinate categories, which have not been mentioned. Nonetheless, this statement does describe, with reasonable adequacy I feel, a portion of mazeway of a kind which it is necessary for a person now in my society to learn, maintain, and use in order to drive himself to work. Thus I have been describing also a piece of culture.

I have also been interested in questions of the magnitude of the logical complexity of culturally institutionalized tasks (see Wallace: 1961b). The exploration of this one technical operation, which involves only a moderate degree of skill and experience for its successful performance, suggests that there is a class of technical tasks in which the complexity of definitions of the situation exceeds the complexity of the available response repertoire. In the case used for illustration, for instance, we can observe a scale of complexity somewhat as follows (see Table 17:3):

TABLE 17:3. *Orders of Complexity*

Category	*Complexity*
Matrix of sensory input	Maximal
Matrix of sensory input attended to	
Matrix of conscious attention	
Matrix of definition of situation	
Matrix of available responses	Minimal

The matrix of responses made available under the particular alerting signal used in the illustration is well within the 2^6 rule discussed in an earlier paper (Wallace: 1961b), but the matrix of definitions of the situation is much larger, on the order of 2^{10}. While obviously arithmetic observations based only on a single example intended to illustrate the probable form of a general process cannot be offered as quantitative evidence, they may be of interest in suggesting that the human organism is more restricted in the complexity of its pattern of output of meaningful behavior than in the complexity of the pattern of meaningful perception. This is certainly true of individual neurons, which can receive and discriminate within a complex pattern of stimuli, but can only respond dichotomously, by firing or not firing. Perhaps a similar process occurs in mazeway and, therefore, in culture, namely, that far more subtle perceptions of situations are possible for men than their available neurological, muscular, and technical apparatus can permit them to recognize in response.

Finally, it may be suggested that the model employed for describing this mazeway segment may be more generally useful in formulating psychologically real, cultural descriptions of technological tasks. The model for driving to work involves five categories of descriptions and analysis: Route Plan (the specification of the origin state, destination state, and intervening transitional states at which instrumental choices must be made); Driving Rules (the specification of general rules for making choices among alternative actions); Control Operations (the specification of the minimal behavioral responses available to the actor); Monitored Information (the specification of the types of data relevant to choice of response); and Organization (the pattern of interpretation employed in relating data to action). Those categories may, more generally, be labeled as Action Plan; Action Rules; Control Operations; Monitored Information; and Organization. This model should be adequate to describe such technical tasks (including physical action) as transportation, manufacture, hunting, warfare, and the like. Whether a homologous frame of analysis would be applicable to behavior in social organization remains to be seen.

Notes

1. I checked the Route Plan for accuracy after drawing it from memory. Two too few lights were inserted in the industrial highway sequence; one too many in the Brookhaven segment.

References

MILLER, G. A., GALANTER, E., and PRIBRAM, K. H.
1960: *Plans and the Structure of Behavior* (New York: Holt).

Kinship

18 COMPONENTIAL ANALYSIS

Ward H. Goodenough

In every society children are quite successful at learning cultural knowledge. One of the first things acquired is a set of categories for classifying kinsmen. This occurs with little conscious awareness that learning is taking place. Seldom can a child, or an adult for that matter, make explicit what goes on. A major premise of ethnoscience is that the investigator is in much the same position as the child, in that he must learn what adult members of a community have learned. In addition he would make this a conscious exercise that can be clearly communicated to his colleagues. Goodenough elaborates on this premise and proposes that componential analysis is a general method for making explicit what children learn. He demonstrates the effectiveness of this method by analyzing one set of kinship terms, and he discusses some of the theoretical issues which have emerged from the application of this method by anthropologists.—EDITOR'S NOTE

What does a person need to have learned if he is to understand events in a strange community as its members understand them and if he is to conduct himself in ways that they accept as conforming to their expectations of one another? To describe the content of such a body of knowledge is to describe a community's culture, according to one of the several meanings anthropologists give this term.

As crucial as such description is, for anthropology and for behavioral science generally, systematic methods for accomplishing it have been slow to develop. Since 1950, however, anthropologists in the United States have been giving greater attention to the methodological problems involved and to their theoretical implications.

To describe a community's culture, in the above sense of the term, one must learn what people in the community have had to learn. To do this, one cannot and need not directly experience everything they have experienced from childhood on up, but one must participate as fully as possible in

Reproduced from *Science*, vol. 156, no. 3779 (June 2, 1967), pp. 1203–1209, by permission of the author and the publisher.

their activities, and one must learn how to communicate with them in their own language. Participation and communication are the channels through which every man learns his native culture, and any other culture. Anthropologists must learn in the same way. But they cannot just leave it at that, unselfconsciously and largely subconsciously acquiring a subjective feel for the rules of the game and for what it is their informants mean by the things they say. If they are to judge the reliability of one another's work, they must develop methods for making cultural learning a conscious exercise and for converting the product of this learning, which for other men is largely a subjective matter, into something that can be an object of scrutiny.

Inspiration to meet the challenge this poses has come largely from the accomplishments of linguistic science. Linguists are able to produce elegant and accurate representations of what one has to know in phonology and grammar if one is to speak particular languages acceptably by native standards. Their procedures enable them to replicate one another's work readily. Application of the basic strategies of descriptive linguistics to the problem of describing other facets of culture is helping to raise the standards of rigor in ethnographic description. These strategies include what is best described as contrastive analysis. Its use for describing how people classify phenomena, insofar as their classifications are reflected in the vocabulary of their language, has led to the analytic method described here (*1–3*.)

The categorizations of phenomena and events (the inventory of ideas) by which a community's members deal with one another and with their surroundings, and which are a major part of their culture, are represented largely, though far from completely, by the words and expressions in their language. People learn what these ideas are through the contextual associations they make with the words and expressions that signify the ideas. A child, for example, seems to form an idea of what *hot, car, love,* and *God* signify from the experiences he associates with their use, abstracting from these experiences a subjective feel for what others signify by these words. He tests its correctness as he uses the words himself, modifying his feel for what they signify until his own use of them corresponds closely enough with other people's use of them for most communication purposes. In this way he learns what he must know if the speech of his fellows is to be intelligible to him, and what he must use to guide his own speech if it is to be intelligible to others. In my own experience, much of my learning of other languages and cultures has followed a similar course. To me, the conclusion seems inescapable that reliable description of other cultures requires us to make this learning process an explicit part of ethnographic method and to try to develop canons for its systematic exploitation. Componential analysis is a method of descriptive semantics designed for this purpose.

To illustrate the method, I confine myself to kinship terminologies. Vocabulary for other kinds of subject matter is also amenable to analysis by this method, to judge from work by Conklin, Frake, and Haugen (*4*, *5*). But it is with kinship terminology that the method has been mainly explored (*1*, *6*)—among other reasons, because the long history of anthropological concern with kinship study has produced a reasonably satisfactory notation for handling kinship data and has also produced a preliminary sorting-out of some of the conceptual criteria that seem to be operative in many kinship terminologies.

Componential Analysis and Descriptive Semantics

Following Morris (*7*), we may say that a linguistic expression *designates* a class of concepts; it *denotes* a specific image or subclass of images within the class on any one occasion of its use; and it *signifies* the criteria by which specific images or concepts are to be included or excluded from the class of images or concepts that the expression designates. What are signified, then, are the definitive attributes of the class, the ideational components out of which the class is formed. An expression *connotes* other images or concepts that people associate with the expression's designatum, and from them people orient themselves affectively and behaviorally; but these connoted images or concepts are not themselves definitive attributes of the designated class. People may agree closely on the definitive attributes—on what is signified—yet disagree markedly on what is connoted or implied.

Componential analysis deals only with signification—with definitive attributes and the ways in which they combine and are mutually ordered (*8*). It differs, therefore, from most other approaches to semantic analysis, which focus on connotation—the "semantic differential" technique of Osgood (*9*), for example. Behavioral and social scientists have been concerned mainly with problems in which connotation is the more immediately relevant kind of meaning. But signification is even more fundamental, for we can understand what a word signifies without reference to what it connotes, but we cannot understand what it connotes without reference to its signification. (This is true for a given point in time only, for, through time, connotation can cause changes in signification.)

The first step in componential analysis is to make a record of the specific images or concepts that informants say an expression may denote. This requires that we already have a metalanguage, or language of description, for recording the denotata. (For many subject matters no adequate metalanguage as yet exists.) The next step is to find a set of definitive attributes that will predict what informants say may and may not be denoted by the expression. We do this by a combination of two operations: (i) inspecting the set of denotata for common attributes and (ii) contrasting the set of the expression's denotata with sets of denotata of other expressions. The latter is the more crucial operation.

The English kinship term *aunt*, as used in much of New England, provides an example. We would list for it such denotata as mother's sister, father's sister, mother's or father's half-sister, mother's brother's (or half-brother's) wife, father's brother's (or half-brother's) wife. By performing the two operations indicated, we might arrive at the following componential definition of what *aunt* signifies: Any relative by blood or marriage who is simultaneously (i) female, (ii) removed from ego by two degrees of genealogical distance, (iii) not lineal, (iv) in a senior generation, and (v) not connected by a marital tie in other than the senior generation of the relationship.

In this way the several disjunctive denotata have been brought together in a conjunctive set and form a unitary class described as a product of the combination of several definitive attributes. That the attributes serve as definitive attributes in this case is evident from our observing that varying any one of them results in a judgment that *aunt* is impermissible as a term of reference. Vary attribute i above (the relative's sex), and *uncle* becomes the appropriate term. *Great aunt* becomes appropriate if we vary ii; *grandmother*, if we vary iii; *niece*, if we vary iv; and *wife's aunt* or *husband's aunt*, if we vary v. In this way it is possible to verify the adequacy of a componential definition.

This example illustrates something else. The definitive attributes forming the significatum of *aunt* are values of conceptual variables whose other values form the significata of other terms. To have to use five different variables in a componential definition of *aunt* may not seem to offer any advantage, from the standpoint of our understanding, over use of the short exhaustive list of denotata. But if the same variables will account for a large number of English terms, there is considerable advantage to be gained from componential definitions. These definitions not only describe the significata of single words, they also show how the significata of different words may be related to one another so as to form an ordered array, a taxonomy in the strict sense of the term.

In the case of *aunt*, *uncle*, *nephew*, *niece*, and so on, the respective significata differ as functions of the common set of defining variables. The respective designata, moreover, are mutually exclusive and complementary. We seem to be dealing with some kind of conceptual or ideal space (call it a genealogical one) that has been partitioned into cells by a set of defining variables, each cell being represented by a linguistic label. All the linguistic labels designating the complementary cells of a conceptual space (or domain, as it is frequently called) form a kind of ordered array or terminological system, one in which the significatum of each label is what makes its designatum different from the designata of the other labels.

The cells of such a conceptual space may be grouped in larger divisions that are also labeled, as the designata of *father* and *mother* are grouped under the label *parent*. An ordered array may include many such cover terms. It may omit them entirely, too, just as English lacks a cover term for the combined designata of *aunt* and *uncle*. The designata of *father* and *mother*, being complementary, are at the same level of contrast. They do not complement the designatum of *parent*, however, but nest within it, just as the designata of *collie*, *dog*, *mammal*, and *vertebrate* nest successively each within the next. They are at different levels of contrast.

Such nesting and complementary relationships among the significata of words are obvious to speakers of English in English examples, but they seem to characterize considerable portions of the vocabulary in every language. Componential analysis helps us to determine, in unfamiliar languages, what words go together in ordered arrays and how their designata are structurally ordered within them. It helps us to avoid arbitrarily sorting words into the conceptual domains of English on the basis of rough translations, or glosses. Thus, componential analysis enabled Frake, in his account of the Subanun religion (*5*), to avoid the mistake of classing together different beings that, by English criteria, would all be "supernatural," and to demonstrate the necessity of a different classification.

Analysis of Lapp Kinship Terms

To illustrate the procedures of componential analysis, I use the following list of Könkämä Lapp kinship terms for designating blood kin (*10*). (No term denoting a blood relationship can also denote a relationship by marriage, according to Könkämä Lapp usage.) The numbers in parentheses in the definitions in the list refer to the numbered relationships of the list.

1) *aččе*, father
2) *aedne*, mother
3) *bardne*, son
4) *nieidã*, daughter
5) *vielljã*, brother
6) *oabba*, sister

7) *vilj-baelle*, any male blood relative in ego's generation except brother (5)

8) *oam-baelle*, any female blood relative in ego's generation except sister (6)

9) *akke*, father's older brother or father's older male blood relative in his generation

10) *akket*, child of a man's younger brother or child of any other younger male blood relative of a man in his generation

11) *čaecce*, father's younger brother or father's other younger male blood relative in his generation

12) *čaeccet*, child of a man's older brother or child of any other older male blood relative of a man in his generation

13) *goaske*, mother's older sister or mother's other older female blood relative in her generation

14) *goasket*, child of a woman's younger sister or child of any other younger female blood relative of a woman in her generation

15) *muossa*, mother's younger sister or mother's other younger female blood relative in her generation

16) *muossãl*, child of a woman's older sister or child of any other older female blood relative of a woman in her generation

17) *siessa*, father's sister or father's other female blood relative in his generation

18) *siessãl*, child of a woman's brother or child of any other male blood relative of a woman in her generation

19) *aeno*, mother's brother or mother's other male blood relative in her generation

20) *naeppe*, child of a man's sister or child of any other female blood relative of a man in his generation

21) *aggja*, grandfather or any male blood relative in his generation

22) *aggjot*, man's grandchild or any blood relative of a man in his grandchild's generation

23) *akko*, grandmother or any female blood relative in her generation

24) *akkot*, woman's grandchild or any blood relative of a woman in her grandchild's generation

First, we sort the terms into reciprocal (rec.) sets, obtaining the following (with reference to the numbers in the foregoing list):

a) 1, 2 rec. 3, 4	*e*) 11 rec. 12	*i*) 19 rec. 20
b) 5, 6 rec. 5, 6	*f*) 13 rec. 14	*j*) 21 rec. 22
c) 7, 8 rec. 7, 8	*g*) 15 rec. 16	*k*) 23 rec. 24
d) 9 rec. 10	*h*) 17 rec. 18	

This reduces the corpus of 24 kinship terms to 11 reciprocal relationships. Analysis will concentrate on the criteria that discriminate among these relationships, then on the criteria that discriminate among the terms within the relationships.

Reciprocal sets *a* through *c* differ in composition from sets *d* through *k*, the former having pairs of terms on each side of the reciprocal equation, the latter having one term only on each side. Sets *b* and *c* differ from set *a* and sets *d* through *k*, moreover, in that the former are self-reciprocating whereas the others are not. Inspection reveals that, in relationships *b* and *c*, "ego" and "alter" are always in the same generation but that in the other relationships they are always in different generations. For the moment, then, we have, as a discriminant variable,

A) Similarity of generation of ego and alter, with the values
  A.1) Ego and alter in the same generation (sets *b*, *c*)
  A.2) Ego and alter in different generations (set *a* and sets *d*–*k*)

Sets *b* and *c* differ in that, in *b*, ego and alter are in the closest possible genealogical relationship, whereas, in *c*, they are in other than the closest possible relationship. This distinction also serves to discriminate set *a* from sets *d* through *k;* it groups sets *a* and *b* together, in contrast to sets *c* through *k*. Thus we have a second discriminant variable,

B) Closeness of relationship between ego and alter, with the values
  B.1) Ego and alter in closest possible relationship (*a*, *b*)
  B.2) Ego and alter not in closest possible relationship (*c*–*k*)

It is not evident from the data presented here that, in the larger corpus of Könkämä Lapp kinship terms, the two sets *a* and *b* (terms 1 through 6) are a unit of reference for deriving other terms and discriminating among still others, much as the English terms *father, mother, son, daughter, brother, sister* are collectively a unit of reference for deriving terms with the prefix *step-* and the suffix *-in-law* (which are not regularly used with any other English kinship terms). Sets *a* and *b*, therefore, stand together as a larger unit whose integrity must be maintained in whatever paradigm we construct for this taxonomic array, just as the integrity of reciprocal sets as natural units within the data must also be maintained.

There remains the necessity of differentiating the several reciprocal sets *d* through *k*. Are there any intrinsic groupings we can discern here? Sets *d* through *i* denote relationships in which ego and alter are always one generation apart, while sets *j* and *k* denote relationships in which ego and alter are always two generations distant. This gives us the discriminant variable

C) Number of generations between ego and alter, with the values
   C.1) Ego and alter one generation distant (*d–i*)
   C.2) Ego and alter two generations distant (*j, k*)

In set *a*, ego and alter are also one generation apart, and in sets *b* and *c*, ego and alter are in the same generation. Could we not add zero distance to the values listed above for variable C and eliminate variable A as redundant? For the portion of Lapp terminology analyzed here we can, indeed, do so; but among the affinal terms, some denote relationships in which alter is never in ego's generation but may be either one or two generations distant. This makes variables A and C both necessary in the larger array of terms, A having a universal application and C a more limited one.

Sets *d* through *i* fall into two natural groups. In one the age of the senior party relative to the age of the linking parent of the junior party is a discriminating factor (sets *d* through *g*), but in the other (*h, i*) it is not. What makes these two groups different seems to be the similarity of sex of the senior party and the sex of the linking parent of the junior party in the relationship. These considerations give us the two discriminant variables

D) Similarity of sex of senior party and sex of linking parent of junior party, with the values
   D.1) Sex of senior party and of parent of junior party the same (*d–g*)
   D.2) Sex of senior party and of parent of junior party different (*h, i*)

E) Relative age of senior party and of linking parent of junior party, with the values
   E.1) Senior party older than linking parent (*d, f*)
   E.2) Senior party younger than linking parent (*e, g*)

This leaves us with the problem of differentiating within each of the pairs of sets *d* and *f, e* and *g, h* and *i,* and *j* and *k*. Clearly, in each pair the difference is in the sex of the senior party in the relationship (regardless of whether the senior party is ego or alter); this gives us the discriminant variable

F) Sex of senior party in the relationship, with the values
   F.1) Sex of senior party male (*d, e, i, j*)
   F.2) Sex of senior party female (*f, g, h, k*)

All the sets of reciprocal terms are now fully differentiated. We can put the array of sets, with their defining characteristics, in a matrix table, with the columns representing the discriminant variables and the rows representing the sets of reciprocal terms, as shown in Table 18:1.

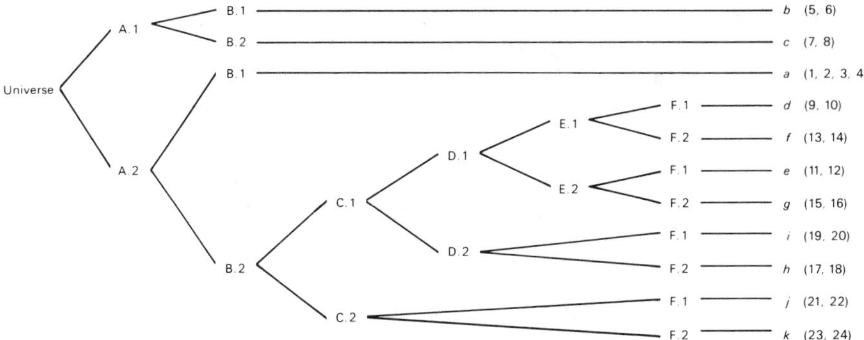

Figure 18:1. Tree diagram of hierarchical ordering of semantic components of reciprocal sets of terms *a* through *k* (*see text*), as represented in Table 18:1.

This brings us to a crucial part of the procedure: the ordering of columns and rows. If the set of sets of reciprocal terms we have been analyzing were completely unordered, there would be no problem. In this example, as in all kinship terminologies with which I am familiar, we are dealing with a partially ordered set (*11*). Only variables A and B partition the entire universe; variables C and F partition the part of it that is both A.2 and B.2; variable D partitions only the part that is C.1; and variable E partitions only the part that is D.1. But variables C, D, and E have no such systematic relationship to variable F. They are unordered with respect to F, just as A and B are unordered with respect to each other.

TABLE 18:1. *Matrix Table for Reciprocal Sets a Through k (See Text)*

Sets of reciprocal terms	Discriminant variables					
	A	B	C	D	E	F
b (5, 6)	A.1	B.1	.	.	.	.
c (7, 8)	A.1	B.2	.	.	.	.
a (1, 2, 3, 4)	A.2	B.1	.	.	.	.
d (9, 10)	A.2	B.2	C.1	D.1	E.1	F.1
f (13, 14)	A.2	B.2	C.1	D.1	E.1	F.2
e (11, 12)	A.2	B.2	C.1	D.1	E.2	F.1
g (15, 16)	A.2	B.2	C.1	D.1	E.2	F.2
i (19, 20)	A.2	B.2	C.1	D.2	.	F.1
h (17, 18)	A.2	B.2	C.1	D.2	.	F.2
j (21, 22)	A.2	B.2	C.2	.	.	F.1
k (23, 24)	A.2	B.2	C.2	.	.	F.2

In Table 18:1, the major variables A and B are put at the extreme left, but their position relative to each other is arbitrary. Consistency now requires that variable C be to the left of D, which must be to the left of E. Variable F must be to the right of A and B, but since it is unordered with respect to C, D, and E, its position at the far right is arbitrary.

The ordering of rows, given a particular order of columns, must be such as to minimize the occurrence of the same values of the same variables in other than adjacent rows. Thus ordered, the matrix in Table 18:1 is identical in structure to the tree diagram in Figure 18:1 and fully portrays the major and minor groupings of the sets of reciprocal terms created by the hierarchical ordering of the discriminant variables. Our principle for ordering rows preserves the integrity of these major and minor groupings by keeping the sets of reciprocal terms within them in adjacent rows.

Consideration of the integrity of subgroups of terms may also be relevant to the ordering of variables that otherwise appear to be unordered. For example, the arrangement of columns in Table 18:1 serves to separate the sets of terms *b* and *a* so that they are not in adjacent rows. Yet the six terms in these two sets themselves form a larger set, as we have noted. To preserve the integrity of this larger set, we must juxtapose columns A and B, as shown in Table 18:2. According to our rule for ordering rows, the sets of terms *b* and *a* now fall in adjacent rows.

Because variable F is unordered with respect to variables C, D, and E, we are free to position it elsewhere, provided it remains to the right of columns A and B. By moving column F over to the left of columns D and

TABLE 18:2. *Reordered Matrix Table for Reciprocal Sets a Through k*

Sets of reciprocal terms	*Discriminant variables*					
	B	A	C	F	D	E
b (5, 6)	B.1	A.1	.	.	.	.
a (1, 2, 3, 4)	B.1	A.2	.	.	.	.
c (7, 8)	B.2	A.1	.	.	.	.
d (9, 10)	B.2	A.2	C.1	F.1	D.1	E.1
e (11, 12)	B.2	A.2	C.1	F.1	D.1	E.2
i (19, 20)	B.2	A.2	C.1	F.1	D.2	.
f (13, 14)	B.2	A.2	C.1	F.2	D.1	E.1
g (15, 16)	B.2	A.2	C.1	F.2	D.1	E.2
h (17, 18)	B.2	A.2	C.1	F.2	D.2	.
j (21, 22)	B.2	A.2	C.2	F.1	.	.
k (23, 24)	B.2	A.2	C.2	F.2	.	.

E, we group together the variables in order of their extent of relevance in discriminating among the sets of reciprocal terms in the array, as also shown in Table 18:2.

It remains now to discriminate among the designata of the terms in each reciprocal set. Two variables account for them all:

G) Seniority of alter's generation, with the values
  G.1) Alter in senior generation (1, 2, 9, 11, 13, 15, 17, 19, 21, 23)
  G.2) Alter in junior generation (3, 4, 10, 12, 14, 16, 18, 20, 22, 24)

H) Sex of alter, with the values
  H.1) Alter's sex male (1, 3, 5, 7)
  H.2) Alter's sex female (2, 4, 6, 8)

By adding these variables to the matrix shown in Table 18:2, we have the complete taxonomic array portrayed in Table 18:3. Variables G and H appear at the extreme right in Table 18:3, because if they were in any other position it would be impossible to keep terms within each reciprocal set in adjacent rows.

By preserving the integrity of these reciprocal sets, we get an ordering of columns that is consistent with different levels of organization, so to speak, within the array. Variables A through F are at one level of organization, discriminating among sets of reciprocal terms, although they vary in the extent of their relevance, and variables G and H, discriminating within these sets, are at another level of organization. Because variables F and H both involve a consideration of sex, and because they are in complementary distribution in the matrix table, it is tempting to think of them as going together in the overall structure of the array; but there is nothing to be gained by so viewing them, because they pertain to different levels of organization.

The order of columns G and H relative to each other in Table 18:3 is determined by another consideration. If we move H to the left of G, the effect is to prevent terms 1 and 2 from being in adjacent rows. Yet terms 1 and 2 are a subset belonging to the same side of a reciprocal equation, terms 3 and 4 going together on the other side. (Terms 1 and 3 complement 2 and 4 but do not reciprocate them.) Having column G to the left of column H preserves the integrity of these subsets in the array.

Attention to the ordering of columns and rows, as illustrated in this analysis, brings out the structural design of a semantic domain (here, kinship). This design is implicit in the way the several terms pertaining to the domain are said by informants to be correctly and incorrectly used. (Note that we do not ask informants to define the terms but ask them only

TABLE 18:3. *Componential Paradigm Representing a Comprehensive View of Lapp Consanguineal Terms*

Set	*No.*	*Term*	*Discriminant variables*							
			B	A	C	F	D	E	G	H
b	5	*vielljâ*	B.1	A.1	.	.	.	.	.	H.1
	6	*oabba*	B.1	A.1	.	.	.	.	.	H.2
a	1	*ačče*	B.1	A.2	.	.	.	.	G.1	H.1
	2	*aedne*	B.1	A.2	.	.	.	.	G.1	H.2
	3	*bardne*	B.1	A.2	.	.	.	.	G.2	H.1
	4	*nieidã*	B.1	A.2	.	.	.	.	G.2	H.2
c	7	*vilj-baelle*	B.2	A.1	.	.	.	.	.	H.1
	8	*oam-baelle*	B.2	A.1	.	.	.	.	.	H.2
d	9	*akke*	B.2	A.2	C.1	F.1	D.1	E.1	G.1	.
	10	*akket*	B.2	A.2	C.1	F.1	D.1	E.1	G.2	.
e	11	*čaecce*	B.2	A.2	C.1	F.1	D.1	E.2	G.1	.
	12	*čaeccet*	B.2	A.2	C.1	F.1	D.1	E.2	G.2	.
i	19	*aeno*	B.2	A.2	C.1	F.1	D.2	.	G.1	.
	20	*naeppe*	B.2	A.2	C.1	F.1	D.2	.	G.2	.
f	13	*goaske*	B.2	A.2	C.1	F.2	D.1	E.1	G.1	.
	14	*goasket*	B.2	A.2	C.1	F.2	D.1	E.1	G.2	.
g	15	*muossa*	B.2	A.2	C.1	F.2	D.1	E.2	G.1	.
	16	*muossãl*	B.2	A.2	C.1	F.2	D.1	E.2	G.2	.
h	17	*siessa*	B.2	A.2	C.1	F.2	D.2	.	G.1	.
	18	*siessãl*	B.2	A.2	C.1	F.2	D.2	.	G.2	.
j	21	*aggja*	B.2	A.2	C.2	F.1	.	.	G.1	.
	22	*aggjot*	B.2	A.2	C.2	F.1	.	.	G.2	.
k	23	*akko*	B.2	A.2	C.2	F.2	.	.	G.1	.
	24	*akkot*	B.2	A.2	C.2	F.2	.	.	G.2	.

to judge the correctness of the way in which the terms are used.) In this case the structural design includes different levels of organization and, within each level, a hierarchical ordering of at least some of its component variables. From left to right in Table 18:3, as we have observed, variables B, A, C, F, D, and E are at one level of organization, and variables G and H are at another. At the latter level, as we have seen, G has structural priority over H; and in the other set of variables, B and A together have priority over C and F, and C has priority over D, which has priority over E. The capacity of componential analysis for bringing out implicit and covert structural designs of semantic domains makes it useful for purposes of comparison as well as description.

Alternative Representations and Their Implications

To the extent that the data analyzed permit us to formulate alternative variables that discriminate equally well among the several terms' respective sets of denotata, we are able to construct more than one satisfactory model of the structuring of a semantic domain. This raises a serious question about the usefulness of componential analysis as a means of constructing scientifically useful representations of ways in which other people see things (*12*).

If we assume that all Lapp people who use their kinship terms in the same way have the same subconscious feel for what these terms mean and somehow share a view that is the one "true" view for anthropological science to discover and describe, then, obviously, we cannot say that componential analysis can guarantee that its products will have this kind of validity. But if we assume that componential analysis is a formal model of the procedures by which people learn what others seem to mean by the words they use, and if we discover from it that more than one product of these procedures may lead to identical overt usages, we must conclude that other people who speak the same language and agree on how its words should be used do not necessarily share a common view but merely have the illusion that they do. If this is the case, then the above question about the usefulness of componential analysis rests on a false assumption about cognitive sharing, an assumption that grants to other humans a capacity for cognitive sharing that equally human investigators lack.

If people who use their terms in the same way may still have somewhat different subjective views as to what the terms signify, and if the same person may have more than one view, any componential representation of what the terms mean, provided it leads us to use them denotatively in the same way others do, is ethnographically adequate. From such a representation we can generate the data that will permit us to construct alternative representations. We select one componential representation over another because of the ease with which we can comprehend it, and because of the ease with which we can use it to understand what others are saying and to make ourselves understood.

We can say, then, that the componential paradigm presented in Table 18:3 represents a comprehensive view of Lapp kinship terms, a view such as an adult Lapp *might* subjectively have arrived at after much experience of using such terms. Certainly a small child does not know any principles for differentiating kinds of kinsmen. Given information about how two people are connected, he cannot correctly state, as an adult can, the category of their relationship. He is taught quite arbitrarily what labels to give to specific individuals. With growing experience he gets successive insights into the ways in which the terminology works, and he develops progressively more elegant conceptions of it. How much progress of this kind any one person makes depends on his experience and his intellectual acuity. Componential analysis leads to the construction of conceptual models of the most adult type—it is hoped, to models that are as elegant as any that can be constructed for a given terminology.

From this point of view, it would be wrong to assume that the model of Lapp-kinship semantics presented here represents the way individual Lapps actually think about the signification of their kinship terms (just as it would be wrong to assume that the formal statement of a language's grammar represents the way individual speakers think about that grammar). What the model represents is a pattern of usage, something each Lapp spends a considerable portion of his life learning to understand. Adequate representations of this usage are bound to help us share understanding with Lapps in the same way that Lapps share understanding with one another—and with the same limitations. Such a degree of mutual understanding is far greater than that obtainable from most ethnographic descriptions that have been made to date.

Alternative Approaches

Not only are there alternative models that can be constructed by the procedures of componential analysis, there are also alternative strategies and consequent procedures for dealing with the problem of describing what words signify. Lounsbury (*13, 14*) has begun to develop a strategy for describing the significata of kinship terms in which he assumes that there is, for each term, a primary denotatum and that the remaining acceptable denotata can be generated through operations on the primary ones. These operations, called extension rules (and including such things as equivalence rules and skewing rules), may be fully or partially ordered, and the minimum set of rules, together with their ordering, that will account for the kinship terminology as it is used portrays the structure of the semantic domain.

Lounsbury's approach can be usefully combined with componential analysis. I have found the use of an equivalence rule of Lounsbury's type essential to defining the way in which the concept of difference in genealogical generation is to be understood as a discriminant variable in the kinship terminology of Truk (see *3*), and Lounsbury uses componential analysis to describe how the primary denotata for a set of kinship terms are to be distinguished from one another (*13*). The two approaches appear to be complementary, therefore, rather than contradictory.

Some Preliminary Findings

Because it is aimed at comprehending total patterns of usage, componential analysis requires, for any particular pattern, a sample of data that exceeds what is often collected. Anthropologists have been reporting kinship terminology for decades, but a survey shows that few reports are sufficiently full to permit us to subject the data presented in them to a componential analysis (*15*). Concern with this kind of analysis should help improve the quality of ethnographic study and reporting.

As we acquire a corpus of kinship terminologies that have been subjected to componential analysis, it becomes increasingly fruitful to review the range of discriminant variables they employ.

Already analysis has produced a wider range of variables than that encompassed by the criteria of kinship noted by Kroeber in 1909 (*16*), criteria that have been standard for anthropologists ever since. By definition, any kinship terminology must employ some variables that reflect the properties of genealogical space. But all the terminologies I have examined employ other variables as well. In many terminologies, these additional variables reflect such human universals as sex and birth order, but in some they also reflect features of social organization, such as clan and other kin-group memberships—things that are not universal human attributes and that in each case derive from facets of the local culture. With such terminologies, componential analyses are impossible without the relevant cultural information.

The several analyses I have made have revealed one striking difference among kinship terminologies. Most terminologies can be analyzed in the two stages illustrated here, the first dealing with reciprocal sets of terms and the second dealing with the several terms within these sets. One terminology that I have analyzed cannot be readily handled in this way (*17*). It does not structure the field of kinship as a set of reciprocal relationships, such as would be appropriate to the structuring of an objective or outsider's view of it, but presents a field of relatives as subjectively viewed by an ego at the center, ego's way of labeling his various relatives having little or no correspondence with the way they label him. Componential analysis shows this basic structural difference clearly—one that, as far as I know, has never figured in any of the vast anthropological literature on kinship.

Componential analysis obviously gives promise of entirely new classifications of kinship terminologies, based on the conceptual variables the terminologies employ and the role these variables play in the structural designs of kinship paradigms. Already it is evident that groupings of kinship terminologies according to these criteria are quite independent of the groupings obtained by the criteria anthropologists have used up to this time. This does not mean that existing typologies of kinship terminology, such as those used by Murdock for comparative study (*18*), are without value. Different typologies reflect different considerations, and any one of them becomes the appropriate one when the considerations it reflects are the object of inquiry. But established classifications of kinship terminologies have been of little use for phylogenetic study. For example, the several kinship terminologies in a set of phylogenetically related languages (as in the Indo-European or Malayo-Polynesian language families) usually include a variety of Murdock's major types (*18*). By contrast, such groupings as I have made, based on similarities of gross structural design of kinship paradigms resulting from componential analysis, correspond more closely with linguistic phylogenetic groupings. Nothing is certain yet, but the preliminary indications are encouraging.

References and Notes

1. W. H. Goodenough, "Property, Kin, and Community on Truk," *Yale Univ. Pub. in Anthropol. No. 46* (1951).

2. ——, in "Report on Seventh Annual Round Table Meeting on Linguistics and Language Study," P. Garvin, Ed., *Georgetown Univ. Monograph Ser. on Languages and Linguistics No. 9* (1957); F. G. Lounsbury, *Language* **32,** 158 (1956).

3. W. H. Goodenough, *Language* **32,** 195 (1956).

4. H. C. Conklin, *Southwestern J. Anthropol.* **11,** 339 (1955); E. Haugen, *Word* **13,** 447 (1957); C. O. Frake, *Amer. Anthropologist* **63,** 113 (1961).

5. C. O. Frake, in *Explorations in Cultural Anthropology*, W. Goodenough, Ed. (McGraw-Hill, New York, 1964).

6. ——, in "Social Structure in Southeast Asia," G. P. Murdock, Ed., *Viking Fund Pub. Anthropol. No. 29* (1960); L. Pospisil, *Oceania* **30,** 188 (1960); F. P. Conant, *Anthropological Linguistics* **3,** 19 (1961); R. Burling, *Man* **62,** 201 (1962); ——, *Ethnology* **2,** 70 (1963); papers by H. C. Conklin, W. H. Goodenough, and L. Pospisil, in *Explorations in Cultural Anthropology*, W. Goodenough, Ed. (McGraw-Hill, New York, 1964); papers by R. Burling, F. G. Lounsbury, A. F. C. Wallace, and W. H. Goodenough, in "Formal Semantic Analysis," E. A. Hammel, Ed., *Amer. Anthropologist Spec. Pub.* (1965).

7. C. W. Morris, in *International Encyclopedia of Unified Science* (Univ. of Chicago Press, Chicago, 1938), vol. 1, No. 2.

8. Some of my colleagues interpret "componential analysis" in a narrower sense than I do. The expression comes from linguistics, where it has a technical meaning. I first used it, in connection with the kind of semantic analysis that is described here, in the title of a paper addressed to linguists (*3*), because it was the best expression I knew of in their vocabulary for giving them a rough idea of what the paper was about. My anthropological colleagues picked it up and used it as the name for the method, but because of its technical meaning in linguistics, they have tended to use it to refer only to the *isolation* of elements of signification and not to the *ordering* of these elements. The expression is used here to refer to a

method of formal semantic analysis that is still in process of development and from which questions of order, structure, and even transformational rules cannot be practically or meaningfully divorced.

9. C. E. Osgood, G. J. Suci, P. H. Tannenbaum, *The Measurement of Meaning* (Univ. of Illinois Press, Urbana, 1957).

10. See my fuller analysis of all Könkämä Lapp kinship terms, in *Explorations in Cultural Anthropology*, W. Goodenough, Ed. (McGraw-Hill, New York, 1964). That analysis is based on data from R. N. Pehrson, "The Bilateral Network of Social Relations in Könkämä Lapp District," *Indiana Univ. Res. Center in Anthropol., Folklore, and Linguistics Pub. 3* (1957).

11. An unordered terminology is a paradigm, and an ordered one is a taxonomy, according to definitions proposed by H. C. Conklin, in "Problems in Lexicography," F. W. Householder and S. Saporta, Eds., *Indiana Univ. Res. Center in Anthropol., Folklore, and Linguistics Pub. 21* (1962). Since most terminologies are partially ordered, and since the word *paradigm* has other established meanings, Conklin's proposed usage is not entirely satisfactory.

12. A. F. C. Wallace and J. Atkins, *Amer. Anthropologist* **62,** 58 (1960); A. F. C. Wallace, in "Formal Semantic Analysis," E. A. Hammel, Ed., *Amer. Anthropologist Spec. Pub.* (1965); R. Burling, *Amer. Anthropologist* **66,** 20 (1964).

13. F. G. Lounsbury, in *Explorations in Cultural Anthropology,* W. Goodenough, Ed. (McGraw-Hill, New York, 1964).

14. ——, in "Formal Semantic Analysis," E. A. Hammel, Ed., *Amer. Anthropologist Spec. Pub.* (1965).

15. B. Klamon, unpublished.

16. A. L. Kroeber, *J. Roy. Anthropol. Inst.* **39,** 77 (1909).

17. This is the Kalmuk Mongol terminology, as reported by D. F. Aberle in *The Kinship System of the Kalmuk Mongols* (Univ. of New Mexico Press, Albuquerque, 1953); see also A. K. Romney, in "Formal Semantic Analysis," E. A. Hammel, Ed., *Amer. Anthropologist Spec. Pub.* (1965).

18. G. P. Murdock, *Social Structure* (Macmillan, New York, 1949).

19. This article draws heavily on work done under NIH grants Nos. M-6126 and MH-06126-02.

Acculturation

19 SEMANTIC ASPECTS OF LINGUISTIC ACCULTURATION

Keith H. Basso

Throughout this book the general nature of cognitive theory and its utility in explaining human behavior has been emphasized. Ethnoscience, as a general method, is useful in the description of cultural knowledge in both complex and primitive societies. It leads to rigorous descriptions, not only of cognitive structures, but also of the dynamic aspects of social interaction. Furthermore, as Keith H. Basso shows in this chapter, it is eminently suited for the analysis of culture change. At the descriptive level he shows how a traditional category system was changed in order to classify the parts of a new object—the automobile. When one society borrows some item from another, the new must find its place within the existing cognitive map of that culture. The author was able to discover the taxonomic location of automobiles and their defining attribute from the Apache point of view and because of this could explain the shift in meaning which occurred.—EDITOR'S NOTE

I

Language[1] is a notoriously flexible instrument, and registers changes in cultural content perhaps more sensitively than any other element of culture. Such changes may affect phonetics, vocabulary, or grammar. But it is in vocabulary that they can be traced most readily, whether they are due to developments within the culture or to the effects of intercultural contact. And yet in recent years the topic of vocabulary shifts has received relatively little attention from anthropologists interested in acculturation. For the most part, earlier studies have focused upon the interrelationship of sociocultural and linguistic factors, with emphasis generally placed upon the former (Beals 1953:635).[2] When linguistic factors are stressed, phonetics and morphology tend to receive much fuller treatment than semantics.

Within the last decade, the development of ethnoscience has provided

Reproduced by permission of the author and the American Anthropological Association from *American Anthropologist*, vol. 69, no. 2, 1967, pp. 471–477.

ethnographers with orderly procedures for describing folk classifications as these are reflected in terminology (c.f. Frake 1961, 1962; Conklin 1962; Sturtevant 1964). Thus far, however, work in this area has dealt almost exclusively with synchronic semantic systems. In the present paper, I suggest that several of the concepts used in ethnoscience may be fruitfully brought to bear upon a type of semantic change that frequently accompanies intercultural contact. In so doing, I will present and analyze data collected among the Western Apache of east-central Arizona.

First, however, it is necessary to consider a more traditional approach to the study of semantic change. In the past, shifts in referential meaning have usually been described by (1) establishing the original meaning, or primary sense, of a given word or lexeme, (2) recording the changes that have altered this meaning, and (3) relating these changes to a set of linguistic, psychological, or historical factors that presumably precipitated them. In short, the basic procedure has been the documentation of a word's history, conceived, as a linear succession of units of meaning (Ullman 1957:164). This approach, which Ullman has aptly labelled "atomistic," operates on the assumption, perhaps most strongly advocated by de Saussure, that whereas synchronic linguistics properly deals with systems, diachronic linguistics must concern itself with single elements. In the semantic sphere, this assumption carries the implication that changes in the meanings of words take place independently of one another or, at best, are only rarely systemically related.

The "atomistic" view thus raises a question of some importance. Namely, is it possible to formulate descriptive generalizations about changes in meaning at a level above that of the isolated word or lexeme? In what follows, I suggest that within certain restricted contexts, verifiable in an operationally explicit manner, such generalizations can be made and that they help bring into sharper focus an aspect of linguistic acculturation that has heretofore remained relatively obscure.

Previous studies, notably those of Herzog (1941) and Casagrande (1954–55), have shown that there are three basic processes by which the vocabulary of a language adjusts to new objects or ideas introduced as a consequence of intercultural contact. First, it may take over words—loanwords—directly from the language that accompanies another culture. Second, it may coin original expressions, frequently idiomatic, to describe the new phenomena. Or, third, existing words and lexemes may be extended in meaning to denote new objects, while the traditional meanings are either retained or displaced entirely.

The literature on loanwords as one aspect of linguistic acculturation, but more especially as a source of lexical interference in bilinguals, has been expertly surveyed and synthesized by Weinreich (1953) and Haugen (1953,

1956). However, the formation of idiomatic expressions, together with extensions of meaning, has received considerably less attention, It is the latter of these processes—meaning extension—that shall concern us here.

Data from the Western Apache indicate that at some point in the not too distant past a body of native words was extended en masse to cover a conspicuous item of material culture introduced by the Whites. Anatomical terms were extended to label various parts of pick-up trucks and automobiles (see Table 19:1).

At this point, let us note that in reference to a specified class of objects (e.g., man, horse, dog) Apache anatomical terms comprise a lexical set; that is, they share exclusively a defining feature of meaning and contrast semantically within a culturally relevant context (Lounsbury 1956, Conklin 1962), in this instance a substitution frame (Table 19:1). The application of anatomical terminology to motorized vehicles illustrates an aspect of semantic extension that is clearly apparent at the level of the set, but that goes undetected if we focus on the individual terms in isolation. Thus a typical "atomistic" interpretation—operating strictly at the word level and failing to consider the internal structure of the lexical set as a whole—would not disclose that together with individual terms a classificatory scheme had

TABLE 19:1. *Western Apache Anatomical·Terms with Extended Meanings*

Anatomical Terms (re: man)		*Extended Meanings* (re: auto)
wos	"shoulder"	"front fender(s)"
gən	"hand+arm"	"front wheel(s), tire(s)"
dɔ	"chin+jaw"	"front bumper"
ke'	"foot," "feet"	"rear wheel(s), tire(s)"
ni	"face"	"area extending from top of windshield to bumper"
ta	"forehead"	"front portion of cab, or automobile top"
čį	"nose"	"hood"
γən	"back"	"bed of truck"
kai	"hip+buttock"	"rear fender(s)"
zϵ'	"mouth"	"opening of pipe leading to gas-tank"
inda'	"eye(s)"	"headlights"
tsɔ̨s	"vein(s)"	"electrical wiring"
ϵbiyι'	"entrails," "guts"	"all machinery under hood"
zιk	"liver"	"battery"
pιt	"stomach"	"gas-tank"
ǰi	"heart"	"distributor"
ǰisolϵ	"lung"	"radiator"
či	"intestine(s)"	"radiator hose(s)"
ƚikɔ	"fat"	"grease"

also been extended. After a closer look at the Apache data, I shall return to this point and discuss it in greater detail.[3]

II

Western Apache is one of seven languages that comprise the Southern Athapaskan (or Apachean) substock of Athapaskan (Hoijer 1938). The other languages are Navaho, Chiricahua, Mescalero, Jicarilla, Lipan, and Kiowa-Apache. Included in Western Apache are five mutually intelligible dialects: San Carlos, Cibecue, White Mountain, and Northern and Southern Tonto (Goodwin 1942). Phonological differences between two of these—San Carlos and White Mountain—have recently been described by Hill (1963). The material for this paper was collected from Apaches living in the community of Cibecue, which is located just south of the Mogollon Rim near the center of the Fort Apache Indian Reservation.[4]

My data come from five Apaches, men, 45 years or older, who speak very little English. All were present on Fort Apache between the years of 1930 to 1935, when Apaches first began to purchase and drive pick-up trucks. Unlike many younger Apaches, who are bilingual, my informants were totally unfamiliar with English labels for automobile parts. This is not to say that the use of extended anatomical terms is confined to members of the older generation. To the contrary, this terminology is part of every Apache's basic vocabulary and is commonly resorted to in daily conversation. Long before an Apache child learns that a truck has a battery, he knows it has a "liver."

Western Apache anatomical terms occur as responses to the query: *X bi' atɛ' hati holzɛ?* ("*X* its parts, what are they called?"), where *X* is a lexeme denoting the object whose anatomy is being investigated.[5] Several hundred lexemes, including *nalbił* ("truck, automobile"), can fill this position, and strictly speaking there are as many anatomical sets as there are substitutable lexemes. The set that refers to "man" (*ndɛ*), for example, cannot be considered semantically isomorphic with the set for "horse" (*łį*), "bear" (*šəš*), or "automobile," even though many of the same anatomical terms are present in all four. This becomes clear when we realize that depending on which set it is in, the same term can have distinctly different referents. Thus, applied to man, the term *kɛ'* denotes "foot," applied to horse "hoof," to bear "paw," and to automobile "tire."

In the presence of multiple anatomical sets, we can only speculate about which one, or ones, actually served as the model for labeling automobiles. A few Apaches maintain that the horse acted in this capacity, which is plausible in view of its functional similarity to the automobile. However, it should be pointed out that none of the terms extended to motorized vehicles is unique to horses. In fact, the extended terms are extremely common, that is, "core" terms shared by the large majority of anatomical sets. With this in mind we shall focus on the set that is probably basic to all the others, that which is elicited in reference to man.

Listed in the left-hand column of Table 19:1 are 19 anatomical terms that occur as responses to the query: *ndɛ bɩ' atɛ' hati holzɛ'?* ("man his parts, what are they called?"). These terms, together with others not extended to automobiles, comprise what we shall call the *anatomical set*. The meanings of the extended terms are glossed in the right-hand column. These latter occur as responses to the query: *nałbil bɩ' atɛ' hati holzɛ'?* ("automobile, its parts, what are they called?"), and make up the *extended set*. The complete anatomical set takes the form of a three-level part-whole taxonomy, with *ndɛ bɩ tsi* ("man's body") serving as the cover term. Approximately half the terms are subsumed under two superordinate lexemes, *ni* ("face") and *ɛbiyɩ'* ("entrails," "guts"), which operate at the second level. It is important to note that even though the extended set contains only 19 terms, its taxonomic structure is identical to that of the anatomical set (see Figures 19:1 and 19:2).

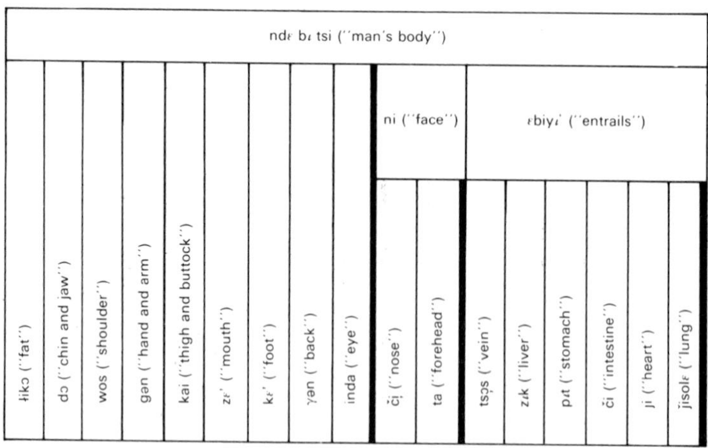

NOTE: Black bars indicate position of additional (unextended) anatomical terms.

Figure 19:1. Taxonomic structure of anatomical set.

III

The semantic range of all the lexemes in a given lexical set constitutes the domain of that set (Conklin 1962, Frake 1962). A domain however limited, represents a segment of a folk classification, that is, a portion of the ideational system of linguistically labeled categories in accordance with which the speakers of a language organize and construe their world of experience. The categories, or segregates, within a domain contrast on the basis of perceptual and/or conceptual criteria whose nature and interrelationship can vary widely from culture to culture (cf. Frake 1962, Goodenough 1964).

Lexemes and the categories they label can change independently and therefore must be separately analyzed (Conklin 1962). In dealing with the extension of a single lexeme, the most that can be shown is that its category has been broadened. (This is perhaps the major shortcoming of "atomistic" interpretations.) However, at the level of the lexical set it becomes obvious that extension involves much more than the acquisition by individual terms of new senses. It involves, as well, the extension of a system of cognitive categories *and* their structural relationships vis-à-vis one another. In short, the process of set extension may be said to occur when an existing classificatory scheme, as embodied in the semantic domain of a lexical set, is mapped onto a portion of the environment that was previously unclassified.

In this connection, our Western Apache data illustrate one point of

nałbil bɨ tsi (''automobile's body'')																
									ni*		ɨbiyɨ' (''machinery under hood'')					
ɬikɔ (''grease'')	dɔ (''front bumper'')	wos (''front fender'')	gən (''front wheel'')	kai (''rear fender'')	zɨ' (''gas pipe opening'')	kɨ' (''rear wheel'')	γən (''bed of truck'')	inda (''headlight'')	čį (''hood'')	ta (''front of cab,'' ''top'')	tsɔ̧s (''electrical wiring'')	zɨk (''battery'')	pɨt (''gas tank'')	či (''radiator hose'')	ǰi (''distributor'')	ǰisolɨ (''radiator'')

*''Area extending from top of windshield to bumper''

Figure 19:2. Taxonomic structure of extended set.

particular interest. Although only a portion of the complete anatomical set was mapped onto motorized vehicles, we have seen that its hierarchical structure was faithfully replicated in the extended set. This suggests the possibility that set extension may be accompanied by a tendency to preserve taxonomic levels at the expense of individual categories.

The concept of set extension is a helpful one. It allows us to generalize about semantic change above the level of the word by suggesting that lexical sets may be extended in a manner analogous to single lexemes. Extension of either sort necessarily calls for the expansion of existing categories to include new referents. But set extension is unique in that it also involves the extension of intercategory relationships. If lexical sets and their associated domains are viewed as representing models of how the speakers of a language perceive the world around them, then set extension is a process whereby old models are used to structure new experience.

A culture has been defined as the sum total of a society's folk classifications (Sturtevant 1964). Whether or not one agrees completely with this definition, it is nevertheless true that culture change includes shifts in folk classifications. As suggested above, lexical sets and their domains may be of singular importance in the categorization of phenomena introduced in the course of acculturation. The changes that result can be rather neatly described by eliciting extended sets. In this way it is possible to specify which particular classifications have changed, how (if at all) their internal structure has been altered, and what new phenomena they have come to designate. The value of this kind of information should be obvious to students of culture change.

A search of the relevant literature has failed to uncover additional clear-cut examples of set extension.[6] This could be interpreted to mean that we are dealing with an extremely rare phenomenon, but more likely it indicates that ethnographers and linguists have simply not been in the habit of searching for extended sets. Herzog (1941) has published a short list of Pima automobile terms, clearly anatomical extensions, which bear some striking resemblances to the Apache material discussed above. However, Herzog's list is of limited comparative value for two reasons. First, we have no way of telling if it represents a complete lexical set, and second, the meanings of the unextended anatomical terms are not presented. Regardless, it is probably safe to conclude that the Western Apache were not alone in classifying automobile parts on the basis of an anatomical model.

Viewed in the context of Western Apache culture the extension of anatomical terms to automobiles was highly functional. It facilitated meaningful communication about a totally foreign object in a familiar frame of reference and (at least temporarily) made it unnecessary for Apaches to contend with a complicated classification that can prove troublesome even to native speakers of English.

IV

In seeking to account for the extension of a lexical set it is not necessary to consider individually the histories of each of the component lexemes. Instead, we treat the set as a unit and assume that an adequate explanation for its extension as a whole serves equally well for any and all of its members. Below, an attempt is made to answer the question: why should one particular lexical set be extended to a particular "foreign" item? Or, in terms of our example, what reasons can we adduce to account for the fact that the Western Apache extended anatomical terms to automobiles?

First, we might offer a functional explanation: after Apaches learned to drive, the automobile came to occupy a prominent place in their transportation system, which had formerly been filled by the horse. Since anatomical terms were customarily employed to describe the horse, they were extended to its mechanized successor. This argument could be supported by additional evidence showing that, indeed, Apaches bring to the care and use of automobiles many of the same values and attitudes that characterize their treatment of horses.[7] And thus the reason for extension would become one of equivalence on a functional level between the object customarily described by the terms in the extended set and the object to which the set is extended.

I do not regard this explanation as wholly satisfactory. In the first place, too much emphasis rests on the functional similarity of horse and car (an assertion that could be disputed), and in the second, it fails to take into consideration the numerous other phenomena that are described with anatomical sets.

An alternative explanation, and one that relates directly to Western Apache semantic categories, rests on the following assumption: when a "foreign" item of culture is incorporated into an existing semantic category, the other members of which are described by a particular lexical set, that set—either in whole or part—will be extended to cover the newly incorporated item.

In the Western Apache folk classification, *nałbil* ("pick-up truck," "automobile") is subsumed under a superordinate category, *hinda*, which also includes man, quadrupeds, birds, reptiles, fish, insects, and a few machines besides the automobile (e.g., bulldozers, tractors, steam-shovels). At the same taxonomic level *hinda* contrasts with the category *dɛstsą̣*, which encompasses all topographical features and almost every item of material culture. My investigation of these categories has been fairly exhaustive, and on the basis of evidence presently available it appears that *hinda* includes only those phenomena that are capable of generating and sustaining locomotive movement by themselves. On the other hand, *dɛstsą̣* labels phenomena that either are immobile or depend for movement upon the intervention of outside forces (e.g., man, wind, rain, etc.). So far as I have been able to determine, anatomical sets are used exclusively in connection with members of the category labeled *hinda*. Members of the category *dɛstsą̣* are not described with anatomical terms, but with different nomenclatures that do not concern us here.

With this information we can offer a semantic explanation for the extension of anatomical terms to motorized vehicles. When the automobile was introduced into Apache culture, it was perceived to possess a crucial defining attribute—the ability to move itself—which prompted its inclusion in the category labeled *hinda*. The traditional practice of describing the other members of this category with anatomical terms was then applied to automobiles, to produce the extended set described above.

Notes

1. The field work on which this study is based was made possible by U.S.P.H.S. Grant MH-12691-01. I gratefully acknowledge this support. An earlier and somewhat modified version of the paper was read by Charles Frake, Frank Cancian, and William Geohegan, all of whom made valuable criticisms and suggestions. The paper as it now stands, however, is the author's responsibility, and his alone.

2. In the 1940's and 50's a few anthropologists, concerned with the relation of lexical change to modifications in nonlinguistic culture, turned to the analysis of contact situations in an attempt to determine when vocabulary shifts were most likely to occur and what areas (domains) of a lexicon were most apt to be effected (Spicer 1943; Hoijer 1948; Dozier 1956). At the same time, scholars like Casagrande (1954–55) were documenting in impressive detail some of the more basic types of semantic change. There was little interest, however, in assessing the effects of semantic change on the structure of native classifications, and, as a consequence, its relevance to cognition was not made sufficiently explicit. In part, this was due to a failure to investigate intensively the terminologies (lexical sets) surrounding specific acculturational foci, e.g. the horse, the automobile, etc. (for an exception see Dozier 1955).

3. For reasons somewhat different from those advanced in this paper, the "atomistic" approach to semantic change has been criticized by other scholars (see, for example, Hoenigswald 1963). Nowhere has it been more roundly opposed than in the writings of the European linguistic field theorists, notably Jost Trier and his followers. For a critical overview and interpretation of field theory, together with comments on its historical development, see Öhman (1953) and Ullman (1957).

4. The Indian population on Fort Apache slightly exceeds 5,000 individuals, and is distributed fairly evenly among eight exogamous settlements. Broadly speaking, a settlement is composed of several matrilineages (or lineage segments), some of which are "related" to one another through imputed uterine ties and thus belong to the same clan (cf. Kaut 1957). The basic residential unit is the matrilocal extended family. Reservation life has brought about profound changes in religious practices. A system that once included ceremonials relative to warfare, hunting, agriculture, moving camp, and curing now focuses almost exclusively on the latter (Basso 1966). Witchcraft, however, persists in undiluted form (Basso n.d.).

5. Western Apache words and phrases are written with the phonetic symbols listed below. Vowel length, stress, and tone have not been indicated.

Vowels: /ɛ/,/ɩ/,/i/,/o/,/ə/,/e/,/a/,/ɔ/
Consonants: /d/,/g/,/b/,/t/,/k/,/p/,/j/,/č/,/s/,/š/,/z/,/ž/,/n/,/w/,/ł/,/γ/.
Glottal stop: /'/
Nasalization:/ ̨

6. It seems probable that the process of set extension has occurred in the evolution of many languages, but the absence of data from nonliterate societies makes this difficult to

demonstrate empirically. Certainly English scientific terminologies are not without extended sets, and it has been suggested to me that this is also true of the philological languages.

An interesting example of set extension, provided by an acquaintance of mine who works as an electrician, involves the extension of botanical terms to the components of complex wiring systems. According to the width of their circumference and their position relative to one another, these components are labeled "roots," "trunks," "branches," and "twigs." Appropriately enough, "roots" are "grounded."

Offhand, it would appear that a limited amount ot set extension occurs in modern everyday American English. In part, this may be attributed to the ease with which old words are dismantled and recombined to provide fresh labels for new ideas and inventions. More important, perhaps, is that owing to the unceasing efforts of advertising agencies most new items come with names already attached. This, of course, would mitigate against set extension.

7. Vogt (1960) describes a similar situation with regard to the Navaho.

References Cited

BASSO, KEITH H.

1966 The gift of changing woman. Bulletin 196, Bureau of American Ethnology, Smithsonian Institution, Washington, D.C.

n.d. Western Apache witchcraft. (To appear in a forthcoming volume on North American Indian witchcraft and sorcery, edited by Deward E. Walker, Jr.)

BEALS, RALPH

1953 Acculturation. *In* Anthropology today. A. L. Kroeber, ed., Chicago, Univertisy of Chicago Press.

CASAGRANDE, J. B.

1954–55 Comanche linguistic acculturation. International Journal of American Linguistics 20:140–151, 217–237; 21:8–25.

CONKLIN, H. C.

1962 Lexicographical treatment of folk taxonomies. *In* Problems in lexicography. F. W. Householder and S. Saporta, eds. Indiana University Research Center in Anthropology, Folklore, and Linguistics Publication 21 *and* International Journal of American Linguistics 28:119–141.

DOZIER, EDWARD P.

1955 Kinship and linguistic change among the Arizona Tewa. International Journal of American Linguistics 21:242–257.

1956 Two examples of linguistic acculturation. Language 32:146–157.

FRAKE, CHARLES O.

1961 The diagnosis of disease among the Subanun of Mindanao. American Anthropologist 63:113–132.

1962 The ethnographic study of cognitive systems. *In* Anthropology and human behavior. Thomas Gladwin and William C. Sturtevant, eds. Washington, pp. 72–93.

GOODENOUGH, WARD H.

1964 Introduction. *In* Explorations in cultural anthropology: essays presented to George Peter Murdock. W. H. Goodenough, ed. New York, McGraw-Hill.

GOODWIN, GRENVILLE
1942 The social organization of the Western Apache. Chicago, University of Chicago Press.
HAUGEN, E.
1953 The Norwegian language in America; a study of bilingual behavior. 2 vols. Philadelphia, University of Pennsylvania Press.
1956 Bilingualism in the Americas: a bibliography and research guide. University, Ala., University of Alabama Press.
HERZOG, G.
1941 Culture change and language: shifts in the Pima vocabulary. *In* Language, culture and personality. L. Spier, A. I. Hallowell, and S. S. Newman, eds. Menasha, Wisconsin.
HILL, F.
1963 Some comparisons between San Carlos and White Mountain dialects of Western Apache. *In* Studies in the Athapaskan languages, H. Hoijer, ed. University of California Publications in Linguistics 29, Berkeley.
HOENIGSWALD, HENRY M.
1963 Are the universals of linguistic change? *In* Universals of language. Joseph H. Greenberg, ed. Cambridge, MIT Press.
HOIJER, HARRY
1938 The southern Athapaskan languages. American Anthropologist 40: 75–87.
1948 Linguistic and cultural change. Language 24:335–345.
KAUT, CHARLES R.
1957 The Western Apache clan system: its origins and development. University of New Mexico Publications in Anthropology 9. Albuquerque.
LOUNSBURY, FLOYD
1956 A semantic analysis of the Pawnee kinship usage. Language 32:158–194.
ÖHMAN, SUSAN
1953 Theories of the "linguistic field" Word 9:123–134.
SPICER, EDWARD H.
1943 Linguistic aspects of Yaqui acculturation. American Anthropologist 45:410–426.
STURTEVANT, WILLIAM C.
1964 Studies in ethnoscience. American Anthropologist 66, no. 3, 2:99–131.
ULLMAN, STEPHEN
1963 The principles of semantics. Rev. ed. New York, Barnes and Noble.
VOGT, EVON Z.
1960 The automobile in contemporary Navaho culture. *In* Selected papers of the Fifth International Congress of Anthropological and Ethnological Sciences. Anthony F. C. Wallace, ed. Philadelphia, University of Pennsylvania Press.
WEINREICH, U.
1953 Languages in contact. New York, Linguistic Circle of New York.

Religion

20 THE LANGUAGE OF SPIRITUALIST CHURCHES:

A STUDY IN COGNITION AND SOCIAL ORGANIZATION

Irving I. Zaretsky

Most studies in culture and cognition deal with knowledge that has as a referent some aspect of the physical world. In the preceding chapters, for example, we have examined concepts for sleeping places, beer, kinsmen, speech behavior, and parts of the automobile. At the same time, ethnoscience methods are ideally suited for research on more abstract symbolic systems. In this chapter, Irving I. Zaretsky examines the meaning of many terms which have no representation in the material world. The special vocabulary, or argot, of Spiritualist churches represents objects, places, and events which are beyond sensory experience. Moreover, Spiritualists do not explicitly define the meanings of the terms they use. This fact necessitated a research strategy largely restricted to observation of natural speech contexts. The author tells how he learned this language in much the same way that novices in the church learn it. More important, he goes beyond description of meaning to indicate many of the functions of language for members of the church. The central importance of messages from the spirit world which take linguistic form gives them a unique identity. Individuals are thus bound together by this common language which is opaque and ambiguous to outsiders. This provides legal protection from prosecution and also functions to induce continued participation, since the longer one stays in the church, the clearer its mysteries become. The language also serves to distinguish positions in the social structure. For example, the use of some verbs is restricted to persons in certain positions. This study is a superb demonstration that language is not merely a separate system of interest to linguists. An understanding of cultural behavior requires a careful analysis of what people know, and much of this is conveyed by means of language.—EDITOR'S NOTE

This chapter has been written for this volume and has never before been published.

In basement temples, in reconverted downtown offices, and in private homes, thousands of Americans weekly pursue the world of spirit communications. They are Spiritualists. They claim that there is no death, there are no dead, and that death is but a transition to a new dimension of life. After the transition called death, individuals continue to exist in the form of spirits with whom communication is possible through the aid of spirit mediums. Spirits, once they have entered *spirit land*, maintain an interest in the people still living on the *earthplane*. Through the instrumentality of the medium in a church service, séance, or home circle, spirits are able to advise parishioners who seek their guidance on personal problems and to instruct them on how to conduct their daily lives in harmony with God's and nature's laws. Spiritualists characterize themselves as "seekers." They come to a medium for help, find hope, often lose faith, only to return to another medium to seek anew. Such cyclical parishioner participation in churches has spiraled for the last 125 years, as Spiritualism has spread from the "burned-over district" of New York State to the receptive environment of California.

The material presented here deals with the Spiritualist movement in Bay City, California.[1] The research upon which it is based has been conducted during the past five years.[2] It has been an unusually long field tour and was aimed to include a comprehensive study of all the extant, formally organized Spiritualist churches in Bay City.[3] There were several topical foci of concentration during fieldwork. However, a systematic and consistent effort was made throughout to collect data on the particular use of language, a Spiritualist argot, within these churches.[4]

Spiritualists have developed a religious argot that is used by both parishioners and church functionaries during church services, as well as outside the church context in discussing church-related topics among themselves or with interested newcomers. The argot includes lexical items which label every facet of the church life and belief system. The more integral an activity or belief is to the functioning of the church, the more elaborate are the labels applied to it. This vocabulary is composed of standard English terms which are used, however, in nonstandard ways. The argot meanings of the terms have been created by Spiritualists and are often not understood by native speakers of English who are unfamiliar with the beliefs, rituals, or social organization of these churches. Because this argot is composed of standard English terms we may view it as phonemically and syntactically one language to all native speakers of English, but functionally as two distinct systems of communication. Non-Spiritualists interpret the argot as an ambiguous, unconventional, and incomprehensible use of standard English. To Spiritualists, however, the language connotes very specific information about church life which the parishioner is able to interpret for himself. On the most general level of Spiritualist meaning, all of the terms in the argot are shared by the formally organized churches in Bay City. However, superimposed on the shared argot are also some specific lexical items and nuances of meaning that are unique and restricted to individual churches.

The thesis presented in this paper is as follows: through their verbal exchanges in the idiom of the argot, Spiritualists create the social organization of the church—the roles, statuses, and hierarchical relationships that articulate the church as a social institution. Once a church is organized and an incipient social structure is made explicit, participants within that structure formulate a grammar of rules for the continued and proper use of the argot by both themselves and newcomers to the church. Abiding by these rules, sanctioning their misuse, and generating new ones allows Spiritualists to control the structural evolution of the church through time. The social structure of the church has to be viewed and understood in terms of the speech events through which participants in the church: (1) define and make explicit their roles and statuses within the church, (2) test and affirm their mobility within the church hierarchy, (3) perceive and announce their own spiritual development, and (4) establish the context markers of church activity within the larger society.

In pursuit of the above task a study has been conducted to collect data on the use of the church argot through the techniques of ethnographic semantics. The lexicographic analysis proceeded through the following stages: (1) isolating the corpus of terms, (2) glossing each term in its natural speech context occurrence, (3) discovering the overall number of senses in which a term is used, and (4) demonstrating the relationships that exist between terms that label identical or similar referents.

The use of language in the church is a topic of great sensitivity to many Spiritualists, for it deals with some of what is considered the most sacred portion of the service, namely, the demonstration of spiritual communication through mediumship. In my analysis I do not wish to either secularize or profane these sacred services, nor to engage in a kind of reductionism and say that all mystery is locked within the spoken word. Rather, my attempt is to present a cultural and social system at work through the vantage point of participants in Spiritualist churches.

I. Social Organizations and Belief-systems of the Churches

Spiritualist churches claim the status of a Protestant denomination with religious and legal rights equal to those enjoyed by orthodox churches.

Spiritualist churches included in this study claim:

> Spiritualism is the science, philosophy and religion of continuous life, based upon the demonstrated fact of communication, by means of mediumship, with those who live in the spirit world. . . . (National Spiritualist Association Manual 1967:40)

These churches consider their activities to be scientific, philosophical, and religious. The scientific aspects consist of both the manifestations of the spirit world experienced or witnessed personally by individuals and the demonstrations performed by mediums in church services or sêances. It is through these experiences in the sêance room and in church services that the faith of both parishioner and medium is sustained and verified. This faith allows the parishioner to acknowledge the authenticity of the experience. The philosophical aspects are all the pastoral teachings and lectures which involve critical evaluation of the style and content of spirit communication and the conclusions derived therefrom. The religious aspects are conceptualized as the attempt to understand and live by the laws of nature, which are said to be also the laws of God.

Within this general definition of Spiritualism fall the activities of a great many churches and splinter groups active in Bay City. Therefore, the churches in this study were chosen not only on the basis of their stated beliefs and religious practices, but also on their organizational structures. All the churches herein described are: (a) legally and religiously recognized as being affiliated with the Spiritualist denomination, (b) regularly convened for religious worship, (c) formally organized as churches, and (d) open to the public at large. Excluded from fieldwork were privately held sêances and other spiritualist gatherings, conducted even by ordained ministers, which were not in a formal church or which did not develop out of some church affiliation of the participants.

All Spiritualist churches in Bay City render two kinds of service to their parishioners. First, there is the medium's *message*, either in the form of a reply to a parishioner's question about personal life problems or in the form of a lecture (sermon) addressed to the whole congregation about the laws for the appropriate conduct of life. (At first appearance, and later when helpful, argot terms are italicized.) Second, there is the *laying on of hands* as a form of *healing* to those who seek such help for physical ailments or mental disturbances. Both messages and healing are part of every church service.

For the purpose of fulfilling these two kinds of service, each church has a staff which is divided into the following categories: *student minister, healer, licentiate,* and *minister-medium*. Any person who belongs to any of these ministerial categories has specific obligations to discharge in connection with which he must resort to specific lexical items that are part of the church argot.

Two characteristics of all the church positions are that they are titular statuses which effect both legal protection for the practice of mediumship and formal division of labor for the church staff. Legally they function to allow a person to engage in counseling or healing without prosecution by the law for fortune-telling. Functionally they serve to indicate specific church jobs and so reduce the conflict and competition for these by the church staff.

The Church Staff

Student ministers are those individuals studying with the pastor in her *development class*. Some of these students are interested in church *work* and in eventually becoming certified as minister-mediums. These student ministers—primarily as part of training—are asked to assist in church work, in giving invocations and benedictions during church services or class meetings. Most student ministers have had previous experience with orthodox churches and consequently employ in their invocations or benedictions traditional Christian terms such as *Jesus Christ* and *Father, Son, and Holy Spirit*. These terms are not part of the accepted church argot, where they are replaced by such terms as *Christ Principle, Infinite Intelligence, Spirit World*, and *Angel loved-ones*. However, student ministers are not criticized for their use of orthodox terms and are told that they will do better as they gain confidence as public speakers and begin to use what they have learned in class, namely, the right terminology for church work. Student ministers do not give either healing or messages in public; hence, they are formally restricted from using certain of the church's religious terminology. They cannot claim in public to *see, hear, feel, sense,* or *intuit*, on the basis of which they can minister to the gathered flock. The use of these terms in public is reserved for the properly ordained ministers, whose *psychic* abilities have been formally recognized. Student ministers who insist on using the argot terms reserved for mediums are regarded as a threat to the church and as usurpers of power. They are sanctioned by the pastor, who may refuse to give them a message or may not assign them a church task. In effect, student ministers cannot use in reference to themselves any verbs such as *see, feel, sense, intuit, receive,* or *get* (which imply fully *developed spiritual powers*) or adjectives such as *sensitive, spiritual,* and *psychic* (which imply that the speaker is in contact with higher *forces* and therefore can recognize such qualities). The proper domain of speech for student ministers is the noun category. They may name those things that they have been taught, but they may not communicate, explicitly or implicitly, that they have personally contacted these *entities* or undergone these *experiences*.

Healers are charged with conducting the healing service, the laying on of hands, for those who come to them with problems of health or personal welfare. The healers utter public prayers for the general good health and welfare of the congregation at large. Such a prayer is usually phrased in the church argot. Healers, however, do not converse with their individual clients. Their job is silently to lay hands on the head of the client and act as a *channel* for the *healing forces* to flow to the client and restore him to "perfect health." In some churches, however, healers do give messages to their clients during or after the laying on of hands. The message is the same kind that a medium gives to a client. In the case of the healer, however, it is called an *independent reading*, since the client did not submit a question to be answered. In giving this message the healer uses much of the same terminology the medium uses. Healers who give such messages are looked down upon by the church pastor. She considers them to be ministering to the congregation beyond their abilities, since they have not yet been certified as mediums. Most of the conflicts in the church are over precisely such instances where members of the church staff usurp the medium's role and give messages in the church argot to the congregation.

Licentiates have the same religious privileges as minister-mediums, except that they cannot officiate at marriages. Within the church context they contribute to church work primarily in giving lectures during the church service. Normally they do neither healing nor message work. The *licentiate* is a transition title between *healer* and *minister-medium*. However, the certificate of licentiate is useful in that it allows its holder to give private consultations and receive referrals from the pastor when she does not want to deal with particular cases. Essentially, the certificate of licentiate allows the individual to counsel as any church minister would and be protected by law. Licentiates can use the full range of lexical items in the church argot. However, since they do not give messages in church, they do not have occasion to use this argot in public. If they insist on giving messages in public, they may be sanctioned by the pastor. Such sanctions may include her refusal to ordain them as full minister-mediums, or her postponement of ordination indefinitely.

Medium-ministers are in charge of the message work. It is in their province to use the full range of the church argot because they have demonstrated their *mediumistic* abilities and have been certified as mediums. Most churches are conducted by women pastors. Although a couple of churches in Bay City are run by men, these are exceptions. However, within Spiritualist circles in Bay City it is more common for men to assume the role of *healing ministers* and women to assume the role of *mediums*.

It is a rule of the churches that any person in one level of the ministerial hierarchy can use the lexical items characteristic of any ministerial level below his, but not of those above. The ministerial levels are hierarchical, with student minister being the lowest level and medium, the highest. Most individuals have to go through each level successively; it usually takes two years from the time someone new to Spiritualism qualifies for ordination as a minister-medium. Each church ordains its pastor's students with certificates of the national organization which chartered the church. It is in the classroom where students earn these ministerial certificates that the movement of Spiritualism is replenished, for each new minister-medium can open her own church and continue to train new people.

The Chartering Organization

All the churches in this study were officially chartered by at least one national Spiritualist organization, and all the ministers permanently associated with churches were certified by similar national organizations. Some churches held charters from more than one organization, under the justification that if one organization folded, the church would still be chartered by another and thus be protected by law in its spiritual ministry. Just as individual Spiritualist ministers have to be certified in order to operate within the law, so churches have to be chartered as official Spiritualist churches if they are to offer mediumship and healing. The charter does not vouch for the quality of the services offered, but it does indicate that the churches chartered and the ministers certified by national organizations have met minimum requirements of competency in the message work or healing.

The national organizations are all recognized federally, by the states, and locally as Spiritualist associations within whose right it is to charter churches, certify ministers, conduct courses on various aspects of Spiritualism, and sponsor Spiritualist camps. Each national organization does not necessarily have a mother church—that is, one that is regarded as the original church founded by the organization or one which serves as a headquarters for the organization. Rather, there exists a national office for each with a board of directors and officers to administer the business of the organization. The national organization functions with respect to the local churches it charters as a legitimizing agency, not a mother church.

Various national organizations are represented by chartered churches in Bay City, and they vary in belief-system, ritual practices, and the use of certain lexical items within the Spiritualist argot. For example, the United States Spiritualist Association (USSA) does not support any belief in *reincarnation*. Consequently, most of the churches chartered by the USSA do not use the Spiritualist argot developed around the notions of reincarnation which are upheld by other Spiritualist national organizations. USSA churches do not use in their service such terms as *reincarnation, karma, reembodiment*. On the other hand, the Universal Spiritualist Association (USA) accepts the giving of communion as part of the Spiritualist service, using the orthodox terminology associated with communion which is not accepted by the USSA. Since these differences exist between national organizations, a minister usually seeks a charter for her church from an organization whose beliefs are in harmony with her own. For the most important job of the national organization, from the viewpoint of the local church, is to stand by its chartered churches and protect them in case of legal action. Spiritualists point to several cases that occurred four years ago in a neighboring Bay City community. Several individuals who had consulted a medium accused her of fraud and turned to the police for prosecution of the medium. The national organization which had certified the medium provided her with legal counsel and succeeded in having the charges dismissed.

The Medium and Her Church

It might appear from the above statements that the chartering organization tends to stamp its own identity on its chartered churches. This is true only in part, because a minister affiliates with an organization that is compatible with her own belief-system and thus is able to shape her church according to her own image of what a Spiritualist church ought to be. For the most part, national organizations do not exercise any effective supervision over their chartered churches which would force them to adhere to any specified format of service.

In fact, individual churches are really centered around the personalities of their medium-pastors and possess many of the attributes of a charismatic cult. A pastor has opened the doors to her own church, which she has organized according to her wants and which she has legitimized by a charter from a national organization to her liking. The church is likely to move when the pastor moves and die when the pastor dies. Through time, the medium-pastor attracts clients, who constitute a personal following which the pastor can call *my people*. The pastor's *people* come to church to *receive the message* from the pastor, more so than from any other *medium working* in the church alongside the pastor. Although each church has an official name, all churches are referred to by the names of their pastors. For example, the Metaphysical Temple of Spiritual Life is known as Reverend Kelly's place or simply as Kelly's. This identification of the pastor's personality with the church as *ecclesia* is further indication of the complete and pervasive authority that the pastor maintains over church activities. Although each church has a board of directors or trustees, the pastor is always president of the board. The members of these boards are usually the pastor's spouse, personal clients who come to the pastor to receive messages, or personal friends who are not likely either to usurp power or to impose their will in church decisions.

Most churches do not have paid memberships. But most pastors have followings. The following is not permanent, however. It is customary for Spiritualists to *travel* from church to church in search of good messages. But at any given time each church does have a small nuclear group which attends it with some regularity. In time, the composition of this nuclear group changes. Once any person within the following of a pastor has entered a conflict situation either with the pastor or with another member of the following, he or she usually leaves the church and looks for another medium from whom to receive the message.

One final feature which is characteristic of all the churches is their geographical location. With one exception, the churches are located in downtown Bay City or in nearby commercial districts. Again, with the exception of two, all the churches are conducted in rented premises. The reason for this is that most pastors do not have the finances to buy a building and convert it into a church. Renting an office or an apartment and decorating it as a church is less expensive and is also less demanding of maintenance. Rented premises also allow a pastor more mobility. She may open a church or move its premises with greater ease according to her will.

II. Typology of Churches

Having pointed out some of the features common to all the churches, I will move now to consider the three types of churches characteristic of Bay City Spiritualism. These may be distinguished by the following criteria:

1. the nature of the Spiritualist organization which chartered the church and the kind of relationship established between the church and its chartering body;
2. the range of activities the church offers to its parishioners; and
3. the internal social organization of the church.

These variables are significant to parishioners when choosing a medium to follow. These organizational features are also significant in our analysis of the contexts and determinants for the use of the argot within the various churches. I visited and became acquainted with all the Spiritualist churches in Bay City. Long-term research, however, was conducted in only a few churches, which served as a sample. Table 20:1 presents an overview of the three types of churches in Bay City. Type A includes two churches in Bay City; in this category. I worked intensively with Reverend Cooper's

TABLE 20:1. *Comparison of Spiritualist Churches.*

	Type A	*Type B*	*Type C*
number of churches in sample	2(1)*	10(6)	8(4)
charter organization	USSA	USL/self-incorporated	A mother church (usually of Type B)
relationship with chartering organization	strong	weak	intermediate
RELIGIOUS ACTIVITIES			
church services	yes (weekly)	yes (weekly)	yes (irregular)
mediumship classes	yes (at medium's initiative)	yes (at client's request)	yes (at client's request)
lyceum	yes	no	no
séances	yes (by church pastor)	yes (by guest mediums)	no
SOCIAL ACTIVITIES			
clubs	yes	no	no
social events (bazaars, card parties, etc.)	yes (regular)	yes (infrequent)	no
INTERNAL SOCIAL ORGANIZATION			
paid membership	yes	no	no
hierarchy	rigid	weak	weak
client-medium relationships	authoritarian	egalitarian	egalitarian
client-client relationships	stratified	nonstratified	nonstratified
BELIEFS			
belief in reincarnation	no	no	yes
syncretistic beliefs	no	yes	yes
SOURCES OF SPIRITUALIST ARGOT			
chartering organization	yes	no	no
medium's teachings	yes	yes	yes
client's preferences	no	yes	yes

*Numerals in parentheses indicate number in sample studied.

Pacific Spiritualist Church. This church is affiliated with the United States Spiritualist Association of Churches. The pastor of the church and all its current ministers were ordained by this organization. The church proclaims the Declaration of Principles published by the USSA. During church services the USSA hymnal is used, as is the USSA *Manual* for any ceremonies, such as christenings or acceptance of new people into membership. This church participates in the state and national conventions of the USSA and abides by the rules and regulations set by the state and national boards. The church pastor always clearly indicates to the congregation that this church is an affiliate of the USSA, which, she states, is the Science, Philosophy, and Religion of Modern Spiritualism. The church upholds the belief-system of the USSA and does not support beliefs in reincarnation. A relatively strong affiliation with the chartering organization is one of the main characteristics of Type A churches.

The Pacific Spiritualist Church offers biweekly religious services and a Sunday morning *Lyceum* (Sunday school) for adults and children. The church further sponsors ladies' and gentlemen's clubs, which work for church-sponsored social activites and which also help sponsor the many and varied church social functions, such as dinners, card games, and bazaars. The Lyceum is frequented primarily by the clients of the pastor. On occasion, however, people new to the church are encouraged to attend, in order to learn more about Spiritualism. The ladies' and gentlemen's clubs are primarily supported by church members. The church social activites are scheduled throughout the year and are open to the public at large. Each of these activities is an annual event, repeated each year at approximately the same time. This church advertises its services weekly in the newspapers and invites the public to church and social events. The church also offers classes in spiritual development, conducted by the pastor, for persons who request them. Private consultations are available with the pastor and with any of the certified ministers. The pastor offers private séances on a very limited basis.

The Type A church is characterized by a high degree of organization. The Pacific Church has a paid membership of about one hundred eighty persons. All social events and church activities are conducted by the students of the pastor, who are organized into committees in charge of various tasks. Authority over all church matters is vested in the pastor and moves downward to the board of directors and the congregation in pyramidal form. The church occupies and owns its own building.

This church's services attract a congregation of about one hundred ten individuals, about sixty-five women and fifty-five men. The congregation is composed of some families and couples, but mostly of single adults. One feature of this church is the diversity of its congregation, which includes nearly as many men as women and a fair number of families and couples. The membership is overwhelmingly white; while there are no minority-group persons in the paid membership, a few blacks and Orientals do attend services.

Theologically, the church supports the teachings of the USSA and those of the pastor, which are reputed to have been given to her directly from *spirit.* Any beliefs upheld by the congregation which are contrary to those of these two sources are not given public expression.

Linguistically, this church shares the Spiritualist argot spoken within all churches. However, this church is characterized by some uniquely defined terms within the generally accepted argot. It does not use publicly any terminology associated with reincarnation, such as *reincarnation*, *karma*, or *reembodiment*. Although such terms are current in the general Spiritualist argot, they are not used in the Pacific Church. Further excluded are such terms (and their derivatives) as *psychic*, *astral*, *cosmic*, *astral travel*, *evil entities*, and *spirit possession*. Again, these terms form part of the shared Spiritualist argot of all churches. Type A churches do not employ the above-mentioned terms for several reasons: First, the strong affiliation of this church with the USSA partially determines the use of language. For example, the USSA continuously emphasizes the use of derivative forms of the term *spiritual* in order to minimally ally Spiritualism with mainstream Christianity. In contradistinction to *spiritual*, such terms as *psychic* or *astral* are shunned because they have a more secular connotation related to some people's talents or abilities, rather than to *church-developed spiritual* values. The USSA further encourages the use of such terms as *medium*, *counselor*, and *spiritual adviser* for the church staff, as opposed to the more common appellations of *reader*, *psychic*, *clairvoyant*, or, in jest, *fortune-teller*. The motivation of the USSA in favoring certain terminology within the Spiritualist argot has been to add dignity to the church staff, so that the public will not treat Spiritualism with the condescension shown to palm readers or roadside gypsies.

Another factor influencing the use of language in Type A churches is the well articulated teaching of the pastor. Reverend Cooper offers classes to her following in which she defines all the key terms used in the church service. During classwork she explains USSA referential meanings of such terms as *medium*, *mediumship*, *healer*, *healing*, *communication*, and *spiritual contacts.* In addition, she defines these terms further in light of her own teachings of Spiritualism. In line with her own teachings, she introduces terms which are not part of the official USSA lexicon but nonetheless are acceptable within Spiritualist circles. Examples are *God-consciousness*, *Godhead*, *soul-knowing*, and *Mind.* Since this argot is dealt with, albeit not explicitly as an argot, in classwork, and since most members of the pastor's following have participated in her classes at some point in their church affiliation, one can safely say that it is the common language that binds the pastor's following and allows them to assume a unique identity *vis-à-vis* other Spiritualist churches.

The determinants of the Spiritualist argot for churches of Type A are: (1) a strong affiliation with the chartering organization, (2) the authority and instruction of the pastor, and (3) the social cohesion of the pastor's following. These three factors allow for the development and maintenance of the church argot, and, conversely, the church argot serves as a platform for cohesive social action.

Often terms that are unique to one church (because they are coined or are given a special meaning by the pastor) are known to the Spiritualist community, because all churches share a clientele of *travelers* who attend, consecutively, all churches and thus serve as a channel for the diffusion of the argot. For example, Reverend Cooper was in the habit of using the term *soulmate* to refer to someone's ideally suited mate, either in this life or in *spirit world.* Individuals who frequented Reverend Cooper's church would use the term *soulmate* even at the church of another pastor. Most mediums in Bay City were acquainted with the term and recognized those who used it as Reverend Cooper's people. Most pastors would not use this term on their own initiative and would employ it only if the term appeared in the question posed by a client. Ultimately, any one church does not have a different Spiritualist argot, but simply a varied degree of use of terms employed by all Spiritualist churches.

Type B Church

Church Type B is the most common variety, in that there are ten in Bay City. I worked intensively with six of them. An example is Reverend Kelly's Metaphysical Temple of Spiritual Life. Churches of this type are affiliated with national organizations like the Universal Spiritual League, which differ from the USSA in that they allow the teaching of reincarnation and exert less control over their chartered churches. Some churches of Type B have also incorporated themselves as Spiritualist organizations empowered to charter daughter churches and ordain ministers under their own auspices. The Metaphysical Temple of Spiritual Life was originally chartered by the Universal Spiritualist League, but two years ago Reverend Kelly incorporated her church into a chartering organization. Thus, she became effectively the pastor of her own church and the president of her own corporation. When the church was affiliated with the USL, the pastor did not announce the affiliation to the congregation at regular intervals during the church service as is done in Type A churches, for the church upheld its own Declaration of Principles, compiled by the pastor. The hymnals used for church services are Cokesbury hymnals, which the pastor bought on her own. The church service is syncretistic, with Spiritualist elements and Catholic borrowings. The church offers communion services and supports beliefs in several saints. The pastor and several of the church ministers hold ordination papers from several organizations to which they have belonged over a period of years. The church never participates in conventions or business affairs of any chartering organization.

Reverend Kelly's church offers religious services three times a week. The church does not have a Sunday school, and very few of the pastor's followers have young children. Further, the church does not have social clubs and offers only a few church-sponsored social events. These social functions revolve around the holidays of Christmas and Easter and usually occur in conjunction with ceremonies of ordination of the pastor's students to some level of the Spiritualist ministry.

The church offers *spiritual unfoldment (mediumship)* classes with the pastor to a limited number of persons whom the pastor approves for classwork. During classwork the pastor instructs her students on aspects of Spiritualism as they have been written about in various sources. She does not claim to have received any teachings from the spirit world. The pastor gives private consultations and sometimes refers some of her parishioners to her student ministers whom she teaches about counseling. The pastor never conducts séances; for the purpose of demonstrating what they are, she invites guest mediums.

The church does not have a paying membership. The congregation is composed primarily of single adults, mostly women. The average attendance at a service is about thirty persons, of whom twenty-two are women and eight are men. Authority over all church matters is vested in the pastor. Various tasks of administering the church are performed by the pastor and her close friends or students who voluntarily assist her. The pastor's following is not organized into any network of committees for church activities.

Theologically the church presents the teachings of the pastor and any version of Spiritualist philosophy that is either acceptable to the congregation or that is expressed by a guest speaker and which is not defamatory of any other group. The pastor is eager to present materials that she knows her congregation and students are interested in. Consequently, the church teachings appear to reflect the attending congregation more than they do an *a priori* selection of ideas by the pastor.

The church rents its premises and has changed location twice in the past several years. The church is wholly dependent on the pastor for the performance of religious services, since no cadre is organized to conduct services in her absence. Compared to Church Type A, this church is more egalitarian in the relationships that exist between pastor and co-ministers and pastor and congregation. The pastor does not view her role as that of an advocate of Spiritualism, but rather as a minister who is charged with helping her flock in their daily problems. Consequently, the church offers many services, like communion, to those persons who wish it who have broken away from orthodox churches.

Linguistically, the church uses the full range of terms within the Spiritualist argot. Although the church is officially nondenominational, most of its staff and congregation acknowledge themselves to be Christian Spiritualists. In their words, "we go with Christ." Therefore, such terms as *communion* or *Holy Spirit* have been given Spiritualist meanings in addition to their traditional denotations. The church is primarily syncretistic, so it is easily able to adopt terms from other religions or philosophies and add Spiritualist meanings to them. The one exception lies with terms specifically associated with Type A churches. Such terms as *Infinite Intelligence*, *Mind*, and *Over-soul* are regarded as unnecessary euphemisms for the term *God* and therefore are not used often. Such terms are characteristic of the United States Spiritualist Association; because churches in Type B wish to define themselves as not being part of the USSA, they avoid them.

Churches of Type B do not have a strong affiliation with a chartering organization and do not, therefore, have any external pressures to use a particular set of terms, as do churches of Type A. It is up to the pastor to indicate any limitations on the argot used.

The pastor is sensitive to the linguistic modes of present-day hip culture, and such terms as *vibration, spiritual, meditation, phenomena, reincarnation,* and *karma* are recognized by her as being not only Spiritualist argot terms, but also part of the hip culture. The pastor clearly indicates that she accepts various usages of these terms within the church context. The philosophy behind the church is "to make people feel at home," so the full Spiritualist argot is accepted, and additional senses for the argot terms are allowed if they are an integral part of the out-of-church life of the clientele.

Type C Church

Type C includes eight churches in Bay City. I worked with four of them, and I shall use as an example Reverend Gilman's Chapel of Divine Truth.

This church is an affiliate of one of the practicing churches in Bay City which was incorporated into a chartering organization. The pastor and several of the practicing ministers of the Chapel of Truth (as it is abbreviated) have all been ordained or certified by the mother church, which is a variant form of Type B. Reverend Gilman uses the hymnals of the mother church and conducts services on the latter's premises. In effect, Reverend Gilman sublets one evening a week from the mother church for religious services of her own. The church abides by the rules and regulations of the mother church, and those rules are usually enforced. The staff of the mother church has easy access to the premises and keeps a watchful eye on the activities of all sublessees. If conflicts arise between Reverend Gilman and the staff of the mother church, Reverend Gilman's charter can be revoked and she can be asked to leave the premises.

Her church offers religious services once a week and offers no social activities, except for an occasional coffee break after services. The pastor does not offer mediumship classes. Private consultations are available with the pastor, but she does not offer séances. The church is not organized on a congregational basis with a regularly attending nuclear following; instead, the pastor announces when services will be held, and those who wish to follow her attend.

Theologically, the church does not sponsor a uniform and codified body of beliefs. It allows its platform to be used by speakers belonging to a number of metaphysical movements which are variants of Spiritualism, such as Science of Mind.

Linguistically, the church uses the full range of terms of the Spiritualist argot and is not distinguishable from church Type B. The only organizational feature which influences the use of language is the right of the mother church to ask the pastor not to use a term which it finds offensive. If the pastor persists in using it, a conflict will arise and the pastor may be asked to move her church elsewhere.

III. The Role of Language and the Spoken Word in Spiritualist Churches

Spiritualist churches share with other American metaphysical movements, such as Christian Science and New Thought churches, a belief in the inner power and meaning of words. Judah (1967:17) has clearly identified this belief as one of the defining attributes of Spiritualist churches when compared with orthodox denominations.

> Most metaphysical groups have a belief in an inner meaning of words beyond their dictionary definition—a meaning that cannot be discovered empirically from the standpoint of usage or etymology, but that is revealed intuitively. This is known by a variety of terms, such as the spiritual, metaphysical, or occult interpretation. Each leader of one of the sects may have his own special definitions which often disagree with the explanations of others. A particular metaphysical sect may make use of the Bible, but its exegesis does not exhibit an awareness of studies in histori-

cal and literary criticism, nor does its interpretation show any dependence upon orthodox theology past or present. To one not acquainted with this intuitional or inspirational method, the interpretation would appear to be allogorical. For the adherent of the metaphysical sect, however, it offers the key to a higher truth, through which the Bible appears in agreement with its particular interpretation.

An examination of the church argot as a set of utterances exchanged between parishioners and church functionaries has to begin with a particular view toward the role of speech (*parole*) within the belief and ritual systems of Spiritualism.

Spiritualists speak of the "power of the spoken word" in both the religious and secular spheres. Their claim is that words, once uttered, have the power to create or effect the referent which they symbolize. This belief is conceptualized by the saying: "words are things; once spoken they are deposited into the ether and will be picked up by like-thinking people." Once a word has been spoken, and particularly in the idiom of the Spiritualist argot, its referent gains an objective reality, a material manifestation, which it might have lacked prior to being verbally uttered.

The implication of this belief for a church participant is that he must use words very cautiously and self-consciously, because through his verbal utterances he effects both a personal and a social reality for himself and his fellow participants in the church. In the context of the church, an individual must not employ those terms restricted in use to an ordained healer or medium, lest he cause himself to believe that he is personally in contact with spirit forces and also convince his listener that he is an instrument for spirit communication. Thereby he may effect for himself the fictitious status of an ordained minister. In a more secular vein, an individual can affect his physical health through verbal communication. If one person tells another that he suspects himself to have an illness such as cancer or heart trouble, he may in fact acquire the illness or force himself to conduct his life as if he had that illness. Therefore, he must not label such things directly, but use a code name, an argot term. In essence, an individual has to be watchful of his language, so that he does not create for himself and others a reality which could be personally harmful or socially misleading. Spiritualists underscore the importance of spoken language in church participation because the *sine qua non* of any Spiritualist ritual is a verbal exchange between a medium and a parishioner. That communication in the form of an argot is the one religious symbol or artifact *sui generis* to Spiritualism.

As was stated earlier, the *raison d'être* of a Spiritualist church is *to bring the message* to its parishioners. Anyone who seeks a Spiritualist church (who is not just a curiosity-seeker) does so because he needs some kind of solution to a problem he faces. The mediums working in the church bring the message in two ways. The first is as a response to a question asked by a parishioner during the religious service. This is called *message work*. In the presence of the parishioner the medium contacts a spirit and is given the relevant information about the parishioner's question or problem. The medium then tells the parishioner what this information is. The medium's statements are called *the message*. Second, the medium may bring a message to the whole congregation on how to lead the good life and get in tune with nature's laws, which are God's laws. Abiding by this knowledge is supposed to prevent the parishioner from being defeated by the life-problems he faces. This message constitutes the church's teaching and is regarded as the philosophical portion of Spiritualism.

These two kinds of messages are the essence of any Spiritualist church, and both are verbal utterances exchanged between medium and congregation. It is essential that these messages be in the form of the spoken word because for the parishioner a message has to be an immediate, pertinent response to his problem at the time of the church service. Any reference to a written text within the message is regarded as preaching or moralizing and is not likely to be accepted. The message must be personally acquired by the medium in the presence of the client. On a congregational level, the message as philosophy of life must be revealed orally by a medium through the form of a *spirit*-inspired address (lecture, sermon, or classwork). This verbal style allows the congregation to accept the message as spirit's assessment of the human condition at the moment of the church service; thus the message assumes a public significance and is understood by each person in the congregation to be also personally relevant. For both kind of messages, the personal and the congregational, a religious argot is used.

The fact that the messages are presented verbally and are couched in terms of an argot is also significant to the social organization of the church. For Spiritualists the word of God is constantly revealed to man via the mediumship of Spiritualist ministers. The medium reveals to her following "the word" and continues for the duration of her ministry to reveal the message anew. Her presentation is always an oral delivery; the word is seldom transcribed. Therefore, to receive the message an individual must be acquainted with the argot in which the message is couched. To learn the argot an individual must continue to participate in church life and thereby to support the church organization financially and socially. The medium as the revealer of the word has prerogatives about the kind of language in which she will deliver the message; she cannot be questioned about the accuracy or content of the message, because she is considered only an *instrument* for spirit and not the initiator of the message. Her authority and privilege in the church are recognized by all, because at any time she can refuse to act as an instrument of the message and thus can deprive her following of *spirit guidance.* Furthermore, her congregation cannot easily refer to any of her past revelations, none of which has been written down, and so there is no binding text to transcend any disagreement within the congregation and keep it unified in the absence of the continuously revealed word of the medium.

Each medium has her own style of speech for delivering the message and is also known for that, as well as for the content or quality of her guidance. The following commanded by any medium is interested not necessarily in Spiritualism as a religion with a body of beliefs, but in the particular medium's version of Spiritualism, her own teachings. Consequently, there is no unified body of ideas that would cement the Spiritualist churches and transcend the individuality of any one.

Spiritualist churches lack a system of three-dimensional religious symbols. They do not subscribe to the use of crosses, figurines of saints, candles, altars, or ritual vestments. In orthodox churches such symbols can be purchased, worn on one's person, or kept in one's immediate environment. These symbols can, among other things, arouse in the individual feelings associated with the church, give him an overt identity *vis-ā-vis* other members of a community, and serve as objects of meditation and silent prayer.

Spiritualism does not use any three-dimensional objects to symbolize any of its beliefs or practices. Spiritualists consider that words perform for them the function graven images do for othodox Christians. They claim that they repeat *affirmations* when they want to experience church-related feelings. Or they choose some term from their argot to meditate or pray silently with. Instead of holding an object, Spiritualists say that one should hold a thought or word. Finally, they recognize each other and present their Spiritualist identity to the community by using the language of the church, the argot.

Orthodox denominations enjoy a sacred space known as the church. The church building is treated with reverence, whether a religious service is in progress or not. Most Spiritualists do not have a church edifice and consequently cannot claim a sacred space that is physically defined. Since their churches are conducted in rented or sublet premises, they must rely on some mechanism that will distinguish the sacred from the profane for the religious service. Such a mechanism is the spoken invocation and benediction by the church pastor, a verbal utterance in the argot of the church which renders a secular space into a sacred one.

Not only is the spoken word of theological and social importance within the context of the church, it is significant also as a practical response by the church to community legal pressures. The churches have created a religious argot that protects the medium from legal prosecution and allows the client to conclude that the medium is in contact with spirits. The argot is based on a set of terms that are sufficiently ambiguous to allow the maximum selective interpretation on the part of the client. The client is expected to make his own equation between what the medium is saying in the message and what he asked in his *billet*. Such an ambiguous terminology would not allow a client to lodge a formal complaint against a medium, for he would lack prima facie evidence against the medium. Also, the argot has a set of terms which can be used in the message to indicate that the information really comes from spirits. An example of a message, in Section VI demonstrates how the argot is used.

What is characteristic about these terms and the way they are woven together into a language is that anyone who is listening to the message, be he a police decoy or the congregation at large, never knows what is referred to unless he wrote the *billet*, in which case he will assume that the medium is referring to his problems. But the rest of the audience is left ignorant of the nature of the problems being addressed. The argot protects the medium. Mediums can and do err in the kinds of information they convey to clients when they are not using argot terms. Mediums can given inaccurate advice, or they can be accused by clients of having given wrong advice. The language is useful in allowing a medium to convey information or to sidestep questions of total strangers whose queries and problems are often unfathomable to her. Finally, the argot allows her to show that she communicates with the spirits. This gives the system of belief a kind of rationale and "logic" which it would lack if answers to questions were given directly in standard daily speech.

IV: Church Contexts for the Use of the Argot

At the core of Spiritualist churches are the *messages* which individuals send and receive. It is impossible to understand Spiritualists without a knowledge of the subtle meanings which are attached to these communication events. But meaning is not revealed from a textual analysis of the messages in themselves. They can only be understood in their context. We have already examined the structural features of the churches and the three types of churches with some of their characteristic argot forms. Now I shall consider the contextual situations in which speech events occur. These include church services, mediumship classes, social events, séances, and private readings (consultations). Then I shall discuss the actual use of the argot, including the persons who are senders and receivers of the messages.

The Church Service

The majority of Spiritualist church services are conducted on weekends. However, some churches meet also during the week, primarily in the evening. Such evening services usually begin around seven-thirty, to accommodate a clientele that commutes by bus. As people enter the church, they find a table by the door upon which are hymnals and two baskets, one for a *love offering* (donation) and one for *billets* (written questions for the medium to answer during the portion of the service called message-work). Most regular attendees of the church prepare billets in the church; however, new people often prepare theirs at home, at work, or elsewhere, in advance of the service. Those who do not know that they must write a question are advised of this by a church secretary, seated at the table, who introduces them to the billet format. This conversation with the secretary is the first contact a client has with the church argot. The secretary socializes newcomers into the terminology of *message* writing and *message receiving*. She uses a series of nouns to describe the billet and the message: *billet, reading, message, psychic reading, independent reading*. The secretary further describes to the client how the *medium works* by using the following verbs: *see, feel, sense, get, give, intuit, read, psychometrize*. Finally the client is told about *receiving* the *message* with a set of verbs such as *accept, welcome, recognize*, and *confirm*. The secretary uses all these terms in referring to the work of the pastor of the church. She does not use any of them in an active voice in reference to what she herself can do, even if she is an ordained medium in her own right. This is the pastor's church, and the church staff does not claim to have the same *powers* as the pastor when speaking to a newcomer. Most newcomers do not understand what the secretary is talking about, but follow the simple instructions of writing down a question to be answered by the medium. If the client returns to the church, in time he or she will learn what the specialized terms mean. The secretary simply uses the church language; she does not define it for anyone. Newcomers show obvious perplexity at this usage.

The client new to the church writes his billet in standard English. Typical billet questions for a newcomer are: Will my rent be raised? Will I be able to pursue my music effectively? Should I stay in Bay City or go back home to Wisconsin or keep traveling, perhaps to the South? However, those who continue coming to the church and who learn the argot used there, learn also to use that argot in their billets. For example: "Just a *message* please." "Will *conditions* improve around me?" "Have you a *message* for me?" "When will I start having *phenomena*?" "What about *vibrations* around the office?" "What about my sister's *spell*?" Such questions indicate to the medium that the client is a regular attendee of Spiritualist churches.

Once a client has submitted his billet, he or she takes a hymnal and chooses a seat. Most individuals do not know others in the church; if they do, anonymity is usually maintained. It is deemed inappropriate to engage strangers in conversation or to pry into others' personal problems. It is these very personal questions that brought clients to the church in the first place, and they are not acceptable topics of casual conversation in the context of the church service or in the few minutes before it begins. Clients usually do not come to church much before the start of the service, so the wait in the church is never very long and is not necessarily conducive to conversation. The mediums do not circulate in the congregation; they are usually seated or standing behind the platform (pulpit), or else they remain in a back room until the service begins.

At the advertised hour the service begins with an invocation by one of the church staff. The invocation contains a series of nominal terms applied to *God*, such as *Infinite Intelligence, spirit force*, and *over-soul;* a series of verbs describing the activity of the *spirits* in coming to the church to *help* the congregation; a series of adjectives naming the quality of help the spirits can offer; and finally a series of nouns labeling the problems that the congregation might have brought to the Spirits for a message.

After the invocation several hymns are sung. Hymns are either traditional orthodox ones like "Rock of Ages" or specifically Spiritualist hymns addressed to *spirit world*. These hymns describe the wonders of spirit world and the joy of the congregation to unite with their *spirit loved-ones*, and they beseech the *spirits* to come to their aid. Such hymns employ argot terms which label spirits, describe aspects of spirit land, and indicate the actions that spirits perform.

A lecture or sermon follows the singing. Lectures deal with the belief-system of the church and instruct the congregation on laws of *right living*. Sometimes lectures are replaced by Bible readings with appropriate commentary on the applicability of certain passages to the congregation's daily lives.

A collection plate is then passed, and a further benediction is uttered over the *love-offering* collected. Such a benediction uses the same argot terms as the invocation. Up to this point the service has lasted about forty minutes; the next portion of the service, the message work, will last for about one hour, or as long as it takes the medium to answer all the billets submitted to her.

During message work the medium uses the full range of argot terms. Each medium has a style of speech of her own. Variations in style exist not only with regard to the actual argot terms used, but also with respect to the frequency and emphasis of particular terms. Following the message work a benediction is uttered, and the congregation disperses.

Some of the essential features of a church service relevant to this study are the following: First, the client can attend a Spiritualist service and virtually not utter a word during his entire stay. If a client does not have any questions on how to write a billet and does not choose to sing hymns, he can remain silent. Second, for about two hours a client has been spoken to by a variety of church personnel, each employing a certain segment of the terms in the general Spiritualist argot. A new client does not understand much of what is said to him. If he returns to the church regularly, he will learn the argot terms. Third, if any conversation takes place between a client and a medium when the latter is giving a message to the former, the conversation never includes a request by the client for the medium to clarify her terms. Mediums do not explain their argot during the church service; they use it. It is up to the client to find out on his own what terms mean. To understand the message, a client must have some command of the argot.

Mediumship Classes

The place where many Spiritualists acquire a familiarity with the church language is in the pastor's mediumship classes. Mediumship classes are known in the argot by several other terms, such as *development classes* and *unfoldment classes.* One speaks of *sitting for development classes.* Each of these terms has certain implications in the belief-system of the church, and the terms are not completely synonymous. For example, *unfoldment* implies that each person contains within himself the abilities of mediumship and *sensitivity to spirit influences*, while the term *development* emphasizes the role of the trainer over that of the trainee. *Unfoldment* implies the spiritual nature of man, while *development* connotes to the Spiritualist a certain artifice and artistry bordering on theatrics. Regardless of how a pastor prefers to name her classes, they usually have similar attributes. A pastor tries to instruct a select group of persons on how to be *receptive* to spirit-contact. The people that attend class are not the anonymous public that comes to services. Usually a person who has been attending church for some time approaches the pastor to ask whether she offers *mediumship* classes. The medium in all cases chooses her students from among the inquiring clients. When enough people have inquired and the pastor can get from eight to twelve persons, she will usually start a class. The classes meet on week nights for about two hours and may continue anywhere from a few weeks to a few months.

During class meetings an individual encounters the first instance of fluent, easy-going social conversation. People are introduced by name and engage in small-talk. At the advertised hour the class begins with an invocation in the argot terms. Students are never told that they must use the argot terms for the invocation; however, they learn to imitate the pastor, which implies learning to use her terminology. In class the student does not learn a set of prescriptive rules for church verbal behavior. He learns, rather in the way a child learns his native language, the practical and customary patterns of speech required for public performance in a Spiritualist church context. After the invocation the pastor begins by telling some funny anecdotes or by singing a couple of hymns. This serves to *warm the atmosphere, raise the vibrations, invite the spirit forces*, or simply to relax and humor the students. Once the mood has been set, the pastor will ask if anyone has anything to report that has happened to him or her during the week. This allows each person to report either his personal tragedies or his joyful events with some comment on how these were anticipated. Such anticipation can be a sign that the individual is becoming *spiritually developed*, or it can serve as a sign that he *received* an accurate *message* from the pastor when he last attended the church service. In the process of this reporting, the students are taught some of the argot. For example, a student will begin by saying; "I had a dream this week. I dreamt that I was back home and there was a storm and I talked to my mother and she was so real just like she was right there." The pastor responds, "That's what we call a *soul flight*. We visit our *loved ones* and are able to *communicate* with them in *spirit world*." When the individual next recounts her dream she will say, "I had a *soul flight* last week, I spoke with my mother." If anyone reports an illness, he is given the term *spell* as a substitute term for either the specific name of the disease or any of its symptoms. If an individual speaks of personal anxieties, of conflicts at home or at work, he is given the term *conditions* as a substitute term. If an individual reports difficulties with roommates, landlords, or residential moves, he is given the terms *environment, home situation*, or *vibration*.

Henceforth, the student will use these terms, and the pastor will use them in return, in giving a message to the student. Once these personal accounts are related, the pastor moves on to present the substantive material to be covered in the class. Such material can be either her own teachings *received by her from spirit* or some published literature about a topic to be covered, such as *meditation*, aspects of the human body which are spiritually significant, or the various *laws of life*. Such material is written in the Spiritualist argot, but it has the distinction of defining contextually the terms it uses. For example, a pastor may say: "We often see *spirits* as *colors*, and different *colors tell* us the kind of *spirit* we are in *contact* with. Yellow means the *spirit* of a *healer*." The argot term *color* is here defined as spirit, and, even though *spirit* is an argot term itself, we are nonetheless able to see the sense in which the term *color* is used and its status as a synonym for the term *spirit*.

Following the presentation of the reading material, which is read aloud by the pastor, is a period of *concentration* and *meditation*. During this period students sit around a table with the lights turned off. After the repetition of an *affirmation* (a prayer which asserts the goodness of the individual and the protection he *receives* from *spirit*) students sit silently and try to *see what they can see and feel what they can feel*. After several minutes each person begins to report what he has *seen, heard*, or *felt*. This reporting involves using argot terms. After this period, which is variably called meditation or concentration or sitting in the silence, a benediction is offered, and class is dismissed.

The essential feature of classwork which is significant from the point of view of language is that the argot terms are presented in a rather full context. Moreover, a kind of substitute definition is given in the pastor's implicitly stating that a given Spiritualist form should replace a given standard form in a given context. The client is given an opportunity to practice using the argot in conversing with his friends and fellow students about topics of daily life. It is this further use of argot terms in social conversation with friends during church social functions which serves to enhance the socialization of an individual into church life.

Social Activities

Social activities such as dinners, bazaars, or card games are not pervasive in Spiritualist churches and are restricted in Bay City to some of the largest churches where the pastor is active in promoting either a membership or a steady clientele for church services. The example here is drawn from Reverend Cooper's Pacific Spiritualist Church. The Pacific Church sponsors activities for which tickets are sold at church services by some of the pastor's students. The work for any church social is done by the church members or the pastor's students, who are organized into small groups which meet weekly to discuss the pastor's teachings and to *meditate* to increase their *spiritual sensitivity*. The main purpose of the social event is to raise money for a particular project within the church, such as improvement of the premises or a building fund.

People who come to the socials are either regular parishioners or new people investigating the activities offered by the church. New people usually do not initiate interaction with the church staff; they wait to be approached and incorporated into a group. The church regulars associate mostly with those who are in their weekly classes. Conversation revolves around the pastor's teachings or the meanings of argot terms. There is very little conversation about personal life or daily activity. This is due in part to the lack of common bonds among many of the individuals who attend the church. The only area of commonality is the church experience, and that experience has a language to describe it, the argot. The social is an opportunity for the pastor's students to reinforce each other's use of the church argot. If one individual will discuss a church matter in standard English terms, he will be corrected and offered a substitute term from the argot. For example, one individual may complain about a parishioner who slammed the door on his way out of church while the service was still in progress, ruining the attention of the congregation. At this point another student will interrupt the speaker to simply say, "*vibrations*," which is the substitute term for the secular description of the church atmosphere, the drama of the *message service*, and so on. During social functions a church client is socialized by his peers into the use of the church argot. Those churches that have no socials usually accomplish this during classwork or in conversation before or after services. Actually, this is not a problem, because most newcomers to Spiritualism first attend one of the larger churches, where they are initiated into the argot, and only with time discover the smaller churches, which usually do not have social events. By the time clients reach the less known churches, they are familiar with the argot.

Séances and Private Readings

The church argot is significant in two other instances, the séance and the private reading. The séance is usually offered by a medium to a select group of clients. Séances are not open to the public at large. There are various kinds of séance. First is the *materialization séance*, where an individual's friends, relatives, or *spirit mentors materialize* before him out of the *ectoplasm* of the medium. Second is the *trumpet séance*, where the same departed individuals speak to the client through the voice *instrumentality* of the medium. *Spirits* are said also to send *apports*, items such as jewelry or personal mementos, to the clients via the *trumpet*, which is a spherical object made out of tin, papier-mâché, or newspaper. Whichever kind of séance a person attends, one factor is paramount: either a person is addressed directly by a spirit in his or her own words and approximate voice, or the medium relates to the client what a spirit is *saying* to him. If a *spirit speaks* directly to a client, then standard English is used with an attempt to reproduce the vernacular of the place and time when the spirit lived. If, however, the medium relates information which she receives for the client, then the Spiritualist argot will be used. The distinction between the voice of the spirit and the voice of the medium is one that is made by Spiritualists. The speaker in either case is the medium; except when the voice of a spirit is heard, it is argued that the spirit is using the vocal cords of the medium. The séance is usually conducted in a darkened room, and a client only hears the voice of the medium and does not see her facial expressions or the movement of her lips.

In private readings the Spiritualist argot is only used part of the time. A private reading is a private consultation which a client secures with the church pastor or some other medium. This is regarded by most Spiritualists as the most desirable form of *communications* with *spirits* because here the medium can speak privately and therefore does not have to shield what the spirits say. Private readings are requested by clients, and pastors grant appointments mostly to those who have previously been to their churches. When an individual comes to a private reading, he usually chats with the medium for a few moments in order to *warm the atmosphere*. Then the medium will ask the client whether he would prefer to talk or be talked to. On some occasions the medium will ask the client to open to a section of the Bible and read. The content of the passage read will serve as an entrée for the medium to start speaking with the client. It is expected that the medium will *bring forth* from *spirit* some information which will pertain to the need, question, or worry of the client. As the information is produced, the client indicates some kind of recognition of whether the information is accurate or whether there is need for further talk by the medium in order to hit the point at issue. Once the problem has been mentioned, the medium will converse with the client about it. During the first part of the interview when the medium is receiving information from spirit, all topics are phrased in the church argot. However, when the medium converses with the client there is a shift to standard English.

As can be seen from my description of the various church activites, the Spiritualist argot is significant in the following ways: first, it is the mode of expression for any information which a medium relates from *spirit;* second, it serves as a social bond for a pastor's clients; third, it allows a Spiritualist church to acquire an identity vis-á-vis both orthodox churches and other Spiritualist churches; and finally, it offers a language which shields the content of the message. Shielding the content of the message is necessary for a medium if she is to avoid conflict with the law.

V. Method and Conceptual Framework for the Analysis of the Lexicon

The relevance of ethnographic semantics to ethnography has been in the study of cognition through the semantic organization of lexical aspects of a people's language. Most lexicographic studies made in the context of ethnographic semantics have dealt with cognitive systems which have as a referent some aspect of the physical world which is three-dimensional, like firewood (Metzger and Williams 1966) or color categories (Conklin 1955), or otherwise demonstrable, like skin disease (Frake 1961). While many scholars have spoken enthusiastically about the importance of such studies (Sturtevant 1964; Kay 1970), other scholars have pointed to the limitations in the literature in terms of both the limited data presented and the methodology used (Frake 1961; Burling 1964; Berreman 1966). The various arguments within the field of ethnographic semantics have been reviewed by Colby (1966). Most recently Berlin (1968) has published data dealing with Tzeltal numeral classifiers, presenting a complete corpus of terms in an attempt to overcome some of the limitations for which the field has been criticized.

My research differs from previous studies in the following ways: Part of the argot deals with referents which have no representation in the material world; the referents are abstract. Such terms as *spirit, spiritual, sensitive, psychic, clairvoyant,* and *vibrations* do not have demonstrable material referents. Furthermore, as conceptual categories they are never explicitly and concretely defined; rather, it is expected that such terms will be understood from observation of their usage in the church contexts. This argot deals with issues and items which are regarded as religiously sacred and about which informants are very secretive.

The methodology used to gather information on this argot has been dictated largely by the sacred nature of this language and by the difficulty of discussing utterances of informants in the speech contexts of church life. I have not been interested in elicited speech, because the quality of information would have suffered. It was my responsibility first to determine the corpus of the argot by itemizing the lexical terms essential to it; then, to isolate instances where each lexical item was used; and later, to gloss each instance of use for its referential meaning and function. I was led to conclude that perhaps the language of Spiritualism and the *séance* room is the one most suitable for analysis by the field of ethnographic semantics, so haunted by the spirit of "hocus pocus or God's Truth."

In considering the methodology and the analysis of the relationships between the terms, some clarification is needed. At the outset of fieldwork I was not aware that Spiritualist churches used an argot in church-related activities. The linguistic material was uncovered only after research in the churches was under way.

Once I realized the existence of the argot, I attempted to elicit information about it from several informants. This initial attempt failed for several reasons. First, I was a newcomer to the church, I did not know many people, and my interest in the church was not yet established. My informants were not sure whether I was genuinely interested in learning about and participating in Spiritualism or whether I was merely a curiosity-seeker who might mock church practices. I had not earned the trust of my informants. Second, the argot is a secret and sensitive area with church personnel. When I originally inquired about argot terms, I was simply refused information. Third, I did not know what the full range of argot terms was, nor did I know the uses to which language was put in Spiritualist churches, and therefore I was not sure what I wanted my informants to tell me. Unlike anthropologists who go into communities and attempt to discover the native categories for such things as diseases or colors, I was not dealing with objects or concepts that I could say *a priori* Spiritualists would have labels for. One can safely assume that every community will have some terminology for colors, particularly those colors in its natural habitat which involve objects of particular social or cultural import. I did not know which concepts or objects Spiritualists deemed particularly significant and so could not ask informants about their labels. Therefore, participant-observation was essential to first acquaint me with those things that Spiritualists had labels for; then I could attempt to discover the meanings of the labels. Fourth, I realized in the initial phases of fieldwork that all the senses of the argot terms were created through the church usage of the terms. Some of these senses are standard to the argot. For example, the term *spiritual* is most frequently used in the sense of "someone who leads a righteous life in accordance with the principles of life, called laws of nature, put forth by a Spiritualist church." But, through creative use of the argot, new senses are given to the standard argot. For example, Reverend Wilkins used the term *spiritual* in the sense of "someone who is psychic, developed to receive spirit communication." This latter sense of the term would have eluded me unless I had observed it in use. Such usages have to be observed in actual occurrence. To interview informants and to elicit information about the argot yields only standard meanings, such as the first sense of *spiritual*. A substantial portion of the innovative usages of the argot are usually not presented. This was my experience with my informants; the generalization may not hold for other research projects.

Observation in natural context leads, also, to direct questioning. The replies of informants are then checked against past and subsequent observations of natural usage. These suggest new questions for direct elicitation which allow one to draw a distinction between the idiosyncratic speech of an informant and the standard usage of the terms.

In one year's fieldwork within the churches, I was able to learn a great deal about the argot through my personal participation in the church. It was after that time that I began to introduce into my interviews questions dealing with the argot. I had established full rapport with my informants, I had compiled a list of argot terms, I had discovered what I thought to be the function or role of such an argot, and my objective was to learn what my informants considered the argot terms to be and how they viewed the role of such an argot in church life. After intensive fieldwork, I could use my own knowledge of the church as a foil for eliciting additional information from my informants.

The initial period of fieldwork undertaken before any linguistic inquiry could be made was essential to acquiring a personal criterion for judging the linguistic information that my informants were at last willing to give me.

Once the argot terms were collected, I attempted to gloss each term. The glosses allowed me to group the terms according to certain relationships. The linguistic analysis has been primarily useful in allowing me to verify ethnographic information that I had collected through observation. The linguistic material offered data that could be verified by other researchers to allow for consensual validation of my thesis.

VI. Lexical Data and Analysis

The argot terms can be grouped into topical categories. The full lexicon consists of several hundred terms, of which I present here only an example of the kinds of terms under consideration. The topical categories for the argot terms have been defined by informants.

A. THE PLACE WHERE *spirits* RESIDE:

spirit world
sphere
astral plane
astral world
atmosphere
ether
summerland

B. THE OCCUPANTS OF *spirit world:*

angel loved one
color
cosmic entity
spirit entity
spirit force
light
spirit
guide
nature spirit

C. PHYSICAL FEATURES OF THE *spirits:*

astral body
aura
vibrations

D. PSYCHIC EXPERIENCES OF PARISHIONERS:

astral flight
astral projection
automatic writing
communication
experience
phenomena
soul flight
materialization

billet is. At the end the medium asks to whom the billet belongs and whether the message made any sense.

Analysis of Argot Terms

To illustrate the analysis of the argot terms enumerated above, we may look at the category labeled "occupants of spirit world," and see the relationships that exist between the terms. One relationship is a paradigmatic one describing how spirits manifest themselves and are thereby recognized by informants. (Diagram 20:1).

	heavenly manifestation	earthly manifestation
Supreme Being	infinite intelligence	truth love
Individual Souls	spirit	voices colors lights

Diagram 20:1

It is of crucial importance to Spiritualists to receive a message from *spirit*. However, it is not only the content of the message that is important, it is also the source of the message. Messages can be said to come from spirits or from Infinite Intelligence (God). Furthermore, in identifying the source, Spiritualists also desire to personally experience a communication from that source. The only way they can experience such communication is to recognize its form. The terms in the grid indicate the forms that such spirit manifestations assume in both the heavenly and earthly spheres.

Another relationship that exists between terms is a part-whole relationship (Diagram 20:2).

The term *band* in Level I is the most general term applied by Spiritualists to include all the spirits in whose province it is to *guide*, *guard*, and *protect* a parishioner. When a medium uses the term *band*, she is indicating to a parishioner that he has attracted to himself *spiritual helpers*, but that his spiritual development has not progressed sufficiently to allow him to know the particular spirits according to their specific tasks or proper names. With the parishioner's additional spiritual development or unfoldment, the

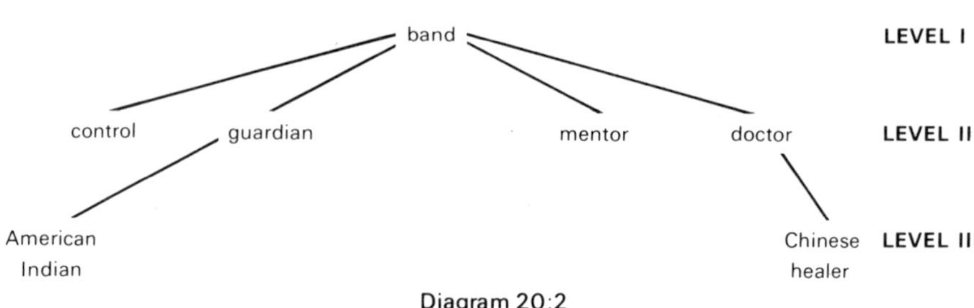

Diagram 20:2

medium begins to factor out for him the particular areas in his secular and religious life where individual spirits are instrumental. Therefore, in Level II we see the specialization of spirits being enumerated. A *control* directs the parishioner's psychic experiences; a *guardian* protects the individual in his daily life; a *mentor* teaches the parishioner the metaphysical laws of life; and a *doctor* guides the parishioner's development as a healer and also heals any physical or mental disturbances he may have. For those parishioners who continue to progress, the medium offers specific names of guides and identifies their ethnic backgrounds. Thus in Level III we find American Indians and Chinese healers, who specialize in guarding and healing the parishioner. Diagram 20:2 indicates the chronology in which parishioners are introduced to members of their bands.

A third relationship is the one organized along the dimension of time—the familiarity of a parishioner with the argot terms from his first visit to church until the time that he receives his own *guides* (Diagram 20:3).

LEVEL I: *God* is the most general term applied to *spirits*. Stated another way, the occupants of spirit land are given the attributes of omnipotence, omniscience, and omnipresence which are exclusively accorded to God in orthodox churches.

LEVEL II: This level indicates the more specific labels for God. *Spirit* as a generic noun for all occupants of spirit land contrasts with *infinite intelligence* and *mind*, which are direct labels for God and do not include spirits.

LEVEL III: *Truth* and *love* further specify labels for God. Both of these terms are regarded as manifestations of God on earth; truth further corresponds to the teachings of a Spiritualist church, and *love*, to the Golden Rule. The two terms allow the speaker to invoke both God and the essential creed of a Spiritualist church. These two labels for God are contrasted with *voices*, which are the earthly manifestations of spirit. Voices heard by a parishioner at certain times are perceived to be spirits attempting to communicate with him.

LEVEL IV: Voice manifestations of spirit over time can become *lights*, or visible manifestations. Voices evolve into lights as the parishioner continues to develop spiritually and communicate with spirits. Hearing voices, or sounds in general, is one of the earliest kinds of psychic experience reported by parishioners.

LEVEL V: Lights turn into *colors* with yet further spiritual development by a parishioner.

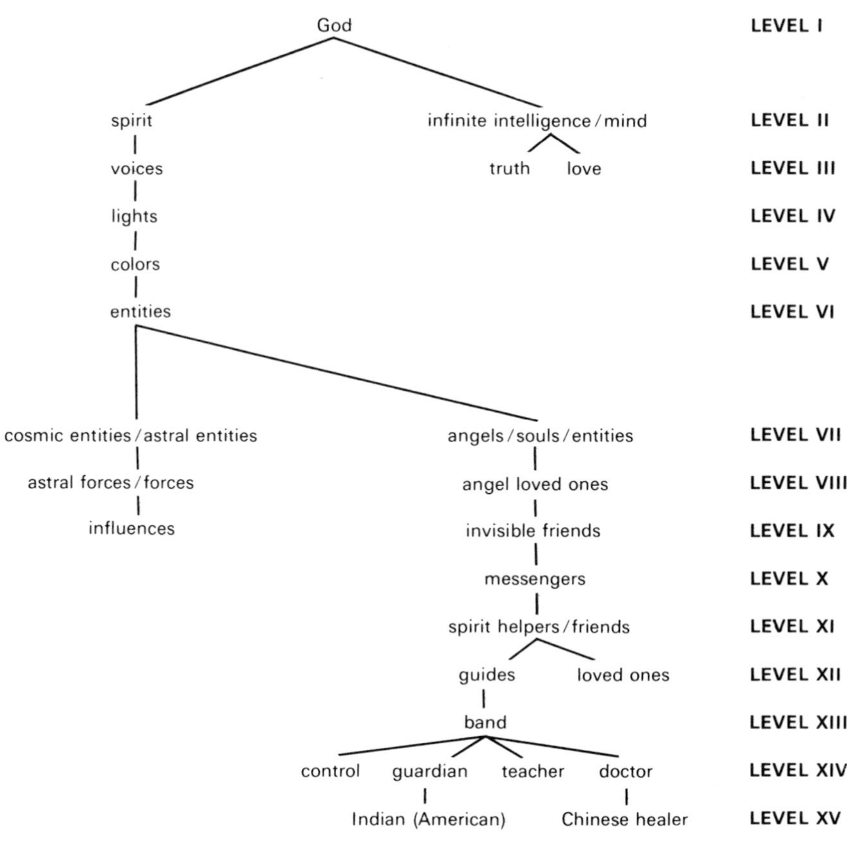

Diagram 20:3

Level VI: The voices, lights, and colors are manifestations of spirit, but some individuals conceive of them as spirits in disguise, and collectively label them *entities. Entities* is the most general term to indicate the existence of a *soul* or *force* in a supraearthly dimension, such as spirit world or astral sphere.

Level VII: Entities are differentiated into more specific categories by the mediums. They relegate entities into two contrasting categories, *cosmic entities/astral entities* and *angels/souls/entities.* Both sets of terms share the characteristic of referring to things that exist in another dimension of life; but the two contrast along a single dimension—their specific geographical or spatial location within that other dimension. *Cosmic entities/astral entities* are souls of individuals who seek to be reincarnated in a living person on this earth in order to atone for misdeeds enacted while the entity was an earth-living individual. Such entities reside in the *astral plane.* However, *angels/souls/entities* are souls of individuals who have entered spirit land and who are able to grow and progress within spirit land and resume "a life on the other side."

LEVEL VIII: *Astral forces/forces* are *cosmic entities* which actively seek individuals on this earth through whom they can either atone for their misdeeds or sate their vices; such *forces* are usually regarded as undesirable or malevolent. *Angel loved ones* are all those souls who pass on to spirit world and seek to help humans in their daily needs; such entities are desirable and helpful. Both sets of entities share the feature of being involved in human affairs, but differ in the nature of that involvement, whether good or evil from the point of view of the parishioner. In effect, an entity aiding the parishioner in his difficulty is an angel loved one, and one which destroys him further is an astral force.

LEVEL IX: *Influences* are forces that actively direct a parishioner's activity, while *invisible friends* offer guidance, but allow the parishioner free will on whether to abide by their guidance. The contrast between these two terms is on the basis of explicit control over the actions of the parishioner.

LEVEL X: *Messengers* are those invisible friends who communicate with a parishioner primarily through the instrumentality of a medium in a message service.

LEVEL XI: *Spirit helpers/friends* are those messengers who are identified by the medium as spirits who take a particular interest in a parishioner and continuously come to his aid.

LEVEL XII: *Guides* and *loved ones* are two sets of spirits that share the status of being spirit *helpers*, but they are contrasted by the medium along the criteria of the relationship each helper had with the parishioner while the former was on the earth plane. Loved ones are always blood or affinal relatives or close friends of the parishioner who have passed on to spirit. Guides, however, can be complete strangers who have taken an interest in the parishioner because spirit cares for the welfare of those left on the earth plane.

LEVEL XIII: All a parishioner's guides are organized into a band, which is a corporate group in charge of the welfare of the parishioner. The identities of the constituent members of the band are revealed to the parishioner by the medium.

LEVEL XIV: This level specifies the kinds of guides within the band. Each category is distinguished by the particular task accorded it in the care of the parishioner.

LEVEL XV: An American *Indian* is an ethnic category singled out as particularly significant for the parishioner because *Indians* are considered to be the most efficacious guardians. Therefore, the category *guardian* is often further specified ethnically by the term *Indian*. Because of a belief in the healing powers of the Chinese, the category *doctor* is often specified by *Chinese healer*.

The terms in this diagram are known and understood by the congregations of the three types of churches discussed in Section I. Church Type A makes use of all the terms, but Types B and C do not employ the labels for God (Levels II and III). Such terms as *Infinite Intelligence, mind, truth,* and *love* are regarded as unique to Type A churches, chartered by the United States Spiritualist Association.

Within each church anyone may use any of the terms if he uses them as nouns labeling referents which are believed to exist on the basis of church teachings. However, the use of these terms following such verbs as *see, feel,* and *sense* in the first-person form, active voice, is restricted to ordained ministers, students of the pastor, or parishioners recognized for their psychic sensitivity. The use of any of these terms following such verbs as *contact, get, have, communicate* is restricted to ordained mediums, who are the only ones who may explicitly contact any of the spirits during the church service.

Terms in Levels I–III are used primarily in invocations and benedictions. Levels II (Voices) through VIII are most frequently used during classwork. Levels IX–XV are properly used during the message service in the church.

The configuration of the diagram is determined, in this instance, by the general meanings of the terms. However, the diagram also reflects both the notion of time from the point of view of the parishioner's involvement with a church and also the levels of stereotypes about spirits prevalent among non-Spiritualists. Any individual who comes to the church for the first time is familiar with and uses terms on Levels I and II (spirit). In order to learn and use terms on Level XV, he must have attended the church for a period of time, for the relationship that a parishioner forms with spirits in Levels III–XV is in large measure determined by the revelation of the medium to him of what that relationship is. Such revelations are offered in messages during the message service or during classwork. Both are available to a parishioner only after he has attended the church for some time.

In similar fashion, Levels I–XV also reflect the length of time a *spirit* has spent in spirit land. A spirit on Level III has only recently departed for spirit land, while a spirit on Level XV is fully developed or progressed and is able not only to manifest or make itself known to the parishioner *voices* (Level III), but can actually participate in the life of the parishioner as an *Indian* guarding spirit (Level XV).

The structure of the diagram, moving from Level I, the most abstract, to Level XV, which is the most specific, reflects the stereotypes of the community at large about-spiritualism. The individual who is least familiar with Spiritualist churches uses terms in Levels I through VI, while any individual who is somewhat familiar with the churches indicates such familiarity by using the more specific terms on Levels VII through XV.

Finally, the diagram mirrors the social structure of the church. Terms on Levels I through VI are used primarily by parishioners; however, once the service begins, the mediums resort to the more specific terms for spirits on Levels VII through XV.

Erroneous use of any of the terms occurs when an individual who is not properly ordained or recognized to be psychically sensitive uses any of the terms with verbs that imply that he is in contact with spirits. Also, any parishioner who has been given a spirit on a specific level and then refers to that spirit by a more general term is disrespectful to both medium and spirit.

VII. Conclusions

In this final section we may consider the analysis of the diagrammatic presentations and the utility of this approach for the analysis of the social structure of the church. We may first draw several conclusions about the argot:

1. Since the essence of this argot is to shield the thing it labels, this argot is most elaborate for those aspects of Spiritualist culture that Spiritualists feel uneasy with. The largest number of terms is offered for the different kinds of *spirits*, the nature of *mediumistic contact*, and the sorts of problems people bring to the church.

2. The criteria for the number of terms a paradigm will have is, first, the importance of the concept or object to the functioning of the church system, second, its legal status, and third, the level of its specificity (does it have a material representation?). The largest number of terms is available for the most important and most abstract terms such as *spirits, mediums, psychic phenomena.*

3. Concepts or objects presented to the public at large are more heavily articulated—for example, the nature of a *mediumistic contact*, *psychometry*, *vision*—while concepts or objects reserved for the faithful are least elaborated—for example, *ectoplasm*.

4. Of the noun, adjective, and verb-form classes, nouns are the numerous category. *Mediums* speak primarily in noun phrases to avoid giving the impression that they are the source of the information presented in the *message*. This is advantageous to the church from the following point of view. Most newcomers to the churches are slightly leary of mediums and suspect the veracity of their claims to mediumistic powers. If argot terms are applied to nouns, or noun phrases, the newcomer will be less suspicious, for most speakers of standard English accept the fact that their vocabulary of nouns might be limited. It is argued that newcomers to the church will be more willing to accept argot terms for nouns than for verbs. Verbs expressed in nonstandard terms, or terms used infrequently in standard English, such as *to psychometrize*, draw attention to the uniqueness of the term and therefore perhaps also to the strangeness of the practice it refers to, mediumship.

5. Most of the argot is composed of standard English terms. Nonstandard English terms are most evident in the noun-form class and least evident in verbs applied to the work of the *mediums*. Such verbs must remain

standard in order not to be offensive to the listener or to make a potentially unreasonable experience, *spirit communication*, appear unreal or abnormal.

6. The argot is used most heavily in the church service and is defined most specifically in classwork.

The argot is essentially oral and is never written. When it is written, as in classwork, where the *medium* dictates her teachings, it is written to preserve its orality, to be used by students in discussing church teachings among themselves. The fact that the argot is unwritten allows the *medium* to avoid being confronted by what she said either by her client or by the law. For the aim of the *message* is not its content, but its effect on the client.

I have pointed out that all the diagrams assume the configuration determined by the comprehensive gloss of each term. However, each particular configuration reveals additional information about the churches, of significance both ethnographically and to the argot. For example, Diagram 3 shows the concern of Spiritualists with time. The particular aspect of time relevant to Spiritualists is the length of time a parishioner participates in the church, the duration of time a student spends with a medium in classwork, and the length of time a spirit has been in spirit land for its progression. Such a concern with time is reflected in the argot. Certain terms may not be used by individuals unless they have spent a period of time within a church. Such time spent in church is measured also by the kinds of activities a parishioner has performed. This is reemphasized by the use of the argot because the most specific levels of meaning are only revealed to a parishioner after a long period of church socialization.

It is important for a Spiritualist church to have a parishioner involved with it for a long time because most churches do not have paid memberships, and so the only way they can be supported is by the continued donation of parishioners at church services or socials. Therefore, the argot is organized along the dimension of time from abstract to specific terms, with the terms most specific, and therefore satisfactory, to the parishioner being defined for him and acceptable for his use only after his lengthy involvement with a church.

The diagram may be reconstituted beyond the configuration based on general meaning. One may regroup the terms along any dimension desired, such as from the viewpoint of a speaker who occupies a particular church position and speaks in a certain portion of the service. Such diagrams can indicate explicitly the frequency with which certain terms are used within particular status positions in the church and also the changing emphasis on the components of meaning of each term according to the context of the speech event.

It is important to keep in mind that Spiritualists make up a community in only a limited sense. Most Spiritualists join a church at a time of crisis in their lives and continue to attend churches on occasions when they encounter personal difficulty. They are not acquainted with the church argot prior to their initial contact with a Spiritualist church, albeit they might know some of the argot terms as these are used in standard English senses. Most Spiritualists are aware that they are using an argot in church, especially since they step in and out of church participation according to the ebb and flow of their success in daily life.

Spiritualists prefer to keep as anonymous in church as possible. Few give their full names, and when they do, they often give nicknames or fictitious names. About 70 percent of the congregation changes from week to week, and one continuously faces a group of persons who either attend the church infrequently or are newcomers. Because of the rapid and continuous changes in the congregations the ethnographer finds that he needs some kind of index to identify the social relationships that exist between the parishioners and the mediums. Such an index is the use of language. Through observation of how an individual uses the argot the ethnographer has an opportunity to assess the relationship of that individual to the church and the pastor.

For the above reasons the methods of collecting linguistic data have to remain inductive and within natural speech contexts. Formal eliciting of specific linguistic information is virtually impossible either from infrequent attendees or from newcomers. In analyzing the material, one has to demonstrate continuously the relationships between lexical items from the point of view of a speaker or from a status position of a parishioner. Since we are not dealing with a community in a formal sense, it is almost useless to give a synthetic diagram that reflects the cultural view of the individuals involved. The only useful and accurate lexical relationships are those which are lodged in particular points of view and which therefore are indicative of the social positions of individuals within the social structure of the church.

Notes

1. All persons and places mentioned have been given fictitious names, and any resemblance between these names and those of actual persons in Bay City is unintentional. The name *Bay City* is borrowed from Lofland (1966). Since I worked in the same location as he did, I have used his name for consistency in the literature.

2. Although this study was conducted principally in Bay City, fieldwork was also done in the New England and mid-Atlantic states, as well as in state and national conventions of Spiritualists. Fieldwork during the past five years has been supported at various times by the following foundations: National Institute of Health Training Grant in Anthropology, grant

number GM 1224; Mabelle McLeod Lewis Memorial Fund; Smithsonian Institution post-Doctoral Research Program; Wenner-Gren Foundation for Anthropological Research, grant number 2514; National Science Foundation Institutional Grant administered by Princeton University. I would like to express my gratitude to these foundations.

3. I would like to thank Professor Elizabeth Colson who advised me during fieldwork and has always patiently and generously discussed with me the various research issues included in this project.

4. I would like to thank Professors Brent Berlin, Paul Kay, William Sturtevant and Mr. Jerrold Guben, who have read and commented upon various sections of this paper and made some helpful suggestions in the analysis of the material.

5. The following are transcript accounts of message work. Parishioner responses are placed within parentheses and punctuation is provided according to voice fluctuation.

Bibliography

BERLIN, BRENT. 1968. *Tzeltal Numeral Classifiers: A Study in Ethnographic Semantics*. Janua, Linguarum 70 (series practica). The Hague: Mouton & Co.

BERREMAN, GERALD D. 1966. "Anemic and Emetic Analysis in Social Anthropology." *American Anthropologist* 68:346–354.

BLUNSDON, NORMAN. 1963. *A Popular Dictionary of Spiritualism*. First American edition. New York: Citadel Press.

BURLING, ROBBINS. 1964. "Cognition and Componential Analysis: God's Truth or Hocus Pocus?" *American Anthropologist* 66: 20–29.

CAPRON, W. E. 1855. *Modern Spiritualism*. Boston.

COLBY, B. N. 1966. "Ethnographic Semantics: A Preliminary Survey (with comments)." *Current Anthropology* 7: 3–32.

CONKLIN, HAROLD C. 1955. "Hanunóo Color Categories." *Southwestern Journal of Anthropology* 11: 339–344.

______. 1962. "Lexicographical Treatment of Folk Taxonomies," in "Problems in Lexicography," F. W. Householder, ed., *International Journal of American Linguistics* 28 (2): 119–141.

CROSS, WHITNEY R. 1950. *The Burned-Over District: The Social and Intellectual History of Enthusiastic Religion in Western New York, 1800–1850*. Ithaca, New York: Peter Smith.

DONOVAN, ROBERT KENT. 1954. "The Ultra-Violet World: Spiritualism in Great Britain, 1852–1898." Unpublished honors thesis, Harvard University.

FRAKE, CHARLES O. 1961. "The Diagnosis of Disease Among the Subanum of Mindanao." *American Anthropologist* 63: 113–132.

______. 1962. "The Ethnographic Study of Cognitive Systems," in *Anthropology and Human Behavior*, Thomas Gladwin and W. C. Sturtevant, eds. Washington, D.C.: Anthropological Society.

GLADWIN, THOMAS, AND WILLIAM D. STURTEVANT, EDS. 1962. *Anthropology and Human Behavior*. Washington, D.C.: Anthropological Society.

HYMES, DELL. 1962. "The Ethnography of Speaking," in *Anthropology and Human Behavior*, Thomas Gladwin and William C. Sturtevant, eds., Washington, D.C.: Anthropological Society.

JUDAH, J. STILLSON. 1967. *The History and Philosophy of the Metaphysical Movements in America*. Philadelphia: The Westminster Press.

KAY, PAUL. 1970. "Some Theoretical Implications of Ethnographic Semantics." *Bulletins of the American Anthropological Association*, volume 3, no. 3, part 2: 19–31.

LAWTON, GEORGE. 1930. "Spiritualism—A Contemporary American Religion." *Journal of Religion* 10 (1): 37–54.

———. 1932. *The Drama of Life After Death: A Study of the Spiritualist Religion.* New York: Henry Holt and Co.

LESLAU, W. 1949. "An Ethiopian Argot of People Possessed by a Spirit." *Africa* (London) 19(3): 204–212.

LOFLAND, JOHN. 1966. *Doomsday Cult: A Study of Conversion, Proselytization and Maintenance of Faith.* Englewood Cliffs, N J.: Prentice-Hall.

METZGER, DUANE, AND G. WILLIAMS. 1966. "Some Procedures and Results in the Study of Native Categories: Tzeltal 'Firewood.'" *American Anthropologist* 68: 389–407.

NATIONAL SPIRITUALIST ASSOCIATION OF THE UNITED STATES OF AMERICA. 1948. *Centennial Book of Modern Spiritualism in America.* Chicago.

———. 1962. *Spiritualist Manual.* Tenth edition. Milwaukee, Wisconsin.

PODMORE, FRANK. 1897. *Studies in Psychical Research.* London.

———. 1910. *The Newer Spiritualism.* London: T.F. Unwin.

STURTEVANT, WILLIAM C. 1964. "Studies in Ethnoscience." In *Transcultural Studies in Cognition*, A. Kimball Romney and Roy Goodwin D'Andrade, eds. American Anthropologist Publication 66. 3: 99–131.

ZARETSKY, IRVING I., and MARK P. LEONE. 1972. *Pragmatic Religions: Contemporary Religious Movements in America.* Princeton: Princeton University Press.

Index